KU-034-301

PERGAMON INTERNATIONAL LIBRARY
of Science, Technology, Engineering and Social Studies
The 1000-volume original paperback library in aid of education,
industrial training and the enjoyment of leisure
Publisher: Robert Maxwell, M.C.

LAND POLICY
AND URBAN GROWTH

THE PERGAMON TEXTBOOK
INSPECTION COPY SERVICE

An inspection copy of any book published in the Pergamon International Library will gladly
be sent to academic staff without obligation for their consideration for course adoption or
recommendation. Copies may be retained for a period of 60 days from receipt and returned
if not suitable. When a particular title is adopted or recommended for adoption for class
use and the recommendation results in a sale of 12 or more copies, the inspection copy may
be retained with our compliments. The Publishers will be pleased to receive suggestions
for revised editions and new titles to be published in this important International Library.

Pergamon Urban and Regional Planning Advisory Committee

G. F. CHADWICK, PhD, MA, BScTech, FRTPI, FILA
(Chairman),
Planning Consultant,
Sometime Professor of Town and Country Planning,
University of Newcastle-upon-Tyne

D. R. DIAMOND, MA, MSc,
Reader in Regional Planning,
London School of Economics

A. K. F. FALUDI, Dipl-Ing, Dr techn,
Professor of Planning Theory,
Delft University of Technology

J. K. FRIEND, MA,
Institute for Operational Research

D. C. GILL, BA, MRTPI,
Director of Planning,
Humberside County Council

B. GOODEY, BA, MA,
Senior Lecturer in Urban Analysis and Perception,
Urban Design, Department of Town Planning,
Oxford Polytechnic

D. N. M. STARKIE, BSc(Econ), MSc(Econ),
Department of Geography,
University of Reading

B. STYLES, BA, MCD, MRTPI,
Divisional Planning Officer,
City of Birmingham Planning Department

LAND POLICY
AND URBAN GROWTH

by

HAIM DARIN-DRABKIN

Director, Institute for Land Resources Planning, Tel-Aviv

PERGAMON PRESS

OXFORD   NEW YORK   TORONTO

SYDNEY   PARIS   FRANKFURT

U.K.	Pergamon Press Ltd., Headington Hill Hall, Oxford OX3 0BW, England
U.S.A.	Pergamon Press Inc., Maxwell House, Fairview Park, Elmsford, New York 10523, U.S.A.
CANADA	Pergamon of Canada Ltd., 75 The East Mall, Toronto, Ontario, Canada
AUSTRALIA	Pergamon Press (Aust.) Pty. Ltd., 19a Boundary Street, Rushcutters Bay, N.S.W. 2011, Australia
FRANCE	Pergamon Press SARL, 24 rue des Ecoles, 75240 Paris, Cedex 05, France
WEST GERMANY	Pergamon Press GmbH, 6242 Kronberg-Taunus, Pferdstrasse 1, West Germany

Copyright © 1977 H. Darin-Drabkin

All Rights Reserved. No part of this publication may be reproduced, stored in a retrieval system or transmitted in any form or by any means: electronic, electrostatic, magnetic tape, mechanical, photocopying, recording or otherwise, without permission in writing from the publishers

First edition 1977

Library of Congress Cataloging in Publication Data

Darin-Drabkin, Haim, 1908-
Land policy and urban growth.

(Urban and regional planning series; v. 16)
Includes index.
1. Land use, Urban. 2. Cities and towns—Planning. 3. Cities and towns—Growths.
I. Title. II. Series.
HD111.D28 1977   333.7′7   76-39912
ISBN 0-08-020401-5 hard

Printed in Great Britain by Thomson Litho Ltd., East Kilbride

Contents

507282

Foreword and Acknowledgements

This book is the result of many years of concern with the theoretical economic problems connected with urban and regional development. This concern was sharpened by the author's work as Director of Research for the Ministry of Housing in Israel, where our studies and our experience showed the enormous impact of land prices on urban growth patterns and housing costs.

A paper on the subject was first presented to a UN conference in Paris in 1965. In that year I was invited by Barry Cullingworth to the Institute of Urban Studies and by Chester Rapkin to the University of Pennsylvania, where I had an opportunity to investigate the complexity of urban land policies in the UK and the USA. In 1970 I carried out a study of Western European land policies and land use control measures which was published by the UN. These studies enabled me to collect a very considerable amount of material on the development of land prices and on the patterns of urban growth. The most important assistance in obtaining material for a comparison of the impact of different land policies on urban growth came from a grant from the Ford Foundation that I received in 1972. This grant has given me the opportunity of completing the present book.

Last, but not least, was my work at the Academy of Contemporary Problems at Ohio State University in 1973, when I had the opportunity to compare developments in land policy in West European countries with the new approaches of different states of the USA.

The author would like to thank all of his many colleagues who, through their discussions and assistance in providing statistical material, helped so much in the writing of this book. My special thanks and gratitude go to the late Charles Abrams, whose warm enthusiasm encouraged me first to undertake this research. I have also received valuable assistance from experts in several countries: in Australia from R. W. Archer; in Denmark from V. R. Nielsen, O. L. Nielsen, S. Gron and P. Dalkier; in France from H. de Fraysseix; in India from C. M. Correa; in Israel from the late D. Thane and J. Slyper; in Mexico from A. Luna Arroya; in The Netherlands from C. de Cler and C. Wegener Sleeswik; in Singapore from S. W. Lim; in Sweden from A. Pahlman, M. Ponzio and C. Berg; in Switzerland from M. L. Voronoff, J. Stvan and H. R. Isliker; in Spain from M. Gomez Moran and J. Fonseca; in the United Kingdom from B. Cullingworth and N. Lichfield; in the United States of America from W. Garces, R. Widner, L. Winnick and J. R. Voss.

For their highly professional editing of various chapters of this book, I am grateful to R. Bucksbaum, P. Josef, Sh. Zaychi and, especially at the most difficult final stage, to S. Schifferes. My thanks go to Mrs. A. Body for her help in preparing the complicated statistical material of the Copenhagen study, and to her and Mrs. F. Zetland for their assistance in correcting some of the chapters. I also acknowledge my gratitude to Mrs. M. Hollander for her efficient technical help in preparing the material for publication.

Special appreciation goes to my son, Dan, for his assistance in organizing the basic scientific material and advising on the architectural aspects related to this work; and finally, to Dan and to my wife, Cesia, my special thanks for their constant encouragement throughout.

H. DARIN-DRABKIN

Introduction

Extraordinary population growth and rapid changes in population distribution are two of the most dramatic phenomena of our times. The rapid urbanization process and the concentration of population in metropolitan areas is a result of the mass migration of people from rural to urban areas. This rapid growth in metropolitan areas has resulted in a number of paradoxes. In spite of the increase in national wealth and personal income, the condition of urban areas is declining. Although the supply of goods and services has vastly increased, the quality of life is diminishing. The rapid influx of migrants into the central cities has resulted in overcrowding. Meanwhile, the movement of middle-class residents to the outlying suburbs has created sprawling suburban communities. The increased use of private automobiles congests traffic and increases travel time. Technological progress which can provide completely air-conditioned high-rise buildings has not yet provided green space, clean air or an appropriate cultural environment. Air pollution is increasing, crime rates are climbing and drug addicts are becoming a feature of modern urban life.

Land use is one of the essential factors influencing the pattern of urban development. The limited space within cities combined with the growing space requirements for different purposes outlines the framework of the struggle for land for different purposes and by different vested interests.

The difficulties in land-use planning result from the contradiction between the rapid technological changes which influence urban growth and the slow process of planning which allocates land use. Land is the basis for structures which, once erected, have a long life, and fix the reality of urban life for a very long time.

There are different levels of contradiction in land-use patterns:

1. the short-term needs of the population for housing, and the long-run consequences of land use decisions;
2. different needs and economic functions which compete for land space;
3. individual private needs, which may be different from collective land-use needs (and also the differing priorities of local, regional and national interests over the use of land).

The use of land is influenced by the interplay of many factors, constantly changing their relationship to one another. Rapid technological changes have created new needs which demand more land, and at the same time new ways of using land. Building technology makes possible a more intensive use of land; the construction of roads, the opening up of new regions, and the utilization of existing space in a more efficient way—all these allow the adaptation of existing land resources to changing and growing needs.

Land use forms the basis of city structure, and urban land patterns are a reflection of a city's social structure. On the one hand, continual socio-economic changes influence the land-use patterns of a city; on the other hand, land use, by determining the location of various city functions, influences the future development of urban society.

The conflicts and common interests of different social strata are expressed in the city as a focus of human contacts. These internal contradictions and common interests influence the use of urban space. Each social group tries to influence the use of urban land to further its economic interests and improve its way of living. The most desirable space is utilized by the most powerful social groups. In this way changes in social relations affect the use of urban space. It may be said that the city is a topographic projection of the social structure.

The competition for land in the city centre and in desirable residential areas reflects the structure of society. Market forces lead to the most central urban space being occupied by the most powerful financial groups—banks, insurance companies, the headquarters of large industrial firms, and high-priced commercial services.

The growing role of the state in society and in the economy has created a need for more space for public buildings in the city centre. The central urban areas are therefore increasingly occupied by the services of public administration as well as by the most important commercial services.

The expected growth of the world's population from the present 4 billion to 6 billion in the year 2000, combined with a doubling of urban population from $1\frac{1}{2}$ billion to 3 billion during the same period, poses some serious questions. The prospects of a population of 10 billion in the year 2050 makes the efficient use of land essential for the future. The unplanned development of urban regions leads to un- necessary land consumption and the destruction of good agricultural land.

The most fundamental question concerns the supply of land for urban development. Is there a danger of a general shortage of land for future urban development or are there simply local shortages?

Given that shortages may exist locally in some areas, are these caused by absolute shortage of land or are they the result of the lack of planned land use and land allocation which results from reliance on the private market?

In addition to examining the private land market it is also necessary to evaluate the public institutions dealing with land-use problems. Are the existing institutions and policies adequate to meet the new demands? Should the role of the public authorities be limited to regulations or should they be given the authority to take the initiative in influencing future urban growth through direct intervention in the land market? Are the present policies, which control what should be built at a given location, able to control the timing of future de- velopment? Is an active urban growth and land-use policy desirable? If desirable is it possible? What can be learned from the experience of different countries using an active land-use policy? Finally, what are the conditions required to adapt the government institutions to the growing needs of the urban society?

The object of this study is to establish the relationships between urban growth patterns, land prices and land policies in countries with market economies.

The study is divided into four parts. First, there is a brief survey of recent patterns of urban growth, which reviews the well-known evidence of the current high rate of urban expansion, and then ex- plores what future land needs might be in the urban areas. The second part is concerned with urban land prices, and seeks to demonstrate the dramatic increases in urban land prices that have resulted from recent urban-development trends (and also other economic trends) in the conditions of private markets in land. Various theories of urban land-price formation are examined in connection with this task. The third part of the book is devoted to public policies toward urban land, and attempts to show the impact of various policy measures on the land market and on the supply and allocation of land. Finally, some alternative future urban land policies are outlined.

One aim of the book is to show the impact of land-price increases on the patterns of urban growth. A concurrent aim is to demonstrate the effects of the peculiar character of the private market in land on land-price formation. Finally, the interrelationships between the market mechanism and government intervention in the urban-growth process will be examined.

At present, the established criteria of land allocation are based on the market mechanism which "allocates" the best use of land to the highest bidder. Therefore those having the financial ability to pay the highest prices are the deciding factor in land allocation. It might be suggested that the present land-use and urban-growth patterns are a result of such a market mechanism functioning in conditions of government regulation too weak to change decisively the dominant role of the private market in land.

But the question which might be posed is what is the alternative, given that the market mechanism is the main factor in the present unsatisfactory patterns of urban growth? What kinds of different mechanisms might allocate land according to the needs of urban development? What are the criteria of needs? How is it possible to measure the needs of society? Do such needs exist for society as a whole, or are there different and sometimes conflicting needs of different groups within society? How much weight should be given to the needs of the present generation, and how much to the needs of future generations?

The definition of the role of public authorities in providing the land needed at the right time, location and price might be defined as a basic goal of public land policy. But this goal might be achieved by different measures which would give different results according to different levels of socio-economic development and political structure within a country.

It is important to establish the definition and classification of land policies and the criteria for effectiveness of these policies before reviewing land policies in different countries and trying to evaluate their effectiveness. Then the interrelationships between different policy measures and their effects on the land market, which in turn influences their effectiveness in achieving their goals can be investigated.

The less-studied problem of the role of the institutional structures—different public decision-taking agencies which are trying to find a solution for conflicting interests in time and space connected with land allocation and distribution—is dealt with in this book. One of the main problems in establishing land-policy measures is the contradiction between the pressure of short-term needs and long-term plans for land allocation. An understanding of the relationship between planning decisions and their effects on the land market—as well as the impact of market on the effectiveness of land-policy implementation—is crucial to achieving results.

Our review of different land policies is not intended to be comprehensive, but is based only on examples of some countries which are trying to introduce new policy instruments corresponding to the new urban imperatives. The selection is based mostly on information published by the UN or obtained from experts on a personal basis. It has to be underlined that the material available for the underdeveloped countries is far more limited.

It should be pointed out that the expression used in this book, "the underdeveloped countries", does not take into account the extremely varied socio-economic structures and economic levels of the countries included in this category. Further, it should be recognized that the expression "underdeveloped" refers solely to the *economic* situation in some countries (which is relevant to their urban situations); we mean no cultural or political judgements by such a term.

After reviewing the general trends of land policies in different countries, we have chosen to analyse land policies in three countries which have a more active land policy than most others. Sweden, the Netherlands and France were chosen as the case studies. The concluding part of the study tries to use the preceding analysis of different policy measures to suggest different possible alternatives that might be adopted to deal with future urban growth.

A very basic question which arises from future growth concerns how land should be viewed by government authorities. Is land primarily an economic commodity or predominantly a natural resource? Related to this issue is the question of the operation of the private land market. Is it able to supply the land required for the growing population?

The quality of urban life depends on the way in which the quantity of land available is used. The relationship between the location of the workplace, the residence and service areas is one of the factors influencing the quality of urban life. The quality of urban life means the appropriate use of land for the whole urban population, not just for some strata of society. The right to quality in urban living includes not only the right to adequate living space, but also accessibility to all city functions—social integration, not social segregation which relegates the lower-income groups only to the outlying areas.

The city changes with changes in society. But the transformation of the city is not just the passive result of global socio-economic changes. The rate of urban growth and structural changes in the economy influence the use of urban space. But the institutional and political structure, the result of the pattern of social relations in a country, also influence the urban structure. In addition, the historical pattern of urban structure affects the pattern of contemporary growth.

The extraordinary rate of growth of the urban population in recent decades has emphasized the urgency of the problem of how to best use the urban space. Rapid urbanization generates a demand for more new land; however, it is the proper planning of all land use which is crucial for ensuring the quality of urban life.

PART ONE

Land Needs in Urbanization

CHAPTER 1

Land-Use and Urbanization Patterns

Knowledge of the basic patterns of urban development is necessary for the formulation of urban land policy. These trends are of major importance for understanding the urban land-development process. An examination of the underlying factors in urbanization patterns will help to determine to what extent they can influence land use, thus creating the problems which land policies are trying to solve.

The basic trends in world urbanization are:

1. An increasing percentage of world population is living in urban areas, the largest cities having the fastest growth.
2. Employment within these metropolitan areas is becoming concentrated in the city centre.
3. Population growth is mainly occurring in the outlying regions of the metropolitan area.

It may be suggested that the rapid technological changes and steady economic growth since the Second World War have been fundamentally responsible for these developments.

Rapid population growth itself is a result of the diffusion of scientific-medical knowledge, and is the underlying cause of the growth of urban population. But the concentration of population in urban areas is also affected by economic growth, which is reducing the percentage of the population employed in agricultural (and rural) pursuits. Further structural changes in employment—the growth of the tertiary (service) sector—have led to increased employment in the city centre, as most service firms need to be centrally located so as to benefit from close interaction with each other. These changes have also had an impact on the distribution of population in the urban areas. The increasing use of the centre for commercial purposes forces population to outlying districts. Improved and new transportation systems (particularly motor

9

transport) facilitate this decentralization. Industry continues to concentrate in the metropolitan area, which has a pool of skilled manpower, access to consumer markets, and a variety of auxiliary commercial services. However, the development of the transportation system has also allowed it a degree of dispersal within the metropolitan region.

Common to all countries is a gap between the existing physical and institutional structure and the rapidly changing spatial requirements which technology has imposed on the economic and social structure. The allocation of city space for different urban uses is based not only on present requirements but also on past structure. Existing public institutions, established by the demands of past development, have become ponderous and bureaucratic, and only slowly do they adapt themselves and the urban structure to new requirements.

1.1. URBANIZATION AND URBAN CONCENTRATION

Urbanization is a world-wide phenomenon. Cities have existed for thousands of years, but recent decades have had such a high rate of urban growth that the human condition itself appears threatened.

The accelerating world population would in itself lead to a great increase in the population of cities. World population took 300 years to double from about AD 1500 to AD 1800 when it had still not reached 1 billion. It then doubled (to 1·8 billion) in the 120 years to 1920, and has doubled again in the last 50 years (to 3·6 billion).

But urban population is growing even faster than world population. It is forecast that by the year 2000 world population will be approximately 6 billion; half of this figure will be urban population. In 1960 there were 3 billion people and only 1 billion were city dwellers. In the next 40 years world population will double, while the urban population will increase threefold. From 1950 to 1970, world population grew by 45%, urban population by 98%. In absolute figures the urban increase was 693 million during this 20-year period; in the preceding 50 years it was only 482 million.

The converse of these figures is that the rate of growth of the rural population is low. In the developed countries a decrease in rural population may even be observed; while in the developing countries, though rural population has continued to increase, it has done so at a much slower rate than urban population.

Table 1.1 shows the difference in urban and rural population growth from 1950 to 1970.

TABLE 1.1.

	Rural population (in millions)			Urban population (in millions)		
	1950	1970	% change	1950	1970	% change
Developing countries	1420	1910	35	284	678	139
Developed countries	376	319	−15	422	721	71

These figures show that the urban population in the developing countries is increasing at a rate twice that in the developed countries. The forecasts for the future show that this trend is likely to continue. A comparison of growth rates from 1950 to 1970 with the predicted growth to the year 2000 shows the severity of the problem (Table 1.2).

TABLE 1.2. Urban Population Growth (in millions)

	Year			% increase 1950–1970		% increase 1970–2000	
	1950	1970	2000	total	yearly	total	yearly
World	706	1399	3090	98	3·5	121	2·7
Developing countries	284	678	2080	139	4·4	206	3·8
Developed countries	422	721	1010	71	2·7	40	1·1

Although the rate of growth of urban population will slow down somewhat between 1970 and 2000, the bulk of the growth will still be in developing countries. Whereas the rate of growth in the developed countries will drop from 2·7% yearly between 1950 and 1970 to 1·1% between 1970 and 2000, in the developing countries it will only drop from a level of 4·4% yearly (1950–1970) to 3·8% (1970–2000).

Urban Concentration

The average figures of urban population growth do not demonstrate the true gravity of the urban population explosion. An analysis of the rate of growth of cities over 100,000—and especially of cities of over 1 million inhabitants—shows that the real problem consists not solely in the high rate of urbanization, but in the rate of *urban concentration*.

According to the available data, cities of over 100,000 will grow by 170% between 1970 and 2000—a compound yearly rate of 3·5%; for cities of over 1 million, the rate will be 234% (4·1% per year). The explosive rate of large-city growth is shown in Fig. 1.1.

These figures show that the greatest urban growth does not occur

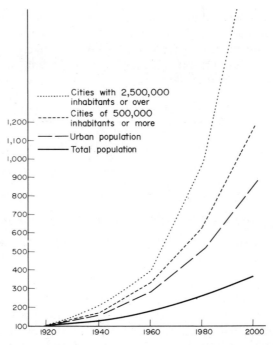

Fig. 1.1. Increase in total world population and in urban populations in different categories (1920 = 100). (Source: *Growth of the World's Urban and Rural Population 1920–2000* (United Nations Publication W(69X1113).)

uniformly in all urban areas, but is concentrated in the large metropolitan areas which are expanding in size and even absorbing adjacent smaller cities. In 1968 there were 153 metropolitan areas of more than 1 million inhabitants—87 of these in the developed countries and 66 in the developing countries.

A comparison of the rates of growth of cities of more than 100,000 shows yet again a higher rate of increase in the developing countries (Table 1.3).

TABLE 1.3. Population Growth in Cities of more than 100,000 (in millions)

	1950	1970	% increase
Developing countries	146	406	177
Developed countries	260	458	76

In 1950 the city population in the developed countries was almost double that of the developing countries; in 1970 the difference between the developed and developing countries was not more than 12%.

The future trend is towards a higher rate of growth of these metropolitan areas in almost all countries, and especially in the developing countries. In the developed countries this has resulted in unbalanced development of different regions of the country, and in social segregation within the metropolitan areas. In the developing countries the lack of economic resources makes it difficult to ensure employment for the continually growing urban population and to erect the needed infrastructure of the expanding metropolitan area.

1.2. CONCENTRATION OF EMPLOYMENT IN THE CITY CENTRE

One of the recent features of urbanization and urban concentration is the increase of service-sector employment in the town centre. This trend is occurring in most countries, regardless of their level of urbanization and industrialization. The growth of the tertiary sector is the most salient fact in the development of the economy of the industrialized countries and is becoming increasingly important in the large cities of the developing countries. The growth of this sector is also correlated with the growth of the world economy, and there is a connection between a country's economic progress and the development of certain services of an international character.

The growth of the tertiary sector in both developed and developing countries can be seen from Tables 1.4 and 1.5.

TABLE 1.4. European Community (The Six):
Distribution of Employment by Major Sectors

Sector	1955	1970
Agriculture	24·3	13·4
Industry	40·0	43·9
Tertiary	35·7	42·7

Source: *The Urban Explosion* by T. H. Elkins, London, 1973.

TABLE 1.5. Latin America: Changes in Active Population by Economic Sector Distribution of Active Population by Sector

	1945 %	1960 %	Change between 1945–1960 %
Agriculture	56·8	47·2	−9·6
Mining	1·2	0·9	−0·3
Construction	3·2	4·1	+0·8
Manufacturing	13·8	14·3	+0·5
Tertiary	25·0	33·5	+8·5

Source: *Espaces et Societes*, No. 3, juillet 1973, Paris.

The difference between tertiary sector employment in developed and developing countries is the structure of the sector and the services performed. In developing countries there is large-scale underemployment (and hence many non-essential services are duplicated), while the large numbers in the tertiary sector in the developed countries reflects newly created needs resulting from a high level of economic growth.

Concurrent with and related to growth in the tertiary sector has been a decline in agricultural employment. This is the result of increased productivity per man which lessens the demand for agricultural labour and of the increasing commercialization of agriculture at the expense of subsistence farming.

Growth of the tertiary sector, then, has been a result of both increased demand and supply—increased demand for services created by growing affluence and by changing patterns of industrial growth; and the increased supply of labour, due to the declining manpower requirement for agricultural and industrial production.

The increase in the size of the service sector has led in turn to an increase in employment in the city centre. This is because the service industries are very dependent on the dense network of intercommunications which only the city centre provides; they need to be centrally located both to take in the largest possible catchment area (which often extends internationally) and also to liaise with each other.

The attraction of service industries to the city centre can be shown by reference to the situation in some of the major Western cities. In London, during the 6-year period from 1955 to 1962, the number of service jobs increased by 260,000 while the population of the city proper fell. By the end of the period 60% of those working in the city centre were doing office jobs; while the amount of office space has doubled since 1939.

In Paris, it is estimated that by the year 2000 the tertiary sector will account for 61% of employment in the region as a whole (an increased proportion of 5%). Within the city of Paris, today, there are 1,500,000 employed in the service sector and 450,000 in industrial jobs, while in the region surrounding the city, the corresponding figures are 900,000 and 1,000,000.

In New York, white-collar jobs increased by 1·5 million between 1950 and 1970 while the number of blue-collar jobs grew hardly at all. In 1960, 35% of the work force of the whole region was employed in the central business district of Manhattan (mainly in services).

The same pattern is evident in the major cities in the developing countries. The percentage distribution of workers in major industry groups in the cities of Iran is as shown in Table 1.6.

In the Republic of Korea, 63·6% of city dwellers were employed in the tertiary sector.

There is an important difference between the situation in the economically highly-developed countries and the less-developed

TABLE 1.6. Major Industry Group and per cent of Total Employed

	Agriculture and production of raw materials	Manufacturing and construction	Business services trade and transport
Teheran	1·1	35·3	63·6
All urban	7·9	37·9	54·2

Source: *United Nations Report on Urban Land Policy*, New York, 1973.

countries. In the former, the large cities and their regions can ensure employment for the population coming in from the rural areas; while in the latter, unemployment in the village pushes the rural population to the city, where there are limited employment possibilities in the services or industry. Thus much of the service-sector employment in these cities is actually disguised unemployment.

1.3. GROWTH OF POPULATION IN THE METROPOLITAN REGION

The concentration of employment in the town centre, the high land prices there, and the need for more space for industrial enterprises all encourage the establishment of new industries in the city region, while the smaller industrial enterprises and handicrafts remain in the town centre. Housing activities also spread to the suburbs because of the high land prices in the centre and the need for more space for personal use.

Industry is still attracted to the metropolitan area, due to the presence of skilled manpower there. But with the new means of transport and power (motor cars and electricity), the location of industry is no longer primarily determined by proximity to raw material and energy sources. Nearness to markets, adequate space for storage and automated production, and the attraction of qualified personnel are becoming increasingly important for industrial firms, and lead industry to still concentrate in the city region, but decentralize *within* the region. Because of these trends, the rate of population growth in the metropolitan region is higher than that in most cities in the world. In the largest metropolitan areas of the more industrialized countries the population of the cities proper has been declining (London, Paris, New York and most other big cities).

With the decrease of population growth in the town, the rate of population growth in the region has accelerated. The average annual population growth in some major cities, as compared with the regions outside those cities, during the first half of the 1960s, is given in Table 1.7. It may be seen that while the population of the city proper has either decreased or increased very slowly, the outer region of the metropolitan area has grown rapidly.

TABLE 1.7. Population Changes per annum in Metropolitan Areas in Selected Cities, 1960–1965
(Percentage)

	Metropolitan area	Central city	Region outside city
Zurich	4·9	0·1	18·8
Munich	3·0	2·6	3·4
Paris	1·7	−1·5	5·0
Stockholm	1·7	−0·6	5·8
Antwerp	0·6	−0·9	1·6
Copenhagen	0·5	−1·1	2·2
London	0·1	−0·3	0·2
New York (1960–70)	1·1	0·0	3·0

Source: Federal Republic of Germany, Ministry of Housing and Town Planning, *Städtebaubericht 1969* (Bonn, 1969), pp. 178–80, and *How to Save Urban America*, New York, 1973.

The same trend is in evidence in the developing countries. For example, population of Mexico City grew by 26·7% between 1950 and 1961. However, the Federal District as a whole (which includes Mexico City and its suburbs) grew by 59·6% in the same period; and it was the small municipalities on the outer border of the FD which had the most explosive growth.

The spreading out of city population to the region as a whole disproportionately affects the size of the urbanized area, as densities are generally lower on average in the suburbs than in the city proper. For example, the built-up area of the New York metropolitan region increased from 1935 to 1962 from 600 to 1740 square miles (290%), while population in the region grew by only 40%.

Transport

The rapid development of the city region at a low density places great strain on the transportation system of the area and creates needs for land for housing and related purposes, for industry and services, for road networks and for recreational facilities. These demands make it very difficult for the large city to absorb new inhabitants. The spread of population to the suburbs adds its weight to the already heavy demands being put on the metropolitan area outside the town proper, especially with respect to transportation. Solution of the traffic problem, due, in part, to the heavy investment involved, is one of the most urgent and difficult tasks in urban town planning. Current trends make the planning of transport in a regional framework a necessity.

Conclusions

Obviously, such a high rate of population growth in the city region must affect the land market. The rate of increase of land prices in the town is high; but in the region outside the town it is considerably higher. Land prices have increased most in countries where the process of transformation from agriculture to industry is still continuing or is just getting under way.

The high rate of population growth in the metropolitan area outside the city poses a problem for the administrative structure of the city region. People live, work and use services in different parts of the city region. As a result of this splitting of the city functions from city to city region, there is an urgent need to adapt urban legislative machinery and administrative structure to the new reality, with city region as the unit of urban development. Some countries have already begun this task.

1.4. IMPACT ON LAND USE

The concentration of service employment in the city centre and the trend towards dispersed industrial location and population growth outside the town have brought about important changes in land use. In the urban centre, the various services compete for land because a very large clientele gravitates towards the centre. This clientele is drawn from the town itself, from the region, from the country as a whole; and if the town is one of international standing, from all over the world. This convergence produces a steep rise in the price of land, which in turn affects other factors. First, the services which are unable to compete are forced out of the urban centre and are replaced by specialist services. The development of the specialist services depends, by and large, upon their being centrally located; they also possess the ability to pay for this privilege. Secondly, building for residential purposes shows a decline for several reasons. Residential building in these areas is costly; however, those sectors of the population able to pay high prices for housing prefer to live in an area where such nuisances as noise and air pollution, which are inherent to the urban centre, do not prevail.

It may be possible according to a planning code to build new residential housing (replacing old buildings) in the city centre. But the high land prices make residential building very expensive and, therefore, uneconomical for the investment of capital. As a result, there are many old houses in poor condition in areas near the town centre. The inhabitants of these houses want to leave these areas for better housing in the metropolitan area outside the city centre. The former residents and new couples are not interested in living in these areas, which are populated by foreign workers, students and people who want to live in town, even though in houses of low maintenance and without modern accommodations. Such a change in the population structure is seen by the local authorities as negatively affecting the socio-cultural development of the town.

Therefore, the high prices in the central business district not only affect a small area in the city centre, but have negative results on the socio-economic development of the city as a whole.

The emergence of the urban centre as a conglomerate of services and facilities encouraging an exclusively commercial function is unquestionably one of the factors causing the separation of place of work from residence. This phenomenon is a by-product of the growth of modern society. It is attributable to the rise in the standard of living, as well as to the expansion of the use and development of public transportation facilities. The service centres, or central business districts, offer a vast choice of employment opportunities, which annually increase along with urban growth development.

The urban centre expands, occupying an even greater area, while the town's land resources dwindle until there is insufficient land to house the people who live in that centre; hence, the construction of new housing estates in the metropolitan area. The extension of housing and building activities to the metropolitan area far from the city centre may not, in itself, have a bad effect. But unplanned building activity transforms large agricultural areas into urbanized areas which provide only housing (mostly social housing) and thereby causes a dependence upon the town for services, as well as for work. In economically less-developed countries, the city attracts masses of former peasants who cannot afford proper housing. They, therefore, must erect for themselves temporary housing (shacks). In this way, quarters are erected without even such elementary services as sewerage systems.

Both planned housing activities, carried out by public authorities, and some unplanned building activities, done by the private sector, use cheap land far from the town for housing projects. This practice unnecessarily extends the urbanized area of the metropolitan region. The result of this extension of housing activities is the rapid increase of land prices in the city region.

This situation has had an impact on the land market and town planning. On the one hand, the landowners do not want to sell their agricultural land; they prefer to wait for future land-use change. On the other hand, there is the pressure of developers interested in using agricultural land for housing projects. As a result of lack of land available on the market, the public authorities are obliged to approve housing schemes in areas far from the city centre and not included in the long-term development scheme. The housing programmes are often implemented not according to planning targets but as a result of the readiness of landowners to sell their land.

Usually, modern housing projects were erected under the pressure of the urgent housing needs, and as a result of lack of long-term town planning and lack of land reserves, new urban centres with all necessary services were simply not provided.

Both the change of agricultural land into urban use and the initiation of building activities in unsettled areas lead to the rise of land prices on large land surfaces between the new urbanized area and the already existing urban areas of the city region.

In all countries, the pressure of population growth in the city region affect the trend for a long-term development scheme for a city region. This pressure also has an influence on the attempt to fix the land use of separate towns on the basis of regional schemes.

The low-density, widely dispersed metropolitan areas not only cause an abnormally high proportion of income to be spent on personal transport, but is also costly in terms of other forms of infrastructure (water, sewers, electricity, telephone).

Even in wealthy countries, living in the "better" or most distant suburbs is so costly that many low-income people live in the areas, generally deteriorated, surrounding the old centre of the city or nearer the industrial areas. Thus arises one of the least defensible consequences of *laissez faire* inequality, the segregation of urban areas by income and the consequent segregation or differentiation of public services and facilities for leisure.

The next two decades need not repeat the mistakes of the past. Urban development, even in large cities, can take a more decentralized form. Planetary cities with satellite new towns; corridor cities organized around transportation and utilities lines; polynucleated cities in which communities focus on distinct urban functions—all are possible ways to manage future urban growth to greater advantage. Transportation technology promises in the next 20 years, not simply the abatement of current environmental pollution from the internal combustion engine, but faster service and lower costs, making possible, cities of high net densities, but with lower overall density, providing greater open spaces. Metropolitan land-use planning can also offer substantial social gains. The balance of city and rural hinterland that has lured urban utopians from Ebenezer Howard to Le Corbusier may actually be achieved. New towns and suburban communities are being planned and created as never before. Despite the institutional, political and economic constraints these innovations must surmount, it would be a great error to assume that the future of cities will be a simple projection of their past.

REFERENCES

"Amt fur kommunale Grundlagenforschung und Statistik der Landeshauptstadt", *Munchener Statistik*, Nos. 4, 6, 1966; Nos. 1, 2, 3, 4, 5, 1968.
Elkins, T. H., *The Urban Explosion*, London, 1973.
Garcia-Pablos, R. "L'explosion urbaine–evolution et révolution du milieu urbain", *Documentos informativos*, No. 797, Serie V, *Arquitectura, urbanismo y vivienda en Espagne*, Madrid, Dec. 1968.
Sauvy, Alfred, *Les 4 routes de la fortune: essai sur l'automobile:* Flammarion, Paris, 1968.
Sclar, Elliot and Schaeffer, K., *Access for All*, Penguin, 1975.
Sharp, Clifford, *Problems of Urban Passenger Transport*, Leicester University Press, 1967.
United Kingdom, Ministry of Housing and Local Government, *The South-East Study, 1961–1981*, HMSO, 1964.
United Nations, *Growth of the World's Population 1920–2000*, New York (UN no. W69X1113).
United Nations, *Future Pattern and Forms of Urban Settlements*, Proceedings of a Seminar held in the Netherlands, 25 Sept.–7 Oct. 1966, 3 volumes.
United Nations, *A Review of World Conditions, Rural Housing*, New York, 1969.
United Nations, *Planning and Development of Recreation Areas including the Development of the Natural Environment*, Proceedings of a Seminar organized by the Committee on Housing, Building and Planning of the UN Economic Commission for Europe in France and Luxembourg, 27 April–10 May 1969, 2 volumes.
World Bank, *Urbanization*, Sector Working Paper, New York, 1972.

CHAPTER 2

Land Needs for Urban Growth

INTRODUCTION

The growing needs for land for urban settlement, transportation and recreation requirements, as well as for agriculture to supply food for a permanently growing population, create a feeling that there is a danger of running out of land in the future. Such dire predictions of "the dangers of progress" have been popularized recently by those who would suggest that technological progress is proceeding *too* rapidly. That is, existing resources are being utilized to such a degree that, if the rate of growth continues in the future as in the past, the natural resource base will not be able to supply the growing needs created by technological progress. The solution to the problem, as proposed, is a slower growth rate.

Certainly, technological progress has influenced the development of new needs, but at the same time it has been responsible for the discovery of new resources. Furthermore, technological progress has led to the exploitation of additional quantities of existing natural resources which were unutilizable in their pre-existing form.

These latter points are overlooked by the "futurologists" who base their prophecies on the knowledge of existing resources and existing technology. If we take into consideration the technological conditions that existed in the past, it becomes quite clear that, then as well, the danger was present that the total resource base would not satisfy growing needs.

From another point of view, the relationship between resources and needs should not be based only on quantities of resources and absolute needs. As the resource base changes with technological progress so needs change as well, not only as the result of technological progress, but also as a result of changes in socio-economic structure. For example, a socio-economic system based on planned action to satisfy the needs of society can affect "needs"—reducing some and increasing others, e.g. more education, more public transport, but fewer private cars, less alcohol, and so on.

Land is one of the natural resources which is limited in quantity. By itself, land is only a basis for satisfying needs, in that labour must be invested to create a set of conditions which allows the land to satisfy needs (e.g. constructing housing which permits a growing number of people to live in a limited space, or building roads which permit the use of land for different purposes). Given that land is a finite resource which must satisfy a multitude of needs, it is crucial that its ultimate use be planned wisely. On too many occasions that are all too visible, this has not been the case. Now, with growing and changing needs, it is even more important to clearly identify the nature and magnitude of land requirements for future urban development. The following sections attempt to estimate future land needs for different purposes, with special emphasis on changing needs resulting from economic growth.

ESTIMATES OF FUTURE LAND REQUIREMENTS

Perhaps the easiest and most effective method for estimating land needs consists of analysing actual urban land requirements for different purposes and comparing these figures with land allocated for different uses in planned new urban settlements. Of course, there will be some difficulties in estimating future needs as a result of differences in the socio-economic level of various countries. For example, in the Stockholm development plan, estimates of future land requirements are based on 2·5 rooms per person for the year 2000. (Presently there are about 1·2 rooms per person.) In Calcutta, where there are presently three persons per room (while 40% of the population live in dwellings without permanent walls), the goal for the year 1980 is to achieve the level of 2·5 *persons* per room.

Estimates of future land requirements will be based on the higher level of the needs of the population, as it is assumed that the present economically less-developed countries will achieve a higher standard of living in the future.

Table 2.1 illustrates the variation in land allocations for different uses in selected cities according to size and stage of development. On the low side are Calcutta ($27\cdot2$ m^2/person) and Madrid ($27\cdot5$ m^2/person) and on the high side are US satellite cities of between 10,000–25,000 population (530 m^2/person), and between 5000–10,000 ($851\cdot2$ m^2/person). It is noted that the actual allocation for different uses may show smaller differences, as the calculations of densities are based on land space within the administrative boundaries of a city. Thus, a city with a high percentage of vacant land and some agricultural land may show a lower density and a higher land allocation per person.

In contrast, land allocations based on the criteria used for new towns and development plans for new urban regions show less variation.

The British new town allocation varies between 149 m^2/person in Cumbernauld and 311 m^2/person in Peterlee. The average for new towns in Scotland is about 172 m^2/person. The land allocation in the Marseilles region is 153 m^2/person. Sizeable differences from the above examples occur in the Copenhagen regional plan, which allocates 370 m^2/person to accommodate a future growth area of 500,000 population, and for US programmes for planned new communities which allocate about 400 m^2/person. A very detailed calculation was made in Switzerland where the estimation is based on the floor space needed for housing, employment and public utility buildings. These figures are correlated with different building and land-use coefficients and different rates of private-car usage. Also, the Swiss approach is based on regional land requirements and, therefore, fixes as a norm 127–261 m^2/person.

In terms of comparison of land allocation for different uses, Table 2.2 shows that the biggest differences are associated with housing, roads and open space. The differences are smaller in the allocations for industrial, commercial and public services land uses.

The differences in planned land use are a result, in some cases, of different rates of private-car use which influence the land allocation for roads and residential land use respectively, while some differences arise from different planning approaches and city sizes.

The published figures on land requirements for particular land uses are different for various cities not only because of the city size but also

TABLE 2.1. Comparison of Selected Actual and Planned Urban Land
Requirements (m²/person)

USA Central cities	50,000–100,000	320·4
	100,000–250,000	321·2
	250,000 and up	201·6
Satellite cities	25,000 and up	230·8
	10,000–25,000	529·6
	5,000–10,000	851·2
English cities	Major industrial	205·6
	Major port	238·0
	Smaller towns	318·0
	Large settlements	298·6
European cities	Zurich	68·0
	London	99·2
	Rome	74·6
	Paris	34·7
	Barcelona	35·8
	Madrid	27·5
	Moscow	55·3
	Stockholm	220·0
	Helsinki	320·0
	Copenhagen	110·0
Developing countries	Calcutta	27·2
	Bombay	58·1
	Cairo	58·9
	São Paulo	428·1
	Porto Alegno	569·0
Planned new towns	UK:	
	London Region	222·8
	Scotland	171·6
	Cumberland	148·8
	Peterlee	311·0
	Hypothetical new towns (Stone)	211·0
	Tapiola (Finland)	169·0
	Obero (Sweden)	231·7
	Chelas (Portugal)	80·0
	Amsterdam (new neighbourhoods)	80·0
	Marseilles	153·0

TABLE 2.2.

	Whole developed area*	Residential	Industrial	Services	Roads	Railway	Playground, parks, open space	Education	Public building institution	Residual
Best	216·8	94·4	13·2	—	—	—	43·6	6·4	—	59·2
Stone (Major industrial towns)	206·0	116·0	22·0	6·0	—	10·0	26·4	8·8	—	17·2
Stone (New Towns)	270·8	153·2	28·8	7·6	—	7·2	40·4	16·0	—	17·6
Bigo (Marseille)	153·3	67·0	18·0	9·19	30	—	17·0	13·2	—	4·8
Switzerland (ORL)	127–261	67–171	—	—	40–50	—	—	—	20–40*	—
C. Clark (USA more than 250,000)	204·0	82·0	18·0	8	50	9·0	17·0	—	19·0	—
(USA under 50,000)	404·0	159·0	23·0	13·0	114	20·0	21·0	—	53·0	—
Cumbernauld	143·0	47·0	27·0	—	9	3·0	47·0	—	10·0	—

Sources:

Robin H. Best and J. T. Coppock, *The Changing Use of Land in Britain*, Faber & Faber, London, 1962. p. 233.

P. A. Stone, "Housing town development costs", *The Estate Gazette*, London, p. 144.

Andre Bigo, *L'Urbanisms face au problems foncier*, Paris, 1968, p. 198.

ORL—Institut fur Arts—Regional and Landplanning ETH, Lrholtung, Aureisherung and Schutz Des Grundwassers, Blatter 516021–516030, Zurich.

* This figure includes green space outside residential areas.

because of the different classifications and definitions of land uses in different countries. The comparison shows that a small town in a big metropolitan area may need less land because it does not contain all urban functions. Thus, its allocation for employment and services may be lower than that of the region as a whole. To avoid these types of irregularities, subsequent allocations will also be based on separate urban functions, based on estimates for planned new towns and neighbourhoods. These estimated figures can only be approximate.

HOUSING

There are substantial differences in the amount of land allocated for residential use in existing cities. In American cities of over 250,000 population the average is $81 \, m^2$/person while in the suburbs between 10,000–25,000 population the average is $271 \, m^2$/person. In English cities the differences in land allocations for residence are not as large. In the major industrial towns the average is $116 \, m^2$/person, while the smaller towns average $149 \, m^2$/person. In London, where a large segment of the population lives in multi-storey dwellings, the allocation is only $38 \, m^2$/person. Other large cities (Zurich, $30 \, m^2$/person; Calcutta with 10–$20 \, m^2$/person) average even less than London.

For new towns and planned neighbourhoods, differences in land allocation result from a reliance on different housing types and planning conceptions. Until recently public schemes were based mostly on multi-storey units in order to preserve open space. The more recent demand for privacy has caused planning authorities to provide a higher percentage of single-family and semi-detached dwellings. Planners have successfully shown that single-family one-storey units do not require large amounts of additional land. For example, research carried out in England, Sweden and Denmark demonstrated that new housing and semi-detached houses require only 8–10% more land than multi-storey dwellings, while one-family housing requires about 20% more. Thus, as all residential use typically comprises 40% of all urban land, the effect of insuring even all one-family houses would be to increase the general land allocation by not more than 8%.

The new neighbourhoods of Amsterdam are significant examples of the provision of good living conditions based on planned land allocation. The ten new neighbourhoods contain a total of 60,000 dwelling units. The average allocation is 250 m²/dwelling or 80 m²/person. The land allocation for different uses is shown in Table 2.3.

TABLE 2.3.

Dwelling area	29 m²/person
Private garden	17 m²/person
Common gardens	37 m²/person
Public institutions	23 m²/person
Roads	83 m²/person
Shops	3 m²/person
Public park and open space	58 m²/person

Larger allocations are found in the development scheme for the Copenhagen region, based upon a larger land allocation. The total allocation is 1000 m²/dwelling or 330 m²/person. The space is allocated as shown in Table 2.4.

TABLE 2.4.

Residential neighbourhood	65% or 650 m²/dwelling
Green space	23% or 230 m²/dwelling
Roads (outside the neighbourhood)	4% or 40 m²/dwelling
Employment	8% or 80 m²/dwelling

The scheme is based upon accommodating a projected population of 500,000.

The Swiss allocation scheme is based upon 61–171 m²/person (the average is 119 m²/person). This figure is designed to yield 30–40 m²/person in floor space (land-use coefficient of 0·7—the land-use coefficient being the ratio of floor space to land area).

In contrast, the Barcelona development scheme is based upon only 27 m²/total/person. This provides 18 m² of floor space per person, and with an average family size of 3.5, a dwelling space of 63 m². With a land-use coefficient of 1.5, each dwelling will occupy 47 m² of land or 13.4 m²/person. In addition to the land needed for the dwelling, space must be allocated for the following items: primary education, 2 m²/person; secondary, 1·4 m²/person; open space, 6·6 m²/person; roads, 3·5 m²/person; thus the total allocation is 26·9 m²/person (though an additional 13 m² must be added for other residential needs).

The British new town of Hook, the French scheme for a new town of 100,000 population and P. A. Stone's hypothetical new towns serve as a more adequate basis for estimating future land requirements. All three schemes use a similar approach. They try to insure a high percentage of single-family and semi-detached houses and plan multi-storey buildings only in the central urban areas. The French scheme proposes the following allocations:

Central zone	70 dwelling units per ha.
Intermediate zone	30 dwelling units per ha.
Periphery	15 dwelling units per ha.
Average	23 dwelling units per ha.

The British scheme allocates:

Central zone	108 d.u. per ha.	15% of population
Intermediate zone	56 d.u. per ha.	45% of population
Periphery	27 d.u. per ha.	40% of population
Average	45 d.u. per ha.	

Stone uses 25 d.u./ha. or 400 m²/dwelling. For an average family size of 3.2, this represents an allocation of 125 m²/person, which appears to be adequate. The British scheme for the new town of Hook uses 220 m²/dwelling or 70 m²/person while the French scheme estimates 435 m²/dwelling or 136 m²/person. Thus, a range of 70–136 m²/person, depending on circumstances, will be used as the base for estimating future urban land needs. Use of a norm 25 dwellings per ha. will insure a high percentage of one-family houses on the basis of allocating 125 m²/person (for an average family size of 3.2). For a larger family size such land allocation would provide family housing only by building multi-storey houses.

GREEN SPACE AND RECREATION

The shorter working week and the increasing availability of free time are results of technological progress and increased consumer income which permit greater expenditure on leisure activities. As the use of free time is becoming increasingly significant in defining living patterns, and given existing overcrowding in most cities, the allocation of green space is quite important. For purposes of estimating land requirements for general recreational pursuits, it is necessary to examine three separate categories.

First, green space needed near the house and in the neighbourhood is taken into account in the estimation of open space needs in residential land use. Second are allocations for playgrounds, urban parks and sports-grounds, which are calculated separately in the estimation of land needs for urban development. Third are allocations for regional and national needs (e.g. national parks).

A recent calculation of land requirements for recreation areas in the Netherlands is presented in Table 2.5.

TABLE 2.5.

	Distance from dwelling (km)	Land needs	Park area (ha.)
Neighbourhood park	0·9	4 m²/person	1
Town quarter park	0·8	8 m²/person	6–10
Town district park	1·6	16 m²/person	30–60
City park	3·2	32 m²/person	200–400
City regional park	6·5	65 m²/person	1000–3000
Park area of regional significance	15·0	125 m²/person	10,000–30,000
Park area of national significance	50·0	250 m²/person	60,000–100,000

Source: G. Van Esterik, *Proceedings of the Seminar on Planning and Development of Recreation Areas*, Vol. 1, Amsterdam, 1969, p. 105.

This calculation shows that 48 m²/person are to be provided for the town inhabitants (12 m²/person for neighbourhood purposes, calculated in the residential requirements), 190 m²/persons in the city region and 250 m²/person for national parks. It is noted that such land requirements were made in a country with the highest population density in Europe (400 persons/m²). By comparison, the following space requirements for regional recreational areas in the densely populated parts of the Stockholm region have been proposed by the Planning Office:

District parks	$20\,m^2$/person
Regional parks	$180\,m^2$/person
Total recreational area	$200\,m^2$/person

These allocations mean that a district park of about $2\,km^2$ serves about 80,000 persons.

The National Recreation Association in the USA suggests $14\,m^2$/person for recreational land inside of urban areas. However, many planners argue that the standards should be raised to $40\,m^2$/person within metropolitan areas with an additional $40\,m^2$/person of state and federal recreational land located within a 2-hour drive from the central city (i.e. excluding the large national parks).

The actual land used for recreational purposes in American cities is as follows: cities greater than 250,000 population, $17\,m^2$/person; cities between 100,000 and 250,000, $17\cdot2\,m^2$/person; 50,000 to 100,000, $21\,m^2$/person; and cities 10,000 to 25,000, $24\,m^2$/person. It is noted that the actual use is quite a bit less than the proposed $40\,m^2$/person.

The actual land use for city parks in European cities is as follows:

Paris	$5\cdot25\,m^2$/person
London	$9\cdot00\,m^2$/person
Rome	$9\cdot00\,m^2$/person
Berlin	$13\cdot00\,m^2$/person
Vienna	$25\cdot00\,m^2$/person

The new development scheme for Milan allocates $24\,m^2$/person for city green space. In Scandinavian cities, the land norms for green space are as shown in Table 2.6.

TABLE 2.6.

Oslo	$45\cdot0\,m^2$/person
Stockholm (in the suburbs)	$56\cdot0\,m^2$/person (1946—$38\cdot0\,m^2$/person)
Orbero (Sweden)	$33\cdot8\,m^2$/person (in comparison with $12\cdot4\,m^2$/person in 1929)
Hook (UK new town)	$43\cdot0\,m^2$/person for city parks
France (planned city of 100,000)	$23\cdot0\,m^2$/person (in addition to $40\cdot0\,m^2$/person of neighbourhood parks)
Marseilles (Bigo's calculation)	$13\cdot3\,m^2$/person

The allocation of green space in cities in developing countries is less than the European and US standard. The Calcutta metropolitan district has no more than $1 \cdot 2 \, m^2$/person. Baghdad allocated $1 \cdot 4 \, m^2$/person. An international standard suggested by experts for developing countries was $16 \, m^2$/person.

From all of the above, it would appear that the Dutch example is the best one to use for calculating the requirements for future urban recreational-land needs, although their projected standard is higher than existing European and US norms ($48 \, m^2$/person in metropolitan areas).

Future allocations must also insure additional space for regional and national parks. As the amounts allocated for these purposes depend upon topographical conditions, the transport network and recreational patterns of the population, there is some cause for variation here. According to Maurer (Switzerland), space for regional and national parks should be equal to the urban settlement space. This would imply $127-261 \, m^2$/person.

The above figure may be influenced by one further consideration, second-home ownership. Congestion and a desire for privacy, combined with the constant tension that exists in the cities, have generated an increasing demand for second homes in rural areas.

The socio-economic composition of second-home owners generally depends on urban living patterns. In countries where the middle and upper income groups live in suburban areas on large lots with single-family homes, only the very rich have a second house. In countries and cities where the middle- and high-income groups are accustomed to residing inside the city, the desire to purchase a second home influences a much larger population segment. In France there are more than $1\frac{1}{2}$ million second-home owners (about 10% of the total population). In Sweden, more than 400,000 summer houses are registered, which indicates that 20% of the population have purchased second homes. In some cases the trend toward second homes may benefit the rural areas; but it may also create problems if second homes are built on previously vacant land, especially if built without prior planning. In undeveloped areas, the erection of second homes may pressure public agencies to develop the infrastructure in regions of the country where growth is not desired. This type of development is a result of the lack of suitable national planning and results in unnecessary land consumption. However, even as the trend toward second home ownership increases, the provision of necessary green space within cities is still the main task of an efficient recreational land-use policy.

Recent schemes for new planned communities have, in almost all countries, insured what appears to be adequate public green space. These allocations vary between 40–56 m^2/person. Thus, in calculating needed green space inside the cities, it may be suggested that these figures be used as the norms for planned future requirements.

TRANSPORTATION AND ROADS

Recent urban development and the forecast of the future pattern of urban life both influence and are influenced by the means of transportation. Generally, the extensive use of private cars combined with insufficient public transport has created a situation where a technological advance has been neutralized by long trips to work and to commercial centres.

While use of the motor car initially allowed for the extension of the city frontier, it reached a point of diminishing returns when there was around one car per family. That is, although the development of the car permitted the achievement of a high level of mobility, the great increase in the number of cars has impeded urban development and the very mobility it was designed to provide. As such, the exaggerated use of the private car in the town is becoming one of the obstacles to future urban development. Certainly, it has limited the development of public transportation which in turn has further increased the use of private cars.

The impact of the increased use of private motor cars on land needs for roads may be seen from the following data on some cities in the Scandanavian countries:

Oslo: needs increased from 21·0 m^2/person in 1948 to 24 m^2/person in 1964.

Stockholm: needs increased from 14·2 m^2/person in 1945 to 19·2 m^2/person in 1962.

Gothenburg: needs increased from 14·4 m^2/person in 1945 to 18·8 m^2/person in 1962.

The basic transportation problem is how to ease the flow of traffic which results from the concentration of employment in the city centre and the dispersion of housing in the city region. The inadequate development of the public transportation system is a common characteristic of almost all the cities of the world. There are, however, differences in the ways cities either neglect the problem or try to find solutions.

It may be suggested that the solution to such difficulties is to limit the circulation of private cars in the city centre and develop public transportation to its required level. It is also proposed that motor cars can be disallowed completely in certain areas in the town centres and pedestrian traffic only be permitted. The results of such restricted area experiments have so far been favourable in Copenhagen and Stuttgart, while the results in Rome have been discouraging.

The extension of the subway is seen in many cities as the essential means of improving public transportation, especially to the town centre. New subways have recently been constructed in such cities as Milan, Montreal, Munich and Rome. Also, an extension of service to the suburbs is being realized in Paris and Madrid. Combined subway and elevated lines are also being constructed in some metropolitan areas. Of course, the private car is still needed to provide mobility in low-density areas. But whatever the solution adapted for the urban transportation problem, the amount of space needed is likely to be greater.

The calculation of transport requirements should take into account three general factors:
1. neighbourhood needs as part of residential land use;
2. requirements for traffic in the town outside the neighbourhood;
3. national transport needs.

For each of the first two the ratio between the amount of land used for dwellings and the amount used for parked cars is a factor relevant to all big cities of the world. For example, a three-room dwelling of 50–55 m² in a seven-storey apartment house occupies 8–9 m² of land. A car also occupies 8 m² of land, not only near the house, but in the work areas of the town. Examples of allocations in some cities are as shown in Table 2.7.

The difference in the figures in Table 2.7 reflect different norms (as

TABLE 2.7. Land Requirement for Roads

American cities, population over 250,000	50 m^2/person
population 100,000–250,000	89 m^2/person
population under 50,000	114 m^2/person
Danish cities, population over 25,000	57 m^2/person
population 15,000–25,000	64 m^2/person
French planned town of 100,000	
(not including neighbourhood roads)	31 m^2/person
Switzerland (estimated needs)	40–50 m^2/person
Zurich (actual use)	24 m^2/person
Hook (planned British new town)	11 m^2/person
Marseille (Bigo)	30 m^2/person
	(25 m^2/person in centre and 5 m^2 for parking)

well as variations in the definition of "roads" between different countries). For purposes of estimating future land requirements, based on sufficient public transport, the planned norms might be estimated as between 30–50 m^2/person.

INDUSTRY

Recently, there have been noticeable changes in industrial location patterns, especially for those industries which are more market/distribution oriented. The most discernible trend has been a suburbanization of light and "clean" industries. There are three primary reasons for such a trend: (1) the growth of freeways and outer belts which has improved the interconnections between all parts of the metropolitan area; (2) the increasing desire of industrial firms for space for production and storage and the need for better accessibility to markets and sources of supply, which in combination with (1) has "pushed" many firms out of industrial parks in interior city locations and on to large sites at outer belt locations; and (3) the desire to be near a skilled work force who are in the city region. While this trend does have some interesting ramifications for land price development, which will be discussed in a subsequent chapter, it is important at this point only to estimate land requirements which must be satisfied if this trend continues.

Again, we must draw on the examples of planned developments.

The Copenhagen development scheme allocates 39–50 m^2/worker floor space for light and medium manufacturing industries (the average being 42 m^2/worker). For a building coefficient fixed at 0.2, 200 m^2 of land per worker is required. In the new town of Hook, the norm is also 50 workers per hectare, or 200 m^2/worker. Swiss estimates for industrial land requirements are between 50–100 m^2/worker, while the Stockholm regional plan uses 100–200 m^2/worker. The Barcelona development scheme estimates 80–125 m^2/worker before 1980 and 100–166 m^2/worker between 1980 and 2010.

In the Calcutta development scheme, for industries located in outlying areas, it is estimated that these industries will need 1 acre for 30–50 workers or an average of 100 m^2/worker of land, though the estimate for "more extensive industries" is 1 acre per 25–30 workers or 145 m^2/worker.

Oslo, Norway, calculates the space requirements for different industries as follows: light industry, 20 m^2/worker; heavy industry, 40 m^2/worker; highly automated industry, 200 m^2/worker. The average for all industries is 40–50 m^2/worker.

From all of the above, and assuming increasingly automated industry, the figure of 150 m^2/worker would appear to be representative. Based upon a 40% active population with 50% of these occupied in industry (as a global industry/non-industry average), the general land allocation for industry is 30 m^2/person for the entire population. Thus, a range of 20–40 m^2/person represents the desirable norms.

THE SERVICE SECTOR

Land requirements for services vary greatly, depending upon location and the means of transportation used by the employees and customers. For example, the actual surface space required for services concentrated in CBD's is quite small as they depend on public transport. In contrast, services in outlying areas where people are more dependent on the use of private cars have parking space allocations which considerably inflate the total surface requirements. The master plan for Iceland's capital, Reyjavik, makes a forecast for land needs for commercial services (Table 2.8).

In Zurich, the development plan allocates 10 m^2/employee. The cal-

TABLE 2.8.

	1962	1983
Offices	1·65 m²/person	2·3–3·0 m²/person
Retail trade	1·1	1·2
Warehouses	1·7	3–5
Totals	4·45 m²/person	6·5–9·5 m²/person

culation of Bigo for Marseille shows that the needed built surface per employee is 25 m² on average. However, taking into account the building coefficient and the percentage occupied in services in relation to the total population, the land needed for services for each inhabitant is 9·2 m²/person. Similarly, in Hook, on the basis of 63% occupied in services, land needs are 3·3 m²/person, while the existing densities in British towns are 6 m²/person in major industrial towns and 7·6 m²/person in new towns (according to Stone).

In calculating land needs for future urban development, more account must be taken of space requirements for typically suburban service development. Suburban residential development has strongly influenced the location of retail trade, particularly for shopping centres whose good freeway connections have made them accessible to customers from a wide area.

Increased demand for goods, self-service procedures and an increase in the variety of goods have all increased space requirements for retail services. The floor space required per employee and large parking areas needed have both increased the amount of land needed.

Similarly, wholesale trade has moved to the urban fringe in search of open land. In contrast, there has been an increased concentration in the CBD of services which require close communication, which results in additional space requirements in an already extremely crowded area.

From the above considerations, future needs for the service sector are estimated at 30 m² floor space per employee. Using the Swiss land-use coefficient of 0·5, and assuming 40% active population, 50% of whom are employed in services, total land requirements are 12 m²/

person. Thus a range of 10–14 m²/person would be a representative norm for estimating future land requirements.

PUBLIC SERVICES

The provision of public services based on the growing needs of an expanding population is one of the essential functions of government. Given that the number and volume of institutional services have been steadily increasing on all fronts, development plans for new urban settlements must insure that land requirements for these institutions are met.

Certainly, large differences exist in the amount of land required among countries with differing socio-economic levels. For example, large differences occur in the amount of floor space allocated for education. The Calcutta development scheme provides 1·92 ha. for educational requirements in a neighbourhood of 25,000. This implies a total of 0·8 m²/person. The French scheme for a new town provides 10 m²/person for the same purpose, while the estimates of land needs for educational purposes in England vary from 6·4 m²/person (Best) to 16 m²/person (new towns—Stone). Calcutta allocates 3·2 ha. for health facilities. This represents only 0·1 m²/person for this function. In contrast, France provides 2 m²/person for administration and 0·8 m²/person for health purposes.

Bigo calculated 23·6 m²/person for all public and institutional land needs in Marseille (or about 15·5% of general land needs of the urban population).

In estimating future needs it should be kept in mind that educational, health and administrative services are likely to permanently increase. Therefore, the requirements of the Swiss development scheme, 20–40 m²/person, seem most appropriate.

CONCLUSIONS ON PLANNED LAND REQUIREMENTS

From previous sections it can be seen that there are large differences between allocations for the variety of urban functions. These differences are primarily a result of differences between levels of economic development, urbanization, and socio-cultural attainment, as well as a variety of individual circumstances associated with each city or area. Given such differences, it is possible only to generalize future land requirements on a global scale. Thus, for each function, the estimated land needs have been presented as ranges, where the "average" allocations can be interpreted as guidelines. As such, the "average" total land requirements for all urban functions are approximately 285 m²/person. It is felt that this figure is sufficient to give a high living standard in the urban region. This figure is based on the estimated land requirements for different uses (Table 2.9).

TABLE 2.9.

	Range	Average
Residential	100–150 m²/person	125 m²/person
Roads	30–50	40
Green space	40–56	48
Public services	20–40	30
Industry	20–40	30
Commercial services	10–14	12
	220–350 m²/person	285 m²/person*

*The norm of 285 m²/person gives an average density of 35 persons per hectare.

It should be emphasized that such estimates of general land needs are only approximate, as actual land requirements will depend on the levels of economic and technological development as well as socio-cultural conditions. Therefore, in an economically less-developed country with a low degree of motorization and with a high percentage of the population employed in agriculture, a larger percentage of space must be allocated for residential area for those rural migrants who prefer one-or two-family houses with ample green space. Generally, less land will be needed for other purposes. It should be underlined that considerably less space may be needed for larger human settlements where the densities will be higher than for smaller towns where the densities are low. The estimated figure is nearer to a maximum required for national planning norms.

National development schemes must insure sufficient space for recreation purposes as well as for the national transport network. It has been suggested by experts in different countries that national, recreational and transportation purposes will require nearly as much space as all the land needed for urban purposes.

The space required for the national transport network varies according to the size of a country and the level of development. Generally more land is needed in comparison with urban requirements in larger countries and less space is required in smaller, densely populated countries. In the United States, roads use as much space as urban settlements (20 million acres). In contrast, in the United Kingdom, roads occupy only 3% of the total land area while urban settlements occupy 7%. The space for the national transport network may be estimated as roughly 40% of the requirements for urban settlements. If the figure of $285 \, \text{m}^2$/person is used for urban space needs, it should be estimated that $114 \, \text{m}^2$/person will be required for the national transport network. Therefore $500 \, \text{m}^2$/person must be taken as a basis for future urban development planning which includes national recreational and transportation needs.

If the estimate of $285 \, \text{m}^2$/person for planned urban settlements is accepted, then 1 million people living in urban settlements and employed in industry and services will need $285 \, \text{km}^2$ of urban land. The Netherlands development scheme assumes that the forecasted 7 million increase in urban population to the year 2000 will lead to a doubling of the present urban space, which is $2145 \, \text{km}^2$. This means an estimate of $306 \, \text{m}^2$ of urban land per person (these figures are based on 50–70% one-family houses).

Using our estimate, an addition of 100 million to the urban population of the US would require no more than $28,500 \, \text{km}^2$ or $11,200 \, \text{miles}^2$ of additional space (at an average density of 8750 persons per square mile). This is approximately the amount of unused idle land area in the North-eastern urban complex. If national requirements are included, the figures increase to $57,000 \, \text{km}^2$ or $22,400 \, \text{miles}^2$.

These figures only prove that the problem of providing land for future urban development has little to do with the quantity of land. That is, given a future world urban population increase of 2 billion, an urban space of $570,000 \, \text{km}^2$ is required. This represents a surface

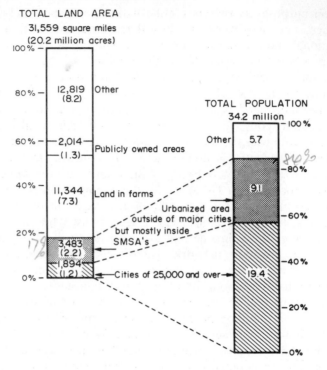

Fig. 2.1. Land use and population in Northeastern Urban Complex, 1960.

area 10% larger than the total area of France, or only 7% of the total surface area of the US.

In spite of these theoretical quantitative calculations using 285 km² per 1 million urban population, actual urban development consumes larger quantities of land because urban settlements are dispersed over large areas. Most of the land between the settlements is vacant. The North-eastern US urban complex provides a classic example of this. Figure 2.1 shows that 84% of the total population of the region live on 17% of the total land surface (57% on just 6% of the land area). Clawson suggests that it might be possible to settle 50–100 million additional people in the north-eastern urban complex by utilizing vacant land without converting agricultural land into urban uses. This illustration serves to show that the problem of insuring land for the future is not a quantitative one, but rather a function of the quality of planning and the level and structure of the public institutions using the land efficiently for the needs of the society.

There are some general factors which influence the demand for more space and affect the increased demand for land in certain regions. The increase of national income creates a need for more space for housing, green areas, sports grounds, national parks and roads. However, the development of building technology allows the erection of structures high above the land surface as well as deep under the earth. This development is especially important for building under-ground roads and parking, and, in some cases, is important for com-mercial and other services. The development of building technology also makes possible the use of space above the land surface for road building on different levels. Therefore, economic development increases the demand for land but, at the same time, provides the technology to partly supply the additional land needs in areas of high density.

The crucial problem of land demand results from the pressure of population concentrating in some regions of the country. The demand is especially great in the metropolitan areas, the regions of rapid economic development. Recently, there has also been an increased demand for land in suitable tourist areas; particularly near the sea, but also in mountain resort areas. In metropolitan regions demand has been increasing for land far from the town, where the prices are still low. The likelihood that the metropolitan area will enlarge in-creases demand even in rural areas far from the town and the city region.

A detailed analysis of land requirements compared to existing land surface in metropolitan areas shows that in most of these areas enough land is available for building purposes, but there is a lack of land available on the market. Even in the most crowded cities there exists a sufficient amount of vacant land or land with low densities. Land-use legislation which would require using the land for construction purposes may increase the building capacity of existing urban land surface. In the last decade, accumulated experience shows that planning may increase the "absorption" capacity of land surface, while a lack of planning may lead to increased land consumption through dispersed building activity in a large area.

REFERENCES

Best, Robin and Coppock, J. T. *The Changing Use of Land in Britain*, London: Faber & Faber, 1962.

Bigo, Andre, *L'Urbanisme face au probleme foncier*, Paris, 1968.

Clark, Colin, *Land Use and Population Growth*, New York: St. Martins Press, 1967.

Clawson, Marion, Burnell Held, R. and Stoddard, C. H., *Land for the Future*, Resources for the Future, Baltimore, Md., 1962.

——, *American Land and its Uses*, New York, 1972.

——, *Suburban Land Conversion in the United States*, Baltimore: Johns Hopkins Press, 1971.

Government of the Netherlands, *Second Report on Physical Planning in the Netherlands*, Part I: *Main Outline of National Planning Policy*, The Hague: Government Printing Office, 1966.

Ibid., Part II: *Future Pattern of Development*, The Hague: Government Printing Office, 1966.

International Federation for Housing and Planning, *Growing Space Needs of Urbanized Regions*, International Conference in Orebo, Sweden, 1965.

Lichfield, Nathaniel, *Economics of Planned Development*, London: Estates Gazette, 1965.

Morrill, Richard, *The Spatial Organization of Society*, Wadsworth Publishing Co., California, 1970.

ORL (Institut fur Orts-, Regional-, und Landesplanning), ETH, Erhaltung, Ancrei-cherung und Schutz des Grundwassers, Blatter 316021-516030, Zurich.

Stone, P. A., *Housing, Town Development and Land Costs*, London: The Estates Gazette, 1962.

PART TWO

The Land Factor in Urban Development

CHAPTER 3

The Development of Land Prices in the Industrialized Countries

INTRODUCTION

The general trend of high rates of land price increase is a common phenomenon for almost all countries. But there are big differences in the *rate* of price increase in different countries and different city areas. Many factors affect land prices. It may be suggested that a comparative study of land price development in some countries may help further understanding of the land price formation process.

Such a comparison should also permit the identification of the main factors which influence land price increases in most countries, keeping in mind the peculiar conditions and circumstances which affect land values in each country during different time periods.

The period since the Second World War has been characterized, unlike preceding periods, by a relatively uninterrupted rise of land prices. While urban land prices also rose in the past with the growth of the cities, in the pre-Second World War period there were many fluctuations and steep declines as well. The post-war period had a permanent price increase in almost all countries, with short intervals of price stabilization. We will investigate the hypothesis that this is related to a change in the type of economic growth. Before the war, the economic cycle included many severe crises. After the war, economic growth has stopped only for short periods of recession until recently, basically due to state intervention in economic and social life.

It may be suggested that other reasons for the constant increase of land prices in the recent period are the inflation connected with economic growth and the process of accelerated urbanization, particularly with regard to the large metropolitan areas.

Data on increases of land prices collected in various countries prove that the greatest increases have resulted from decisions by public authorities to change land use from agricultural to urban land. In such cases, the increase of land prices is measured by hundreds, sometimes thousands, of percentage points.

One of the economic results of the increase of land prices is the growing importance of land in expenditures for housing and for industrial and service buildings, which cancel out some of the effects of technological progress in the building industry and of the decrease in building production costs. Land prices are especially important in the high expenditures for housing (land costs now compose 30–50% of housing costs in big cities). This leads to the siting of social housing far from employment and essential services. The comparison of land price development in countries having different land policies may help to understand the role of land policy measures in the formation of land prices.

EVALUATION DIFFICULTIES

A comparison of land prices within the same country, given definitional problems and data insufficiencies is a difficult enough proposition. Cross-country comparisons, given varying standards of living, stages of development, and constantly changing currency exchange rates, are even more difficult, though it is possible to draw some general comparative results. One of the main difficulties in collecting material about the development of urban land prices derives from the diversified character of land prices which differ not only between cities of the same country, but between sites in the same quarter and street. Fixing an average price cannot, therefore, express the real value of the land. Furthermore, a serious difficulty results from the fact that public authorities in some countries do not, as a rule, publish statistics on land prices.

Statistics are partially available, however, from two sources: land transactions, and land evaluations made by special officers of the taxation office for the purposes of taxation. Transaction figures are difficult to compare because they occur in different places at different times.

Although a comparison of prices made by evaluation is less reliable about the real market price than transaction figures, it gives a more exact picture on land-price development trends, because evaluation is made at the same time throughout the country and to the same criteria over time. Evaluation figures are, however, seen as confidential in most countries. In fact, only Denmark published land-value maps for the entire country every 4 years. Very reliable material can also be found in research studies on the development of land values in different cities, in particular some cities in France, Milan, the city and region of Zurich, some US cities, Israel, Japan and India.

It is suggested that the best method of measuring the development of land prices is by comparing changes in the price of the same site at the time of change of ownership. This method eliminates the large variations in land prices resulting from the different locations. The changes in land prices, even of the same site, may be not only a result of the general trend of land price increase, but an effect of some development of the region or of more intensive use of the land of the investigated site. The same method that illustrates the impact of different factors on the price of the same site also allows the measurement of the general increase of land prices.

A comparison based on prices in countries of different levels of national income and gross national product also make comparisons difficult. Similarly, differences in land-use coefficients between different cities is another factor which presents evaluative problems.

We have presented our figures in current prices, making adjustments for inflation by giving separate figures for the increase in consumer prices. In order to collect information for this study, use was made of available official material. Information was also collected through interviews in various countries with different experts: surveyors, evaluators, builders, architects and government officials dealing with land-use planning. The material collected, however, has informative value only. Therefore, any comparison of land prices only shows the trend of price development rather than the real level of land prices.

All of the information collected is presented below in the following form:

(a) average increase of land prices over a long period;

  (b) differences in rate of increase of land price in metropolitan regions;
  (c) comparison of residential and commercial land-use prices.

It should be kept in mind that figures based on aggregate city and country value are more relevant for comparison over different time periods than others calculated by current transaction prices. For comparing absolute price levels among cities, we are using the highest price level in each city which, for comparison among different cities, may be better than the average of transaction prices.

LONG-TERM TRENDS IN LAND-PRICE DEVELOPMENT

We have been able to locate material on urban land prices over a long time period for only a very few countries. Only for the USA and France is it possible to present data going back very far into the nineteenth century. There are a number of countries in which information goes back to the period around the First World War—Denmark, Switzerland, the UK and Japan (only from 1936). After 1950 data is available from a number of countries. In choosing which countries' data to use, we have also tried to select a range of different development patterns. Therefore we have presented material from recently industrialized countries (Italy, Spain, Japan), countries with varying types of state intervention in the economy and in the land market (the Netherlands, Sweden, Denmark, France, the UK), and countries with more *laissez-faire* governments (Switzerland, USA).

There are two general points in our material. The first is the difference in the pattern of land-price development before and after the Second World War, shown by all countries for which we have information. The second is the difference in the *rate* of price increase in the post-war years, ranging from a relatively low rate in the USA, the Netherlands and Sweden to a very high rate in Japan. The relationship between various economic indicators and these post-war land-price increases will be discussed in a separate section below, after our survey of country-by-country land-price trends.

The United States

Homer Hoyt, in *The Urban Real Estate Cycle: Performances and Prospects* (Urban Land Institutes, 1960), shows that over a period of 150 years, from the beginning of the nineteenth century until 1960, the urban real estate cycle was about 18 years in length from peak to peak and from trough to trough. He found that:

> The rising trend in real estate values lasted much longer than the fall. The downturn was sharp and swift. The upward movement in real estate prices persisted from 1819 to 1836; 1860 to 1872; 1894 to 1907; 1908 to 1925; or for periods of from twelve to seventeen years. The periods of sharply falling real estate values were from 1818 to 1819; 1837 to 1840; 1857 to 1859; 1873 to 1875; 1892 to 1894; 1907 to 1908 and 1929 to 1932, or a duration in time of one to three years. The main upthrust in real estate values was also of short duration, or from 1816 to 1818; 1834 to 1836; 1852 to 1854; 1867 to 1869; 1887 to 1890 and 1922 to 1925. The urban real estate cycle has been closely associated with the general business cycle; but as shown by the chart on Chicago land values in Fig. 1 [shown here as Fig. 3.1], which is typical of real estate, values were not appreciably affected by the numerous minor fluctuations in the business cycle. Real estate prices moved slowly and did not reverse their trends until a major business crisis occurred, such as the panics of 1819, 1837, 1857, 1873, 1893, and the financial debacle of October 1929.

Generally, land prices follow only the periods of very deep economic crises, while recent wars and changes in economic life have had no such direct impact on real estate trends.

In his book *One Hundred Years of Land Value: The Chicago Real Estate Cycle*, Hoyt makes a more detailed analysis of the relationship between various business indices and land prices. He shows the dramatic difference in the magnitude of oscillation between the general business cycle and the land market (see Table 3.1).

Hoyt also makes the point that commodity, land and stock speculations do not occur at the same time but tend to alternate. He suggests that "the movement of each (speculation) may be enhanced by the concentration of funds upon each in turn instead of the diffusion of capital over all of them at the same time. Speculators who reaped large profits from the rise or fall of commodity prices may invest in land. It is significant to note that some of the largest fortunes in real estate have been made by men who were not primarily real estate operators."

Hoyt distinguishes between the period of 1790–1933 of some monetary stability, and after 1933 with a permanent rise in the wholesale

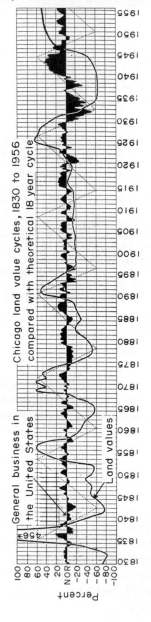

Fig. 3.1. Chicago land-value cycles, 1830 to 1956. (Reproduced by courtesy of Urban Land Institutes, 1960.)

TABLE 3.1.

	% Maximum deviation		% Average deviation		Maximum years of period		Length of period		% of entire period above normal
	Above Normal	Below Normal	Above Normal	Below Normal	Above Normal	Below Normal	Above Normal	Below Normal	
Business activity in US annually	16	41·6	5·1	7·5	7	6	3·0	2·0	58·8
Chicago land values 1830–1933	456	80·0	58·4	30·0	9	26	6·0	16·3	29·0

Source: Hoyt, *op. cit.*, table lxviii, p. 415.

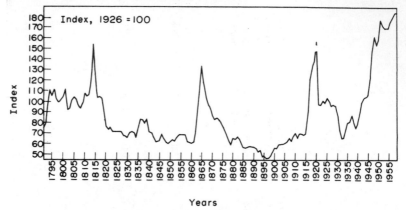

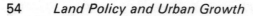

Fig. 3.2. Wholesale prices, United States Bureau of Labor Statistics, 1791 to 1959. (Source: Hoyt, *op. cit.*)

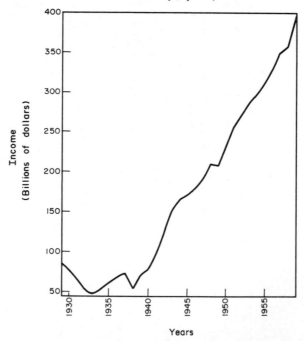

Fig. 3.3. National income, United States, 1929 to 1959. (Source: Hoyt, *op. cit.*)

price index (Fig. 3.2) and a permanent rise in national income (Fig. 3.3). He mentions that after the sharp decline of national income from $86 billion in 1929 to below $50 billion in 1933 national income did begin to permanently rise—achieving $400 billion in 1959. Rapid urban population increase between 1790 and 1960 also had a large influence on the increase of land values (Fig. 3.4). In all, the per-

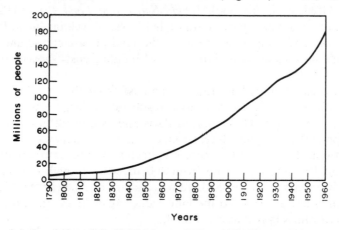

Fig. 3.4. Population of the United States, 1790 to 1960. (Source: Hoyt, *op. cit.*)

manently uninterrupted economic growth and increase in national income together with urban population growth are factors which have conditioned the permanent rise of urban land prices after the Second World War.

We have other data for the average annual changes in land prices in the US in the later period. These estimates are as follows:

1920–30   the total increase was 19% or 2·1% per annum
1930–38   there was a decrease of 2·1% per annum
1938–45   +3·7%
1945–56   +5·0%
1956–66   +5·5–6·9% per year

Source: Milgram, *U.S. Land Prices—Directions and Dynamics*, Washington 1968.

It must be kept in mind that the above figures are aggregate national estimates. The difference in land price changes among different cities are enormous. Newly urbanized and rapidly growing areas, such as in Southern California, Arizona and Florida, had price increases several times the average.

France

J. J. Grenelle, in his book *Urban Space and Land Prices* (Paris, 1970), presented voluminous data on land-price development in Paris since 1860. The comparison between the land-price increase and the index of consumer prices and the index of building costs shows a more independent trend.

Land prices show a high rate of increase from the middle of the nineteenth century up to 1910, as a result of the large urbanization works carried out by Haussman in Paris and as a result of economic development. The highest level of land prices was achieved by 1910, and between 1910 and 1920 there was decline in real terms. Between 1920 and 1929 the index rose from 400 to 2030, though during the depression years in the 1930s there was a sharp decline (i.e. to 770) in 1937. Only in the 1950s did the land values again reach the previous high 1910 values in real terms (Fig. 3.5).

From the 1950s to 1965 prices rose in Paris by 17 times (a rate of 21% per year). The period 1959–62 showed the highest rate of increase (26% per year). Since 1965 prices have risen by only 5·8% annually. These trends are similar in provincial cities; for example, in Marseilles the highest rate of price increase was between 1954–63 (24% per year).

Grenelle suggests that there is a definite relationship in this period to the rate of economic activity. Both reached their highest rate of increase in 1963, and subsequently both were lower (Fig. 3.6).

Grenelle also presents information in his Paris study on the relationship of land prices in the different districts of the city. He found a continuously decreasing ratio in the long term; in 1830 the relationship of prices in the city centre (1^e and 2^e Arrondisements) to the rest of the city was 50 : 1. By 1900, despite a phenomenal rise in prices in the city centre (25 times), the ratio was reduced to 25 : 1, as the average price increase was even higher. From 1900 to 1965 prices in the most exclusive districts (e.g. the 9^e Arr.) actually declined in real terms, while those in the poorer districts (e.g. 14^e and 15^e Arr.) and outlying

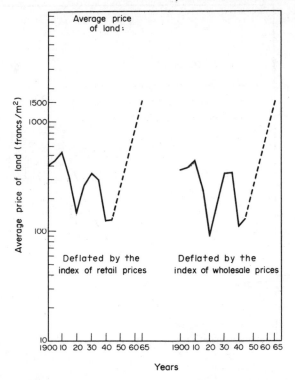

Fig. 3.5. Land price trends (in real terms) in Paris, 1900–1965. (By courtesy of J. J. Grenelle, *op. cit.*)

areas (Boulogne) rose by 4 or 5 times even in fixed prices; thus the ratio of land prices in the most expensive and least expensive areas was further reduced to 8 : 1.

The overall analysis of land-price development in Paris shows most strongly the effects of continuous growth and change in structure on prices. Unlike Chicago, prices never declined very much and reached new highs at each rise. It may be suggested that this could be related to the lack of other profitable investments in France, as well as the concentration of activity there in a single capital city.

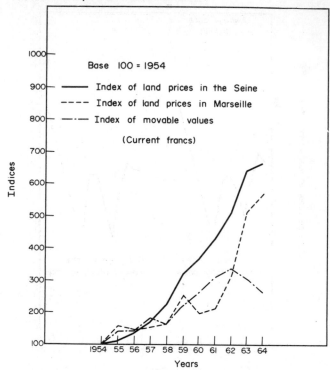

Fig. 3.6. Index of land prices (current prices) for Paris and Marseille from 1954 to 1964. (By courtesy of J. J. Grenelle, *op. cit.*)

The United Kingdom

E. A. Vallis has recently presented some information on trends in land prices in the UK from 1892 to 1969, based on transaction prices at auctions but with a small sample.* His figures include commercial, industrial and residential land prices, but mainly pertain to London and the South-East. The long-term average price rise for the whole period was 2609% (6·8% p.a.), or 329% (3·0 p.a.) in fixed prices. However, this average figure disproportionately weights commercial

---

*E. A. Vallis, "Urban land and building prices", *Estates Gazette*, Vol. 222, pp. 1015–19, 1209–13, 1406–7, 1604–5, 13 and 20 May, 3 and 20 June, 1972.

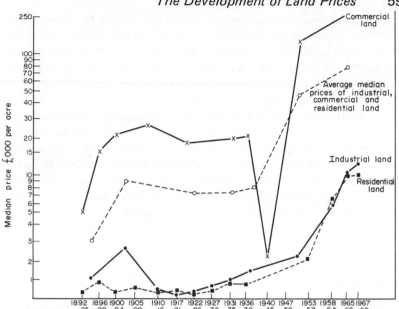

Fig. 3.7. Industrial, commercial and residential land prices in the United Kingdom, 1892 to 1969. (Source: E. A. Vallis, *op. cit.*)

and industrial land; for residential land alone the increase was much greater—8053% (19·7% p.a.) or 1161% (5·2% p.a.) in fixed prices.

The other important point is that nearly all the price increase was concentrated in the post-war period, and even more particularly in the post-1952 period (when the betterment levy was abandoned). Even in current prices it was not until after the Second World War that land prices exceeded their pre-war peaks (which occurred in 1899, 1905 and 1910 for residential, industrial and commercial land respectively). From 1892 to 1914 land prices fluctuated irregularly; during the First World War they fell (more markedly for commercial and industrial land). In the interwar years there was a slow rise after 1922, and then a dramatic fall (particularly for commercial land) during the Second World War (presumably as a result of bombing). From 1945 to 1969 there was a steady and accelerating increase in all land prices (see Fig. 3.7).

Two points with special regard to the UK might be made. First, commercial land in the pre-1914 era was probably already relatively expensive in London, the financial and trade centre of the world (and the sample is biased towards London). Secondly, land prices were possibly stabilized for the whole pre-1945 period by the existence of profitable alternative investments abroad, which led to less speculation in land (and hence smaller price swings) as compared to other countries.

Finally, when residential land prices are disaggregated by regions, the higher priced residential districts in London (NW, W) show a lower over-all increase in prices for the period as a whole than either the rest of London or the south-east region. This again is similar to the Paris data. But keeping in mind the restricted sample size, these figures should be seen as first approximations only.

Switzerland

Information is available on the average sale price of land in the Zurich municipality from 1901. These figures (see Table 3.7) are basically similar to the trends for other West European countries. Prices fluctuated erratically before the First World War, reaching a peak in 1913. During the First World War there was a sharp decline, followed by a recovery which took prices almost to their pre-war peak by 1930. Another sharp decline followed, and a slow recovery was interrupted only mildly by the war. By 1949 prices had exceeded their historic highs, and continued upwards until they increased that level by over 10 times in 1968. The period of fastest growth was 1960–5, 1965 being the new historic high.

Again the data shows a very close relationship between the economic cycle and land prices. As Zurich is an international centre for finance, it is particularly sensitive to disruptions of international capital movements, such as occurred in the First World War and during the 1929–31 economic crisis. (We suggest that some of the highest bidders for land are normally these outside financial sources.) On the other hand, the fact that Switzerland was neutral in both world wars meant that to some extent it was insulated from the great fluctuations in land prices that took place during and immediately after both wars (due to war destruction and political uncertainty).

Denmark

Denmark has the most comprehensive data on land prices in the world—since 1924 the public authorities have published land-value maps every 4 years giving the price of land for every site. This is extremely useful for our study, since it shows that the price *trends* for all types of land (agricultural as well as urban) are similar.

The fluctuations in the price-development trend (from 1920 to the end of the Second World War) are a result of economic cycles. Three periods may be observed: two periods of moderate rate of increase (10·1–12·1% between 1920–4, and 1932–45) interrupted by a period of lower rate of increase (4·5–5·1% from 1924 to 1932).

The trend from the end of the War up to 1965 was a high rate of land-price increase which corresponded to steady economic growth and the permanent increase in the price of all commodities which encouraged people to invest in real estate as a hedge against inflation.

Thus, the highest price increase (140%) took place in the period 1960–5, compared with 35% during the 5-year period just after the War.

A comparison between land-price increases in Copenhagen and the provincial towns shows that on the whole the trends of price increase are the same during 1920–65 period, but the rate of price increase is higher in the smaller towns.

In the earlier period the differences are negligible but recently it has become significant. The provincial towns showed an increase of 148·7% between the years 1960 and 1965, compared to Copenhagen's 90·0% during the same period.

A further point is that after 1932 the land-price increase in the communities around towns was higher than the increase in the towns proper, although the trends are the same. Thus, in 1932–6 the land-price increase was 27·9% in the Copenhagen County Region, compared to the 10·1% increase in Copenhagen itself. During the same period, there was a land-price increase of 19·5% in the suburbs of the provincial towns, compared to 12·2% in those towns proper. During the years 1960–5 the differences between the rate of price increases in the suburbs as compared to the cities became far more noteworthy.

Japan

Japan is the only Asian country for which adequate and systematic information exists on urban land prices from before the Second World War. This data is published periodically by the Japan Real Estate Institute, Tokyo, and our information is drawn from their September 1974 *Indices of Urban Land Prices and Construction Costs of Wooden Houses in Japan.*

Several periods with distinctive trends may be seen from the figures. From 1937 to 1945, the land-price index reached 210, but the consumer price index was 302 (1936 = 100 for both indices). From 1945 to 1951 the rise in the consumer price index greatly exceeded the land-price index's increase (by a factor of 4). Between 1951 and 1955 land prices caught up with the consumer price index and reached equality in real terms. From 1955 land prices continued to rise at an accelerating rate while consumer prices remained virtually stationary. Since 1973 the consumer price index has suddenly begun to increase, and since 1974 land prices have stabilized.

Despite the very high rate of increase of land prices over the entire period 1955–74, there have been great fluctuations in the rate of increase in different years. As Table 3.2 shows, these fluctuations are greater in the big cities.

TABLE 3.2. Land Price Increases in Japan
(yearly rates)

Year	All urban land	Six big cities
1955–6	6–8%	6–8%
1956–60	11–13%	13–14%
1960–1	17–18%	29–30%
1962–4	6–9%	8–10%
1965–6	2–3%	1%
1966–72	5–8%	3–6%
1973	15–16%	14–19%
1974	1–7%	0–4%

We have also disaggregated figures for residential, commercial and industrial land which show that over the entire period (1936–74) residential prices rose the most, though in the period of economic growth (1955–74) industrial prices had the highest increase. The highest priced land (commercial) had a *rate* of price increase less than the average.

The data for Japan particularly well illustrate the different relationships of land prices to a high rate of inflation (in the immediate post-war years and today) and to steady and rapid economic growth (in the 1955–74 period).

The Netherlands

From 1945 to 1963 the price of land per dwelling in the Netherlands rose by 132% or 4·8% yearly. During the period from 1951–3 to 1957–9, the cost of developed land per dwelling increased by 82·3% (10·5% p.a.) but the cost of raw land in the same time period increased by no more than 27% (4% p.a.). From 1954 to 1966 the cost of raw land has risen by 8% yearly.

Sweden

A study of land prices undertaken in 1966 by the Ministry of Justice of Sweden shows a relative stability of land prices due to the active land-acquisition policy of the municipality. According to the study of the three major towns, Stockholm, Gothenberg and Malmo, there is a similar price development in the three towns; and the highest price increase is observable in redeveloped areas situated in the centre of the towns.

Prices of building sites for one-family homes in Sweden developed as shown in Table 3.3 during the period 1957–63.

In the other countries, the price increase was from 4 to 21% during that 6-year period. A higher price increase was significant for sites for summer homes in certain municipalities which have a particularly good location. In such localities,* the price increase during the 6 years

* United Nations, "Seminar on Supply", Development and Allocation of Land for Housing and Related Purposes: *Country Monographs*, vol. II, p. 245.

TABLE 3.3.

Location	Price increase for period 1957–63 (%)
County of Stockholm	46·0
County of Uppsala	38·0
County of Sondermanland	30·0

was 82–96%.† The prices in Stockholm show an increase of 7% yearly during the period 1967–74. The price of raw land purchased by the Stockholm Municipality has increased during the period of 1938–66 by 6·6% yearly.

Italy

During the 15 years between 1948 and 1963 there was a continuous increase of land prices in Italy. The period 1963–5 showed some stabilization of land prices as a result of recession. During the period 1966–8 there was a slow rise of prices; and during the recent period 1969–70 there has been a halt in the trend of price increase. According to some experts, this change is probably the result of new urban land-use legislation.

A study of the development of land prices at Milan and in its region in the period 1946–62 shows the following price increase for different urban areas: (a) central business district, prices increased 8 times; (b) central zone, 9 times; (c) peripheral zone, 12 times; (d) exterior zone, 9 times.*

Spain

During the 13 years between 1950 and 1963 the average land price

---

* Instituto Lombardo per gli Studi Economici e Sociali, *Indagine sul valore elle agre fabbricabili in Milano e nel suo territorio del 1956–1962* (Milan, Luglio, 1963), chap. V, pp. 8–10.

in Spain increased ten-fold. In one district at Madrid, land prices increased by 7 times during the 8-year period 1961–9.*

DEVELOPMENT OF LAND PRICES IN COMPARISON WITH SEVERAL NATIONAL ECONOMIC DEVELOPMENT INDICES

In order to understand some of the factors which influence land prices, we have given in Table 3.4 some relevant macro-economic variables. Our data pertains mostly to the post-war period, as it is

TABLE 3.4. Rates of Increases of Land Prices, Consumer Prices, and National Income *per capita* for Selected Countries (yearly percentage)

	Period	Land price increase (current prices)	Consumer price increase, 1948–67	National income *per capita* 1948–67
Denmark (Copenhagen)	1956–69	11·4	4·2	6·5
France (Paris)	1950–66	21.0	4·3	5·5
Italy (Milan)	1950–62	12·0–19·0[a]	3·0	5·6
Japan	1955–69	19·9	0·8	8·2
Netherlands	1945–63	2·6–10·5[b]	3·4	3·8
Spain (Madrid)	1950–69	20·5–27·5[a]	5·3	7·5
Sweden (Stockholm)	1957–63	6·6	3·5	4·2
Switzerland (Zurich)	1950–68	13·0	1·9	3·0
United Kingdom (London)	1960–69	12·0	3·7	1·7
USA	1956–66	6·0	1·5	6·0

[a] Figures for central and outlying districts of the city.
[b] First figure, raw land; second figure, developed land.

only in this period that there is data on land-price development for enough countries to make a comparison worthwhile. We have used current prices in our table, as we are interested in a *yearly* rate of increase and we explicitly take into account the effect of inflation by including the consumer price index as one of our variables.

* *Op cit.,* UN Seminar on Supply, p. 297.

There are a number of weaknesses in the data presented. The land-price figures may not always be strictly comparable, as they are calculated on a different basis in different countries. It would also have been useful to have a more detailed breakdown of land prices in different areas, not just an overall average; likewise, our crude index of economic activity could have been supplemented by more specific indicators relevant to land such as the rate of interest, building activity, etc. Nevertheless the rough and preliminary analysis we are able to make will show that no one economic factor is adequate to explain land-price increases; many political and economic factors must be taken into account.

The countries with the highest rates of land-price increase are Spain, Japan, France and Italy. Spain and France have the highest rate of increase in the cost-of-living index. Japan and Spain have the highest rate of national income per capita, and France and Italy are among the highest. Japan has the highest rate of increase in the urban population. Though not shown in the table, it should be noted that Spain, Italy and France have all shown a particularly high urban population growth rate in certain large centres (Milan, Barcelona, Madrid and Paris). Tourism is also an important part of the economy in these countries.

The lowest rates of land-price increases are to be found in the Netherlands, Sweden and the USA (see Table 3.4). The USA has a high rate of economic and population growth, but a low rate of inflation. It also should be noted that the USA is much less densely populated than the European or Asian countries we have been considering, and furthermore displays a rather more dispersed pattern of development. In the Netherlands and Sweden political factors are relevant, namely the active intervention of the state in the land market (in both countries the municipalities are the major buyers of development land through a policy of advanced land acquisition). This has served to restrain the rate of land-price increase in these two countries whose economic indices would seem to indicate that they would show a higher rate of increase.

The middle two countries, Denmark and Switzerland, together with the UK show the difficulty of any single-factor explanation of land prices. Despite almost similar rates of land-price increase, Denmark has a rate of inflation and of economic growth double that of Switzerland. For Switzerland the heavy investment of foreign capital and the great importance of tourism may have raised land prices, while in Denmark active public involvement in development may have restrained prices more than economic indices would lead one to predict. In the UK previously accumulated capital, now without other profitable assets, may have been invested in land.

CONCLUSIONS

By using the whole range of data we have presented, a number of points about trends in land-price development might be made. The first is the interrelationship between economic cycles and land prices. In the pre-Second World War era the USA provides the most striking example of this, with dramatic collapses in land prices closely related to general business panics. But it can also be illustrated in the post-war era in a less extreme form. For nearly all countries for which we have data, the highest rate of land-price increases occurred in 1960–5, with 1963 the peak. Prices stabilized from 1965 to 1968, increased again from 1969 to 1972, and have collapsed in the last 2 years. This is roughly the pattern of the most recent cycle of economic growth. The swings of land prices are greater in both directions; and it is where prices have risen fastest that they also have collapsed the most.

Secondly, we are able to observe the long-term relationship between urban concentration, economic growth and land prices. The study of Paris is a good example of this, though in recent years Japan, Spain and Italy all show the correlation between an increased rate of industrialization and urbanization and a long rise in land prices. The high rate of land-price increase in some countries may be modified by the existence of more profitable investments, alternative investments, either foreign (UK) or domestic (USA).

The reduction of alternative investment possibilities in their colonies may also help explain the high rate of increase in land prices in European countries after the Second World War. Other factors which might explain the higher rate of post-war land price increase in Europe than in the USA include the need for massive reconstruction after war damage and the greater state responsibility that was assumed for housing. On the other hand, the active land acquisition policies of some European countries, as we have seen, have served to restrain the price rises.

This brief and fragmentary discussion may at least serve to suggest that urban land prices are affected by two main kinds of factors, those connected with land as a production factor in building (e.g. urban population growth and national income growth leading to greater demand for housing) and those connected with land as a financial investment (e.g. inflation, taxation policies, and alternative investment possibilities). The fact that fluctuations in land prices have always been more marked than those of other economic indicators, as demonstrated by Hoyt, may serve to show the importance of the latter (speculative) factors. But it is the complex interrelationship of many factors which determine land prices; furthermore, the dominant factor may change with time.

RELATIONSHIPS BETWEEN LAND PRICE INCREASES IN CITY CENTRES AND OUTLYING AREAS WITHIN THE CITY REGION

Given that the dominant share of metropolitan population growth takes place elsewhere in the city region than its centre, it is useful to try to determine how such dispersed growth influences land-price development trends throughout the city region. Of particular interest are price increases which result from changes in land use. Some examples from selected countries are presented below as indicative of existing trends in land-price development.

Denmark

A study of the Copenhagen region shows that rates of land price increase between 1956–69 were 11·4% yearly in Copenhagen, 19·8% in the Copenhagen region and 26–33% in some rapidly growing communities in the region. Some individual areas within the latter show rates of increase as high as 100–1000 times (47–80% yearly) for the 12-year period where land has been converted from agricultural to urban use. The same trend may be observed in Copenhagen—high rates of increase at the city outskirts and for previously low-value areas. The trend of higher rates of increase for outlying areas as compared to central areas in Copenhagen is also demonstrated by comparing the locations of high land-value districts and their distances from the city centre. Generally, such a comparison shows significantly large land-price differences at the same distance from the city centre, indicating large land-price differences at the same distance from the city centre, indicating that distance from the centre *per se* is only one of many factors which influence land values. Particularly in the Copenhagen region, environmental features and amenities and the socio-economic structure of individual neighbourhoods appear to play a more dominant role in land price formation.

Paris

During the past 20 years land prices in France have increased on the average from 12 to 20 times the level of 1950. In the Paris region, in the period 1950–65, land prices increased about 17 times, or an average of 21% per year. Land prices in the more fashionable quarters of Paris show a lower rate of increase in comparison with districts populated by lower-income groups, where land prices were originally lower (Table 3.5).

TABLE 3.5. Paris: Change in Land Prices, 1950–65

	Price per square metre (current francs)				Average increase per annum (percentage)			
	1950	1958	1962	1965	1950–8	1958–62	1962–5	1950–65
Zone A[a]	210	690	1550	2200	17	25	15	18
Zone B[b]	30	175	800	1300	25	39	18	29
Zone C[c]	33	220	550	850	27	34	16	24
Average	72	315	790	1200	20	26	15	21

Sources: For 1950–8, Information and Documentation Centre for the Building Industry; for 1962–5, National Federation of Builders.

[a] Districts 6, 7, 8, 16 and 17.
[b] District 15, Boulogne.
[c] Other districts of Paris.

Between 1950 and 1965 the prices increased ten-fold in the central areas (zone A). In zone B, the price increase was highest, 43 times. In zone C, the increase was 26 times. The difference in the rate of increase is mainly evident in the earlier part of the period. From 1962 and 1965, by which time the lower value districts had reached high levels, the *rate* of price increase was virtually the same in all districts.

According to a recent study done by J. Grennelle,* the rate of increase in Paris between 1965–8 was 27% yearly, compared to the more peripheral areas where the rate of increase was 45%.

Milan

Research carried out by the Instituto Lombardo per gli Studi Economici e Sociali (ILSES) on land values in the central and metropolitan areas of Milan between 1946 and 1962 demonstrates the same trend as in Paris (Table 3.6).

TABLE 3.6. Milan: Development of Land Prices in Various Areas
(Italian lira per square metre)

	Milan				Metropolitan region			
Year	Central business district	Central zone	Peripheral zone	Exterior zone	Zone 1	Zone 2	Zone 3	Zone 4
1946	82,000	47,000	20,000	11,000				
1950	169,000	83,000	31,000	16,000				
1956	350,000	185,000	64,000	40,000	6,300	1,430	970	740
1962	643,000	374,000	240,000	96,000	23,000	8,360	3,430	2,290
Increase from 1956 to 1962 (percentage)								
	84	102	275	140	271	476	244	209
Relation between central business district and other areas								
1956		1·89	5·47	8·75	56	241	361	374
1962		1·72	2·68	6·70	27	77	193	281

Source: Instituto Lombardo per gli Studi Economici e Sociali, *Indagine sul valore delle aree fabbricabili in Milano e nel suo territorio del 1956–1962* (Milan, Luglio, 1963).

* *Le marche des terrains à Paris de 1960 à 1969.*

The investigated areas were categorized on the basis of distance from the centre. The peripheral zone is an area inside a municipal area and near the boundaries of the town; the exterior zone is the area nearest to the town frontier and outside the municipal area. Zone 4 is about 30 km from the boundaries; zones 1, 2 and 3 are between zone 4 and the exterior zone.

The data show a continuous rise of prices—higher in the metropolitan areas and the peripheral quarters than in the central areas of the town. The ratio between the prices in the most central areas and the other areas decreased with time although there was an absolute increase of prices in all areas.

Zurich

Data from a study on the impact of development works on land values in the canton of Zurich are given in Table 3.7.

TABLE 3.7. Zurich Region: Prices of Land Transaction of Unbuilt-up Sites, 1946–67 (Swiss francs per square metre)

	Year	Average price of total area	Price index (previous period = 100)	Yearly rate of increase (%)
Geroldswill	1946–50	2·55		
	1956–60	23·32	914	25%
	1966–67	56·90	244	10·5%
Opfikon	1946–50	8·12		
	1956–60	42·09	518	18%
	1966–67	166·62	396	16·6%
Uitikon	1946–50	6·26		
	1956–60	52·76	843	24%
	1966–67	164·59	312	14%

Sources: Statistisches Amt der Canton Zurich, *Freihaundverkaüfe von Unbauten Grundstücken nach Bauzonen 1946–67.*

Land prices show an extreme increase in 1956–60, in comparison with 1946–50, and a very strong increase in 1966–67, in comparison with 1956–60, though not to such an extreme as the former. The increase from a low starting-point to a higher one is a result of changed use from agricultural to urban. This increase is extremely high in comparison with the rate of increase in Zurich, 13·4% p.a. from 1948 to 1957 and 10·8% from 1958 to 1967.

Geneva

Some selected transaction prices comparing 1955–7 to 1965–9 will show the difference in magnitude between different types of land transactions. In the city centre, land which was sold at 1900 Fr/m^2 in 1955 fetched 7300 Fr/m^2 in 1971, an increase of 350%. Land in a good residential district (Plainpalais) doubled its value in the same period. But land formerly outside the city, which was worth 10 Fr/m^2 in 1955, was sold for between 100 and 270 Fr/m^2 in the late 1960s.

The USA

Selected US studies of land price changes in different areas indicate that the rate of increase associated with the conversion of agricultural to urban land is between 6 and 7% p.a.

Allen Schmid, in his publication *Converting Land from Rural to Urban Uses*,* illustrates many examples of high rates of pure increases. Quoting the results of a study by Sherman Maisel for the San Francisco Bay Area between 1950–62, he shows that price increases for raw land for single-family lots were 221% over the period, or 10·2% per year. If we look at the value of Californian agricultural land, we see that it is about $200/acre. The average value of irrigated orchard/vineyard land is $2300/acre. Yet urbanized farms land achieved an average of $10,000/acre after conversion, more than 4 times the value of the highest value in agricultural use.

A case study in Lisle, Illinois, shows that, for agricultural land values at $360/acre in 1961, after conversion to urban use and *after* deducting development, capital and interest costs, the same land achieved a price increase of $2363/acre, almost 7 times its original value.

* See Further Reading, p. 424.

Similarly, a 1973 survey of land prices in the north-west part of Columbus (1965–70) showed 20–40% annual rates of increase between 1965 and 1973 after conversion to urban use, compared to an average 6% increase in value prior to conversion.

Some magazines have reported the doubling or tripling in a single year of raw land which has a potential for development in much sought after residential or recreational areas (e.g. Florida, Vermont, near Western National Parks).* It should be mentioned that the average price increases in the USA is estimated at only 6–8% yearly for the period 1952–68.

DEVELOPMENT COSTS

In view of the high rate of price increases for the newly urbanizing outlying regions of the city, it may be of interest to calculate the "economic cost" of newly developed urban land, made up of the cost of development works and the raw land (the cost of the raw land previously in agricultural use). Such a comparison will show some differences in the ratio of these two costs (Table 3.8).

TABLE 3.8. Development Costs and Costs of Agricultural Land (in US dollars per square metre)

	Price of agricultural land (1)	Price of agricultural land near the large towns (2)	Primary development costs (3)	Ratio (2–3) (4)
Germany (FDR)	0·62	12·50	5·75	2·2
Italy	0·30	1·5 – 5·00	10·50	0·7 –2·0
The Netherlands	—	1·00	10·0 –20·00	0·1 –0·2
Spain	0·05	10·0 –17·00	3·0 – 4·00	2·5 –5·6
Switzerland	0·20	7·50– 9·0	7·50–10·00	0·75–1·2

Table 3.8 shows that in most countries the costs of raw land exceeded the cost of development works in newly urbanized areas. The explanation is that the prospective change in use of agricultural land

* *Time* Magazine, 1 Oct. 1973, pp. 80–100.

drives up the prices of such land located near large towns far above its agricultural-use value. The exceptionally low figure for raw land prices in the Netherlands is due to the fact that the municipalities themselves are the principal buyers of development land and have a decisive influence on the land market. Such figures may show the potential of public authority land policies based on acquiring land for future urban growth at its economic cost.

CONCLUSIONS

The enormous rise of land prices in the metropolitan areas in comparison with the central city areas show how the average land prices for city regions are only of a relative value.

Keeping in mind that the population growth and the industrial development occurs in the metropolitan area outside the city—these land-price-development trends are more significant for urban land-price increases and land problems than the price development within the city.

The interesting feature is that the diffusion of high land prices throughout large metropolitan areas has not stopped prices from increasing in the city proper, though it had restrained the *rate* of increase there in comparison with the outlying metropolitan area.

The examples given of some few cities are significant for almost all city regions in the world. It may be suggested that the rate of land-price increase in city regions with a high rate of population increase and land markets less regulated by public authorities would be even higher. A study of land-price increases in the newly urbanized areas resulting from changes in land use from agricultural to urban will show that these are considerably higher than the *average* rate of price increase as shown in the Copenhagen study.

REFERENCES

CREDOC (Centre de recherche et de documentation sur la consommation), *Etude du marche des terrains dans l'agglomération de Marseille de 1954 à 1963*, Paris, 1965.
Grenelle, J. J., *Le Prix du sol et l'espace urbain*, Paris, 1970.
Hoyt, Homer, *The Urban Real Estate Cycle: Performance and Prospects*, Urban Land Institute, Washington, 1960.

———, *One Hundred Years of Land Values: The Chicago Real Estate Cycle*, Chicago, 1940.

Instituto Lombardo per gli studi economici e sociali (ILSES), *Indagine sul valore delle aree fabbricabili in Milano e nel suo territorio dal 1956–1962*, Milan, July 1963.

Japan Real Estate Institute, *Indices of Urban Land Prices and Construction Costs of Wooden Houses in Japan* (at the end of September 1972), Tokyo: Japan Real Estate Institute.

"Price movements for residential land: 1965–1969", *Chartered Surveyor*, 1969.

Societe d'étude pour le développement économique et social (SEDES), *Annex au rapport d'étude dur marche foncier a Lyon de 1954 à 1963*, SEDES, Delegation de Lyon.

Statistisches Amt des Kanton Zurich, *Untersuchung uber die Entwicklung der Grundstuckpreise in Zurich.*

———, *Freihandverkaufe von unbebauten Grunstucken nach Bauzonen 1946–67, Opfikon, Uitikon, and Geroldswill.*

"Suelo Urbano", *Ciencia urbana*, No. 3, May-June 1969, Madrid.

United Nations, *Urban Land Policies and Land Use Control Measures*, Vol. III: *Western Europe*, New York, 1973.

Vallis, E. A., "Urban land and building prices", *Estates Gazette*, 13 May, 20 May, 3 June and 20 June, 1972 (Vol. 222, pp. 1015–19, 1209–13, 1406–7, 1604–5).

Vurderingen af landets faste ejendomine (Assessment of Real Property), Dansk Statistik, Copenhagen.

CHAPTER 4

The Impact of the Land Factor on Urban Growth in the Developing Countries

The urbanization process in the developing countries takes place under more difficult conditions than in the older industrialized countries. The key factors contributing to these difficulties are a high rate of population increase, especially of urban population, low income *per capita* and an inequitable distribution of wealth. Since 1920 the developing countries have had a rate of urban population growth considerably exceeding that of developed countries. (From 1940 to 1960 the urban population increased by an average of 4·5% per year in the former, and by only 2·0% in the latter.) In the large cities (over 500,000) the difference is even more: 6·9% per year increase as compared to 2·6% per year in the same period.

While economic development rates have increased over the last two decades, income *per capita* has not increased appreciably. The gap between the developed and developing countries is very wide. In terms of wealth, the developing countries (two-thirds of the total world population) account for only 18% of the total wealth of the world. On average, in 1970 each "developed" inhabitant produced $3743 as compared to the $317 for his "developing" counterpart. There are, of course, large differences in the *per capita* GNP (those of Latin American nations being about double, and those of African nations half of the average for the developing countries), but the overall relationship between the two groups remains roughly stable. The large difference between developed and developing countries in income *per capita* is further compounded by the very unequal distribution of national wealth within the developing countries. A very small segment of the population controls the overwhelming majority of wealth. Such large disparities have a marked effect on the patterns of urban development in the developing countries, particularly where urban land-price trends are concerned.

LAND-PRICE TRENDS

There is insufficient published material available on land-price development in the developing countries. Generally there is only some information available on land prices in different city areas and for different time periods.

The figures used are collected from the study on Urban Land Policies and Land-Use Control Measures published by the UN in 1973, and also from material on some Asian countries published by the John Lincoln Institute (Hartford University, 1971). Additional material on land-price development trends has been published by the Israeli Land Research Institute.

Table 4.1 illustrates the high rate of land price increase in some of the developing countries.

TABLE 4.1. Comparison of Land Prices Increase of Selected Developing Countries

City	Period	Location	% increase per annum			
			Land prices (current prices)	Land prices (fixed prices)	Con-sumer prices index	GNP *per capita*
Taipei	1956–68	Average of 6 areas	26	10·5	14	—
Teheran	1940–60	Average of 18 districts	23	10	12	6·2
Tel Aviv	1951–71	Average of 4 districts	28	21	6	5·9
Seoul	1953–66	Average of all land in city	41	18·7	19·2	4·6
Jamaica	1965–71	Average of all urban land	22	17	4	3·8
Mexico	1939–58	Average of 2 districts	23	15	7	3·7
New Delhi	1959–67	Middle-class residential district	18·6	17	1·3	0·5

It should be kept in mind that the different time periods over which the price increases have been measured means that comparison cannot be exact. But material from other countries for a shorter time period shows the same general trend. The rate of increase in land price in the cities and countries shown varies from 21% to 28% yearly (except for Seoul with an increase of 41%). But in constant prices the rate of increase is between 10 and 21% yearly, with Tel Aviv (21%) the highest. The rate of land-price increase shows some correlation with the consumer price increase and GNP *per capita*, but it has to be underlined that other very important factors influence the formation of land prices, such as the rate of urban growth, the amount of foreign investment in land purchase, and various land-policy measures.

COMPARISON WITH SOME INDUSTRIALIZED COUNTRIES

The very high rate of land-price increase in some countries and cities shown in Table 4.1 may be better understood by comparison with land-price increase of the industrialized countries (Table 4.2).

TABLE 4.2.

| City | Period | % increase per annum | | | |
		Land prices (current)	Land prices (fixed)	Consumer prices	GNP *per capita*
Paris	1950–66	18	12	4·6	5·5
Madrid	1950–69	24	17	5·3	7·5
Milan	1950–62	15	11	3·0	5·6
Amsterdam	1945–63	6	2	3·3	4·0
Stockholm	1957–74	7	3	3·0	5·0
USA	1956–66	6	4	1·5	6·0

This comparison allows us to make some conclusions regarding the effect of land policies on land-price formation. Spain, France and Italy show the same rate of increase (in fixed terms) as the developing countries. These more recently industrialized countries probably also have larger financial investments in land, due to relatively restricted investment possibilities, than the early-industrialized countries (USA).

They also have a high rate of urban population concentration in one city. In both of these ways they are similar to the developing countries. But the low rate of price increase in Stockholm and Amsterdam cannot be explained by a lower rate of urban population growth. (Stockholm grew by 5·8% yearly, and Paris by 5% per year, between 1960–5.)

PRICE FORMATION IN THE METROPOLITAN AREA

The high rate of land-price increase in the cities of the developing countries does not yet express the role of the land factor in urban growth. As a result of the high land prices in the big cities, rapid population growth is concentrated in the regions outside the big cities. There the rate of land-price increase is considerably higher than in the city.

Some examples from different countries may show the extraordinarily high increase in land prices resulting from a change in land use from agricultural to urban.

India (Calcutta). Between 1950 and 1965 the price of land in undeveloped areas within the municipal borders has increased by 900%, while the price of land on the outskirts of the city has increased by 1300%.

The Philippines (Manila). Land in the metropolitan area showed an increase between 1940 and 1969 of 2000 times or 30% yearly in one outlying area (the Escolta), and an increase of 100 times (12% per year) in a more central area.

Iran (Teheran). The new Mehrabad area has shown a price increase of 262% annually from 1952 to 1957. Teheran also provides a good example of the close relationship between land prices and the building of new roads. In 1960 before the Amir Kabir Road was extended, land in the outlying area was worth $20/m^2$; after its extension, $106/m^2$. The same pattern was seen with the extension of Avenue Ekbatan, where land immediately quadrupled in value.

Taiwan (Taipei). The increase in the price of agricultural land near the city frontiers is as follows: 1956—$0.04/m^2, 1968—$1·20/m^2 (a 30-fold increase in 12 years). Prices in the new developed Nankin East Road area were $33/m^2 in 1956 and $1000/m^2 in 1969 (a yearly increase of 33%). In another newly developed area there was a 9-fold increase from 1962 to 1968 (or 44% yearly).

Israel (Tel Aviv). In suburbs 30 km from the centre of Tel Aviv the following price increases were shown: Kfar Saba: 1957—$0·7/m^2, 1971—$35/m^2; Rananna: 1957—$0·3/m^2, 1971—$25/m^2 (a 50–83 times increase during 14 years, or 32–37% yearly).

These high increases in land prices are not typical of all parts of the metropolitan area. At the same distance from the city, areas have changed from agricultural to urban use, others are still in agricultural use but planned for future urban development, and a very high percentage of land lies vacant, used for neither agricultural purposes nor under construction.

The uncertainty factor of the timing and location of the change in land use from agricultural to urban affects the rate at which land prices increase, and accounts in great part for the differences in the rate of increase in the city where the restricted land supply pushes land prices up. This could be dealt with by an appropriate taxation system, efficient land-use legislation and an active municipal land-supply policy with appropriate institutional machinery for policy implementation.

SOME FACTORS INVOLVED IN THE HIGH RATE OF PRICE INCREASE IN THE DEVELOPING COUNTRIES

Vacant Land

One of the significant factors which create a shortage of available land is the high percentage of vacant land in the metropolitan area despite the high demand. Some examples will show that this phenomenon plays a major role in the high rate of land-price increases.

In Buenos Aires, according to a 1971 UN report, 70% of land was vacant in the metropolitan area. In Teheran in 1958 there were 12,760 ha. of urbanized land, 6637 ha. of mixed-built and vacant land and 19,687 ha. of vacant land planned for building. In Tel Aviv (where some people live 30 km from the centre) 30% of the land is vacant within the municipal borders. In the metropolitan area the percentage of vacant land is as high as 40% to 50%.

The existence of large vacant areas in a city region and a very high land-price increase in such an urban area may be seen as two inter-related phenomena.

The expected profit from future land-use changes restricts the supply of land to the market. A taxation system which does not impose a high tax on the vacant land needed for future urban development makes the capital costs of maintaining vacant land low.

The economic decision to invest in land will be based on the expected profit and the prevailing interest rate. Generally, in countries with restricted investment possibilities and a high rate of urbanization and of land-price increase, the holding of vacant land is one of the most profitable economic enterprises. This is especially the case in countries with permanent inflation.

Such a situation might change when the rate of inflation and the interest rate become very high, as a shortage of capital in the financial market may force some of the landholders (mostly developers) to sell their land. This could even lead to some price decreases in areas which formerly had very high land-price increases. This has recently occurred in Japan, England and Israel.

Foreign Investment

Finally, emphasis must also be laid on the important role played by foreign firms in establishing high land prices: when a branch of a New York or London bank or a large industrial firm locates in a city of a developing country, representatives of these firms are not overly con-cerned with apparently high land values, for in most cases, the prices paid are considerably lower than in their own countries. The net effect is an artificial bidding up of land prices, which ultimately affects all categories of land.

Similarly, resident foreigners and the wealthy have the ability to pay high rates for residential properties, especially in desirable locations, but these prices affect prices throughout the metropolitan area. Land located within the city proper which enjoys complete infra-structural facilities is much more expensive than the large surrounding areas of vacant or undeveloped land.

EFFECTS OF LAND-PRICE INCREASES

Housing Costs

The continuous and high rate of increase in land prices has many effects. First of all, the increasing cost of land is reflected in a general rise in housing costs, of which land costs are one component. This puts a strain on the low-income groups in the population, forcing them to acquire housing further away from the city (with higher transportation expenses and travelling). High land prices are also responsible for high densities within the city and lack of open spaces for parks and re-creation. Finally, these high prices lead to many not being able to afford any land, and hence squatting.

There are only limited data on the role of land in housing costs (mainly from seminar reports and UN publications). The following examples are typical of cities in developing countries:

South Korea (Seoul). In 1957 the proportion of land costs in total housing expenditure was less than 20% in the peripheral suburban area; in 1967 land constituted 50% of the cost of low-income housing, and 70–80% of housing costs in better locations.

Nigeria (Lagos). In the metropolitan area land costs are 3–4 times higher than construction costs, making the former 75–80% of the total housing costs.

Philippines (Legaspi). The costs of erecting a small house from bamboo is only $100, but the 40 m^2 of land for such a house costs $3000.

Israel (Tel Aviv). The price of land increased during one year (1973) by 25–50% (100% in newly urbanized areas). The proportion of land in housing costs reached 60% in the city centre and 35–55% in the metropolitan area.

Land-price increases had most effect on housing costs, as they increased more than any other factor. The gap between the rapidly rising housing costs and the relatively static income of the majority of the population is increasing throughout the world. In the industrialized countries governments are attempting to solve the problem through subsidizing public housing. The solution to the housing problem is much more difficult in the developing countries because of more limited financial resources of their governments and the higher housing costs relative to income. Table 4.3 shows the relationship between the price of a dwelling and the income *per capita* in developing and industrialized countries.

TABLE 4.3. Price of Dwelling Expressed in GNP *per capita* in Selected Countries in 1956

Country	GNP per capita in $	Price of social housing dwelling in $	Space of dwelling in m²	Price of m² built space in $	Price in yearly GNP per capita	
					dwelling	built m²
USA	2,126	12,225	116	105	5·7	0·05
UK	957	4,760	90	52	5·0	0·05
India	62	1,262	55	22	20·0	0·36
Pakistan	70	1,845	56	33	26·0	0·47
Burma	47	1,427	49	29	30·0	0·60

Note: For the developing countries, these dwelling space figures refer to mostly *middle-class* dwellings. The low-income groups can only afford a space of 20–30 m².

An inhabitant in a developing country therefore has to spend 4–6 times as much of his lower income for a dwelling as does a US or UK resident. The difference is even greater when we compare the cost of a built square metre of dwelling space. Although this price in monetary units is 2 to 4 times higher in the industrialized countries, in GNP units it is 7 to 12 times more in the developing countries.

The following are some examples of the gap between low-income and higher housing costs in the developing countries.

In Taipei a worker employed within the city borders earns on average \$60/month: he could pay a maximum of \$10 monthly or \$120 yearly for a dwelling. On the basis of an 80% mortgage (at 6% for 20 years) a family could afford to buy only $17 \, m^2$ of land (at \$30/m^2) even in an area far from the city centre. The land costs would still be \$510, 30% of the general housing costs. The family will then have to spend \$1200 for building costs (53 m^2 at \$22/m^2). With the given land, the dwelling would have to be constructed on a building coefficient of 3—which means erecting four-storey houses at a density of 560 *families* per hectare. Thus at best the Taipei worker could provide his family with only a very small dwelling in an area of very high density outside the city.

Squatting

In all, the high land prices make it difficult for many of the new urban dwellers to find even the most modest housing facilities, and forces them to live in almost subhuman conditions, with a lack of piped water and sewerage with inadequate transport links to the city.

The low rate of industrial development in the cities has meant that there are not enough jobs for the new immigrants. Many at best find a part-time job which does not provide enough money to pay for even low-standard housing (which must be erected on residential land which is relatively high priced). A large part of the new urban population must provide housing for itself on areas of vacant land outside the city, erecting shacks, huts, tents, etc., without essential services. Such make-shift (though often permanent) housing conditions are in direct contrast to the highly developed, high-standard commercial and residential areas within the city.

Some figures compiled by the UN show that this is a widespread and increasing problem in the developing world. For example, in Rio de Janeiro the percentage of the city's population living in "uncontrolled settlements" increased from 20% in 1947 to 27% in 1961. In Lima the number of squatters increased even faster: from 9% to 36% during 12 years (1957–69) of rapid growth. It should be noted that these percentage increases are even more significant when it is realized that the cities as a whole are growing very fast in population. Many of the largest cities in the developing world (Calcutta, Djakarta, Taipei, Seoul, Dakar, Mexico City) now have a squatter population of between one-quarter and one-third of the total population.*

Economic Consequences

The accumulation of capital resulting from high land profits leads to increased expenditure for housing by a large strata of the population, and decreases their purchasing power while increasing the wealth of the landowners and developers. In some cases the economic result of such a capital accumulation is the investment of part of the land profits in the housing industry, in the building materials industry, and in other industrial enterprises. This has been the case in Mexico and is described in a very clear way by the well-known Mexican economist Edmondo Flores. Such a process has also occurred in other developing countries where the urbanization process led to the primary accumulation of capital which financed the first stage of industrialization.

But for the most part the developing countries, which need capital to invest in industry and in the modernization of agriculture, are not able to make use of the huge amount of capital tied up in land transactions. The high rate of profit in land in comparison with other economic sectors and the permanently increasing demand for land attract capital for reinvestment in land where future urban growth is expected. Land sometimes attracts capital away from banks because the rate of interest there is lower than the average rate of return from land transactions. The large middle-income strata may invest their savings in land rather than in the banks.

The negative impact of the high profits of land speculation is not limited to the permanent reinvestment in land. The surplus capital thus gained is also used in large part for luxury consumption. Countries which need foreign exchange to pay for the import of essential goods for rapid economic development use part of the profits from land to pay for the import of luxury consumption goods. Some part of the profits are also invested in building luxury residential palaces,

* World Bank, *Urbanization*, Sector Working Paper, Jan. 1974, table 6, p. 82.

while at the same time there are no means to satisfy the minimum housing needs of the low-income groups. Economists of different countries suggest that a considerable part of these profits also find their way to banks in foreign countries, at a time when the developing countries need foreign currency desperately.

The process of redistribution of capital as a result of the land market was described in a very clear way by Paul Vielle in his book *Marche des terrains et société urbaine*. The author emphasizes that the state does not play a role in restraining speculation, but rather it is the public authorities' decisions which allow further speculation. This is done by permitting more profitable land use through planning changes. For instance, fixing a higher land-use coefficient, allowing commercial use, or constructing roads all increase land value; while taxation methods which would take some of the land profits and use them for financing urban growth costs are not employed. The fact that the interests of powerful landowners are well represented in state and municipal institutions concerned with planning is also one of the factors which is responsible for this situation.

ALTERNATIVES TO HIGH RATES OF LAND-PRICE INCREASES

Various policy measures have been used in different countries to restrict the exaggerated land-price increase. All the countries mentioned in our examples have had some form of taxation and land-use regulation policies to this end. But the fact that the land-price increase in these countries has been so high shows the lack of effectiveness of these measures. On the other hand, our previous examples of those developed countries which have adopted a policy of advanced land acquisition by the public authorities, coupled with an effective land-use plan, may be of some interest to the developing countries. Obviously no policy measure can be mechanically translated from one country to another. We will try only very roughly to investigate the possible effect of such a policy were it to be adopted in the developing countries. Our calculation is that a policy of advance land acquisition could reduce the percentage of land costs in total housing costs from the current 30–50% to 10–17%. This policy would therefore not be a financial burden, but of financial benefit to the public authorities.

The goal of such a policy would be to reduce the cost of newly developed land on the city frontier by buying it before its price increases to near urban levels.

The average price of agricultural land in the rural areas in the developing countries is $0·05–0·20/m^2$. But even at 30 to 50 km from the boundaries of some large cities (we have data from Teheran, Taipei, Tel Aviv and Tokyo) the price of agricultural land has already been pushed up through speculation to $15–30/m^2$.

There is no doubt that agricultural land is more valuable if it is in the vicinity of a large city, but a policy of advanced land acquisition will prevent the authorities from paying a vastly inflated price for this land. For the developing countries, we estimate that agricultural land costs near the city should initially be 2 to 3 times the average agricultural land prices. As agricultural land prices (as given above) in the developing countries average $0·05–0·2/m^2$, this gives a range of costs that the public authorities must pay for land of between $0·15 and $0·4/m^2$. Capital costs (interest lost through buying this land and holding it in advance for 10 years) are estimated to be equal to the original price paid, giving a total land cost of about $0·4–0·8/m^2$ (in contrast to the $15–30/m^2$ paid today).

The effect of these lower land prices on the total costs of building new housing can be seen from the following figures. The total housing costs for new developments are made up of construction costs, infrastructure costs and land costs. Construction costs in the developing countries are roughly $20–30/m^2$. There is insufficient information on infrastructure costs in these countries; however, they can be estimated as 5–12% of construction costs (a figure derived from surveys of some Western countries). Thus, infrastructure costs would be $1–4/m^2$. In total, the cost of developing this new land by the public authorities (infrastructure plus land costs) would be $1·4–4·8/m^2$. These development costs therefore reach 10–17% of total costs.

The contrast with the current situation of unplanned development—where land costs are 30 to 50% of total housing costs—is striking. We may conclude by saying that these figures show that it is possible to supply land for urban development even in those developing countries whose government have limited financial resources. The lack of land for urban development in these countries is not a result of the lack of financial resources, but a result of the failure to implement a policy of advance land acquisition. It is probable that this is partly because of the influence of powerful economic groups who want to hold land as a very profitable investment, even if this will prevent the supplying of the needs of the majority of the population.

Today the effect of the land factor on urban growth patterns is expressed in the underdeveloped countries by a high rate of land-price increase in suburban regions, continuous expansion of the area of urban settlements often without vital services, and extremely high densities in some central urban areas. Our rough calculation shows that it might be possible to reduce considerably the high land prices (which particularly effect the living conditions of the less well-off) through the active intervention of the public authorities in the land as well as the housing market.

The increase of urban land prices is a world-wide phenomenon, but the social and economic consequences are, without doubt, more serious in the developing countries. The high rate of land-price increase in the developed countries has led to a decline in the quality of urban life. The high land prices in cities in the underdeveloped countries are one of the factors that have led to the exclusion of a large segment of the population from any housing possibilities whatsoever. At the same time the greater amount of speculation in land in these countries has hampered their economic development by syphoning off scarce capital from more productive investment.

REFERENCES

Bairoch, P., *The Economic Development of the Third World Since 1900*, London: Methuen, 1975.

Bose, Ashihi, "Some aspects of rising land prices and land speculation in urban Delhi", UN Regional Preparatory Conferences for the Habitat Conference on Human Settlements, Vancouver, Canada, 1975.

Darin-Drabkin, H., Poznanski, A. and Zaretsky, S., *Patterns of Land Use and Land Tenure in Israel*, Ministry of Housing, Tel Aviv, 1972.

International Union of Local Authorities, *Urbanization in the Developing Countries*, The Hague, 1968.

Lim, William, *Equity and the Urban Environment in the Third World*, Singapore, 1975.

United Nations, *Urban Land Policies and Land Use Control Measures, Asia and the Far East; Latin America*, New York, 1973.

Vielle, Paul, *Marche de terrains et société urbaine*, Paris: Maspero, 1973.

Woodruff, A. M. and Brown, J. R., editors, *Land for the Cities of Asia*, Hartford, Conn., John Lincoln Institute, 1972.
World Bank, *Urbanization*, Sector Working Paper, New York, May 1972.
——, *Housing*, Sector Working Paper, New York, June 1975.

CHAPTER 5

International Land-Price-Level Comparisons

Comparing land prices between different countries, and even between different cities in the same country, is a complicated task because of the large variations in price of the same kind of land at different locations within the same city. It is easier to compare land-price *development* trends between different countries and cities than the absolute prices expressed in monetary terms. The use of the *highest* land prices for each type of land can, however, serve as a barometer of the price of commercial land in the CBD and of land in the most expensive residential areas. It has been shown that the highest prices follow the same general trend as the average prices. One must be aware, however, that land prices expressed in monetary units per space unit does not reflect the true land value, as one must take into account the building coefficient (which has a very marked influence on the value). It must be understood that the highest prices are limited to a very restricted area with the price level dropping considerably even a short distance from the area. The topography of a city, and especially that of the most central commercial and residential area, influences the relationship between the highest land prices and the average land prices in the city.

Thus the data collected and presented here have limited application and are intended to illustrate some of the factors influencing the formation of commercial and residential land prices. The data can be analysed to reveal, for instance, the relationship between the size of a city and a country and the formation of commercial and residential land prices. The data can also be used to investigate the relationship between national economic levels and land prices, whereby land prices are adjusted to take into account differing per capita levels of gross national product (GNP). However, very specific factors also have to be included in an understanding of the level of prices in different cities. Thus, although the data in Table 5.1 have definite limitations, they are valuable within those restrictions, and provide the basis for a comprehensive study in the future.

COMMERCIAL LAND PRICES

An examination of Table 5.1 shows that there is no direct relationship between the level of the highest commercial land prices and the size of a city or city region and the population of a country. It appears that the main factor influencing the commercial land prices is the level of economic activity and the role of the city in international trade and finance. Generally, the biggest cities of the largest countries in the world serve also as centres of international trade and finance. There are, however, large cities with a lesser role in international trade; these are for the most part cities in countries with a very low GNP *per capita*.

Among the top five cities in commercial land prices, four are the biggest cities in the world: New York, Tokyo, London and Paris. But the highest level of commercial land prices is found in Zurich, a city of 400,000 population (800,000 in the city region), while the total population of Switzerland is 6·5 million. Beirut, a city of 800,000 in a country of 3 million, also has one of the highest commercial land prices. Both cities, Beirut and Zurich, are centres of international finance and foreign currency markets.

On the other hand, two of the largest cities in the world, Buenos Aires and Mexico City, show lower commercial land prices than other smaller cities and countries. Thus there is a relationship between commercial land prices among cities of similar size only when they are of the same character (i.e. industrial, commercial, financial centre, etc.).

For example, the tourist city of Lugano, Switzerland, with a population of 70,000, has a higher maximum commercial land price than the industrial city of Milan, with a population of 1·7 million, only 100 km away. The same comparison can be made between Geneva (120,000 population), where the highest commercial land price is $10,000/m^2$,

TABLE 5.1. Comparison of Highest Land Values in Selected Cities in 1970

City	Commercial values $/m²	Residential values $/m²	Ratio residential to commercial values	GNP per capita 1971 in $	Land values in yearly GNP per capita		Increase in % 1953–70	
					commercial	residential	GNP per capita	consumer price index
1 Zurich	14,000	350	1:40	4158	3·4	0·08	97	50
2 Tokyo	11,000	850	1:13	2450	4·5	0·35	359	97
3 New York	9,000	1000	1:9	5110	1·6	0·20	75	46
4 London	8,000	160	1:50	2653	3·0	0·06	58	80
5 Paris	7,000	1200	1:6	3449	2·0	0·35	143	90
6 Beirut	4,800	120	1:40	580	8·2	0·20	—	—
7 Munich	4,500	600	1:75	3791	1·2	0·16	176	48
8 Madrid	3,500	700	1:4	1154	3·0	0·60	230	150
9 Milan	3,000	600	1:5	2001	1·5	0·30	147	71
10 Amsterdam	2,700	170	1:16	2990	0·9	0·06	131	86
11 Buenos Aires	2,600	200	1:13	1111	2·3	0·20	87	4122
12 Mexico City	1,800	180	1:10	689	2·6	0·266	—	146
13 Tel Aviv	1,700	500	1:34	1852	0·9	0·27	370	110
14 Stockholm	1,000	150	1:7	4690	0·2	0·03	100	85
15 Helsinki	1,000	170	1:6	2457	0·4	0·07	115	72
16 Copenhagen	1,000	100	1:10	3612	0·3	0·03	103	105
17 Taipei	1,000	140	1:7	416	2·5	0·35	116.	478
18 Lima	300	50	1:6	480	0·7	0·10	—	139
19 La Paz	200	40	1:5	225	1·0	0·18	74	5624
20 Calcutta	160	16	1:6	100	1·6	0·17	84	133

and Lyon (1 million population) located only 200 km from Geneva, where the highest commercial land price is $2000/m^2.

The lack of correlation between population size and commercial land values is even more evident when one compares cities within one country which differ in economic character. The highest commercial land prices in Cannes on the Cote d'Azur (population 70,000) are 50% higher than in the big city of Lyon. This comparison shows once again that the role of a city in the international trade, finance and tourism is one of the most important factors in determining the height of commercial land values. Another important element is the degree of concentration of international trade in one big city in a country. In the USA and the Federal Republic of Germany, for example, international trade is shared by several cities—Chicago, San Francisco, New Orleans and New York in the USA and Dusseldorf, Hamburg, Munich and Berlin in Germany. Therefore, the potentially high land prices are dispersed over several cities and not concentrated in New York and Berlin. Some examples of concentration of international trade in one city in a country are Buenos Aires, Mexico City (the classic example), Copenhagen, Helsinki, London and Stockholm.

No direct relationship was found between the highest commercial land prices and the GNP of a country. Although Switzerland has the third highest GNP *per capita* (after the USA and Sweden), as well as the highest commercial land prices in the world, the second highest prices are in Tokyo (which is only eighth in GNP *per capita* among the selected countries). Finland has the same GNP *per capita* as Japan but Helsinki is fifteenth in commercial land prices. Beirut is an even more telling example; with a GNP *per capita* in Lebanon three times lower than in Israel, Beirut's highest commercial land price is three times higher than Tel Aviv's. This proves once again that it is the role in international trade and not the economic level of the inhabitants of a city which is the dominant factor influencing commercial land prices.

When the highest commercial land prices (per m^2) are divided by GNP *per capita*, New York has the same relative prices as Milan and Munich. Mexico City, Buenos Aires, Madrid, London and Tokyo have higher values than New York. The rich Scandinavian countries have the lowest commercial values expressed in these terms. Here again one sees the strong influence of a country's role in international trade, as opposed to the economic level of the local population, in determining commercial land prices.

The topography of a city and its commercial centre is an additional factor influencing land prices. The small area of the CBD in cities in Switzerland in comparison to the large area of Manhattan, New York, along with building regulations which allow high-rise buildings in New York and limit the height in Zurich, Geneva and Lugano have a considerable importance in explaining the high land prices in Switzerland in comparison with New York.

RESIDENTIAL LAND VALUES

A look at Table 5.1 shows that of the five cities with the highest commercial land prices, three of them have also the highest residential land prices—$1200/m^2 in Paris as compared to $1000/m^2 in New York and $850/m^2 in Tokyo; while in regard to commercial land prices Paris is less expensive than Tokyo and New York.

It is interesting to note that Zurich, with the highest commercial land prices in the world, is in the middle category of residential land prices while London falls in the category of relatively low residential land prices.

The building regulations and the topography of the city and region influence the comparatively lower residential land values in Zurich and London. In Zurich the highest building coefficient is 2·5, and population growth has been in the environs of Zurich with their natural beauty and excellent transportation network. In London residential areas are based on a low building coefficient (mostly single or semi-detached family houses with a small garden).

The building coefficient for exclusive residential areas in Paris, New York and Tokyo is high in comparison with Zurich and London. The higher residential land prices in Paris, as compared with New York, may be explained by the fact that a large percentage of high-income New Yorkers prefer to live outside the city, while the comparable Parisians prefer to live in the city (and to have a second house in the country for weekends and vacations). Madrid, Milan, Munich and Tel Aviv are cities with very high residential land prices ($500–700/m^2); and in these cities too the high-income strata like to live in the city. There are considerable differences in the GNP *per capita* in these four countries in relation to the comparatively smaller differences between the highest residential land prices among them. This may be explained by the large gap between the high- and medium-income strata in Madrid, Tel Aviv and Milan which means that the effective demand for the most exclusive housing is much the same as in Munich. A common feature of the four cities is a policy which pushes the low- and even middle-income strata of the population outside the city, while land speculation (not controlled by the public authorities) contributes to high residential land prices in the centre. This is in contrast to the Scandinavian countries and the Netherlands where active public authority policies have resulted in the highest residential land prices being only $100–10/m^2 (in spite of the high GNP *per capita* in these countries).

The highest prices in terms of GNP are found in Madrid, Paris, Tokyo, Milan, Tel Aviv and Mexico City. These six countries share in common a very high rate of increase of GNP *per capita* during the period 1953–70. Germany also had a high rate of GNP increase but its very high GNP *per capita* makes the level of residential prices computed in GNP units only 0·16. New York, in spite of the high residential land price of $1000/m^2, has a land price/GNP *per capita* ratio of only 0·20, because of the high GNP *per capita*. The Scandinavian countries and the Netherlands show the lowest ratios due to the relatively low residential land prices. London also has a ratio of only 0·06, because of the low residential land prices ($160/m^2). Zurich, where residential land prices in monetary terms are more than twice that of London ($350/m^2), with the GNP deflator has virtually identical prices because of the high annual GNP *per capita*.

A most significant example is Calcutta where land prices are only $16/m^2, yet the ratio to *per capita* GNP is 0·17 (because of a $100 annual GNP *per capita*). A comparison of Stockholm and Calcutta shows that the highest-priced residential land in Calcutta is three times more expensive for the local population than in Stockholm, where the annual GNP *per capita* is 47 times higher. La Paz, Lima, Taipei and Beirut also show high residential land in GNP units. It is more difficult for the population of these cities to pay the low residential land prices than it is in countries with high levels of both GNP *per capita* and land prices. The high level of residential land prices in the GNP units in these cities may be related to the high rate of inflation over the 1955–70 period. The continuously diminishing power of money in these countries and others (Israel, Mexico, Spain and Argentina) is one of the main factors encouraging land speculation, which reduces the amount of land on the market (and thus pushes up prices).

THE RELATIONSHIP BETWEEN COMMERCIAL AND RESIDENTIAL LAND PRICES

The commercial land prices in all the cities studied are many times higher than the residential prices. The ratio of residential to commercial prices range from 1:3·4 and 1:4 in Madrid and Tel Aviv to 1:50 in London.

Considerable difference was found between the commercial and residential prices in the same section of Copenhagen in this research, and in earlier studies of other cities carried out by R. M. Hurd (1924) and P. F. Wendt. According to Hurd the ratio varies from 1:3 and 1:5 for *average* commercial and residential prices in different neighbourhoods, but declines 1:10 for the *highest* commercial and residential land prices.

As illustrated in Table 5.1, three cities show an exceptionally high ratio of commercial to residential land prices (1:40): London, Zurich and Beirut. All three of these cities have very high commercial land prices, but Beirut and London have lower residential land prices than Zurich. As we have seen, residential land prices are unusually depressed in these cities, and their commercial prices are also elevated by their importance as international financial centres.

The lowest ratios of commercial to residential land prices are seen in Tel Aviv (1:3·4), Madrid (1:4), and La Paz (1:5). Slightly higher ratios (1:6) are seen in Calcutta, Lima, Helsinki and Paris while the other cities studied show ratios of from 1:7 (in Taipei) to 1:16 (in Amsterdam). The low ratio in Tel Aviv, Madrid, Paris and Milan can be explained by the very high level of residential land prices, due in part to the preference of the affluent there for a central location. La Paz and Lima show a low ratio because of the lower commercial land prices in comparison with other cities. It must be noted here that, in

GNP units, these latter two cities show a high level of residential land prices and a medium level of commercial land prices.

The Scandinavian cities and Amsterdam have almost the same residential land prices, but differ in the ratio of residential to commercial prices because Amsterdam has higher commercial prices.

While the commercial land prices do have some influence on the level of residential prices, the comparison of commercial to residential land prices show that the relationship between the two is a result of many factors, including the topography and economic character of the city, its building regulations and policies for implementing them, and the locational preferences of the population. The comparisons between cities with differing rates of increase of GNP *per capita* and consumer prices show the impact of macro-economic factors on the level of urban land prices.

CHAPTER 6

Price Formation in the Copenhagen Region, 1956–69

WHY A STUDY OF THE COPENHAGEN REGION?

Recent urban growth has been nothing short of phenomenal. Such growth has created a variety of burdensome problems which urgently require new land-use policies to provide guidelines for accommodating continued growth. Policy formulation, however, requires a more complete understanding of urban growth processes than currently exists. In particular, little is known concerning land-price development trends as they affect or are affected by urban-development patterns and land-use changes occurring in cities and city regions.

Most previous studies concerning price formation have dealt with "stationary" cities, looking at price changes *within* fixed municipal boundaries. Little has been done concerning land-price formation in rapidly developing metropolitan areas and city regions. It is suggested that an investigation of land-price development, especially in the context of city/city region, will permit the identification of those key factors which influence price formation. Once identified, the research question then becomes one of learning how to control and manipulate such factors from a public policy standpoint.

As a case study, an appraisal of the historical development of Copenhagen and its broader functional region has many relevant policy implications. Because of the excellent data available, the city serves well as a research example. Most studies dealing with land-price formation tend to be spatially restricted; that is, the collection and evaluation of detailed transactions data for specific areas rarely permit the extrapolation of identified trends to other areas. Thus, when undertaken for large urban centres and large metropolitan regions, such piecemeal findings fall short of attempting to explain the more complex interrelationships involved in the urban growth process. In this sense, Copenhagen represents a windfall in that time-series data for the entire metropolitan region are available.

The Danish system of evaluating all land property every 4 years and publishing evaluation results on land-value maps for each locality (which give the price of each site) allows the comparison of land-price changes for the same sites and areas over time. Average land prices are calculated on the basis of such transactions as have occurred in different locations where no transactions have occurred, adjustments are made if development works have been built. Thus, the average land price is influenced mostly by the area location and the type of land use associated with the occasional transactions. It may be suggested that average land prices based on transaction prices only are far from showing the real trends of land values. Evaluation cannot exactly express the real market price; but evaluation executed at the same time using the same evaluation method may provide the most valuable material about the relationship of land prices at different locations and different times. Since the bias is similar for all evaluated sites, the evaluation gives a real development trend of the distribution of land prices through space and time.

The main sources of information for this investigation were:

(a) Statistical books on assessment of real property in Denmark for the years 1956 and 1965, and statistical reports from the central evaluation office for 1969. These books contain the land areas and the land value according to land use for all of Denmark.

(b) Evaluation maps are published by the Bureau of Statistics in Denmark for the years 1956, 1965 and 1969 for all communities and real estate in Denmark. In these evaluation maps the price of every site is recorded. The land use of these sites is not indicated on the evaluation maps; but, by comparing the average price per square metre in the maps with the information given in the books on the assessment of real property, it is possible to determine the nature of the land use of a particular site.

Additional information was received through the assistance of the chief of the planning department/of the Danish Ministry of Housing, and both the national and Copenhagen chief evaluators' offices were most helpful in providing a better understanding of the published figures.

Scope of Study

The study has two points of departure:

1. a comparison of *aggregate* value changes for different types of land use in Copenhagen, Copenhagen County, and three investigated communities in the county;
2. a detailed investigation of the land evaluation maps for the three communities and for the city itself.

The municipality of Copenhagen (including the administrative "island" of Frederiksberg) reached its maximum population in the early 1950s (890,000 inhabitants), representing at that time considerably more than half the population of the Copenhagen region. In the mid-1950s the population of the municipality began to level off and decline. By 1969 the population of the city of Copenhagen had declined to 747,000, but the total population of the Greater Copenhagen Region was 1·7 million, or about one-third of the total population of Denmark.

The Greater Copenhagen Region includes Copenhagen, Frederiksberg, and the three surrounding counties: Copenhagen County, Roskilde County and Frederiksberg County. This region, comprising 2850 km² (1100 miles²) which represent 7% of the area of Denmark, includes about fifty-two municipalities, some forty of which are highly urbanized, while others are still small and rural. Land use is still dominated by agriculture, forests and lakes, the urban zone comprising only 18% of the area. We have chosen for investigation only Copenhagen County out of the region as a whole.

For the purpose of this study, three out of the twenty communities comprising the Copenhagen County Region have been chosen for detailed analysis: Ballerup, Hoje Taastrup and Herstedernes (see Figs. 6.4, 6.5, 6.6). These communities, located in the western part of the county region, cover about 114 km² of the total 520 km² of the

Copenhagen County Region. The western part of the county region is experiencing a faster rate of growth than the northern section in which development has previously been concentrated.

The development of the regions is conditioned by the planning effort to link the urbanization and industrialization process together. Thus, planning authorities are designating areas in the region for industrial centres, commercial centres, recreation areas, residential one-family areas combined with multi-storey housing projects, and planned community social centres. Integrating all of these needs is the transport network which must permit ease of access in terms of both distance and time to the totality of regional functions. At the same time, efforts are being made to maintain the role of Copenhagen as the social, cultural and economic centre of the region and the country.

In this study, it is of interest to observe the effects of the planning of the social and economic development of the region on land-use patterns and land prices. This is especially so keeping in mind that the plan includes efficiently implemented macro- and micro-zoning legislation which does not permit the use of agricultural land for urban development until land previously allocated for urban uses is recognized as being insufficient for supplying future needs.

This study of the Copenhagen region should be regarded as a case study of the impact of the urbanization process on the formation of land prices in a metropolitan area and especially the role of land-use changes in land-price increases and the creation of additional land value.

TRENDS IN LAND-PRICE DEVELOPMENT IN COPENHAGEN AND THE REGION

We begin by investigating the changes in the *aggregate* land value that have occurred over our 13-year period in Copenhagen, in the investigated communities, and in the county in which they are located. The comparison between the aggregate-value increase for Copenhagen and the Copenhagen County Region, as well as for the investigated communities, shows a great difference in the rate of price increase between Copenhagen and the other areas. Although the distance from Copenhagen to the investigated communities is no more than 15 km,

TABLE 6.1. Aggregate Land Value Increases in Fixed 1969 Prices

	Aggregate land value in 1,000,000 Kr				Percentage Increase			Total	Yearly rate of compound increase in %			Overall
	1956	1960	1965	1969	56–60	60–65	65–69	56–69	56–60	60–65	65–69	56–69
Denmark	22,000·0	28,571·5	53,000·0	67,371·0	29·9	85·5	27·1	206·2	6·8	16·7	6·2	9·0
Copenhagen	5,231·8	6,375·6	9,509·0	11,760·0	21·87	49·1	23·7	124·8	5·1	10·5	5·5	6·4
Copenhagen County	2,109·4	3,491·5	10,422·7	14,666·1	65·5	198·5	40·7	595·3	13·4	31·5	8·9	16·1
Total for the investigated communities	158·8	290·4	1,769·6	2,128·3	75·0	675·0	19·8	1451·1	14·9	64·2	4·6	23·0
Ballerup	90·5	176·8	864·6	1,046·3	95·4	389·0	21·0	1056·8	18·2	48·5	4·9	20·6
Herstedernes	21·7	34·6	425·1	474·0	59·4	1128·6	11·5	2085·0	12·3	87·0	2·8	26·6
Hoje Taastrup	46·4	79·0	479·9	608·9	70·3	507·5	26·9	1211·5	14·2	57·0	6·1	21·9

land-price development trends differ greatly between an existing, developed, stationary city and surrounding urban settlements which are in the stage of rapid urbanization. During the 13-year period (1956–69), the price increase in Copenhagen was 125%, or 6·4 yearly, generally lower than the total land price increase in Denmark as a whole, 9% yearly on the fixed 1969 prices (Table 6.1).

In the Copenhagen county region during the same 13-year period, the increase was 595%, or 16·1% yearly. Whereas in 1956 the aggregate land value of Copenhagen was 150% higher than for the Copenhagen county region, in 1969 the aggregate land value for the region was 20% higher than for the city (Table 6.2, Fig. 6.1).

TABLE 6.2. Aggregate Land-Value Increases in Current Prices

	Aggregate land values in 1,000,000 Kr				Yearly compound rate of interest 1956–69 in %
	1956	1960	1965	1969	
Denmark	12,503·0	17,175·0	41,085·0	67,371·0	13·8
Copenhagen	2,906·6	3,832·5	7,259·1	11,760·0	11·4
Copenhagen County Region	1,171·9	2,098·8	7,956·3	14,666·1	19·8
Total for the investigated communities	88·2	174·6	1,350·9	2,129·2	28·8
Ballerup 1956	50·3	106·3	660·0	1,046·3	26·2
Herstedernes	12·1	20·8	324·5	474·0	32·6
Hoje Taastrup	25·8	47·5	366·4	608·9	27·5

The rate of price increase in the investigated communities is indicative of the high rate in the Copenhagen region, even though it is higher than the average regional rate. The least developed community in 1956, Herstedernes, shows the highest rate of price increase— 2085% over the 13 years, or 27% yearly. In the other two communities, the average yearly rate of increase was 21–22%, as compared with the 16·1% in the Copenhagen region as a whole.

There are considerable differences in the rate of land-price increase for the earlier and later parts of our period. From 1965 to 1969 the rate of increase in the three investigated communities is lower than in Copenhagen or the county as a whole, while in the previous 5 years

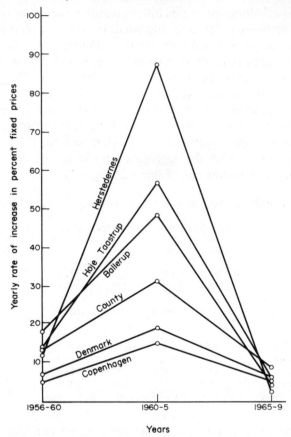

Fig. 6.1. Yearly rate of increase in percentage fixed prices, 1969, Copenhagen study.

their rate of price increase reached a peak which far exceeded Copenhagen's. The best way to explain these figures seems to be that in these newly urbanized communities initially there is a very high rate of price increase as land changes from agricultural to urban use. It is that phenomenon which accounts for the great part of the massive increase in land value; thus after new development has been completed, there is little further rise in prices. This will be investigated in more detail below. But first we must consider other possible factors which contribute to urban growth and thus to land-price increases.

LAND PRICES, POPULATION GROWTH, AND ECONOMIC ACTIVITY

Several factors influence the increase in urban land prices. Among them are the rate of population growth, the rate of economic growth, the increase in the purchasing power of the population, and the rate of inflation.

Permanent urban growth is accompanied by the investment of public and private capital in the infrastructure and in public and private services; these factors serve to enhance the urban environment and increase the value of urban land.

This study will attempt to investigate the role of public authority decisions on land use, especially the decision to change the land use from agricultural to urban. Our assumption is that while general urban growth creates additional land value the greatest increase in value is created through the change of land use.

The rate of population growth is one of the factors which affects land prices. However, by itself it is not an explanatory variable, as the same rate of population growth may lead to widely variable rates of land-price increase. Similarly, a higher rate of population growth in one community must not necessarily lead to a higher rate of land-price increase in comparison with another community with a lower growth rate (see Table 6.3). For example, Ballerup, whose population increased by 299%, and Hoje Taastrup with a 114% population increase show the same land-price increase of 21–22% yearly.

The decline of Copenhagen's population as compared to the 49·6% population increase in the region during the 15-year period may explain the higher rate of land-price increase in the Copenhagen county region (16·1% per year) than in the city (6·4%). Population growth exerts pressure on the land market, making demands for land for residential and related purposes, such as public and private services. However, the relationship is not a direct one. The example of Herstedernes shows this clearly. In 1960–5 the population grew in the community by 123%, and in 1965–9 by an additional 169%. But land prices increased by only

TABLE 6.3. Population Growth

| | Population in absolute numbers | | | | Percentage increase | | | |
	1956	1960	1965	1969	1956–60	1960–5	1965–9	1956–69
Denmark	4,448,400	4,585,256	4,767,597	4,920,966	3·1	7·2	3·2	10·6
Greater Copenhagen	1,518,600	1,596,700	1,663,600	1,716,500	5·1	9·5	3·2	13·0
Copenhagen	871,139	835,662	788,919	746,883	−4·1	−9·4	−5·3	−14·3
Copenhagen County Region	398,227	486,139	555,019	595,781	22·1	39·4	7·3	49·6
Totals for investigated Communities	25,699	36,038	59,920	88,785	32·6	129·9	78·6	304·5
Ballerup	11,405	19,582	35,663	45,507	71·7	212·7	27·6	299·0
Herstedernes	3,291	3,600	7,350	19,778	9·4	123·3	169·1	501·0
Hoje Taastrup	11,003	12,856	16,907	23,500	16·8	53·6	39·0	113·5

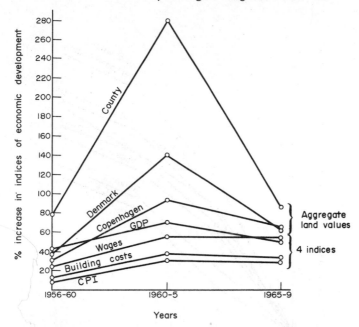

Fig. 6.2. Economic development indices and aggregate land values (current prices), 1956 to 1969, Copenhagen study.

11·5% in 1965–9 after increasing by 1128% from 1960 to 1965. One of the explanations for this is that the greatest price increases occurred where land was being newly developed (changing from agricultural use) but it was not actually settled (with the consequent population increase) until several years after the land prices rose. Thus there is a time lag between land-price increase and population growth.

Population growth influences the land values indirectly through increased demand for land, but it is not the amount of vacant land in urban areas but the amount of developed land approved for construction by the authorities which is relevant to the land market. An additional factor is the level of public and private services, including transportation connections and environmental features for each community. This may explain some of the anomalies between the rate of

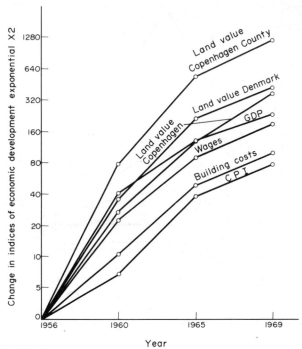

Fig. 6.3. Aggregate index changes, 1956 to 1969, Copenhagen study.

population increase and land-price increase in the Copenhagen county region.

The comparison between the rate of land-price increase in Denmark and Copenhagen and some items of economic development show that the rate of increase in gross domestic product most closely parallels that of land prices. A comparison of different time periods shows that the years 1960–5 have the highest rate of increase in both gross domestic product and land prices; while there is a decline in the rate of increase of both during the period 1965–9 (see Figs. 6.2, 6.3 and Table 6.4).

A comparison of the rate of land price increase with the rate of

TABLE 6.4. Comparison between Land-Values Increase and Indices of Economic Development

	Index				Percentage increase			Total increase in %
	1956	1960	1965	1969	1956–60	1960–5	1965–9	1956–69
Gross domestic product at market prices	100	142	243	366	42·0	71·1	50·6	266·0
Consumer price index	100	107	139	178	7·0	29·9	28·1	78·0
Wages per hour for unskilled workers	100	124	192	295	24·0	54·8	53·6	195·0
Building costs of residential buildings	100	112	154	205	12·0	37·5	33·1	105·0
Aggregate land-value increase in Denmark	100	137	329	539	37·0	140·1	63·8	439·0
Aggregate land-value increase in Copenhagen	100	130	250	405	30·0	92·3	62·0	305·0
Aggregate land-value increase in Copenhagen County Region	100	179	679	1251	79·0	280·0	84·2	1151·0

increase in the consumer price index and the gross national product shows that the additional land value created exceeded the increase in other indices of economic development. Although these influenced land prices, the additional increase may be said to be the differential rent created through urban growth. The increase in land prices is a measure of the overall attractiveness of the city. The analysis of land price changes disaggregated for particular land *uses* may allow us to isolate the importance of land-use changes in creating additional value.

LAND-USE AND LAND-VALUE CHANGES IN THE
COPENHAGEN COUNTY REGION

A comparison of the rate of aggregate land-price increases and changes in land use in the Copenhagen County Region will serve as a background for the more detailed analyses of the three investigated communities.

There are some difficulties in making such a comparison because of administrative changes during the 13-year period. The space of the county region has grown by 7·7% due to the inclusion of additional areas (probably 2800 ha. of forest) into the administrative limits of some communities of the region. There was also a change in the classification and evaluation of agricultural land. Until 1969 the agricultural-use prices were evaluated according to the level of the prevailing market prices; from 1969 they were based on the existing agricultural-use price in the rural areas without taking into account the actual prices, which are higher near urban areas as they include some part of the prospective higher value from a change of land into urban use. The difference is not as large as in other countries because of legislative and taxation measures.

The average market price for agricultural land was about $4 \, \text{Kr/m}^2$ in 1969, the average evaluation was $2·5 \, \text{Kr/m}^2$. This change in evaluation method makes it difficult to compare the agricultural values for the years 1956 and 1969. In spite of this problem in data analysis, the small percentage of agricultural land-use values in total value enables us to investigate the changes that occurred in the region's land use and land values, especially for urban land uses (residential, residential mixed with commercial, commercial and industrial).

As illustrated in Table 6.5 and Fig. 6.3 (showing land-use changes in the county), the space in urban land use increased by 85%—from 5597 ha. in 1956 to 10,533 ha. in 1969. The value of this urban land increased by 2288% (from 644 million Kr in 1956 to 10,167 million Kr in 1969). This rate of increase is higher than the average rate of aggregate land price increase in the region (1065%). This is composed of the increased price for 5597 ha. urban land and 4613 ha. of land that changed from agricultural to urban use.

For particular land uses (Table 6.13) commercial values show the

TABLE 6.5. Land-Use and Land-Value Changes in Copenhagen County Region, 1956–69

Category of land use	1956 land use + value			1969 land use + value			Changes 56–69 in %		
	Area (ha.)	Av. value (Kr/m²)	Agg. value in 1000 Kr	Area (ha.)	Av. value (Kr/m²)	Agg. value in 1000 Kr	Area	Av. value (Kr/m²)	Agg. value in 1000 Kr
Agriculture	12,957	0·4	51,744	11,049	2·5	272,000	−15	525	341
Urban use	5,597	12·3	644,551	10,951	93·62	10,167,000	157	758	2288
Building sites and non-built sites	2,531	3·9	99,360	5,380	29·5	1,589,000	113	656	1494
State and community property	7,911	1·9	142,210	4,230	27·7	1,109,000	−47	1439	743
Other uses	10,176	2·2	229,044	7,783	19·4	1,514,000	−24	782	561
Totals	39,172	3·0	1,166,909	39,393	34·5	14,651,000	37	832	1065·4
Forestry	—	—	—	2,801	0·5	15,000	—	—	—

largest increase (4784%), while for industrial use the increase is 1762%, for residential 1408%, and for residential mixed with commercial 1201%. The fact that commercial values show the highest rate of increase may be explained by the relatively low level of commercial land prices in 1956.

The average price for the four urban uses increased from 12·2 Kr/m² in 1956 to 103·2 Kr/m² in 1969 (an increase of 774%). In absolute terms the difference is 91 Kr/m²; calculated in fixed 1969 prices the difference is still 83 Kr/m².

For agricultural land use the absolute price difference is very small. In 1969 there was a difference between the market value (4 Kr/m²) and the evaluated value (2·45 Kr/m²). In 1956 the evaluated 0·4 Kr/m² corresponded to the existing market value. The difference between 1969 and 1956 for agricultural land use values is therefore 3·6 Kr/m² (4 Kr/m² − 0·4 Kr/m²) instead of 2·05 Kr/m² (2·45 Kr/m² − 0·4 Kr/m²) according to the evaluation. The enormous difference in land prices between agricultural use (4 Kr/m²) and urban use (103 Kr/m²) creates the basic element of urban land rent.

LAND-USE AND LAND-VALUE CHANGES IN THE INVESTIGATED COMMUNITIES

An examination of land use and land value change in the three investigated communities shows in more detail the effect of land-use change on land-price formation (Table 6.6 and Figs. 6.2 and 6.3).

One sees first of all a general decline in agricultural land use in all three communities during the investigated period (1956–69). The largest change occurred in Ballerup, where the space in agricultural use declined from 51·2% to 16·4%. A lesser but still significant change took place in Hoje Taastrup where land in agricultural use declined from 67·6% to 36·1%. Herstedernes, the least developed community initially, with 82·2% agricultural land, still had 50·5% of land in agricultural use in 1969 (though part of this land is planned as a park). Ballerup, with the highest aggregate land value, has the highest percentage of land devoted to urban uses (residential, industrial, commercial), 27·4% of the total space associated with 56·5% of the aggregate value. The 16·4% of space in agricultural use has only 1%

TABLE 6.6. Main Land-Use and Land-Value Changes in the Investigated Communities

Land uses	Ballerup				Herstedernes				Hoje Taastrup			
	1956		1969		1956		1969		1956		1969	
	Area (ha.)	Value (Kr)	Area (ha.)	Value (Kr)	Area (ha.)	Value (Kr)	Area (ha.)	Value (Kr)	Area (ha.)	Value (Kr)	Area (ha.)	Value (Kr)
Agriculture	1575	5,088	485	11,469	1978	6,327	1258	17,603	1742	5,529	895	22,006
Urban uses	226	19,412	848	609,294	56	2,028	406	259,004	224	12,902	442	323,798
Building sites and unbuilt areas	253	7,845	543	179,485	94	1,182	309	89,119	152	2,459	442	158,591
State and community property	203	3,514	256	72,556	97	1,416	146	23,339	124	2,017	118	25,696
Others	818	14,392	834	173,505	181	1,098	371	84,888	335	2,890	581	78,761
Totals	3075	50,251	2966	1,046,309	2406	12,051	2490	473,953	2577	25,797	2478	608,852

of the aggregate land value. Hoje Taastrup has 17·8% urban space, with 53·2% of the total aggregate value, while agricultural land use composes 36·1% of total space and only 3·7% of total value. Herstedernes in 1969 has 50·5% of agricultural and recreational area associated with 3·7% of aggregate value, but an aggregate value of 54·5% for the 16% of land space devoted for urban uses. It may be suggested that public authority planning decisions on change of land use are the *main* factors of land-price increase and the deciding factor in creating the urban land value. A more detailed analysis of land-use change at the *same* sites may illustrate the role of public authority decisions more clearly.

To this point, figures for land prices according to different uses were based on the *average* price of different land uses by aggregating all sites of the same use according to different locations and summarizing all the values for different locations for the same use. This permitted an evaluation of the aggregate land value of each land use. However, the published evaluation maps for the investigated communities allow the measurement of land-price development of the *same site* and thus illustrate much more clearly the role of public authority in the actual creation of land value and/or urban land rent.

In order to illustrate the price changes which occurred during 13 years at the same site, we have randomly chosen one page of the evaluation book for each of the three investigated communities. The evaluation maps publish the value of each site in kroner per square metre (7·0 kroner = approx. one US dollar in 1969). This price for each site is fixed at the time of evaluation which is carried out every 4 years. The uniform criteria for evaluation for the entire country allow an exact comparison of the value changes occurring in the same area over extended time periods. Each page comprises between 100 to 160 hectares, or 250 to 400 acres. For each page we compared the price changes that took place during the 13-year period on the same sites.

Referring to the maps (Figs. 6.4, 6.5 and 6.6), the first thing one notes from the land value changes on the evaluation pages is the enormous price increase in one small area of one evaluation page, ranging from 7–250 times in Ballerup, 15–360 times in Hoje Taastrup, and 5–1000 times in Herstedernes. An interesting feature is that within a distance of a few yards the value of one site increased from

$0.40 \, Kr/m^2$ in 1956 to $40 \, Kr/m^2$ in 1969—an increase of 100 times, while across the road (where no change in use was permitted) the increase was only from $0.50 \, Kr/m^2$ to $1.50 \, Kr/m^2$. In another part of the same map the land value change was $0.30 \, Kr/m^2$ to $300 \, Kr/m^2$, or 1000 times, while on a nearby site the value change was only from $0.30 \, Kr/m^2$ to $40 \, Kr/m^2$. This same phenomenon may be observed on all other pages of the evaluation maps.

The comparison of evaluation maps shows in a concrete way the role of public authority decisions on change of land use in not only influencing but actually creating land value, which in turn is the basis of urban land rent. This analysis also reveals the "lottery" nature of future land values, whereby one landowner makes a considerable capital gain on his property, while that of his neighbour remains virtually unchanged. Common to both these landowners is that neither of them engaged in any economic activity in order to influence the land price increase. The increase or non-increase in land value resulted only from the decision of the planning authorities to change the use of a particular piece of land. Obviously, such decisions are a result of socio-economic development and the constantly growing need for land for urban growth.

The next part of this study consisted of measuring the value and area of every site in the three communities and the price changes over the 1956–69 period. The first step was the measurement of all sites with the same land value in 1956 on every map of the evaluation book of the particular community (there are 27 such maps for Ballerup, for instance). Then, these sites were compared with their land value 13 years later. Thus, it was possible to observe how sites with a common price in one period have split into five or six different land-value categories by the later date. These results were added together and recorded in a table which shows the summarized results for each of the three communities.*

* *Note.* As evaluation maps do not actually list the *type* of land use, but just the land prices for different sites, we have had to substitute categories of land prices (based on the range of land prices for each type of use given by the Danish assessment books) for actual land-use categories. As agricultural land prices almost never overlap urban land prices, either in 1956 or 1969, this assumption will not lead to great difficulty, though it must be noted that comparisons of different categories of urban land is more problematical.

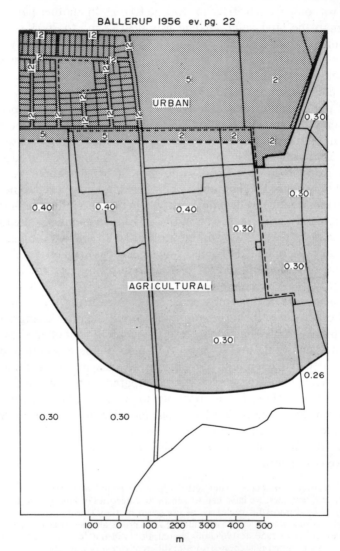

Fig. 6.4. Land usage and land prices, Ballerup, 1969.

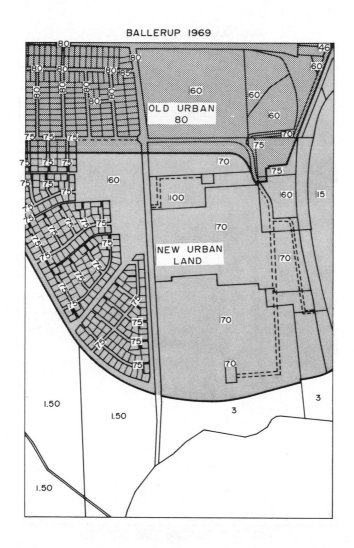

Fig. 6.4. (*cont.*)

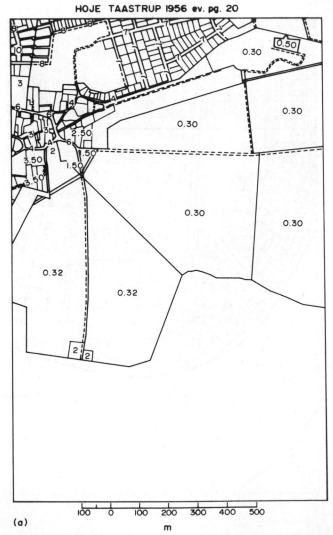

Fig. 6.5. Land values in Hoje Taastrup, 1956 and 1969—a comparison.

(b)

Fig. 6.5. (*contd.*)

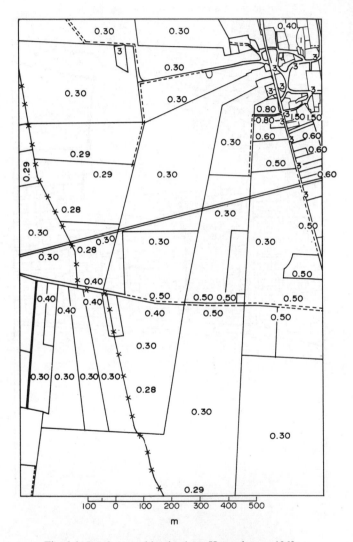

Fig. 6.6. Land use and land values, Herstedernes, 1969.

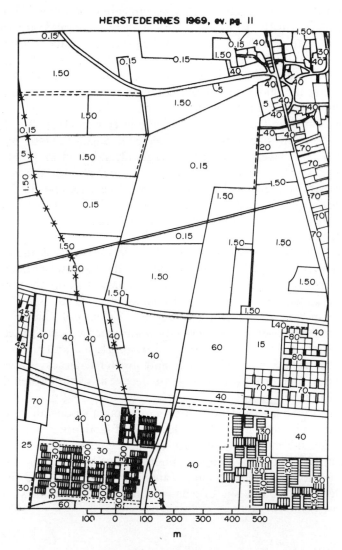

Fig. 6.6. (*contd.*)

Tables 6.7 and 6.8 show the percentage of the area in a particular type of use in 1956 that has changed use and that amount that has remained the same, each category's aggregate land value in 1969, the percentage growth of the land value at each new price category, and the aggregate growth for all sites of the same land value in 1956.

From Tables 6.7 and 6.8 one can see the role of the different categories in price increases, and their role in the change in land use in the aggregate land value of the community. The average aggregate increase in land value between 1956 and 1969 is 21 times in Ballerup, 23 times in Hoje Taastrup, and 39 times in Herstedernes. But the rate of increase varies according to the sector in which the land belonged in 1956. The lowest-valued sector (agricultural land in 1956) shows the highest rate of increase. The rate of increase for this sector is 96 times for Ballerup, 44 times for Hoje Taastrup, and 51 times for Herstedernes. The highest-value sector in 1956, which represents already developed land or land planned for development, shows the lowest rate of increase.

The most interesting results are obtained by analysing the changes which occurred between 1956 and 1969 within the lowest value sector (i.e. formerly agricultural land). Such an analysis shows the impact of changes in land use on the rate of increase in land value. In 1969 the rates of increase for Ballerup range from 8·8 (for land which remained in agricultural use) to 424 times (for land which was converted from agricultural to highest land price use); in Hoje Taastrup the rates changed from 8·5 to 703 times; and in Herstedernes from 3·1 to 922 times. The lowest rate of increase occurs in sectors which did not change in use.

Thus, in the highest land value sector (roughly equivalent to commercial land) while there is a wide range of land price increases, nowhere are the magnitude of price changes greater than for formerly agricultural land. In Ballerup the highest-value land increased in price from 3·9 to 43·7 times, in Hoje Taastrup from 7·3 to 33·5 times; in Herstedernes the one site of 5 ha. of high land value shows a price increase of 7·9 times.

TABLE 6.7. Land-Use Values and Sectors—Total Changes, 1956–69

Land use type	Value range (Kr/m²)	Ballerup		Hoje Taastrup		Herstedernes		Total area value	
		Area (ha.)	Aggregate value (Kr/m²)	Area (ha.)	Aggregate value (Kr/m²)	Area (ha.)	Aggregate value (Kr/m²)	Area (ha.)	Aggregate value (Kr/m²)
1956									
Agricultural	0·10–0·50	1466	5,088	1644	5,529	2159	7,425	5269	18,042
Development	0·60–1·99	1021	17,906	609	7,177	191	2,592	1821	27,675
Residential	2·0–5·9	277	9,182	194	10,351	51	1,635	522	21,168
Commercial	6·0–14·5	202	18,075	31	2,735	5	393	238	21,203
Totals		2966	50,251	2478	25,792	2406	12,045		
1969									
Agricultural	1·0–2·5	485	11,469	956	24,057	1258	17,612	2699	53,138
Development	13·0–33·0	1633	475,540	582	78,995	742	124,656	2957	679,191
Residential	36·0–97·0	790	496,844	888	404,499	372	260,400	2050	1,161,793
Commercial	130·0–400·0	58	112,400	52	101,800	34	71,400	144	235,600
Totals		2966	1,096,253	2478	609,351	2406	474,068		
Times increase 1956–69			21·8×		23·6×		39·3×		

TABLE 6.8. Land-Use Values and Changes, 1956–69

| | 1956 sectors and values | | 1969 sectors and values | | | | | | | | | | |
	Area (ha.)	Value (1000 Kr)	Agriculture Area (ha.)	Agriculture Value (1000 Kr)	Development Area (ha.)	Development Value (1000 Kr)	Residential Area (ha.)	Residential Value (1000 Kr)	Commercial Area (ha.)	Commercial Value (1000 Kr)	Totals Area (ha.)	Totals Value (1000 Kr)	Totals Times increase
Agriculture													
Ballerup	1466	5,088	485	11,469	522	136,178	453	285,437	6	10,200	1466	443,284	96·1 ×
Hoje Taastrup	1644	5,529	956	24,057	262	35,552	414	169,918	12	20,420	1644	249,947	44 ×
Herstedernes	2159	7,425	1258	17,612	572	96,096	295	206,500	34	71,400	2159	391,608	51 ×
Sub-total	5269	18,042	2699	53,138	1356	267,826	1162	661,855	52	102,020	5269	1,084,839	60 ×
Times inc.		6·8 ×		6·8 ×		54·8 ×		156·0 ×		638 ×			
Development													
Ballerup	1021	17,906	—	—	781	204,259	240	150,548	—	—	1021	354,807	18·8 ×
Hoje Taastrup	609	7,177	—	—	182	24,723	417	208,887	10	16,993	609	250,603	34 ×
Herstedernes	191	2,592	—	—	140	23,520	51	35,700	—	—	191	59,220	22 ×
Sub-total	1821	27,675	—	—	1103	252,502	708	395,135	10	16,993	1821	664,630	25 ×
Times inc.						18·8 ×		42·4 ×		203·7 ×			
Residential													
Ballerup	277	9,182	—	—	230	59,576	35	20,504	12	20,400	277	100,480	9·9 ×
Hoje Taastrup	194	10,351	—	—	138	18,720	38	14,584	18	37,335	194	70,639	5·8 ×
Herstedernes	51	1,635	—	—	30	5,040	21	14,700	—	—	51	19,740	11·7 ×
Sub-total	522	21,167	—	—	398	83,336	94	49,788	30	57,735	522	190,859	9·4 ×
Times inc.						4·6 ×		15·5 ×		45·8 ×			
Commercial													
Ballerup	202	18,075	—	—	100	25,532	62	40,405	40	81,800	202	147,732	7·2 ×
Hoje Taastrup	31	2,735	—	—	—	—	19	11,110	12	27,052	31	38,122	13 ×
Herstedernes	5	393	—	—	—	—	5	3,500	—	—	5	3,500	8 ×
Sub-total	238	21,203	—	—	100	25,532	86	55,015	52	108,852	238	189,354	9·4 ×
Times inc.						3·9 ×		7·2 ×		28·3 ×			
Grand totals	7850	88,087	2699	53,138	2957	629,196	2050	1,161,793	144	285,600	7850	2,129,682	24·1 ×
Times inc.						20·5 ×		55·3 ×		228·8 ×			

CALCULATION OF ADDITIONAL VALUE

A look at some land-value changes gleaned from previous tables shows more clearly than the evaluation maps the impact of land-use changes on value increase, on the creation of additional land value and the formation of urban land rent. It should be noted that there are additional factors contributing to the urban land rent especially the growing attractiveness of already urbanized areas but on the basis of the figures gathered in the tables we can calculate the amount of additional value created by the change from agricultural to urban land use. For this purpose we use the aggregate prices of lowest-priced land in the year 1956 ($0 \cdot 10$–$0 \cdot 50\,Kr/m^2$), although there is agricultural land in the next bracket ($0 \cdot 60$–$1 \cdot 99\,Kr/m^2$) as well.

In order to calculate added land value created by urban growth it is necessary to calculate the added value of the area still in agricultural use.

The total area devoted to agricultural use in the three communities in 1956 was 5269 ha. The area that has still remained in agricultural use in 1969 (the area represented by the value of 1–$2 \cdot 5\,Kr/m^2$) is 2699 ha. The area that was converted from agricultural use in 1956 to urban use in 1969 is 2570 ha. The aggregate value of this 2570 ha. in 1956 was 8,822,000 Kr, or in 1969 prices, 15,800,000 Kr.

In 1969 this space which became urban land was worth 1,031,701,000 Kr, an increase of 65 times. The additional value created in this comparatively small area was 1,015,901,000 Kr. Furthermore, the 2570 ha. that changed from agricultural use in 1956 to urban use in 1969 are made up of two sectors: 1356 ha. evaluated between 13–$40\,Kr/m^2$, representing in 1969 land planned for urban uses where development works had not been completed; and the rest, 893 ha., evaluated at over $50\,Kr/m^2$, representing land already in urban use.

In order to calculate the additional urban land value, the estimated value of the accomplished development works must be deducted from the total additional value. The estimated average cost of development works in 1969 was $25\,Kr/m^2$. Thus, the total cost of development works in the area that was changed to urban use is 223,250,000 Kr (893 ha. $\times\,25\,Kr/m^2$).

The added urban land value in the 2750 ha. that changed from agricultural use to urban uses is thus 792,550,000 Kr (1015·9 million minus 223·25 million), or 113,500,000 US dollars.

This increased urban value was accumulated not by the 90,000 inhabitants of the three communities, but by the 461 landowners (figures based on the statistical evaluation book of 1956) who in 1956 owned 5280 ha. of agricultural land totalling about 18 million kroner, or 2·57 million US dollars in value. The average amount of urban land surplus per landowner, then, may be estimated as 246,000 US dollars.

It should be noted that high price increases resulting from land-use changes are significant for all rapidly developing settlements in city regions throughout the world. Similarly, keeping in mind that the Copenhagen Region is not the most rapidly developing region in the world, and that its population and economic growth rates are not as high as in many other city regions, the high amount of additional value and urban land rent accumulated is at least as significant in other city regions.

LAND-PRICE DEVELOPMENT IN COPENHAGEN

An analysis of land prices in Copenhagen indicates two distinct trends—of the residential and commercial land-use prices. Such an investigation of the separate trends for residential and commercial land prices is important, as most studies have investigated either *aggregate* or residential land-price trends; few have investigated commercial prices, or the relationship between residential and commercial prices.

There exists an essential difference between land-price relationship for different land uses. The analysis of the commercial land prices show a big difference between the very high average land prices in the two CBD districts (Borsen and Voldkvart) and commercial prices in the other parts of the city (Table 6.10).

The prices in 1969 in these districts were, respectively, 2809 Kr/m^2 and 2257 Kr/m^2, while in the next two districts the prices were 729 Kr/m^2 (in Tilboden) and 629 Kr/m^2 (in Vesterbore). The prices in the next four districts were 329–399 Kr/m^2, while the five districts of the lower priced commercial land prices range from 168–246 Kr/m^2. In one district the prices reach a low of 130 Kr/m^2.

TABLE 6.9. Commercial and Residential Land Value and Use in Copenhagen

	Commercial				Residential			
	Area		Value		Area		Value	
	in ha.	%	As value in 1,000,000 Kr	%	in ha.	%	As value in 1,000,000 Kr	%
CBD Borsen Voldkvart	36·8	2·2	932·1	27·0	13·7	0·8	97·6	2·9
Inner Districts Tilboden Norrebros Osterbros Vesterbore Frederiksberg	39·3	2·3	191·0	5·6	298·7	17·6	799·3	23·3
Outer Districts Bronshoj Vanlose Utterslev Husum Valby Sundbyvestre Sundbyostre	42·2	2·5	88·6	2·6	1263·0	74·6	1575·4	38·4
Totals	118·3	7·0	1211·7	35·2	1575·4	93·0	2472·3	64·6

The interesting point is the large role played by the highest-priced commercial land in the urban land market. The area of the CBD is about 30% of the total area of commercial land use in Copenhagen but represents over 80% of the aggregate value of all commercial land.

It is also interesting to compare commercial land prices in the period 1956–69. The average price increased by 121% (from 448 Kr/m^2 in 1956 to 991 Kr/m^2 in 1969). In comparison with other urban land uses, the rate of increase for commercial price is low (because of the already high commercial price of land in 1956).

A significant feature is a high rate of increase for the highest commercial values. The highest price in 1969 was 2809 Kr/m^2, showing an increase of 211% over the highest 1956 price of 910 Kr/m². However, the highest rates of increase were shown in the medium-price districts. In spite of the high rate of increase of areas with low commercial land prices the ratio between the highest commercial value and the average Copenhagen commercial value increased during the 13 years from 103% in 1956 to 183% in 1969. This indicates that in spite of the development of new commercial centres in the region, the role of the most centrally located commercial services was still salient. (The increased ratio can be explained by the fact that the *amount* of lower-priced commercial land increased, thus lowering the average price.)

An analysis of the commercial and residential values shows different trends of development (Table 6.10). Residential land values increased considerably during the 13 years, 368%, while commercial land values increased only 121%. The high rate of increase in residential land results from relatively low average residential land values in 1956— 28 Kr/m², while the commercial average was very high even then— 448 Kr/m².

It is noteworthy that the residential land prices for seven districts of the city comprising 91% of residential land are almost identical (98–110 Kr/m²); for four districts containing 7·8% of the space the prices are a little higher (171–286 Kr/m²); the highest residential price of 840 Kr/m² occurs in only 0·7 ha. or 0·05% of the residential land surface; and the other two high prices are 505–585 Kr/m², which occupy no more than 1·4% of space (20·6 ha.).

The fact that high-priced residential land occupies only a small percentage of total residential land area, while high-priced commercial land occupies a very large proportion of total commercial land area, shows the important role in the urban economy of high-priced commercial land in the most central districts of the city.

The very high commercial values in comparison with the highest residential values show the monopolistic character of commercial land in CBD. The demand for some commercial services which are interested in the most centrally located districts cannot be satisfied by the supply of land in other areas of the city. Residential land prices are more affected by various environmental factors and are less influenced by central locations. Therefore well-planned new residential areas in the

TABLE 6.10. Comparison of Commercial and Residential Land Prices in Copenhagen

Copenhagen districts (by distance from CBD)	Area				Average price						Comparison of commercial to residential values			
	Commercial (ha.)		Residential (ha.)		Commercial			Residential			Ratio		Absolute terms (Kr)	
					Kr/m²		Change in %	Kr/m²		Change in %				
	1956	1969	1956	1969	1956	1969	1965–9	1956	1969	1965–9	1956	1969	1956	1969
Borsen	22·2	24·7	0·2	0·7	910	2257	148	354	840	137	2·6	2·7	556	1417
Voldkvart	5·4	12·1	8·7	13·0	904	2809	211	131	585	342	6·9	4·8	773	2224
Toldboden	8·3	13·2	8·1	7·6	148	729	393	108	505	368	1·4	1·4	40	224
Vesterbros	2·1	5·3	27·4	26·8	275	629	354	40	171	327	6·9	3·7	235	458
Frederiksberg	5·7	7·9	166·8	181·2	96	399	303	46	205	246	2·1	1·9	50	194
Norrebros	2·5	5·5	20·4	25·8	167	344	177	73	286	292	2·3	1·2	94	58
Osterbros	6·0	7·4	68·5	57·3	82	329	247	46	221	380	1·8	1·5	36	108
Bronshoj	2·0	1·6	116·6	158·6	65	333	412	23	107	365	2·8	3·1	42	226
Vanlose	1·7	1·5	168·4	166·3	51	246	372	21	109	419	2·4	2·3	30	137
Utterslev	3·9	6·3	162·2	160·9	61	212	247	27	110	307	2·3	1·9	34	102
Husum	0·3	2·1	180·4	211·0	48	197	310	17	98	476	2·8	2·0	31	99
Valby	1·6	24·0	227·8	251·2	68	168	147	22	108	390	3·1	1·6	46	60
Sundbyvestre	1·7	2·8	121·2	159·7	61	184	202	25	98	292	2·4	1·9	36	86
Sundbyostre	1·8	4·2	151·9	155·3	51	130	155	26	100	285	2·0	1·3	25	30
Copenhagen total	65·2	118·6	1470·6	1575·4	448	991	121	28	131	368	16·0	7·6	420	860

city region may restrain the land-price increase for residential use within the city, thereby weakening the monopolistic character of the residential urban land market. The monopolistic character of commercial land in the CBD is shown by its considerable role in the urban land market as a whole. The CBD commercial land is 2·2% of the total urban space, yet it contains 27% of the total value.

An essential difference in the factors influencing commercial and residential land prices may be observed by comparing commercial and residential prices within all districts of Copenhagen.

One of the most interesting findings of the Copenhagen study is the fact that there is a "permanent distance" between commercial and residential land prices; that is, commercial land prices are always higher than residential prices in the same area (Table 6.10). This is correct not only when comparing the most central land in the CBD with the highest residential land values in the city, but also when comparing the commercial and residential land values within districts outside the centre. Such a "distance" existed in 1956 and still exists in 1969.

The average commercial and residential land prices were 448 Kr/m^2 and 28 Kr/m^2 respectively in 1956, a difference of 420 Kr/m^2 or a ratio of 1:16; in 1969 the average prices were 991 Kr/m^2 and 131 Kr/m^2, a difference of 860 Kr/m^2 or a ratio of 1:7·6.

In spite of the considerably high rate of increase in residential values, the difference has grown in absolute terms by 104% (though the ratio has diminished). The difference between commercial and residential prices does vary according to district; it is greatest in the most centrally located districts where the commercial values are highest, where the difference has grown by 168–380%. In other districts the difference has increased by only 88 to 268%. Only in two districts, one of high land value and the other of very low land value, has the difference grown absolutely by only 30 to 44%.

This phenomenon of the existence of a continuous "distance" between commercial and residential land values in the same location increasing in absolute terms over time emphasizes the monopolistic character of commercial land in all locations (but with differences in magnitude). This is central to the study of land-price trends in urban regions.

HYPOTHETICAL COST–BENEFIT ANALYSIS OF ADVANCE
LAND ACQUISITION

The findings of the case study of the three communities in the
Copenhagen Region may allow some conclusions about trends in land
prices in city regions of most countries of the world.

The available published statistical data of periodical land evaluation
in Denmark allowed investigation of the impact of planning decisions,
especially with regard to the change from agricultural to urban use,
on the land-price increase in the rapidly developing communities of
the city regions.

In all countries the highest rate of land-price increase is observed
with the change from the agricultural to urban use. Using data collected for the UN report on Urban Land Policies in Western European
Countries, it may be shown that in general the rate of land price
increase is 30–200 times for land converted from agricultural to urban
uses. Therefore, the results of the case study of the three communities
of the Copenhagen region which show a yearly rate of increase of
21–27%, during the 13-year period from 1956 to 1969, and 30–1000
times total increase in the case of land changed from agricultural to
urban use, are significant for almost all city regions of the world. The
material available for this study allowed not only the evaluation of the
rate of land price increase, but also the amount of urban rent land
created as a result of the urbanization process.

The additional value was collected by few landowners, while the land
values and the urban land rent were created by the decisions of
public authority to change land uses (and therefore to carry out development works and eventually social services). Nevertheless they
have to struggle to find the financial resources for investment in and
maintenance of continually expanding urban services.

The contradiction between the huge amount of private additional
value created through the urbanization process and a lack of public
means to ensure urban growth is an international phenomenon.
Therefore, it might be of some interest to carry out a hypothetical
cost–benefit calculation of the potential results from the collection by
the public authority of the additional value created as the result of the
public authority decisions to acquire lands in the city region currently

in agricultural use and which are to be converted to urban use after some period of time. The available material of the case study in the Copenhagen region allows the presentation of such a hypothetical cost–benefit analysis.

Obviously, it must be kept in mind that in order to create a land reserve for future urban development, considerably more land has to be acquired than such areas which in the future might be changed into urban use. The unknown factor of continually changing needs does not allow the exact forecasting of the amount and the location of areas which will be devoted in the future to a specific urban use. Therefore, the land reserves prepared for future urban development must include land space which will be used in the future for recreation and other kinds of open space.

Therefore, for our hypothetical calculation we will consider not only the cost–benefit of the part of agricultural land use changed to urban use in the investigated communities, but also the land in agricultural use in 1956 and still not changed into urban use in 1969.

Taking into account the unknown factor of the rate of urban growth, we will base our calculation not on the period of 13 years, but of 20 years. For the costs of needed capital investment for the advance land acquisition, we will calculate the 1956 prices at fixed 1969 prices, multiplying the 1956 prices by the 80% increase in the consumer price index from 1956 to 1969. As a rate of capital interest we will use 8% which includes the 6% rate for interest prevailing for this period in the financial market, adding 2% for administration of advance-acquired land reserves. A more detailed cost–benefit analysis has to take into account the cost of the lost property tax from the acquired agricultural land (which is usually low) and the benefit from income derived by leasing land to be changed into urban use during the 20-year period.

The total space of agricultural land use in 1956 in the three investigated communities was 5269 ha., of which 2570 ha. were turned into urban use, and 2699 ha. remained in agricultural use in 1969. The value of the 2570 ha. transferred into urban use was 8·8 million Kr in 1956, or 15 million Kr at fixed 1969 prices (Table 6.11).

The value of this area in 1969 increased to 1031 million Kr. The additional created value during the 13 years was 1015 million Kr. After deduction of the 223 million Kr invested in development works, the

TABLE 6.11.

	Ballerup	Hoje Taastrup	Herstedernes	Total
		Hectares		
1. Total agricultural area in 1956 (2+3 = 1)	1,466	1,644	2,159	5,269
2. Total area that remained in agricultural use in 1969	485	956	1,258	2,699
3. Total area that changed from agricultural use in 1956 to urban uses in 1969 (4+5 = 3)	981	688	901	2,570
4. The amount of land that changed from agricultural use in 1956 to urban uses in 1969 belonging to value sector 13–40 Kr/m²	522	583	572	1,677
5. The amount of land that changed from agricultural use in 1956 to urban uses in 1969 belonging to value sector above 50 Kr/m²	459	105	329	893
		Value in 1000 krone		
6. The aggregate value in 1956 of the total agricultural area in 1956 (7+8 = 6)	5,088	5,529	7,425	18,042
7. The aggregate value in 1956 of the area that has remained in agricultural use in 1969	1,682	3,228	4,310	9,220
8. The aggregate value in 1956 of the area that has changed from agricultural use in 1956 to urban uses in 1969	3,406	2,301	3,115	8,822
9. The aggregate value in 1969 of the total agricultural area in 1956 (10+11 = 9)	443,284	249,947	391,608	1,084,839
10. The aggregate value in 1969 of the area that has remained in agricultural use in 1969	11,469	24,057	17,612	53,138
11. The aggregate value in 1969 of the area that has changed from agricultural use in 1956 to urban uses in 1969 (12+13 = 11)	431,815	225,890	373,996	1,031,701
12. The aggregate value in 1969 of the area that has changed from agricultural use in 1956 to urban uses in 1969 belonging to value sector 13–40 Kr/m².	136,178	152,132	96,096	384,406
13. The aggregate value in 1969 of the area that has changed from agricultural use in 1956 to urban uses in 1969 belonging to the value sector above 50 Kr/m²	295,637	73,758	277,900	647,295

urban land rent was estimated at 793 million Kr, or 113 million US dollars.

In our calculation we will try to estimate what might happen if this land had been acquired by the public authority in 1956. For this purpose we have to take as a basis not the costs of the 2570 ha. converted to urban use, but rather the entire area of 5,269 ha. which was in agricultural use in the three communities in 1956. The value of this land in 1969 was (in fixed 1969 prices) 32 million Kr. If the land had been acquired in 1956, the value after 13 years, on the basis of capital costs of 8% yearly, would be 87 million Kr in 1969, and after 20 years (in 1976)—150 million Kr.

The difference between the overall cost resulting from advance land acquisition and the additional value received by the private landowners over 13 years is 643 million Kr (793 million—150 million).

In order to illustrate the advantage of planning and the financial possibilities in the case of advance land acquisition by the public authority, we will investigate the costs of eventual acquisition of the whole agricultural land in Copenhagen County Region.

The area occupied by agricultural land in this region was 12,957 ha. in 1956. The value of this space was 111 million Kr in fixed 1969 prices (Table 7). On the basis of 8% capital costs the value is 517 million Kr after 20 years. This calculation shows that on the basis of capital costs of 8% yearly linked to consumer price index, the land prices increased 2·72 times in 13 years and 4·66 times in 20 years.

As a result of advance land acquisition the cost of capital invested by the public authorities would be considerably lower (35%) for a space of 12,957 ha. kept as a reserve for 20 years for urban development than the additional value (793 million Kr) collected by 461 landowners during the 13 years for a space of 2570 ha.

This hypothetical calculation may serve as a model for detailed cost–benefit analysis of advance land-acquisition policies by public authorities. A comparison might be made between the costs of advance land acquisition, the GNP, and the national budget. This might prove that the main obstacle in carrying out a policy of advance land acquisition is not the lack of available public funds, but a lack of awareness by the public authorities of the need for advance acquisition of lands for future urban development.

Keeping in mind that future urban populations will be diffused throughout city regions, and not just in the city itself, the collection of the large amounts of additional land value (urban land rent) created by the conversion of agricultural land to urban use, has a special importance.

COMPARISON OF COPENHAGEN AND THE REGION

The formation of land prices in Copenhagen and the Copenhagen County Region illuminates the effects of urban growth on the land market. The rapid development in the region influenced the high land-price increase in areas of former agricultural use. However, this development did not affect the prevailing Copenhagen price levels in the same manner; on the contrary, without rapid development in the region the rate of price increase in Copenhagen might have been higher.

The lower rate of increase in Copenhagen itself (6·4%) occurred at a time when aggregate land values in the other three communities had increased 21–27% yearly. An analysis of land-price development in the city over the 13-year period (1956–69) would suggest then that urban growth has an impact on the interrelationship between the rate of increase on land prices and the different land uses in the city and its outlying region.

The formation of land prices in the region is influenced by the structure of land prices in Copenhagen and by the well-developed transport network connecting the regional communities with Copenhagen. Generally, the price of land in a community within the urban region is influenced by the existing prices for the same use in the city, and *not* by the prevailing land prices for previous land use in the community. It would appear that the main factor which affects land values in the urban area is *land use*, though within limits. However, large differences also exist in the framework of the same land uses. For example, residential land-use values in the same urban region are differently affected, according to land-use intensity, social structure of neighbourhoods and environmental features. Obviously, the transport network initially influences residential land prices since, in locations far from the city centre, all other factors being equal, land prices will generally be lower. However, an efficient transport network may serve to restrain price differences within the same land uses by shortening the time spent in travel to and from centres of urban activity.

Despite the tendency of decreasing differences between land prices according to land uses in the city and the county region, in 1969 there is still an important difference between the land prices of commercial land between the city and the county region, though lower than the difference in 1956 (1 to 7·3 in 1969 instead of 1 to 39 in 1956). For residential land the difference decreased from 1 to 2·5, in 1956 to 1 to 1·4 in 1969, and for industrial land from 1 to 6 in 1956 to 1 to 3 in 1969 (Table 6.13).

The relatively small differences in average residential land values between Copenhagen and the county region may be explained by the better environmental features in the county region.

The comparison of land-price developments in the county region and in Copenhagen shows that there is a very high rate of price increase in the period of rapid development of the small communities within the city region during the years 1956–65 (Table 6.12). However, the rate of increase is diminishing with the development of the urban settlements, and has become even lower than Copenhagen in the years 1965–9 (Table 6.1).

The first period shows the highest rates of urban land-value creation. Regional land prices are influenced by, but are lower than, the existing prices for the same use in Copenhagen. The differences became smaller with time as a result of the higher rate of increase in the region and the slower rate of price increase in Copenhagen.

The changes in total space allocated for different land uses in Copenhagen and the Copenhagen Region during the 13-year period, 1956–69, are shown in Table 6.13.

The comparison of the changes in land use which occurred in Copenhagen between 1965–9 shows a trend towards diminishing land area for industrial use and increasing land area for commercial and residential use (Table 6.13).

The changes in area for different land uses show the important role of commercial activity in the urban economy as well as the continued importance of residential land use in the city, despite the increase in the residential housing in the outlying region.

The rate of increase in the amount of space allocated to the four

TABLE 6.12. Comparison in Aggregate Land Values in Copenhagen's Neighbourhoods in 1956–65

Name	Area		Value 1956		Value 1965		Value increase in %		
	In hectares	%	In 1000 Kr	%	In 1000 Kr	%	1956–60	1960–5	1956–65
Neighbourhoods									
Toldbodens	461·6	2·1	300·1	10·3	719·7	9·9	36·0	76·3	140
Borsen	84·0	1·4	451·9	15·6	840·7	11·5	15·2	61·5	86
Voldkvart	135·6	2·3	329·8	11·4	883·6	12·1	33·0	101·5	68
Vesterbros	371·6	6·5	248·2	8·5	598·7	8·2	29·0	86·9	41
Valby	699·5	12·1	167·2	5·8	515·0	7·1	44·9	112·5	208
Norrebros	317·6	5·5	297·1	10·2	606·0	8·3	25·4	62·7	104
Osterbros	347·5	6·5	191·1	6·6	550·5	7·5	29·7	122·1	188
Utterslev	523·3	9·1	171·2	5·9	380·6	5·2	26·5	75·8	122
Bronshoj	253·0	4·3	58·8	2·0	171·3	2·3	28·8	126·1	191
Husum	469·6	8·2	62·8	2·2	220·6	3·0	50·7	133·2	251
Vanlose	246·3	4·3	60·7	2·1	189·0	2·6	32·9	134·5	211
Sundbyvestre	871·0	15·2	105·0	3·6	376·4	5·2	51·7	136·3	258
Sundbyostre	377·9	6·6	116·7	4·0	303·6	4·1	34·7	93·2	160
Frederiksberg	564·0	9·9	346·0	11·8	953·0	13·0	—	—	—
Total incl. Copenhagen	5722·0	100·0	2907·0	100·0	7309·0	100·0	30·2	90·6	152

Table 6.13. Land-use Allocation, Aggregate and Average Value in Copenhagen and the County Region, 1956–69

Category of LV	Area (ha.)			Aggregate value in 1,000,000 Kr			Average price in Kr/m²		
	1956	1969	Change 56–69 in %	1956	1969	Change 56–69 in %	1956	1969	Change 56–69 in %
Copenhagen County Region									
Residential	4388	7,625	74·0	487·4	7352·0	1408·0	11·1	96·4	768·0
Res.+Comm.	517	1,090	111·0	89·3	1162·0	1201·0	17·3	106·6	516·0
Comm. only	43	180	319·0	5·0	244·1	4785·0	11·5	136·0	1083·0
Industrial	649	1,459	125·0	57·8	1077·1	1762·0	8·9	73·8	729·0
Totals	5597	10,354	157·3	639·5	9835·2	2289·0	12·2	103·2	774·0
Copenhagen									
Residential	1479	1,575	6·0	413·9	2066·1	399·0	28·0	131·2	36·9
Res.+Comm.	854	849	–1·0	1002·4	3136·8	313·0	117·4	369·5	215·0
Comm. only	65	119	83·0	291·2	1179·5	305·0	448·0	991·2	121·0
Industrial	561	482	–14·0	269·5	1031·0	248·0	52·9	213·9	304·0
Totals	2959	3,025	18·5	1977·0	7413·4	316·3	161·6	426·5	252·3

urban uses in the region (85%) is greater than the regional population growth rate of 50% (Table 6.3). This may be explained by a greater *per capita* allocation of land for each type of use (e.g. more land per residence unit).

The planning efforts of the regional authorities in fixing the macro- and micro-zoning are directed toward avoiding a fragmented urban development and ensuring an adequate supply of land for the needs of a growing population. While land prices in the region are obviously increasing as a result of increasing demand, the continually growing supply of land to the market does not allow land value to increase beyond certain limits. The higher rate of land-price increase in the region may be partially explained by the peculiar factors which influence the high rate of price development in the rapidly growing urban settlements in the city region as compared to the more "stationary" big city.

REFERENCES

Dansk Statistik, Grundvaerdikort (Land Evaluation Map) *over Ballerup-Malov Kommune (Del) ved 15 Alm. Vurdering, Pr. 1 Apr. 1956; 1 Apr. 1965; 1 Apr. 1969.*

——, *Grundvaerdikort over Hederenstanes Kommune ved. 15 Alm. Pr. 1 Apr. 1956; 1 Apr. 1965; 1 Apr. 1969.*

——, *Grundvaerdikort over Hoje-Tastrup Kommune ved. 15. Alm. Vurdering Pr. 1 Apr. 1956; 1 Apr. 1965; 1 Apr. 1969.*

——, *Grundvaerdikort over Kobenhavn og Frederkisberg Kommuner, ved. 15 Alm. Vurdering, pr. 1 Apr. 1956; 1 Apr. 1965; 1 Apr. 1969,* Uggivet pa Foranstaltning af Statens Ligningsdirektorat.

——, *Vurderingen af landets faste ejendomine* (assessment of real property), *Pr. 1 Sept. 1956,* Copenhagen, 1959.

——, *Vurderingen af landets faste ejendomine, Pr. 1 Aug. 1965, Statistiks Tabelvaerk 1970:* II, Copenhagen, 1970.

Municipality of Copenhagen, *A Short Description of the Origins of Copenhagen, the City's Physical Structure, and Planning,* 1973.

CHAPTER 7

Doctrines and Models in the Sphere of Urban Land

INTRODUCTION

Land-price increases are related on one side to macro-economic factors such as rapid urbanization, population growth, and economic cycles, and on the other side, to the peculiar factors which influence the land market. These various factors have led to many schools of thought who have tried to explain urban land values. This interest came later than the interest in agricultural land. It may be suggested that this is due to the fact that agriculture was of primary importance to the economy of most countries for hundreds of years, while urbanization has been a relatively recent phenomenon. This short review will try to give a picture of the diversity of factors which have been used to explain urban land prices which means in effect that many important theories have not been mentioned.

ORIGINS OF URBAN LAND THEORIES

The first school of economists to have a definite concept regarding land and land revenue were the physiocrats of the eighteenth century. Their interest centred around questions of agricultural land, while they gave little or no thought to urban land.

At the beginning of the nineteenth century, David Ricardo published his work, *Principles of Political Economy and Taxation*, in which he made a basic and all-embracing analysis of agricultural land issues. His concepts were similar to those of Malthus and Richard West, and they served later as a basis for various land doctrines, such as those of John Stuart Mill, Karl Marx, J. H. von Thunen and Alfred Marshall.

According to Ricardo's approach, a farmer wishing to lease a piece of land is in competition with other farmers, and obviously, he will be able to rent it only if he makes the best offer of which he is capable. To enable the farmer to pay such a rent, the output of his plot needs to be higher than the input; that is, a certain agricultural surplus must be created in relation to the input, and this surplus is the economic rent of the land (known as Agrarian Rent).

As the market price of the crop is not dependent on the quality of the land yielding it, the farmer can pay a higher rent for more fruitful land. This is because fruitful land ensures better crops with the same input of capital and labour, which will increase the surplus and the agrarian rent.

Furthermore, Ricardo believed that the farmer can pay a higher rent if his land is nearer to the market, because the transportation costs of bringing his goods to the market are thereby lessened.

On the other hand, there is marginal land yielding such poor crops, or which is so distant from the market, that the farmer is unable to pay any rent, or can pay only a token rent. In other words, different rents are obtained for lands of different qualities.

The concept of rent derived from market proximity was extensively developed by J. H. von Thunen. According to his doctrine, agricultural land is arranged around a market through a process of competition in which one piece of land will be more profitable than the others. The saving in transportation costs, which occurs when cultivating a site located at a short distance from the market, determines the rent each site can ask. Cultivated areas farthest away from the market do not ensure such savings, and therefore are unrentable. On the other hand, the nearer the cultivated areas are to the centre, the higher rent they can demand because of the savings in transportation costs.

Applying von Thunen's reasoning to the urban land market, Hurd published in 1903 his *Principles of City Land Values*. Hurd's belief was that as a city develops, use is made of more distant and less valuable land. The difference in the demand for the two classes of land—first-class land in the city centre and second-class land on its periphery—is what determines the level of the ground rent for first-class land. With the further development of the city and the beginning of building on even more distant land (third class) first-class ground rents rise and a rent for second-class land is created. In this way, a kind of hierarchy of ground rents is created so that all the land within the city limits has a certain ground rent, while the land outside the city is, in effect, devoid of value. What Hurd says in this connection is illustrative: "As the value is dependent on the economic rent, the rent is dependent on location, the location—on convenience, and the convenience—on proximity, it is possible to disregard the intermediate stages and determine that the *value is dependent on proximity*." The reference being, of course, to proximity to the centres of economic activity.

Alfred Marshall, who also dealt with the problem of urban land value, placed emphasis on the location of land within the town. He introduced the concept of "location value", which is expressed in the financial advantage deriving from the site location. In his opinion, the site value was equal to the agricultural rental and the location value; that is, the basis for the worth of land is its value as agricultural land, and the urban land value is determined by adding the location factor to the agricultural land value. Another factor increasing the value of urban land is the amount of floor space in the building (i.e. a higher density through more floors). In effect, this analysis of Marshall already contains the basis of the present doctrine of urban land prices. The implication is that there is a parallelism in the prices of urban and agricultural land, while on the other hand, there is competition between potential users of the land, and it will go to the highest bidder. One of the defects of Marshall's approach is that he gives no explanation of the value of residential land.

Following Hurd and Marshall, and emphasizing the strong connection between rent and transportation costs, R. M. Haig put forward his theory in 1926. He states that *rent is the payment collected by the owner of urban land for the savings in transportation costs made possible by the use of that land*. The basis for this is that transport is the means of overcoming what has been called "spatial friction". The better the transport, the lesser the friction. Haig also attempts to analyse the various economic uses of the land, and concludes that in agriculture and industry, location is determined by the desire to lessen the "friction" as much as possible; that is, to reduce transportation costs to the greatest possible extent. This is not true with regard to other sectors, such as retail trade, banks and other businesses. Here business turnover is very dependent on location. The businessman will, therefore, be prepared to pay a high rent if the location of the concern assures him a satisfactory income. As for the prices of residential land, R. M. Haig contends that the determining factor is what the resident is prepared to pay for accessibility to economic activities and places of entertainment and social life. In other words, a person buys "accessibility" just as he buys food and clothing and he weighs this expense against other consumption expenses.

Haig's approach underlines the role of prospective income from services erected on the land in the formation of land prices. The dominant role of the locational factor in commercial services is a result of the ability to achieve a higher turnover in one location in comparison with another. The locational factor plays therefore a more important role for commercial land use than for residential. The concept of "accessibility" shows the importance of the location of services and employment in the formation of residential land values.

Another school of land theories is rooted in human ecology and reaches conclusions concerning land prices based on ecological concepts. The starting-point of their theory was sociological, while the preceding ones were mainly economic. The ecological theory sees land prices as the result of the competitive process between potential users of the land—a process which, in effect, determines the siting of the various land uses in the town. According to this theory, *land prices are the principal factor influencing and determining utilization of the land.* The main concern of this theory is with problems of residential land. Hawley, who developed this theory, contends that houses are largely distributed according to the prices of the land, producing the following paradox: on the one hand, many houses in a poor condition are found on expensive land; this is because the land is close to commercial and industrial areas and its owners refrain from selling it for speculative reasons (in anticipation of further price increases), while they are not interested in spending money on improvement or building new houses. The houses are therefore old and of low standard and let at a low price. The very fact of their proximity to business activities is the cause of the low rentals for these dwellings. On the other hand, new dwelling houses are erected on land for which there is not alternative commercial use, and which is obviously cheaper. As rents of the new houses are relatively higher, *we can see that rents of dwellings change inversely to the land prices.* This results in the paradox of low-income families living on expensive land, while wealthy families are living in houses on relatively cheap land.

It might be added that this phenomenon is proof that the value is affected not by present use but by the prospects of a land-use change from residential to commercial. The value is based not on the rental income but on the prospective higher income from future commercial land use.

The following are models which try to answer different urban land problems methodologically and systematically, mainly through a quantitative expression of the relationships they describe. The models will be reviewed according to two categories: urban land models which are mainly concerned with the spatial distribution of land uses, and urban land models which are mainly concerned with land prices. The former can be further divided into descriptive and dynamic urban structure models; the latter into three models which use individual land prices to explain structure, and those which seek to explain the changes in aggregate land prices themselves.

URBAN STRUCTURE MODELS

The first models reviewed are essentially descriptive and initially derived from the ecological approach.

The Concentric Zone Model

This model was developed by E. W. Burgess at the beginning of the 1920s, on the basis of data collected in Chicago. The model conceptualizes the city as a series of concentric zones encircling the centre. Burgess maintains that the process of the radial expansion of the city from its Central Business District can best be understood by identifying five successive zones:

Zone I. The Central Business District.
This district contains the city retail centre, and the centres of economic, social, cultural and political activities. Encircling the

core of the district lies the Wholesale Business District, with its markets, storage buildings, etc.

Zone II. The Zone in Transition.

This zone contains areas of residential deterioration caused by the pressures of businesses and institutions in Zone 1, and an inner belt of factories. It is characterized by first-settlement immigration colonies, rooming-house districts, homeless-men areas, diverse outlaw activities, etc. Families and individuals escape this zone as they prosper, moving into Zone III and farther.

Zone III. Zone of Second-generation Immigrant Settlement.

The residents of this zone are mostly independent working-men of the second immigrant generation, who desire to live near their place of work and near the Central Business District with its amusements. Their social and economic expectations are directed towards Zone IV.

Zone IV. Middle-class Residential District, or the Zone of Better Residences.

This is the zone in which the majority of middle-class native-born Americans live, e.g. small businessmen, professionals, etc.

Zone V. High-class Residential District.

This is the commuters' zone. It is an area of highly segregated communities, in which the wife and mother become the centre of family life. It consists of a ring of small towns and hamlets which are mainly dormitory suburbs.

To sum up, Burgess's concentric models describes the mosaic of a city. Although in his original paper he did not indicate how this process took place, later he explained the mechanism of expansion through the process of invasion and succession, in which one group succeeds another in the use of an area, through ecological competition.

The Sector Model

The sector model was developed by H. Hoyt at the end of the 1930s. It is also a descriptive model, developed inductively and based on information collected in about 204 urban settlements in the USA. Its starting-point is a criticism of the concentric zone model. In accordance with the data he had, Hoyt maintained that:

1. The CBD is not the only commercial and cultural centre, and its boundaries are not always as explicit as in the concentric model. There are strips of commerce extending from the CBD along main roads.
2. The wholesale district does not usually completely encircle the CBD.
3. Industrial areas tend to stick to the periphery of the city, where they follow railroad lines, river valleys, ocean fronts, etc.; the industrial land patterns usually differ drastically from the concentric model.
4. Working-men's homes have no tendency to encircle the CBD.
5. High-standard residential areas are sometimes adjacent to the CBD.
6. The commuters' zone does not have the homogeneous features as described in the concentric model, as different social groups are found in it.

In accordance with the above criticisms, Hoyt developed the sector model, which conceptualizes the city in terms of rent areas tending to conform to a pattern of sectors instead of to a pattern of circles. These rental areas are determined by the average rent level, and Hoyt distinguishes between high, intermediate and low rent areas. Socio-economic groups allocate themselves in these rent sectors, and Hoyt deals with their location within a discussion of the city growth and the changes in residential-area characteristics. Hoyt mostly analyses the distribution of the high rental residential areas, and from it he generalizes to the other sectors.

Multiple-nuclei Model

This model was developed by Harris and Ullman in the middle of the 1940s. The authors of the model claim that, in contrast with the concentric and sectoral models which postulate a single-core city, it is possible that a city with separate nuclei would arise.

Four reasons are given for such a phenomenon:

1. Some uses need special facilities which must be allocated out of the CBD.

2. Activities of one kind often cluster in one district due to external economies (such as the office district, the legal district, etc.).
3. Certain activities are detrimental to each other, such as noxious industries and high-status residential areas.
4. Certain activities cannot afford to pay high rents for the most accessible locations, thus forming their own clusters.

All these factors may, over time, lead to a model of a multi-nuclear city, in which each centre specializes in a certain activity.

URBAN DEVELOPMENT MODELS

The following models attempt to determine the dynamics of city structure by deriving it from a few basic factors, with transportation costs to the workplace usually being the most important.

The Lowry Model

The Lowry Model is an operational model which seeks to derive one set of activities, namely residential and local services, from another set, basic employment. It then allocates the derived activities in the urban spatial system, thus achieving a spread of urban land uses. The model distinguishes between two categories of activities: basic employment activities that include industry, business and administrative institutions, all of which serve non-local demand; and non-basic employment activities including retail businesses and other sectors which serve local demand.

It is assumed that the location of basic employment is independent of non-basic employment, whereas non-basic employment is locationally dependent on the basic-employment location. That is to say, that the population allocates itself around the basic employment centres according to travel time functions, and non-basic employment allocates itself in accordance with the residential locations and the job locations.

The model operates as follows: First, total employment (E) is calculated through basic employment, using economic base relationships. Then total population (P) is calculated. The population is allocated by a potential model in the following form:

$$P_j = PE_i f^1(C_{ij})/_{ij}E_i f^1(C_{ij})$$

where $f^1(C_{ij})$ = function of generalized travel cost from i to j. Non-basic employment is then calculated from this population allocation and allocated in the following form:

$$S_i^k = S^k(g^k P_j f^2(C_{ij})q^k E_i)/({}_{ij}g^k P_j f^2(C_{ij})q^k E_i),$$

S_i^k = non-basic employment in category k allocated in zone i,
g^k, q^k = empirically determined weights,
$f^2(C_{ij})$ = function of generalized travel costs.

The equations above can be solved if a given system of basic employment and travel cost functions are known. If the distributions of population and employment predicted by the model differ from these used as independent variables in the potential models, the predicted distributions are fed back as independent variables, and the model is run in an iterative fashion until consistency between input and output variables is secured.

An Opportunity–Accessibility Model

The Opportunity–Accessibility Model is an operational model developed by G. T. Lathrop and J. R. Hamburg. It seeks to allocate different future activities to different sites in the city, thus obtaining the city spatial arrangement. These allocations serve later as inputs to a transportation model which has to evaluate different transportation alternatives.

The model maintains that it is possible to rank the sites in a city according to their distance from the urban centre, defined in terms of time. Each of these sites has a number of opportunities for allocating a certain activity, the opportunity defined in terms of land-use intensity of the activity, i.e. its density. Hence the urban spatial system is viewed as a system of geographical sites, on which an opportunity surface of a certain activity is superimposed. The actual distribution of an activity is a product of a successive evaluation of the alternative opportunities for the sites. The object of this evaluation is to find the optimal opportunity for each site. According to the model:

$$A_j = A(e^{-lO} - e^{-l(O + O_j)})$$

A_j = the amount of activity to be allocated in zone j,

A = the aggregate amount of activity to be allocated,

O = the opportunities for siting a unit of activity rank ordered by access value and preceding zone j,

l = probability of a unit of activity being sited at a given opportunity,

O_j = the opportunities in zone j.

In the model the sites are ranked according to their level of accessibility from the centre. The opportunities are defined in terms of density, which is achieved through balance between land prices and transportation costs. All of this makes the model sensitive to the form of the accessibility system. In other words, the transportation system becomes an important determinant in the distribution of activities over the urban spatial surface. The parameter l indicates the probability that a unit of activity will be sited at a unit of opportunity. The larger this value is, the more tightly packed the region will be. Thus, it is a measure which describes the relative importance of central positioning within a city.

The model distributes growth increments across the opportunity surface, which is rank ordered by time-path values to the centre. After each increment of growth is allocated, the available land is reduced by the amount of land required to site the increment of activity, thus decreasing the opportunity surface, and the activity inventory by zone is updated.

Mills's Model

This model is a mathematical model which explains the sizes and structures of urban areas. These are explained in the model as market responses to income and production conditions in the city. Empirical findings show that the size and growth of cities can be explained as responses to income and employment opportunities provided in them. Likewise, it was observed that land-use intensity differs between cities and within a city due to factor substitution. This justifies the analysis of the model in which production functions will explain the observed factor substitution.

What distinguishes this model is the high importance it casts on the production opportunities, expressed in production functions, in determining the size and structure of the city.

Mills maintains that a city will not exist, but consumers will spread evenly over the land surface, if we consider a general equilibrium model in which an arbitrary number of goods is produced for production and consumption; the only non-produced goods are labour and land, which are homogeneous; the production functions have constant return to scale; input and output markets are competitive; utility functions have the usual properties and have a specified amount of inputs supplied and products consumed.

If the city exists, it is due to relaxations of two assumptions, namely—the homogeneity of land, and the constant return to scale of the production functions. The non-homogeneity of the production functions enters his model through the definition of efficiency parameters which have locational effects. In addition, the model assumes increasing and decreasing returns to scale.

The model defines the production conditions by assuming that only three activities take place in the city, as follows: (1) the production of goods expressed through a Cobb–Douglas production function; (2) intra-city transportation in which the percentage of land used for transportation systems is defined; (3) housing activity which is also expressed in the form of a Cobb–Douglas production function.

Secondly, the model determines market conditions and the different marginal productivity conditions for different activities, where the wage rate and the rental rate of capital are assumed to be exogenous.

Thirdly, it assumes certain links to market conditions, e.g. the housing consumption per worker; the fraction of workers employed adjacent to their place of residence; the cost per passenger mile of transportation; the link between transportation and housing costs.

Finally, other conditions are also specified: within the CBD land is used to produce goods and transportation and housing; there is no obstruction to a circular city; and all workers must live somewhere within the city.

All the conditions mentioned above, namely production conditions, market conditions and other conditions are expressed in mathematical formulae, and the solution of these brings about the determination of the size of the areas for the different activities, and their structure in relation to each other. The importance of this model is its ability to explain the differences between the aggregate land value of different cities as a result of the level and structure of production and services sectors.

All the models so far reviewed are geographical models concerning the development of urban land-use patterns. These models do not contradict each other, but on the contrary—they constitute a spectrum of successive levels of development of a city. The specific kind of land-use patterns a city will follow depends on its size and the complexity of its socio-economic system.

LAND PRICE AND CITY STRUCTURE MODELS

In contrast to the above-discussed models, the ones below tend to *explain* phenomena of urban land use by means of economic relationships, mainly residential demand for land. The trade-off between desirable location and desirable size of plot is one of the important elements to emerge from this analysis.

The L. Wingo Model

L. Wingo has recently evolved a theoretical analysis which relates urban land value to transportation costs in the town.* Transportation costs and ground rent appear related in his system by an incremental formula, with each complementing the other. Their total is a fixed amount equivalent to the costs of transport to the furthest residential district in the given town. That is, a person is ready to pay a higher amount for the land if its proximity to the town centres enables a corresponding saving to be made in the associated transportation costs. This saving is not only in actual travelling costs, but also the financial equivalent of the time lost in travelling. This equivalent is determined by the marginal value of the rest time, that is, by the income a person is prepared to forego in order to obtain an extra hour of rest. Wingo's analysis, therefore, falls into line with Haig's outlook regarding the complementary relationship of land rent and transport expenses—which is, incidentally, reminiscent of the von Thunen agricultural model.

* Landon Wingo, *Transportation and Urban Land*, Washington, 1961.

As the base for his model, Wingo uses a town with a homogeneous population from the point of view of income and consumption. At the same time, he assumes its possible application to more realistic cases of population with differing income and consumption patterns. Serving as the essential basis of the model are the transportation costs, including the cash outlay for transport and the travelling time value.

It is possible to present the Wingo model thus: we denominate the transportation costs as K, and the distance from the home to the town centre t. We present K as a function of t; that is, $K(t)$.

The rent of the building plot is defined as the product of the land unit price (p) by the amount of land (q); that is, $p \cdot q$. A resident of the town views the transportation costs and rent for the plot as complementing each other. He expends the same amount on rent and transportation costs as a single item, without taking the plot location into account. Because this fixed amount is equal to the transportation costs to the most distant dwelling t_m (where the price of the land equals 0), the following equation is obtained:

$$p \cdot q + K(t) = K(t_m), \tag{1}$$

and hence

$$p \cdot q = K(t_m) - K(t). \tag{2}$$

Now, Wingo assumes the following function regarding the demand for land:

$$q = \left(\frac{a}{p}\right)^b \tag{3}$$

when a and b are parameters and p the land unit price. In effect, the meaning of this function is that the consumer will buy less land at a higher price. Equation (2) thus determines the amount of money expended on land and equation (3) the amount of land purchased and the price. With the solution afforded by this set of equations we arrive at the conclusions regarding the price of the land, size of the parcels of land, etc.

So far, we have found the equilibrium solution regarding the individual land user. It may be determined for the whole population of a town by the next formula:

$$n = 2\pi \int_0^{t_m} \frac{t}{q(t)} \, dt \qquad (4)$$

where t is the distance from the town centre and n indicates the total population of the town. In effect, this equation determines that the population of a city is equal to the integral of population crowding $1[q(t)]$ relative to the total city area (defined in the simplest way as the areas of a circle t^2).

All the elements of the equation are known apart from the limit t_m of the integral. The above equation is solved in order to find the distance t_m that is the distance from the centre to the furthest periphery of the city (settlement limit).

The W. Alonso Model*

One of the important urban land models has been developed in the USA by W. Alonso. It is based, as are many others, on commutation costs. The value of the land appears in it as the amount of annual ground rent.

Basic to the model is the assumption that the town is situated in a plain, that there are no topographical singularities and that there is equal transport facility in all directions. The model makes the following main assumptions:

(a) All employment and services in the city are concentrated in the centre, and the value of dwelling plots is solely dependent on distance from the centre.

(b) In choosing a dwelling, the householders face the following alternatives: whether to prefer a larger plot of land for their home, or lower travelling expenses, or a reduction in the costs apart from the ground-rent.

(c) The expenditures of the householders are equal to their income. It then follows that

$$R = P(r) \cdot q + K(r) + Pz \cdot Z,$$

*W. Alonso, *A Model of Urban Land*, 1960.

$R =$ the total income of the householder,

$P(r) =$ price of 1 m^2 of land at distance r from the centre,

$q =$ area of the plot occupied by the householder,

$K(r) =$ transportation costs to the centre,

$Pz \cdot Z =$ total other expenses.

Alonso continues by calling the arbitrary location of a householder as $S(r, q, z)$, which he defines as the facilities corresponding to the coordinates r, q, z. Then he shows that if the rent (P_0) that the householder is prepared to pay at a distance r_0 is known, it is possible to determine for this householder a demand curve defining the price P which he will agree to pay at any distance v from the centre. The demand curves of various householders make it possible to fix the location of the dwellings and the price they pay for the land. Householders will prefer a more distant location whenever their demand curves have a stronger slope in the vicinity of the centre. On the other hand, land on the border of the town, occupied by dwellings, will be equal in price to agricultural land, because agriculture represents the only other effective possible use.

W. Alonso makes four additional assumptions in his analysis:

Fourth Assumption: Complete competition exists between householders.

Fifth Assumption: Every householder can find a place where the price of the land does not exceed P_r; that is, the price appropriate to his demand curve.

Sixth Assumption: The land area available for dwellings exactly satisfies the demand.

Seventh Assumption: The landowner receives the full rent deriving from the location of the division.

In other words, Alonso's model is indubitably one of equilibrium, for it assumes that there is complete market competition and that the supply of land exactly meets the demand. Alonso also shows that an improved transport network brings about, relative to the land values, a decline in the centre and an increase in the outskirts.

However, these axioms are only correct in relation to residential land and not for land used for business and office purposes. The model bases itself, in effect, on American conditions where certain social groups (that is, the wealthy classes) prefer to live on the out-skirts where the urban land is cheaper and they can have a larger plot.

The Penn–Jersey Model

The Penn–Jersey model bears a different character than those of Wingo and Alonso. Its purpose is not to find an explanation for present land values, but to arrive at a forecast of future values by starting from an initial time it arrives at a forecast of land values at $O+t$. The model takes into account corrections resulting from the developments in the period, such as the establishment of new enterprises in the vicinity or public authority activities.

The initial assumption of the Penn–Jersey model is that a town is divided into a number of districts, within which there are no transportation costs. The plots of land in every district are equal and dwellings of every type may be built on them.

An additional assumption of the model is that the householders interested in acquiring dwellings are divided into homogeneous groups of low, medium and high income: all the householders of such a group have the same attitude regarding location and demand for land.

The model predicates the existence of a number of districts: $Z_0, Z_1, Z_2, Z_3, \ldots, Z_n$. Assuming that the householder agrees to pay a rental of S for a dwelling in District Z_0:

$$\text{in } Z_1 \text{ he will agree to pay } S+P_1$$
$$\text{in } Z_2 \text{ he will agree to pay } S+P_2$$
$$\text{in } Z_3 \text{ he will agree to pay } S+P_3$$
$$\text{in } Z_4 \text{ he will agree to pay } S+P_4$$
$$\text{in } Z_n \text{ he will agree to pay } S+P_n$$

According to the definition, P can be both positive and negative. The series $S, S+P_1, S+P_2$, etc., represents what may be called "Potential Offers" relative to the various districts. These offers are indicated as O_{ij} and two householders belonging to the same social group will have equal offers. The model assumes that the initial position is known and that its purpose, therefore, is to arrive at a forecast regarding period t, and this is done by the method of maximization according to the linear programming technique. The model's purpose is to arrive at the O_{ij} maximum.

The model assumes that the attitude of householders is dependent on three criteria: (a) size of dwelling; (b) attractiveness of the residential district; (c) transport inconvenience. The "potential offers" of each group of householders vary as a function of distance from the centre.

Some examples show the reciprocal connection between the readiness of a given group to pay for land (as rent) and the distance from the centre. It emerges, that the low-income group can obtain the maximum benefit from a district that is about 5 miles from the centre. The medium-income group attains the maximum at about 5–10 miles, while the high-income group attains the maximum at about 15 miles, that is, in the suburbs.

Dynamic Urban Land-price Development Models

Finally we come to those models which seek to explain the factors responsible for the overall changes in urban land prices. These may include urban growth, and the macro-economic factors which affect prices, and also financial and planning factors which affect the land market.

An interesting model of land prices has been developed by four research scholars of the University of Pennsylvania. This model attempts to examine the influence of the processes of urbanization on the prices of undeveloped land. The model is based on the assumption that land prices reflect the capitalized value of expected future use. It is suggested that before formation of the town, the rent for urban land is nil, while with urbanization a rent is created depending on: (a) technological factors; (b) institutional factors; (c) taxes; (d) development costs.

The investigators start with the assumption that the price of land reflects the capitalized value of the anticipated future course of the rent. If the rate of interest is r and R_i is the net rent of the land at time i, the value of the land at time t (V_t) is

$$V_{t=1} = \frac{R_i}{1(1+r)^i} \tag{1}$$

A typical characteristic of vacant land is that until it is developed the return on the land is nil, and if taxes and other expenses are taken into account, there is even a negative return. On the basis of this formulation, the following formula is obtained:

$$V_t = \frac{n}{i} + \frac{R_{uj}}{1(1+r)} i+j+n+1 \frac{R_{dj}}{(1+r)^j} j \qquad (2)$$

where $n =$ the year in which the development is implemented,

$R_{uj} =$ the net rent before the vacant land is developed,

$R_{dj} =$ the net rent after development of the land.

That is, the inclusive capitalized value is the amount of the capitalization before development plus the capitalization after development.

If it is assumed that $R_{ui} = 0$ and R_{dj} is constant from the year $n+1$, the value of the land at times t and $t+1$ is

$$V_t = \frac{R_d}{r}(1+r)^{(t-n)}, \qquad V^1 + {}^.1 = \frac{R_d}{r}(1+r)^{(t-n+1)}. \qquad (3)$$

If these two equations are divided by each other, an interesting conclusion is obtained regarding the dynamics of the free land price. For it emerges that:

$$\frac{V^{t+1} + 1}{V_t} = 1+r. \qquad (4)$$

That is to say, the annual rate of growth of the value of vacant land is equal to the rate of interest.

For the above, the authors also arrive at conclusions regarding the mechanism of land speculation in that, in addition to the typical imperfections of the land market, there are differences in anticipated rent (R_d) and in maintenance costs (R_u) and also in the interest rate (r). These anticipated differences change, of course, the capitalized value of the land—a process reflected by speculative phenomena.

The effect of the anticipated differences in value R_d on the value of the land is expressed by the equation:

$$\frac{dV_t}{dR_d} = \frac{(1+r)^{(t-n)}}{r}. \qquad (5)$$

This model demonstrates the extent to which urban land rent is created through the urbanization process.

The Concepts of Sherman I. Maisel

Also worthy of close attention are the investigations of Sherman I. Maisel, of the University of California, regarding the factors influencing urban land prices. These investigations relate to land prices for single-family houses in the USA, but they have a wider significance regarding the rising prices of urban land in general.

Maisel's model shows that the development of urban land prices depends on the following principal factors:

(a) *Population growth of the cities*, resulting from the general growth of the population. The cities expand and embrace new, more peripheral areas. The inhabitants of these new, distant districts bear, of course, higher transportation costs to the city centre (travelling to work, entertainment, study, etc.). This process of increasing transportation costs in the city brings about a rise in land prices.

(b) *Increased incomes.* An increase in the real incomes of the population has, as is known, an even clearer influence on rising land prices.

(c) *Inflationary trends.* An important reason for rising land prices is an inflationary trend. This is because over a long-term period the ground-rent tends to adjust itself to the general price level of the economy.

(d) *Artificial land shortages.* There may be periods, in the short or medium term, when the demand rises above the supply of land; that is, an essentially artificial shortage is created. The reasons for this shortage are two-fold. Firstly, while undeveloped land is plentiful in American cities there frequently happens to be a shortage of developed land which may be built on without delay. Secondly, in periods of marked land-price increases, plot owners in the desired areas frequently refrain from selling or developing their plots, preferring to wait for land prices to rise further. As a result, an artificial land shortage is created and prices rise to a level considerably exceeding the real value of the land.

(e) *Speculative long-run factors.* In addition to the speculative factors from the supply side, speculative factors are also active from the demand side. When the population grows quickly and there is a constant rise in income levels, people become accustomed to the idea that there will be a constant rise in the demand for land. This encourages many people to speculate in real estate and buy land not because of present demand, but from forecasted increased demand in the future.

This analysis of some factors influencing land prices shows the important role of macro-economic factors as well as of general development trends.

The René Mayer Model

One of the most important land price theories is that of the French expert René Mayer. It is based on the assumption that the land value reflects at the same time the value of the transportation time and the price of land.

The value of time includes the element of distance and the level of discomfort from travel. Therefore the value of time might be connected with the reduction of travel time and thereby of discomfort. It is noteworthy that Mayer's model includes not only the journey to work, but all the householder's journeys, including those for entertainment purposes, purchases, etc. As a result, social values are clearly inserted into the price of land. For example, if someone lives in a neighbourhood unsuited to his social standing, this brings about an increase in transportation costs, for in such a case he will have to make more journeys in order to maintain his social connections. Conversely, the value of the land in a neighbourhood increases if the person can come into contact with people of his own social circle (i.e. without having to travel far).

Another characteristic of this model is the introduction of the land-shortage factor, considered as a result of scarce land. Thus, Mayer puts into his model the capitalized value of the future profits from land. At the same time he underlines the role of the increased urbanized area on the land values in the existing city. According to his theory each additional area transformed from agricultural into urban use increases land values in the whole city. He explains the impact of the different factors influencing the land price in the following model: the price of land on the periphery is composed of four elements:

the agricultural land value a, the cost of infrastructure works l, capitalization of the additional rent due to urban growth L and the capitalization of the additional rent due to scarcity of available developed land on the market d. At the frontiers of a city the price of land QL may be formulated as follows:

$$QL = a+b+c+d.$$

Within the city the price of land in any place M is increased by a factor $Q(t)$ whose value increases with diminishing time (t) of the access to the centre of the city. Thus the total price (Qm) may be expressed as follows:

$$Qm = QL+Q(t).$$

This means that the price of land in any location of the city Qm is composed of the price of land of the city frontier QL and increased by the factor of the reduced access time to the centre $Q(t)$.

Therefore, land prices depend, on the one hand, on the relationship between permanent process of urban growth and the availability of developed land on the market, and on the other hand on the transportation network and the location of services and employment.

From this model the following conclusions might be drawn: that land prices are affected by the rate of urban growth but at the same time public authority policies may act as a factor in increasing or restricting land prices, through measures aimed at increasing the supply of land to the market, and by the planned allocation of land for different purposes.

Wendt's Model

Wendt's starting-point is a sharp criticism of Haig's land-value theory. Haig derives the rent charged by the owner of a site from the saving in transportation costs which occurs when a site has a relative accessibility advantage over other sites. Wendt contends that, on the contrary, the urban land market is not so undifferentiated (one site cannot be always substituted for another) to make comparisons of transport costs the determining factor, and besides, other factors (such as the level of services and environmental features of a site) are also important in land-use allocation.

Following these criticisms, Wendt suggests another theoretical framework, according to which urban land values represent the expected future net returns of the sites. These aggregate net returns are the remainder of future expected revenues minus future expected costs capitalized over time

$$V = \frac{R_x - C_x}{r}$$

where V = expected net returns,
R_x = expected revenues,
C_x = expected costs,
r = rate of capitalization.

Factors influencing revenues are: population (P), average amount of income spent on urban services (Y), competitive pull of urban area (Pu), supply of competitive land (S), and public investment (PI):

$$R_x = f_x(P, Y, Pu, S, PI).$$

The expected costs are the sum of the following: local taxes (T), operating costs (O_c), interest on capital invested in present and future improvements (i_{im}), depreciation on present and future improvements (D_{im});

$$C_x = (T + O_c + i_{im} + D_{im}).$$

The capitalization rate is dependent on interest rates (i), investment risk (R), capital gain possibility (C_g):

$$r = f_x(i, R, C_g).$$

Thus the expected net returns which represent land prices will be as follows:

$$V = \frac{f_x(P, Y, Pu, S, PI) - (T + O_c + i_{im} + D_{im})}{f_x(i, R, C_g)}.$$

Many factors therefore influence the expected future revenues and costs. The basic approach, that the present values are affected by the future expected profits, may explain the fact that though in the long-term technological building improvements have increased the built space in a limited land area—this has not led to a diminishing of land values. The monopolistic character of land market restrains the supply to the market. of land where there is an expectation of a future land price increase.

This approach to land values in a dynamically changing city makes them a function of urban growth and not of stationary city areas. Such an approach, along with an estimation of the macro-economic factors affecting the land values, may allow a better understanding of the variety of factors influencing the formulae of urban values.

Pöyhönen's Model

This model was elaborated in Finland in the middle of the 1950s by Penti Pöyhönen. Unlike Wendt's model, it stresses the importance of building rights and the size of the site as determinants of land prices. It is evident that by bringing in the building rights factor, Pöyhönen focuses the attention on the local authorities which determine these rights, and so may have an important role in the determination of land prices.

The following expression represents Pöyhönen's model of land-price formation in urban land market:

$$P_t = \frac{aA_t 10^{(cR+bT')}}{r^h} 10^S$$

where P_t = price of the site per square metre in the year t,

A_t = population (in 1000) of the locality in the year t,

$R = \dfrac{E-\bar{E}}{r_0+r}$ where R = measure of the building rights, E = utilization value of the value of the site in question, $\bar{E}$ = average utilization value of sites in the locality, computed separately for inside and corner sites, r_0 = a statistical parameter and r = the so-called distance of location from the centre of the city.

$T' = |T-T_0|$ where T' = measure of the influence of the size of the site, T = area of the site under consideration, and T_0 = a statistical parameter, in $1000 \, \text{m}^2$.

$r = r_1 + a_2 r_2 + \ldots + a_k r_k$, where r = the so-called distance of location from the centre of the city, r_i = distance along route r, and a_i = the corresponding weight indicative of the significance of this route. The measuring is started from the business centre, defined as a point, and carried out along such a route which reduces r to a minimum. The last term of the expression is derived from the depth of the site, multiplied by a suitable coefficient.

a, b, c and h are statistical parameters, the values of which are determined separately in each locality.

S = random variable.

The price parameter a can be split further into common and local index-number factors and factors explicable by means of business turnover and degree of construction activity. In the case of inside and corner sites at least the parameter a is determined separately.

The measure of the influence exerted by the building rights is represented in the equation by the expression 10^{cR}, where the parameter c acts as a proportional factor.

In the measure of the location and shape of the site, l/r^h, the possible variations in price caused by the irregular structure of the city centre are accounted for by the parameter h.

The measure of the size of the site is the expression 10^{bT}, which reaches its maximum when the site area if T_0, decreasing with both towards larger and smaller site areas. The parameter b acts as a proportional factor.

The use of statistical parameters in the equation is of great advantage as an indicator of how far the model thus obtained conforms with reality. In so far as nearly equal values are obtained for corresponding parameters in different localities, the employed measures of the factors in price formation can be considered successful. In cases where no natural explanation can be provided for the differences observed, the model has to be considered unrealistic, either entirely or in part.

Salmela's Model

This model was designed by Arto Salmela of Finland. The starting-point of this model is the following function:

$$y = f_1(r) \cdot f_2(e_r) \cdot f_3(I)$$

where y = price of the site according to the equivalent of floors in square metres,

r = the distance from the town centre,

e_r = the building coefficient of the site,

I = the annual change in land prices.

One of the interesting findings obtained from this model relates to the dynamic development of land prices. It appears that there is a very close link between the development of the prices of individual sites and the general rise of the land-cost index. The model attempts to express this phenomenon by aid of the following formula:

$$y = \frac{1}{r+r_0} \cdot y'$$

where y = price of land,

r = distance from the centre,

r_0 = the specific fixed distance for each town,

y' = other factors influencing price of the land.

For r_0 there is a different value in each town. In provincial towns this distance is between 0·2 and 0·4 km, while in larger cities this distance grows. In Helsinki, for instance, it reached 27 km in 1962.

The significance of the above formula is that while there is an inverse relationship between the price of the plot and the distance from the centre, there is no direct proportionality, and the variations in land prices with distance from the centre are slower than the increase in distance from the centre.

A further attempt was made to formulate the model of land prices in diverse cities. Out of it emerged, for example, that if the number of residents grows by 10%, the average land price rises by 8–9%. Another conclusion was that reduction of the building coefficient brings a reduction of land prices. It also became clear that the rise in land prices in the vicinity of the centre of Helsinki would be more or less in conformity with the capitalized value of the reduced travelling and transportation costs.

Salmela's inclusive formula in this sphere is:

$$h = \frac{I_e \cdot I_t \cdot V_1 \cdot e_t - V_2}{r+r_0}$$

where h = price (in money units) per m² (of floor space equivalent),

I_e = index of building costs,

I_t = land prices index,

e_t = building coefficient,

r = distance (in km) from the central point of the business
centre (measured along the streets),

V_1, V_2 = fixed allowances.

This model is based mostly on comparison of cities of the same economic structure and does not take into account the different effects on land prices of a varying level of commercial and other services in a city of the same size.

RESUMÉ

This review of some urban land-value theories and models show the variety of factors influencing the formation of urban land prices and also influencing urban land values. Some of the theories deal with urban-growth patterns, and may explain the basic factors influencing urban land values as a function of land uses. These theories explain the allocation of land space according to different uses as a result of the dynamic development of a city.

The theories on land prices deal with two kinds of factors which influence the formation of urban land prices. These are macroeconomic and national socio-economic trends which influence the general level of land-price development; and particular factors which influence the land prices of various sites in some urban areas and for different urban uses.

Generally, there is more attention paid to the theory of residential than commercial land prices, in spite of the important role of commercial land values in the urban economy.

More attention is paid to the formation of land prices in a "static" city than in a rapidly developing, dynamic urban settlement. There is little attention paid to the role of planning decisions which affect the formation of land prices. Probably one of the reasons is insufficient material on the theory of urban land policies and their impact on the patterns of urban growth.

Such a difference between a great number of theories of urban land prices, and the few theories which consider urban land policies, is a result of an approach which considers the market mechanism as the essential basis for regulating land prices. The restricted amount of material on land-policy theory is especially astonishing considering the rich published material on the theory of urbanization and on urban development patterns.

REFERENCES

Alonso, W., *A Model of Urban Land*, New York, 1960.
Burgess, W. E., *The City: Selected Essays*, University of Chicago Press, reprint of 1925 edition.
Haig, R. M., *Regional Survey of New York and its Environment*, New York, 1925.
Hurd, *Principles of City Land Values*, New York, 1903.
Marshall, Alfred, *Principles of Economics*, London, 1925.
Pöyhönen, P., *An Econometric Investigation of City Land Market Prices*, Helsinki, 1964.
Ricardo, David, *Principles of Political Economy and Taxation*.
Wendt, P., *Theory of Urban Land Values*, Land Economics.
Wingo, L., *Transportation and Urban Use*, Washington, 1961.

CHAPTER 8

The Peculiar Nature of the Land Market

Land prices are influenced by many factors. One set of factors concern the changes in the urban economy and society itself, and another set relates to macro-economic factors, principally economic growth and its side effects. Both are influencing the formation of land prices, but their respective importance changes with changes in the world economy and urban growth trends. An understanding of how these factors are inter-related and the role each plays in determining land prices is important to understanding the functioning of the urban land market. As the nature and extent of these relationships will vary through time, it is necessary to develop a dynamic approach to the study of land prices. Indeed, the problem becomes even more complex when it is considered that the relationship among the variables varies in different countries with different levels of economic and social development. Similarly, there is a difference in the role of the same factors in different categories of cities according to their significance in the country and even in international economic relations.

Some theories and models have attempted to identify and explain the specific factors influencing urban growth and land values. Many of these models have investigated only the effects of one particular factor, mentioning other factors but without looking at the interactive effects with all these other factors. Thus it is important to understand and to determine which factors are dominant and which common factors exercise the most influence. In particular, insufficient attention has been paid both to the different factors affecting residential and commercial land prices, and to the implications of the fact that land is extensively held as a financial investment.

WHAT IS THE BASIS OF URBAN LAND VALUE?

What is the attraction of a city for an individual or for a firm? A person looking for a residence in an urban area is seeking not only enough land for housing, which could be found anywhere, but, as R. M. Haig has emphasized, *accessibility* to the superior level of job opportunities and the variety of services (personal, commercial and cultural) than are to be found in the city. Thus there are several factors involved in an individual's choice of location which may work in different directions: first, accessibility (which includes the effects of transportation and distance to city functions); but also pleasing *environmental features* (which includes both the social and physical environment, e.g. quiet, absence of pollution, but also a neighbourhood with a congenial life-style).

The role of location is even more important for commercial land. The value of a location to a commercial firm is related to the prospects of the *turnover* that a particular site can command. A more central location with a larger catchment area will command a higher value. Services which are oriented to regional, national and even international clienteles and are highly specialized need central locations in order to compete with similar firms for a small number of customers.

Though we will not discuss industrial location in detail, the attraction of an urban location is, as for residential land, a function *both* of an adequate space for a site (increasingly important for modern production methods) and accessibility to markets, raw materials and a skilled labour force.

The role of locational factor and accessibility to urban functions may depend on the level of attractiveness of a human settlement. This is influenced by the variety of employment opportunities and the level of services. Many factors affect land values. The location factor, which is one of the most important, includes the accessibility to different activities. However, the factor which accumulates to itself the effect of different factors is the expected or actual income from structures built on the land surface. The "constructibility" (the possibility of using the land for construction purposes), or the intensity and kind of land use, determines the urban land value.

It is suggested that investment in the infrastructure and in public and private services (or the economic cost of land) creates the basis of urban land value. The difference in aggregate land values from this economic cost might be seen as one of the basic meanings of urban rent. These investments create a variety of employment opportunities and services which attract people to some areas more than to others. The level of attractiveness creates the demand for space for commercial as well as for residential use in some areas more than in others. Therefore the process of urban growth creates an additional land rent. This rent is created not by the additional investment of the landowner, as in agricultural land, but by the additional general investment in a large urban area. This additional investment creates the addition to urban land value which the particular landowner gets as land rent.

Therefore, the impact of the land-use policies of the public authority, which play the deciding role in fixing both the land use and the intensity of use, is one of the main factors in setting the urban land value. Taking into account the dominant role of land use in setting the land value, the term "value" is used mainly to underline the kind of land use (residential, commercial, industrial and recreational land values). Land "price" may be defined as land value expressed in monetary terms in the market economy.

But the same land values may reach different prices according to the factors affecting the land market. As a rule, in a perfectly functioning free market, the law of supply and demand fixes the price. Due to the peculiar character of the land market, however, the law of supply and demand does not function here as with other goods and products. The *expected* land use and expected demand have an influence on the land market, as do the taxation policy, the rate of interest, and various other factors. The land price is therefore an expression of land value and a result of supply and demand in the framework of the peculiar conditions of the land market.

Some urban activities which provide the essential basis for social life find little or no expression in the urban land market. For example, cultural institutions (theatres, museums, concert halls) are needed to satisfy an increasingly better educated population. Such institutions require a central location to provide access for a large public. The provision of such institutions, however, present an interesting value question. In a market economy where economic value is fixed by actual or prospective income, centrally located land is occupied by institutions which are able to pay the highest prices (banks, insurance companies, etc.). Thus, in discussing urban land values an additional factor, the social utility factor, must be introduced. This is measured neither by the turnover of goods and services nor by the actual or expected profit, but by the social benefit to the community which is using the land to satisfy the collective needs of its residents. As such, the social utility value is neglected by the market which is unable to regulate land prices on the basis of free competition.

A high level of cultural services increases the attractiveness of a city and thus its aggregate value. Parks and the provision of green space also favourably influences land prices. The additional value, which is not created by the action of any private individual, is exploited by private interests in the form of higher land prices in cities with developed cultural and recreational facilities.

While the value of urban land is a "good" belonging to society, because the value is created not by individual effort, but by the investments and planning decisions of that society, this value is usually expropriated by private individuals.

THE URBAN LAND MARKET

The urban land market is influenced by the peculiar character of urban land. That is, the general law of supply and demand does not influence the urban land market in the same way as it does other commodities. The demand for and the supply of land is always related to the characteristics of specific locations. Location affects land values in accordance with the use to which the land is put, and, as a general statement, it exerts a greater influence upon commercial land use than upon residential land use.

The Peculiar Character of Land

Some of the unique qualities of land which distinguish it from other goods are:

(a) Land is physically undepreciable and is not influenced by time, while the quality of virtually all other commodities depreciates with time. There is, of course, a distinction between raw land and developed land. Raw land is physically undepreciable. The structures built on land are depreciable, but the land on which this development occurs is undepreciable. In fact in some cases the depreciation of a structure may increase the value of the land because of an expected change in use when a new structure would be built as a replacement.

(b) Land is not transportable. Even if the use of land can be changed, the land itself is stationary. Thus, it is hardly possible to talk of a national market for land in the same way as one might speak of, for instance, a national market for different goods. Even in "regional" terms, as land cannot be transported, the price of land is fixed by the demand for land in certain areas, *not* by the availability and demand for land in the entire region. Most spatially fixed are commercial uses, where the price of commercial land is mainly determined by the supply and demand for land in the centre of the city or in neighbourhood centres.

(c) Land is limited in quantity and its supply cannot be increased (with the exception of, for example, land reclaimed from the sea). However, the intensity of land use may be increased. This serves as a substitute for additional quantities of land.

(d) Land is used not only for production purposes but also as a long-term investment or as a basis for savings. The scarcity of land and the physically undepreciable character of land make it profitable to hold large reserves without using them as a basis for production. In contrast, investors in depreciable physical commodities will be forced to sell after some time, since their value diminishes with the physical depreciation of the goods. Obviously, money invested in land has its maintenance costs such as interest charges and taxes, but such costs are often minimal in comparison with the expected capital gains of sale. Such uses restrict the supply of land which might otherwise be used for building purposes. This is especially true in countries with inflationary pressures and limited investment opportunities (typically the case in most of the developing countries).

These unique characteristics of urban land—the fact that the amount of land in the desired place is inherently limited, and the fact that land can *not* be used for production purposes with relatively little penalty (unless either tax rates or interest rates become prohibitive)— may lead to a permanent disequilibrium in the land market between supply and demand. As demand for land increases, its price rises; but paradoxically, this higher price does not necessarily always increase the supply (as with other goods), but may reduce it, as landowners where new development might take place will withhold their land from the market in the expectation that future rises in prices will bring even larger profits. They can do this because they have almost no "production costs", urban land being mostly developed by public money. The landowners' perceptions here are generally correct in that, as the amount of urban land in limited by public authorities (both by planning regulations and by their willingness to undertake development works), land which does *change in use* (from agricultural to urban, or from residential to commercial) will become many times more valuable. However, not every landowner will benefit from this as inevitably in some cases the public authorities will not allow development or redevelopment. But every landowner will hope for such large profits, and thus the *expectation* of a change in use leads to the reduction of the supply of land to the market. And as the price of land is fixed not by the potential amount of existing or unbuilt-upon land, but mainly by the quantity available on the market, land prices will rise. Thus landowners, though acting individually, produce the same results as a monopoly in classic economic theory—higher prices and reduced supply.

Ironically the more willing the public authorities are to allow land-use changes, the more prices of land will rise over a wide area which is not yet developed or redeveloped (since all areas can expect a change in use) generally more than balancing out the lowering effect on prices of already developed land. For example, in some developing and developed countries where there are not strict building codes restricting where commercial buildings can be erected, residential land prices in a very wide radius from the city centre are high due to the expectation of a change to commercial use.

Thus only a dynamic approach, taking into account *prospective* changes as influencing the land market (as in other financial investments) and also taking into account the role of public authorities, can hope to understand the workings of the urban land market.

SOME DETERMINANTS OF URBAN LAND RENT

The economic character of urban land was initially explained with reference to the theories of Adam Smith and Ricardo concerning the origins of agricultural rent. The famous assumption that the price of land is affected by the price of corn is still applied to urban land by some who are convinced that the price of a house is influenced not by the price of land, but by the payment possibilities of prospective dwellers which then affects land prices. This view is only partially correct, based as it is on the assumption that the land market functions like all other markets.

For agricultural land, the crucial factor in deciding whether to bring more marginal land into production is the price of the agricultural goods produced; if the price rises, it becomes economical to farm less productive land (that which gives a lower output for a given input). As the more marginal land produces less, there is now a differential rent accruing to the better land which gives a higher income.

But what is the good produced by urban land? It is the different types of urban land use (residential, commercial, recreational, etc.). This "good" is not homogeneous in the same way that agricultural produce is, with roughly one price in a national market. There is no national or even regional market for urban land; new urban land in Scotland is not a substitute for the lack of urban land in London. Also, it is very expensive (relative to the price of the land) and takes a long time to bring more land into urban "production" (including changing residential to commercial) and this decision, taken by public authorities, cannot usually be reversed. This "stickiness" of urban land production possibilities further restricts the possibility of urban land markets responding closely to demand.

Neither is urban land a homogeneous good, in the sense that the same land in different uses will command vastly different prices (due to the different prospective income from different uses). It is this fact which gives rise to speculation in land which, as we have seen, further drives up prices. The division of the land market into price-use sectors (the most important being commercial and residential) has important consequences for the land market. The extent to which public authorities succeed in isolating sectors from each other will have a great influence on whether high prices from one sector will influence lower-priced sectors (due to the expectation of a change in use). Thus one would lower prices in one (high-priced) sector at the expense of raising them in another (low-priced) sector. This direction of influence (higher priced land influencing lower priced) also occurs within sectors, as we shall see, and it is the opposite of the Ricardian theory of rent, where it is the cost of the least productive land that determines the differential rent of the better land.

There are some differences between the commercial and residential sectors, stemming basically from the fact that there is no substitute for some types of commercial land (particularly in the CBD). This leads to a monopoly element in CBD commercial rents. This is partly because many firms located in the CBD could not relocate in outlying areas, as they must be close to their (international) clientele and to their rivals and auxiliary services. The amount of land available in the CBD (which is influenced by building regulations and topography) also affects the degree to which monopoly conditions obtain.

The higher prices of commercial rather than residential land may be affected by building regulations which restrain the extension of commercial land use. Generally the growing role of the tertiary sector in national and urban economy exerts a pressure to extend the space for commercial services. The limitation of commercial land in a restricted area within the city must therefore increase the land prices considerably, and at the same time leads to pressure to change land regulations, extending the high commercial land prices to new commercial centres erected within the city area or in the city region. The enormous extension of the services sector may be seen as one of the factors in the high rate of land price increase in recent years.

There are substitutes for residential land; however, as some land is more desirable than others, there is a differential rent accruing to that land. Desirability is not measured solely by distance, or even by accessibility (which accounts for the effect of an improved transportation system) but also by pleasing environmental features. Thus some suburban land is more valuable than inner city land if transport connections are good.

But it is most important to understand that in residential land as well there is a "chain effect" by which high residential land prices affect the lower-priced residential land throughout the city. It is true that the ability of a small segment to pay high prices for particularly desirable locations (either centrally located or suburban) pushes up prices in those areas. (This is the Ricardian housing-to-land-price theory.) The higher residential prices in certain areas influence land prices in adjoining areas as owners expect a change to a higher-price use. But the majority of the population has rather limited payment possibilities for housing (as it is already a rather large part of the total individual's expenditure). Therefore they are forced to move to less desirable (usually distant) locations or to accept a worse standard of housing where they are (e.g. through overcrowding). This relentless search for cheaper land for housing, in turn, affects prices throughout the city region (where it is expected that more land will be turned to urban use): while land will still be less valuable than closer urban land, it will still be much more valuable in urban than in any non-urban use.

The prices already existing in the urban area therefore influence the formation of land prices in newly urbanized areas. The urban land rent may be seen as the difference between the existing urban land prices and the economic cost of newly urbanized areas (agricultural land prices plus development costs). Obviously some coefficient of accessibility to city functions should be kept in mind, which results in lower prices in the newly urbanized areas than in the city proper. Thus in the urban land market with its limited supply possibilities a small segment of the market can have a large effect.

ROLE OF PLANNING DECISIONS

All of the capital gains which result from changes in land use are only made possible by the decisions of public authorities to allow development. It is the investment in infrastructure which creates the aggregate increase in value of land in newly developed areas but it is the planning decisions which determine the distribution of those windfall gains to particular individuals. One piece of land will increase in value a hundred times, while an adjacent piece (on which development was not permitted) will be little more valuable. Therefore, there is great pressure for landowners to try to influence planning decisions, sometimes through illegal means.

Studies indicate that the highest land price increases are produced by public decisions which change the land use. For example, enormous price increases are correlated with the construction or improvement of highways. Additionally, the decision to increase the density of land use, that is, to erect high-rise buildings in formerly low-density areas, is another example which automatically increases land prices. It is well known that the decision to change agricultural land into urban land immediately creates increases in the price of this land, often by hundreds of times their former level. This same phenomenon occurs when unused land, sometimes even very poor agricultural land, is transformed into a new town.

A distinction should be made between land values in the existing city and in newly urbanized areas or rapidly growing small cities. Generally, growth in population and economic activities and the forecast for future development permanently influence increasing land values. However, the rate of growth is higher in the fast developing new urban settlements and in rapidly growing small towns than in older cities. Therefore, the rate of land-price increase is generally higher in the newly developed urban areas than in the existing city (and thus the public authority decisions to change land use and invest in infrastructure works are most critical here).

More recently, the growing tension as a result of physical and social congestion in the city has created new value criteria which influence land values. The search for better environmental features, more quiet conditions of life, and more security have increased the value of areas possessing these characteristics. This has resulted in a general increase in values of suburban land while the increase in land values in overcrowded city areas has shown a much lower rate of growth. It might be that such values would actually show a diminishing price trend if not for the influence of commercially used land. Here, the rapid growth of the tertiary sector which required more space in central city areas, negated the effect of the environmental factors on the residential values in central city areas. Again, this type of effect underlines the difficulty of defining the role of separate factors in the formation of land values.

CONCLUSIONS

Many different factors have an influence on land prices, and the importance of different factors varies with time under different macro-economic and urban development trends. The main sets of factors are those which affect the demand for land (economic activity and urban growth) and those which affect the land market (maintenance costs of land and existence of alternative investments). Both are affected by the overall socio-economic pattern of development of a country.

The value of most products and goods is affected by the amount of labour and capital invested in the production of these goods. The economic value of urban land is also affected by this factor.

The basis of aggregate land value is the overall investment in the urban area which have been carried out by public and private investments. In a market economy this aggregate is alloted to individual owners, basically through a lottery system run by the public authorities (through their planning decisions).

As urban growth continues, one would expect that land prices would continue to rise. Their fluctuations are in part due to variations in effective demand for land, principally as the result of general economic fluctuations. But some types of cities are less influenced than others by regional or international economy. This can affect both commercial and residential prices in tourist and financial centres, though usually commercial prices more. Especially in undeveloped countries is the ability of foreigners to pay high prices significant.

Also generally more significant for the less-developed countries is the importance of land as a financial investment. Land becomes attractive for investment where there are few profitable alternative investments and permanent inflation (which discourages holding cash assets). On the other hand, a suddenly high rate of inflation with its accompanying high interest rates will squeeze speculators who bought land on borrowed money and, if this is widespread, cause a collapse of the speculative market. This has happened in the last year in some Western countries. Higher taxation on vacant land would have the same effect.

In summary any theory of urban land must include these three points:

1. urban land has an inherently monopolistic character due to location effects;
2. the *prospective* change in use is the most important factor in increased land prices;
3. it is public authority decisions which determine many of the conditions of the land market; however, the question is whether public decisions today are more successful in influencing the land market than the land market (through high prices) is in affecting the implementation of the public authorities' plans.

PART THREE

Land Policies for Urban Growth

CHAPTER 9

Criteria for Evaluating Land Policies

1.1 SOCIO-ECONOMIC FACTORS IN URBAN LAND POLICY

Urban land policy is a part of urban-development policy and must be viewed within the framework of general development policies. One of the goals of development policies is to mobilize the resources of a country in order to achieve socio-economic objectives. The basic goal of urban land policy is to achieve the socio-economic maximization of land use.

The difficulty of establishing a land policy results from the nature of urban land. Land is both one of the natural resources of a nation and one of the essential goods necessary for the existence of the individual. Land is a basis for urban settlements where people live, work and use services. Therefore, a land policy has to be based on a socio-economic approach.

One of the goals of urban land policies may be defined as supplying land needed for urban development in the appropriate location at the right time. Because land policies are a part of development policies, they are influenced by the socio-economic and political structure of a country and its level of development.

The level of socio-economic development, the rate of urbanization, and the historical background are the factors creating the problems which land policies seek to solve. The rapid process of urbanization which is occurring in almost all countries in the world has created the problem of land scarcity in metropolitan areas, while the character and urgency of this problem depends on the socio-economic structure and the development level of a country.

The urbanization process as well as urban-land policies have a different character in countries with a federal structure and a system of autonomous local authorities than in countries with centralized government. Further, the concentration of population in a small number of large cities creates different problems than the development of a large number of medium-size cities. Finally, different problems are created for new urban dwellers in the old industrialized countries than for the new urban migrants in agricultural countries currently in the process of rapid industrialization.

Other important factors influencing land policies are the physical and demographic characteristics of a country. A small and densely populated country is apt to be more willing to accept planning and efficient land-use measures than a country with large unpopulated areas. Additional factors influencing urban land policies include the momentum of historical development and the role the state plays in both the economy and society of the nation. Clearly, then, there are many interacting elements which determine the land policies which a nation follows. Consequently, generalizations are difficult and one must be cautious about setting up any land-policy typology. Nevertheless, some central tendencies do seem to exist among groups of countries, but one must always keep in mind the limitations of such statements.

Countries with a strongly centralized political authority responsible for providing essential services and for the development of the national economy have different land policies than those countries with a federated structure and where private initiative is an important factor in development.

Urban-land policies are formulated according to the level of general national planning. In countries of planned economies the general comprehensive planning system has an impact both on urban development and on urban-land policies. Urban development is planned according to national economic development needs and the main objectives of the general plan are to use rationally all of the resources of the nation in order to achieve a higher level of economic development, and to increase the standard of living of the population.

The urban land policies of countries with different types of socio-economic structure are based on adapting different measures in order to achieve similar land-policy objectives. Policies and control measures are changing with the development level and changing socio-political structure of the country.

1.2. DEFINITION OF LAND POLICY

Policy may be defined as a set of measures aiming to achieve the goals formulated by the public authorities. The goals and the measures are influenced by the social and economic structure of a country and by the level of development.

Land policy is a part of the development policies which are influenced by various factors acting in the framework of the historical background of a country. Development policies will change with time as a result of a change in the factors influencing them. But in each period there exists a dominant factor influencing the definition of the development policy and goals.

Land policy might be seen as one of the means to achieve the goals of the development policy. At the same time the land policy is one of the factors influencing the development process. There generally exists a certain gap between the planning programme and its implementation. Land policy may be seen as one of the factors influencing the implementation of the development aims.

In each historical period the goal of land policies is defined according to the main purposes of the development process. Some examples may illustrate this assumption. In the USA the opening of new territories was one of the main goals of the development policies in the eighteenth and nineteenth centuries. The transfer of land from federal ownership to the railway companies at the cheapest prices was one of the incentives for attracting capital to erect the railway system which allowed the development of enormous new territories.

The Soviet Union is trying to achieve a high level of industrial production and exploit their natural resources in Siberia and other unpopulated regions, and have concentrated their efforts in establishing new towns near the natural resources. The immediate economic goal, with its promise of achievements to be enjoyed by future generations is the principal aim, while the level of services and the human living conditions in the new towns were secondary factors in the first stage of development. Only after achieving the primary economic results were human conditions improved. In contrast, in the Scandinavian countries today with a welfare-state system, the provision of land for housing is of first importance in land policy. Recently the decline in the quality of urban life has led to land policies in many countries whose aim is to ensure a decent urban environment in the future.

1.3. THE GOALS OF LAND POLICY

Foley* identifies three categories of planning goals: (1) "planning's main task is to reconcile competing claims for the use of limited land so as to provide a consistent, balanced and orderly arrangement of land uses"; (2) "planning's central function is to provide a good (or better) physical environment; a physical environment of such good quality is essential for the promotion of a healthy and civilised life"; (3) "planning, as part of a broader social programme, is responsible for providing the physical basis for a better community level".

The first category consists of general social goals of economic efficiency and social equity. These indicate that the plan at some time in the future is intended to provide a better life for people by achieving "balance and prosperity in the sub-regional economy and the greatest social welfare" and "the best living and working environment throughout the sub-region" together with ensuring "the greatest choice of opportunities".

The second category consists of a number of specific aims by which the general objectives can be achieved. These aims closely reflect the operational aims of physical planning as stated by Foley. For example, there are a number of aims which are concerned with the solution of land-use conflicts and the efficient use of land resources. These include aims that minimize the loss of good-quality farm land; avoid the loss of workable mineral resources; and keep the cost of utilities and land-development schemes to a minimum. There are also aims which relate to the provision of a good environment essential for the promotion of a healthy and civilized life. These include the location of new housing areas in pleasant surroundings and the location of new development in areas which will not be adversely affected by atmospheric and noise pollution.

The largest single group of objectives coincide with the concern of physical planning in providing the framework for a better basis of

* D. L. Foley, "British town planning: one ideology or three", *British Journal of Sociology*, Vol. 11, 1960.

community life. Such objectives include: locating new development so that there is the greatest possible choice of jobs available to all workers; increasing the potential range of shopping facilities available and providing the greatest possible accessibility to them for all residents; and providing sufficient roads and public transport to meet the future travel needs of the population.

1.4. CRITERIA OF POLICY EFFECTIVENESS

The effectiveness of policy measures depends to a great extent on the coordination of policy measures in order to minimize the side effects due to the interrelationship between different policy measures. The results achieved by a particular policy measure is a function not only of its efficient implementation but also a result of the effects provided by other, different measures.

The role of the institutional structure as a framework for implementing policies is one of the factors influencing policy results.

The policy programme is implemented on national, regional and local levels; therefore conflicts between national, regional and local authorities may hamper implementation. The effective participation of the local level in establishing the regional plan, and the efficient control by the national and regional level of implementation at the local level, is one of the main factors leading to policy efficiency. Local authorities must have restricted competence to change land use, yet the ability to influence the release of land needed for urban extension and renewal. The allocation of adequate financial resources for the implementation of local and regional plans by the National Regional Authority is important for the implementation of policy plans according to policy programmes.

Based on past experience, the establishment of public agencies responsible for carrying out different land-development schemes might be seen as one of the factors leading to efficient policy implementation.

1.5. KNOWLEDGE OF PLANNING LIMITS

Planning can never be perfect or all-encompassing. The power and ability of plans to bring about desirable changes is much more limited than is generally realized. The danger of exaggerating the extent to which policies may alter trends in population or employment should be recognized. There is a danger of adopting unrealistic time scales within which to bring about changes and trends in the short- and medium-term needs. The long-term possibilities are subject to still higher levels of uncertainty. We have to accept that the information available in a form which is useful, for example, to monitor change, and in particular to measure and evaluate the effects of various policies, is extremely limited. We have to accept that uncertainty, complex problems of values and valuation, as well as political decision, are involved in the calculus. Scientific knowledge may provide fundamental advances in scientific theory but it cannot provide all the answers for the formulation of social policy.

In view of such considerations, the planner should be sure that the process of effective synthesis between economic, social and spatial aspects is explicitly directed towards operational ends. This will result in a more modest strategy which has fewer hopes for the perfectability of man and is more conscious of the problems which face us in the here and now.

Classification of Land Policy Measures

The three types of land policy measures might be distinguished as follows:
1. legal measures influencing private land-use decisions;
2. taxation methods influencing private land-use decisions;
3. direct action by public authorities.

1. Legal measures influencing private land-use decisions

1.1. Land-use planning fixing space for different purposes in national, regional and local framework. National and regional long-run planning fixing areas for urban, agricultural, re-creation use. Local medium-term plans for the detailed allocation of land for different uses within the planned urban area.

1.2. Zoning control specifying permitted land uses and defining norms for different land-use categories. The fewer the number of categories the more freedom for developers and less control.

1.3. Subdivision of control through reparcelling the private sites according to the approved development scheme. Transfer to public authority of land needed for public purposes. (First introduced in Germany—readjustment—and recently carried out in Japan.)

1.4. Planned allocation of land for different urban purposes through fixing norms for collective needs (green space, public utility services) in relationship to population figures (Italy).

1.5. A greater degree of zoning, obligating the use of land according to the development scheme within a fixed time period. Introduced in some states in Germany and Spain.

1.6. Concentration of public investment in infrastructure works in some areas, forbidding building activity outside specified sites. Declaration of some areas as of future development, where land transactions are frozen (France).

1.7. Priority purchase rights for public authorities in the case of a landowner interested in selling his property (Sweden, France, Germany).

1.8. Expropriation and compensation methods and procedures.

2. *Taxation methods*

2.1. Property taxes.

2.2. Taxation on land profits.

2.3. Taxation for planning purposes. Taxes on vacant land planned for urban use or insufficiently used according to the planned scheme. Introduction of a higher rate of tax for holding a site unused in spite of the planning.

2.4. Evaluation methods and procedures.

3. *Land acquisition by public authorities*

3.1. Infrastructure works carried out by the public authorities in order to supply building land to the market.

3.2. Land acquisition by national, regional and local public authorities to carry out the planned development schemes.

3.3. Land acquisition for carrying out short-term development schemes (housing projects).

3.4. Advance land acquisition for creating reserves for future urban development as well as for other purposes (recreation).

In the following chapters we will be reviewing some examples in different countries of the more effective land policies in each particular category. Specifically, examples have been chosen in each category to illustrate the present limits of public authority intervention in the land market. Characteristic of the present situation is the uneasy coexistence between the private land market and the public sector.

CHAPTER 10

Land-Use Planning Controls

The current pattern of fragmented urban development, consuming large areas of land and leading to the declining quality of urban life and the destruction of good agricultural land in the vicinity of the city region, has led many countries to reassess their land-use planning controls that are now based mainly on local zoning ordinances.

Land-use planning arose in some countries as a part of national planning policies (UK), but in others (e.g. in the USA) it was a way of ensuring the highest land prices for urban and suburban plots by preventing undesirable adjacent development, and in some cases also promoting social class segregation. Recently, however, even in countries where the private land market is pre-eminent a change in the climate of opinion is becoming evident, as in Switzerland and the United States. There is a growing understanding that land must be treated as a natural resource, which people are given the privilege of using, rather than as a commodity which the owner has the right to use as he sees fit.

The most important new policies of land-use management employed recently by different countries (and to be discussed in detail below) are:

1. Long-term national and regional land-use planning (including environmental conservation).
2. Readjustment schemes (compulsory reparcelling of land in a given area).
3. Special land-use controls in areas of development.
4. Positive land-use controls (requiring development).
5. Pre-emption rights.
6. Methods of expropriation and compensation.

Many countries have set up long-range urban-development programmes by introducing a classification scheme for different parts of
the country according to the expected land use in the future. This
system differentiates between urban land use, future urban land use
(reserves for development), recreation areas, and agricultural land.
This classification has been introduced, for example, in Denmark,
The Netherlands, Spain, Taiwan, Korea and Japan. Other countries
are now beginning to follow this pattern but have not yet reached
the same level of sophistication as the above countries in the closeness
of control of actual land use on the basis of future planned use. The
aim of precise classification is to prevent the establishment of fixed
land uses which may be contrary to future urban planning. More than
that, the aim of this policy is the full utilization of land within the
boundaries of the urban plan.

This is the basic reason why building permits for urban development in the above countries were not given for those areas which
were planned for future urban development until full utilization of the
land within the jurisdiction of the existing urban communities was
achieved.

In most of the countries, as a result of the rise in the prices of land
in the big cities, in spite of unused land areas within the city, permits
are given for building in areas that are located far from the city. This
is the main reason for the vast urban sprawl outside of the city in many
countries while there exists unused land within the city.

To prevent this, *France* introduced the declaration of certain areas
as priority zones where unplanned development is prohibited and
public authorities have pre-emption rights. These are areas where
public authorities concentrate their efforts in carrying out development
works and building public housing schemes.

National and local authorities use various planning measures in
order to restrain the economic development of big city centres and to
encourage the development of less economically developed areas. In
the *United Kingdom* and *France*, special taxes were introduced on
erecting new industrial and office buildings, and building permits were
refused in congested areas, such as London and Paris. An interesting
example of using legal powers not only to fix land use but also to
impose use of land according to town-planning schemes was intro-

duced in Spain. Different countries and different conditions yield different proposals and solutions.

LONG-TERM NATIONAL AND REGIONAL PLANNING

Due to the recognition that planning only at a local level does not take into account the side-effects on adjacent areas (in particular areas of future urban expansion), the trend today is for more comprehensive planning which will control urban development throughout the country. There are different national land-use allocation schemes. First, only general outlines must be fixed, and then more detailed plans can be prepared. These functions may well take place at different levels of government. Therefore to be effectively implemented a long-term national scheme has to be flexible enough to change with changed conditions of growth, but not so flexible as to be set at will by public or private vested interests. This involves effective coordination between the various levels of government.

In the future, planning an urban region should replace planning for the separate agglomerations making up a city region. Additionally, future town-planning must not only be based on the planning schemes of a city region, but must be coordinated with development schemes at different administrative levels. This change of scale gives a development plan in the form of a general outline which serves as a basis for detailed plans (medium-term execution schemes) and municipal master plans.

Long-term planning *must* cover all possible features of urban life for a period of 20–30 years: population; standard of living; employment structure; means of transport; and areas required for the various amenities. It must also find various ways to adapt traffic conditions to the new needs of urban and city region growth; ensure land for housing, industry and recreation; account for the possible changes in need, and forecast different alternatives of future growth. In essence, development schemes providing for future needs must provide the detailed basis for urban development.

Many countries have recently introduced legislation obliging local authorities to produce long-term development plans requiring the approval of the central authority, which can then formulate regional and national development plans and coordinate all of the local plans. The local long-term development scheme approved by the Government serves as the basis for preparing the detailed execution schemes, specifying details of land use and setting the coefficients of land use in different urban zones. As a rule, the detailed scheme does not need the approval of the central authority; but representatives of the central authority usually supervise the implementation of the scheme to see that it satisfies the criteria of the central authority for town development and of the approved long-term development scheme. In certain countries, detailed execution schemes must be changed when they are in conflict with regional or national long-term planning schemes.

For example, the basic legislation in the Federal Republic of *Germany* was formulated in the Federal Construction Law of 23 June 1960; and amended by the Law of Construction Use of Land of 26 June 1962 and by the order of 26 November 1968. Basically, the Federal Law distinguishes between two kinds of town development schemes—surface-use schemes and built-up schemes.

In surface-use schemes, the general use of land is decided, while, in the framework of the municipalities, built-up schemes specify in detail the way in which individual sites will be used. The law concerning built-up schemes differentiates between municipal areas where building activity is allowed and municipal areas where such activity is forbidden. The law also forbids subdivision of a site without a special permit to avoid making small sites so that construction, planned according to the development schemes, will not encounter difficulties.

In *France*, the land-use policy law of 30 December 1967 takes into consideration recent developments in socio-economic planning by reinforcing the power of public authorities in dealing with the activities of development and urbanization. This law distinguishes systematically between the forecasting aspect of urban planning and the legal aspect of short-term plans. This distinguishing factor is carried out by replacing the *Plans directeurs* and the *Plans details d'urbanisme*, both dated 31 December 1953, by two new tools, the layout scheme of planning and urbanization, and the land-use plan.

The layout scheme consists of general directives for long-term urban development. It establishes general land uses, urban infrastructure and transport organization, and locates public services and other important town activities. Another aspect of the layout scheme is the location of areas for development and sectors for renovation.

The plan is intended to ensure equilibrium between the planned future and the existing present. The layout scheme, by its nature, is an undetailed document requiring further work. The plan provides directives for planning in the subsequent 10 years, but it obviously must take into consideration development beyond that period. The scheme is drawn up by interested public bodies, local authorities and government ministries, in coordination with their own diversified plans. Once published, the layout scheme has only administrative power; but the different authorities must act accordingly.

The land-use plan contains two basic, but contradictory objectives: urban development and urban protection. The plan determines the urban boundaries for the relatively short period of 5–10 years. Within the urban area, the land-use plan fixes two elements for each district: the type of land use and the maximum land-use coefficient (the relation between the built-up area and the surface of land). In extreme cases, the land can be exploited beyond the determined coefficient; but, obviously, enough of the land can be developed to a lesser extent.

The plan is legally binding on both the individual and the authority, and thus is an important tool in regulating the matters of land ownership.

Despite the rigid boundary that it draws between agricultural and urban land, the land-use plan determines the land reserves for future urban development. This "reservation" is carried out according to conclusions derived from the layout scheme.

According to the Lege Ponte (bridge law) in *Italy*, municipalities that are on the list of local authorities are required to submit a development scheme (General Regulation Plan) to the General Council of Public Works (highest national planning authority), which has to formulate its remarks within one year, while the municipality has to carry out the recommendations within 180 days. If the municipality does not implement the ordinance of the General Council, the regional representative of the central authority has to nominate an expert to prepare a town-planning scheme in accordance with the remarks of the central authorities.

The Lege Ponte states: "Restrictions must be scrupulously observed in respect of building density, height, distance between buildings, as well as maximum relation (proportions) between spaces intended for residential and productive establishment and public spaces of those reserved for collective activities, public gardens and parking, must be observed in all Municipalities with a view to forming new town planning instruments or revising the existing ones".

Article 3 of the Decree establishes the maximum proportions between areas intended for residences and public spaces, and those intended for collective activities: public gardens or parking (exclusive of streets). The minimum apportionment that must be "scrupulously observed" is $18 \, \text{m}^2$ per resident (an average volume of $80 \, \text{m}^3$ assigned, equalling $25 \, \text{m}^2$ of gross habitable surface).

Emphasis in the *Netherlands* is on a maximum of autonomy at the provincial and municipal levels of government, with coordination being the task of the national level of government. The Physical Planning Act of 1965 provides the legal basis for the town and country planning policy of the government, specifying the National Physical Planning Agency, which is assigned to draw up the policy of the Ministry of Housing and Physical Planning. The Housing Minister must report to Parliament once a year on the policy pursued. The Agency does not prepare national plans, but simply sets down general policy guidelines, while the formulation of plans is left to the municipal and provincial governments.

The municipalities are additionally obliged to draw up a development plan for sections outside the built-up area. These plans then constitute the basis for granting building and construction permits. The municipalities are also empowered to draw up a structural plan for the municipal territory indicating its future development. The provinces can, at their discretion, draw up a regional plan for one or more parts, or for the whole of the territory of the province, indicating in outline form the future development of the area. The structural plans of the municipality, as well as the regional plan of the province, can be regarded and treated as development programmes. Approval is required only for the municipal plan; and, to this end, it must be submitted for review to the provincial administrative body.

Provinces can compel the municipalities to draw up or to revise a structural or development plan, within a given period of time; in addition, they can give directives for the contents of a development plan, if supermunicipal interests are involved. The Minister of Housing and Physical Planning can, in turn, compel the provincial administration to draw up or to revise a regional plan within a given period of time, as well as give directives with respect to the contents of a regional plan. In so far as supermunicipal interests demand, the Minister may also give instructions with respect to the contents of the directives that the provinces must give to the municipalities.

The fundamental functional tool in *Spain* is the Municipal Plan of Urbanization and its development into partial plans and urbanization projects. The council of the corresponding municipality is usually in charge of its preparation, and its approval goes through the following stages: (1) initial approval by the municipality; (2) publication for a period of one month; (3) provisional approval by the municipality; (4) sanction by National Council or the Provincial Commission of Urbanization (when it refers to plans related to capitals of provinces or cities with more than 50,000 population) and publication of the final approval in the Council Bulletin.

Furthermore, if the municipality does not promote the elaboration of urbanization plans within the periods established by law, the Central Commission of the Provincial Commission for Urbanization can order its preparation by the technical organs of the Ministry of Housing or by its Provincial Deputation.

In *Sweden* the Building Act contains four types of plan: regional plan, master plan, town plan and building plan. All detailed plans have to be ratified by regional and national authorities while comprehensive plans seldom go further than approval by the municipal authorities and thereby provide only non-official guidance for the expansion of municipalities. About 3000 detailed plans are ratified every year, half of which are town plans, with municipal responsibilities for implementation, and the others building plans, where the responsibilities devolve on the landowners jointly.

After a detailed plan has been ratified, real-estate formation has to take place in accordance with the intentions of the plan. Only after that can the municipality grant a building permit. One prerequisite for land being used for urban settlement is that a detailed plan has been approved for the area. Outside such an area building permits for urban purposes may, in principle, not be granted. As resources for planning activities are sometimes inadequate, exception may be granted by the county administration if special circumstances exist. If a building permit is refused, the landowner has no right to compensation. This applies to to urban as well as rural settlements, the latter according to amendments to the laws as recent as 1972.

Parallel with comprehensive physical planning, all municipalities have to prepare yearly residential building programmes for the next 5 years. This has connections with the national housing policy as the programmes provide, besides particulars on housing, the basis for planning social services, building of roads and mains and for development agreements with landowners on land acquisition. In order to be able to carry out planned expansion, the municipal authorities have a number of means at their disposal for the acquisition of land where deemed necessary.

Control of building in rural areas rests primarily with the municipalities in granting building permits. If areas are considered to be so valuable that they should be preserved more or less in their natural state, the Nature Conservation Act contains provisions for protecting these assets. It is the county administration and its board which declares areas as nature preserves or protected shores in order to preserve the landscape. New building within such areas requires permission from the county administration as well as from the municipal authorities.

In *Denmark*, the cornerstone of the 1969 reform was the Urban and Rural Zones Act which, with effect from 1 January 1970, divided the whole of Denmark into urban zones and rural zones together with "summerhouse" (second home) districts. *Urban zones* (and summerhouse districts) are those areas which are allocated for urban development in (1) approved town plans or (2) approved building ordinances, or (3) approved urban development plans. (Thus the "urban zone" concept was linked to specific types of public authority plans and not to subdivision agreements, sewerage, street works, etc.) The remainder of the country is defined as a rural zone.

In urban zones and summerhouse districts, development must take place in accordance with the town plan and other rules. In rural zones, only development for agricultural, forestry and fishery purposes can take place freely. All other development and likewise the change of use of undeveloped areas for purposes other than agriculture, forestry and fishery requires permission. In areas covered by an urban development committee, such permission may be granted by this committee, in other areas by the county council. *That is to say, the power to grant permission is not vested in the communes but in a regional authority.*

Appeals can be lodged with the Ministry of Housing by the owner, by the appropriate commune, or by the countryside conservation committee.

However, as urban growth continues (and must continue) to take place, the urban zones must naturally be capable of being continuously extended; and in order to limit speculation in land values, it is expected that at all times enough land will be included in urban zones to provide 12 years' supply. Such extensions are effected by proposals for one of the above-mentioned types of plans, which result in the creation of an urban zone. Leaving aside urban development plans, it is the commune that makes proposals for a town plan or a building ordinance, and then the Ministry of Housing considers whether the plan should be approved and the urban zone established.

To summarize, it is the regional authorities, county councils, and urban development committees, who decide whether in individual cases permission shall be granted (within zones) for plot subdivision, development or change of use. But it is the commune and the Ministry of Housing who decide whether large new areas shall be changed from rural zones to urban zones (or summerhouse districts).

The *United Kingdom*'s urban planning and development programme emphasizes local government authority over detailed planning, leaving the central government to formulate broad planning strategies. The Town and Country Planning Act of 1968 makes a distinction between "structure" plans—broad indications of future policies which require ministerial approval—and "local" plans, which are the sole responsibility of the local planning authorities, and do not require ministerial approval in detail. Other legislation (e.g. the Civil Amenities Act of 1967) details large-scale comprehensive positive planning of whole areas of special historic or architectural interest, as opposed to the mere preservation of individual buildings. Development of recreational facilities in the country was given encouragement by the Countryside Act of 1968.

Each local planning authority must produce a development plan for their area, and this plan requires the Minister's approval. The plan consists not only of maps showing in urban areas the places where different kinds of development are intended to take place, but also written statements of policies applying to urban and rural areas. The development plan has to be approved by the Minister, and, in this way, there is a means of coordinating policies.

In the future, the Minister will be concerned only with the broad strategy and not with detailed local allocations. If a local planning authority proposes to grant planning permission contrary to the provisions of the development plan, they must advertise the application and send a copy of it to the Minister, so that the public will have an opportunity to express their view on the application, and so the Minister may, if he wishes, exercise his power to call the application in and deal with it himself.

Under the 1968 system, the entire country will, in due course, be covered by structure plans setting out broad principles for land use, but, in addition, many parts of the urban areas and some parts of the rural areas are likely to be covered by local plans, giving much greater detail and precision.

Perhaps the most significant development in urban land-use planning in recent years has been the realization that the control of road traffic must be regarded as an essential feature of urban planning generally, following the principles laid down in Professor Buchanan's Report, *Traffic in Towns*.

India. It is very difficult to summarize or generalize the position regarding land planning laws because the statutes governing or affecting land-use planning and their contents are varied. Thus, for instance, there are, in addition to the planning acts, a number of others including slum-clearance acts, periphery development control acts, restriction of land-uses acts, housing board acts, municipal acts and so on. Subject to this limitation, the present position stated is that in most states the existing planning legislation is rather old. In the southern Indian states of Andhra Pradesh, Tamil Nadur and Kerala, the basic planning law dates back to 1920 when the Madras Town Planning Act was enacted and even earlier to 1913 when Travancore Planning Regulations were passed. In a few other states such as Rajasthan, Bihar and Orissa, the relevant act appends the planning function to improvement trusts which exist in very few urban areas. In all of the old acts, the planning jurisdiction remains severely confined to municipal limits and the administrative jurisdiction of the improvement trusts which are generally smaller than the municipalities.

Taking into consideration the lack or inadequacy of proper planning legislation, the central Town and Country Planning Organization prepared for the guidance of the state governments a "Model Town and Country Planning Act". It is based on British planning principles and practices, as contained in the country's Town and Country Planning Act of 1947. As the Model Law emanated from the central Government's Town and Country Planning Organization, all the laws enacted after or those presently being drafted have generally followed or are likely to follow this model.

In view of its influence some salient features of the Model Law should be summarized. It provides for the establishment of a State Town and Country Planning Board to advise the state governments on town planning matters and to guide, direct and assist local planning authorities in the preparation and enforcement of "Development plans". It permits the designation of a local body as the planning authority. It requires a present land-use map and register to be prepared for every planning area. Thereafter it requires an "interim development plan" to be prepared followed by a "comprehensive development plan". At every stage there is provision for public objections and hearings and the state governments' approval. After the enforcement of the plan no development or change of use of land is to be undertaken except with the prior permission from the local planning authority. It stipulates the levy of a development charge for the grant of planning permission. Detailed provisions have been made to regulate the contents of the plans, procedure for the enforcement of planning controls and the assessment and levy of the development charge and ways to deal with violations of the plans.

The above sketchy description of planning legislation would not be complete without mentioning the Maharashtra Regional and Town Planning Act of 1966. It is not only the latest but perhaps the most comprehensive of the Indian laws on the project. It provides for the establishment of "regions" in the state of Maharashtra as well as the establishment of regional planning boards. These boards consist of a chairman, the Director of Town Planning of the state government, not more than four members drawn from the local authorities within the planning region and not more than six persons possessing special knowledge or experience of planning, industry, commerce and agriculture—all appointed by the state governments. The Act provides that the contents of the regional plans may include allocation of land for various uses and land reservations for certain authorities, such as transport and communication, water supply, drainage and sewerage, reservations of sites for new towns, relocation of industry and population from overpopulated areas, etc.

The Act constitutes the local planning authority though it provides for special planning authorities for any area within the jurisdiction of one or more local authorities. It provides for joint development plans or joint planning schemes to be prepared by the special planning authorities. Next in the hierarchy of plans are the development plans which are prepared by the local authorities within the framework of the regional plan. It enables town planning schemes to be prepared for certain smaller areas within the jurisdiction of a local planning authority. Unlike the model, this legislation makes it optional for the local authorities to prepare an interim development plan unless the state government directs them to do so. The planning procedure is the same as in the Model Act. The act also provides for the designation of sites for new towns and the establishment of new towns development authorities.*

Indonesia. The law and rules governing land-use planning activity is the Town Planning Ordinance of 1948. The salient features of the ordinance are that it provides for the preparation of two types of plans,

---

*UN, *Urban Land Policies and Land Use Control Measures,* Vol. II; *Asia and the Far East,* New York, 1973.

namely, town plans and detailed plans. The former are in the nature of broad land-use plans showing designation of areas for public housing, industrial and commercial uses, public structures and social amenities, circulation systems, protection of historical and cultural monuments, open spaces and green areas, etc. The town plans also must show the types of buildings to be constructed or permitted in certain areas. The detailed plans are expected to show detailed provisions governing building and ground works according to building regulations. The ordinance also obligates the councils to divide the building areas into restricted zones for projected construction within which no building licences for building construction, renovation, alteration, expansion, addition or for particular kinds or types of buildings are to be granted.

The planning procedure provided in the ordinance requires that the mayor and alderman consult with various governmental departments, higher government authorities and public utilities undertaking works within the municipality. After these consultations the town plan is adopted and submitted through the resident and the director to the national government.*

Japan.† A new City Planning Law, which abrogated the then existing law on this subject and the Law Concerning Building Land Development Projects, was enacted in 1968. Briefly, the law provides for the designation of any area, including a built-up area in a city, town or village, for which integrated development, improvements and construction as a unified urban area is necessary. The criteria for the selection of such areas are provided by a cabinet order. A city-planning area extending over two or more prefectures is designated by the Minister of Construction after hearing the opinions of the prefectural governors. A city planning area within a prefecture is designated by the prefectural governor after ascertaining the opinion of the cities, towns and villages concerned and of the local city planning councils.

Two types of planning areas are envisaged, the urbanization promotion areas and urbanization control areas. The former means an existing built-up area or such an area where preferential treatment has

* *Ibid.,* p. 89.
† p. 90.

to be given for systematic urbanization in the course of 10 years or less. The latter is an area where premature urban development should be curbed. Every city plan should decide zoning areas and districts and urban facilities as listed in the law. The city plan may contain one or more of the following types of built-up area development projects: land readjustment projects, new residential built-up area development projects, industrial estate development projects and built-up area renewal projects.*

Singapore. The legal basis for physical planning activity is provided by the Planning Ordinance of 1959 and the Master Plan (prepared in 1955 and approved in 1958 under the provisions of the Singapore Improvement Ordinance) together with all subsequent alterations and additions approved by the Governor-General or the Minister. The Planning Ordinance provides for the appointment of a competent authority for enforcing the ordinance or any of its parts or provisions. The authority for matters concerning the Master Plan and development rest with the Chief Planner and for matters relating to land development the authority resides with the Chief Building Surveyor.

The ordinance provides that the Master Plan (of 1958) shall be reviewed at least once in every 5 years. However, proposals for its alteration or addition may also be submitted by the competent authority (i.e., the Chief Planner) to the Minister at any time. Additions to the Master Plan may take the form of proposals for comprehensive development or redevelopment of any area which in the opinion of the Chief Planner should be developed or redeveloped as a whole for the purpose of dealing satisfactorily with conditions of a bad layout or obsolete development or for the relocation of population or industry, etc. Section 7 of the Act empowers the minister to make rules prescribing the form, contents and procedure to be followed in the preparation, submission and approval of additions or alterations to the Master Plan.

Another aspect of the ordinance is that it provides for the levy of a development charge for planning permission given by the Chief Planner which permits development in excess of the average density prescribed

* *Ibid.*, p. 96.

in the town map or the central area map of the Master Plan or in excess of the average density of 50 persons per acre in the Island map of the Master Plan and certain alterations to the Master Plan. The development charge may be levied at different rates. Certain exemptions from the payment of the development charge are, however, provided and it is levied at different rates.*

In general land-use planning has been less comprehensively applied in the developing countries. For example, in Latin America a UN report states:

> To summarize, then, with the exception of Venezuela and Chile, although the regulation of land has been an issue for some time, there are few fully comprehensive, coherent and functional urban land control regulations in existence in Latin America. Even in the case of these two countries the practical results are only relatively successful due to the lack of sufficient legislation. Brazil is in a similar situation at present. It is impossible in such a short time to judge how successfully the new system of control of land subdivisions will be applied.
>
> In the majority of cases in South America, since practically all of the urban master plans are out of date, zoning at the present time and until the above-mentioned prerequisites are met, will be totally inadequate. Even in those cases where the plans include zoning standards they are frequently not applied in practice. Some plans are only partially completed in order to avoid dealing with complicated problems that are frequently politically explosive, or because of the demoralizing impacts of prolonged legal procedures that offer little hope for success. Indeed, this latter point arises because of conflicting philosophies in the basic legislation and in its legal interpretation.†

In spite of the shortcomings it may be said that Venezuela patterned its urban planning activities more or less like that of Europe. The starting-point for urban planning may be taken as the year 1947, when a number of master plans were prepared. They were undertaken without a full knowledge of the facts and the results obtained were not very appreciable. Since 1959 a new effort has been made to adjust the plans, this time with more satisfactory results. At the present time, master plans exist for the majority of the cities. All cities of 30,000 inhabitants or more either have an operational master plan or are engaged in preparing one.

The national government influences these master plans indirectly, as the plans must be submitted by the municipalities for approval with

* *Ibid.*, p. 98.
† UN, *Urban Land Policies and Land Use Control Measures,* Vol. IV: *Latin America,* New York, 1973, p. 51.

respect to their fulfilment of sanitary regulations. By means of this informal channel the national government is able to exercise significant control over the plans even though the control is not established by law. This enables it to standardize the criteria used by the local governments and to follow a rational urban development policy. In the majority of cases, the Directorate of Planning provides technical and financial assistance to the local governments. The conditions under which this assistance is granted enables the national authorities to exercise direct control during the preparatory stages of the plan-making process.

The first master plan for Caracas was drawn up in 1938 and was updated in 1952 and 1958. A new plan with projections up to 1990 was recently prepared for the metropolitan area, the federal district and the district of Sucre.

In 1965 *Chile* created a Ministry of Housing and Urbanization (Ministerio de Vivienda y Urbanismo), the major objectives of which are "the planning of urban development and improvement so that the *poblaciones* may become organic units, provided with the services necessary to permit their full development".

Of the 270 municipalities existing in Chile, 80 have master plans in force, although many have required updating in recent years. The Ministry of Housing has been helping the municipalities in the preparation of their city plans. Moreover, all municipalities with over 1000 inhabitants are required to have a master plan.

In Chile, it is evident that the real control over land-use is exercised by the national government through local master plans, which it must, in all cases, approve. Everything connected with the planning and implementation of the intercommunity plans is also its responsibility. In the case of intercommunity plans, problems in regulating the use of land can easily be controlled by the national government as well. In these cases it can control the use of the land not only within the city limits but also on surrounding rural land. The Directorate of Planning simply requests information from the National Office of Planning (Oficiano de Planificacion Nacional) as to the prospects and projections in the area under study. The plan was enacted in 1958. An example of an intercommunity plan is in Valparaiso.*

* *Ibid.*, pp. 40, 49.

Uruguay may be considered among those countries that have urban development plans and policies. Montevideo has a master plan which for many years has been in use and continually updated, despite the high degree of urbanization reached by the country and concentrated in this capital city. There it has been possible to maintain a relatively high degree of regulation within the city limits and in the adjacent areas. Plans are in use or in preparation by the offices set up for this purpose in Paysandu, Salto, Melo, Fray Bentos and Colonia, but these efforts are limited in scope or incomplete in contrast to Montevideo.

In Uruguay, the "Townships Law" (*Ley de Centros Poblados*) was enacted by the Parliament in 1946. It was applied only in the city of Montevideo. Although procedures were established for its implementation, exceptions were permitted when approved by a majority vote of the departmental council. This deprived the system of most of its potential force. The "Townships Law" applied only in Montevideo and was an effective mechanism for land-use regulation. As a consequence, the city growth was rational, taking note of the serious problems of other urban centres of Latin America which were not controlled in the past.*

ENVIRONMENTAL PLANNING

The concern in recent years over the deteriorating quality of the environment, both through the destruction of areas of natural beauty near urban areas and the loss of historic areas of cities, has led several countries to introduce measures to ensure the preservation of buildings of historic or architectural interest and, more important, to ensure enough green space in the urban region. The United Kingdom has been a pioneer in Green Belt schemes: but recently even countries with a federal structure and local autonomy (the United States and Switzerland) have introduced measures on a national or regional level to ensure land use which preserves the environment.

The Green Belt programme in the *United Kingdom* was started in 1947 as a result of the Town and Country Planning Act of that year. It was perhaps the first comprehensive long-term national planning programme ever to be implemented. Based on the Greater London

† *Ibid.*, p. 50.

plan of 1944, which sought to control urban growth through compulsory land-use controls, all development was permanently prohibited in a contiguous zone up to 10 miles deep surrounding London. Most of the land in the Green Belt remains in private ownership, but with less than 10% of the land in urban or industrial use. Existing urban areas within the Green Belt could "round off" their boundaries, and approximately 1·4 million people now live within the area. The government attempts to secure public access to private non-urban land in the Green Belt areas by the payment of a small consideration to landowners.

Another innovation in UK land-use environmental planning is the complete control over land-use exercised by the Peak District National Park, located less than 50 miles from seven of the ten largest cities in England.

The *United States* has had one of the weakest tradition of government land-use controls in the world, particularly above the local level. However, even there a number of regional and state planning agencies and regulations have, recently, been introduced to control land-use in the interest of a better environment, and a bill is pending in Congress (the Jackson Bill) making such state-wide planning mandatory in all states and supplying federal funds for this purpose. Generally those states which have experienced the most rapid growth in recent years have been the ones which have introduced more comprehensive and stringent land-use controls.

Hawaii has had a state-wide regulation of land use since 1961. The Land Use Law mandates a State Land Use Commission to determine land-use in the islands according to four categories—conservation, agricultural, rural and urban. Within each urban area land use is determined by pre-existing local zoning procedures; in the other areas, however, any changes in land use must be approved by the Land Use Commission or (for conservation land) by the state Department of Land and Natural Resources. The purpose of the law was to conserve agricultural land and natural features from the pressures of growth in a state that was experiencing rapid population growth and the expansion of tourism. A further purpose was to allow compact and efficient land use in urban areas; to this end the designated urban areas included what was considered enough land for urban growth for 10 years in the future. However, as much land has been held vacant in the designated urban areas for speculative purposes, land prices and housing costs have increased. It has been suggested that the goals mentioned above in the Land Use Law are somewhat conflicting.

Vermont adopted an Environmental Control Law in 1970 setting up a state Environmental Board. This Board prepares a state land-use plan, and all development above a certain size and in certain areas of natural beauty must have a permit from the Board (which for administrative purposes has set up seven districts—regional commissions). Vermont has also attempted to limit speculative land purchase (mostly of second homes by residents of the nearby north-east US urban region) by taxing more heavily land recently bought.

Florida, also an area of natural beauty threatened by rapid retirement home development and tourism, has recently (1972) passed a Land and Water Environmental Management Act which sets up an Administration Commission directly responsible to the governor. Unlike the other states, this commission can only designate (by recommendation to the governor) certain areas (limited to 5% of total state area at any one time) as "areas of critical state concern" in which the state requires and oversees the implementation of detailed land-use controls. In addition, any land development which would have an impact on more than one county can be designated a "development of regional impact" which requires a development permit and a regional impact study by the regional authority concerned.

Other states which have recently enacted environmental legislation (mainly to protect areas of natural beauty, such as shorelands and wetlands) include Maine, Massachusetts and Wisconsin.

On a regional level, two prominent examples of environmental planning are the San Francisco Bay Conservation and Development Commission and the New England River Basins Commission. The San Francisco Bay Commission has the power to control all development on the shoreline of the San Francisco Bay, in the interests of preserving it for water-oriented uses. It has been able to successfully block the filling in of a good deal of the wetlands area of the Bay by developers. The New England River Basins Commission has prepared plans for land-use in the watershed area of the major New England rivers, on the basis of coordination and cooperation with the appropriate state and Federal authorities.

Certain local authorities in suburban areas threatened by urban growth have also taken more positive action in limiting development and requiring that it be coordinated with the construction of infra-structure works (Ramapo, NY) and with the preservation of out-standing environmental features of natural beauty (Boulder, Colorado).

Currently there are several bills before Congress which would en-courage states to prepare comprehensive land-use planning. The strongest is the Jackson Bill (S. 268), introduced by Senator Henry Jackson (D-Wash), which would require states to develop a land-use planning process within 3 years, and a land-use programme within 5 years. Federal funds would be available for this purpose, and the government would monitor progress after 5 and 8 years. Still under debate is whether there would be financial sanctions (withdrawal of other Federal aid) against non-complying states. Other bills currently under consideration would set up either a federal National Growth Planning Council (Hartke Bill) or an Office of Balanced National Growth and Development (Humphrey Bill) to oversee national land-use planning and coordinate efforts to this end.

The Switzerland Experience

In March 1972 the Federal Assembly decided to decree and to carry out immediately some urgent space-planning measures. The federal decision, which will be effective until 31 December 1975, has laid upon the Cantons the obligation to determine, and to convey to the know-ledge of the competent federal department, a plan concerning "pro-visionally protected zones" covering territories, the occupation and utilization of which, as to construction purposes, must be limited or prevented. In accordance with the decision, the following areas must be declared "provisionally protected zones": the shores of rivers and lakes, picturesque sites or beauty spots, historical places, natural and cultural monuments, recreation areas near agglomerations, threatened regions. A space planning delegate and an advisory committee have also been appointed.

Late in May 1972 the Federal Council approved and referred to the Federal Assembly a bill which will provisionally contain the main operative parts of Article 22 of the Constitution. The purpose of the bill is to ensure space planning by the Cantons and by the Confederation, by promoting and coordinating their efforts in this domain. In particular, the law tends to mark the boundaries of the territory that must be occupied, to ensure its wise utilization, and to maintain the character and beauty of the landscape, and to create recreation zones. The Confederation will determine the basic principles, whereas the Cantons will ensure the space planning itself. The Federal Assembly have now approved these measures.

The Local, Regional and National Planning Institute of the Federal Technical University in Zurich issued in spring 1973 its voluminous Final Report concerning the national land planning picture for Switzerland. The Report had been ordered by the Federal Economy Department in accordance with the federal law concerning measures for the promotion of the construction of dwellings of 19 March 1965, and with the corresponding executive ordinances; the Report should constitute an essential basis of optimum settlement in Switzerland.

According to the provisions of the federal decree concerning urgent space planning measures, land plans had to be established by the Cantons and returned late in November 1972 to the federal department involved indicating the territories whose occupation and utilization—for construction purposes—had been provisionally limited or prevented. In accordance with this procedure, the Cantons have assigned to the federal requirements specific interpretations. In the French-speaking region of Switzerland, for instance, a definite difference has been found between Geneva, which is a city-canton and which is progressive in matters of space planning, and other cantons, which interpreted the urgent measures in quite a broad way. Although the space-planning problems have been treated very differently from canton to canton, it already seems that the urgent decree, which will be followed by a federal law, has exerted an accelerating effect everywhere.

As a result of Article 20 of the Federal Water Protection Law, and Article 15 of the corresponding Water Protection Ordinance, building is no longer allowed in all Switzerland, starting from 1 July 1972, except in already constructed zones, or in an area within authorized general sewerage projects. This was regarded as an historic turning-point. In determining what constitutes the last-mentioned category, at most a doubling of the existing population can be allowed in the context of locally suited development of industry, trade and tourism over a maximum 15-year period. Thus preservation of water resources has become an important space-planning instrument.

The federal decision of March 1972 concerning urgent measures in the field of space planning is not only of considerable importance for the preservation of the still unspoiled landscape, but also, to some extent, for the protection of irreplaceable centuries of old local buildings within towns.

The coordinated space-planning office of the two *Basels* published in July 1972 the regional plan "Landschaft" in a sketch form. This is one among several regional plans and is closely related to the settlement plan published in 1970. Its purpose is the protection, the orderly utilization, the arrangement and equipment of the still unsettled free spaces. The protection requirements regarding landscape, nature, water, agriculture, recreation and monuments were taken into account. After an extensive petition process, the revised plans were presented to the two parliaments for a binding decision and came into force in 1973. The text is the first parliamentarily decided cantonal *landschaft* plan in Switzerland, and serves as an overall directive plan in line with the urgent federal decision concerning space planning. In 1974 the settlement and transportation plan became legally binding.

As a result of the proposal of a representative of the Cantonal Council, the development committee of the Canton of *Geneva* passed unanimously in November 1972 a bill that modifies the law regarding land use. According to this bill, the wood and forest zones and green areas are more accurately defined, identified and protected against constructions and transformations. Furthermore, the State Council would have to extend the green zone in proportion to the increase of the needs of the city agglomeration.

A bill has been brought in at the Central Council of Geneva in 1972 and is in the process of study by the parliamentary committee. The bill has to do with prohibiting the building of villas or other so-called country seats in agricultural zones, even on properties exceeding $40,000\,m^2$ on which it is permissible to build at present. It has been found that the freedom granted to the owners of the last-mentioned grounds are the sources of difficulties, since villas or mansions have been built on elevations which are detrimental to the harmony of the environment. It is a matter of deciding whether a radical, or a less absolute, decision, authorizing only very definite construction on defined building sites, is preferable.

In order to protect its landscape against the detriment caused by the construction of buildings, the Canton of Vaud has chosen to interpret very strictly the urgent federal space planning decree. In its enacting regulation, the State Council of the Canton of Vaud has decided to subject to protective regime all the territories located outside the extension zones that are legalized at present or are about to become so, and outside the present perimeters of the localities. The same applies to the portions of these zones or perimeters which are probably not to be occupied, or in which such occupation is not desirable, while taking into account the foreseeable development of the locality during the next 10 years and a sensible and purposeful occupation of the territory. Furthermore, the decree authorizes the State Council to withdraw the building permits delivered before the coming into force of the decree if their utilization might compromise the purposes of the decree.

A law of the Canton of Vaud, which came into force in January 1972, contains the following article: "The zones assigned for the extension of an agglomeration must be justified by the foreseeable development of the community or of the region during the next 10 years. The access highways, the inlet, disposal and treatment of wastewaters must be anticipated and executed within this time limit. The 10-year period starts on January 1, 1972, for the zones that were previously authorized." Furthermore, a construction permit will be given only when the real estate is ready for building including means for the treatment of wastewaters.

READJUSTMENT PROGRAMMES

Readjustment programmes provide for the compulsory seizure of land needed by the public authorities for development, with compensation given in the form of equivalent plots of land in the same area. The land-readjustment method has been extensively used in *Japan* and the Republic of *Korea* with a commendable measure of success. In *Japan*, this method is called *Tochi Kukaskuseri*. Based on the German *Lex Adickes*, the concept was first introduced in the Arable Land Readjustment Law enacted in 1909. The concept was subsequently incorporated into the City Planning Law of 1919 and the method has been used extensively since. It is reported that land readjustment covering 1500 km² or about 27% of the country's total urban land area has been already executed or is being carried out.* Between 1920 and 1945 land readjustments were undertaken for some 600 km². These included the rehabilitation projects after the great earthquake disaster in 1923. From 1945 to 1965 another 900 km² were developed or redeveloped using this technique. Included were sizeable areas along the new Tokaido line of the National Railways between Tokyo and Osaka and in the cities of Hashima and Yokohama. On the basis of the experience gained, particularly from the projects carried out following the great earthquake of 1923 and after 1945, a separate law on this subject, the Land Readjustment Law, was enacted in 1953.

Land-readjustment projects are carried out within a city planning area. Their main objectives are to provide a specified area with adequate public facilities (roads, parks, water supply, sewage), to rearrange properly the land uses and to effect a reallocation of housing sites on the basis of a new layout. These projects do not drastically affect the rights of the land owners and the holders of other rights. Land within the project area which is required for public uses is obtained through *Cenbu*, or the offer by the landowners of part of their land for public uses, and *Hoyuchi*, i.e. a land reservation for meeting the project costs. Since the area of land for public uses in a new layout is generally more than before, the reconstituted plots are to some extent smaller. However, the provision of services and facilities and the improved layout frequently results in the reduced plots being valued at equal to or more than the value of the original plot.

These projects are carried out either by public organizations, such as national government agencies, local government bodies, and public corporations, or by private organizations usually called Land Readjustment Associations which are organized by landowners and other

---

* *Tochi Kukaskuseri, Land Readjustment in Japan*, 1968.

rights holders in the project area. In both cases the procedure for executing the projects is the same and is governed by law.

In *India*, land pooling and readjustment, which are undertaken as a part of some approved "town-planning scheme", are used successfully by a few cities such as Gujarat and Maharashtra. This technique involves the pooling together of land and then a subsequent redistribution of plots to the landowners on the basis of a new layout. Before redistribution the land is properly developed and serviced, and the land required for public uses such as roads, "*tot*-lots", parks and schools, etc., is deducted from the total pool. The redistribution of land is proportionate to the original size of the plots held by the owners and a land-value assessment is made before and after the execution of the town-planning scheme. The difference between the value of an owner's original plot and the proportionately reduced but developed and serviced plot allotted after the execution of the scheme is adjusted by the payment of cash compensation. Important advantages of this measure are that it minimizes compensation and development costs and causes less displacement of people than is the case in outright compulsory acquisition. Yet it has been difficult to employ this measure in built-up areas because of resistance from tenants, if not from the landowners.

SPECIAL LAND-USE CONTROLS IN DESIGNATED AREAS

The most comprehensive programme along these lines has been established in France. Legislation enacted in 1958 and 1962 provided for "zones a urbanizer à priorité ZUP", i.e. priority urban development zones, and "zones d'amenagement differé ZAD", i.e. zones of deferred development.

Priority urban-development zones (ZUP) are designated by decrees of the Minister of Housing, after consultation with the local authorities within whose jurisdiction the zones are located. For builders, in zones decreed as ZUP, (a) building licences on land within a certain distance from the zone may be refused if it is insufficiently developed land, or if the contractor can obtain equally suitable sites within the zone; (b) any housing development of more than 100 units must be located within the zone.

For the landowner, the ZUP decree gives the right of the public authority or its representative to stipulate the land uses within the zone. For 4 years from the date of publication of the decree, any land up for sale within the zone must first be offered to the public agency concerned.

However, not even the device of "priority urban development zones" could stem speculation. Demand for land increased in areas adjoining ZUPs since land values in these areas rose perceptibly.

To limit such occurrences, a further law passed in 1962 created "zones of deferred development", ZAD, which are larger areas designated for future urban growth. Within them all new development is frozen, though building licences in previously developed areas cannot be refused.

The creation of special planning areas influenced the stabilization of land prices inside the areas, but shifted speculation to neighbouring areas. Therefore, in order to limit speculation, and especially to avoid the impact on land prices of planning decision, planned areas have to be made as large as possible. On the other hand, although the right of pre-emption stops speculation within the area, it does not lead automatically to acquisition of needed land. Practice shows that the landowners are not ready to sell their land at the prices proposed by the public authorities, and therefore the expropriation procedure must be used. It may be that the 8-year limit fixed for pre-emption rights inside the ZAD is one of the reasons for the small percentage of voluntary transactions. The landowners may expect that at the end of the 8 year period, a free land market in the area will be resumed. Thus, the amendment prolonging the pre-emption right period for 14 years will help to create the needed land reserve in areas of urban development.

The different kinds of planned zones for different tasks—residential planned zones, industrial planned zones, tourist planned zones— needed a framework to which some common legislative measures could be applied. Such a framework was created by Article 16 of the 1967 Land Orientation Law, which includes a provision particularly important for zones of new urban development and areas of urban renovation. This exempts these zones or centres from strict adherence to the detailed land-use plans, by virtue of the special conditions under which the development infrastructure and building operate.

An interesting provision in *Sri Lanka* is that the minister makes a "General Interim Development Order" with respect to the interim development of land situated in the area for which a planning scheme is to be prepared. The minister may also make any "Special Interim Development Order" concerning any specified area. The effect of such interim orders is that no development, subdivision, construction, alteration, demolition or similar physical changes can be made without the prior permission of the planning authorities.*

The *Syrian Arab Republic* adopted a building regulation in 1969 which imposed heavy restrictions on the use to which property within the urban centres might be put. This regulation has classified dwelling houses into ten categories with a height limitation ranging from one to four storeys. In order to control the density and overcrowding of the neighbourhood, the built-up portion in a plot has been limited so that it will not exceed 70% of the plot area. Also, in order to control the density of the population in areas where apartments were permitted, a density of occupancy of 16–24 m is allowed per person depending on the size of the plot. It is clear that the new Syrian regulation attempts to control population density not only by height and area requirements but also to control directly land per person or family in residential districts. Multi-family districts are subject to greater area and lesser height requirements. In the Syrian regulation, specific requirements for off-street parking space for automobiles is established for access to certain types of businesses, places of assembly and multi-family residences. Neighbourhood business districts restricted to retail shopping and small service establishments are to be created at a ratio of 1–1·5 m^2 per person.†

* *Urban Land Policies and Land Use Control Measures*, Vol. II: *Asia and the Far East*, New York, 1973.

†UN, *Urban Land Policies and Land Use Control Measures*, Vol. V: *Middle East*, New York, 1973, p. 24.

IMPOSING LAND USE ACCORDING TO DEVELOPMENT SCHEMES

Land-use legislation in almost all countries is based on the principle of regulating what is not desirable. In a very detailed way, it fixes the way land is used, the height of buildings, the distance of buildings from roads, etc., and is intended to ensure quality and desirable building structures.

Zoning regulations fix the way land is used by limiting the landowner in what he can do with his land, but he is free *not* to use the land in his ownership. There are no regulations requiring that the landowner use the land according to development schemes, thus, in most cities of the world, there exists overcrowded areas side by side with vacant, unused land.

In order to encourage a landowner to use the land for construction purposes according to the development plan, in some countries there exists a higher rate of taxation of vacant land in urbanized areas. Spain was the first country to introduce legislation requiring the land owner to use his land within a fixed time for construction purposes in areas declared as urbanized.

Spain. As a result of the principle of subordination of the exercise of the property right to the compliance of its social function, in Spain the right to build is considered not only a right, but also a duty (Articles 67.3.b and 114 and the following articles, Land Law Ordinance of Forced Building and Municipal Register of Plots of 5.3.1944).

When a detailed plan has been fixed for a particular area to become newly urbanized, a landowner must build according to the plan within 2 years (or sometimes 3 years from the start of infrastructure works) or his land will be expropriated.

When a plot of urban land thus becomes a building site, i.e. when it satisfies the conditions specified above, the owner is required to surrender, without compensation, the area necessary for laying streets, parks and gardens in the sector in accordance with the plan in force, and is also obliged to build on the remaining area, in accordance with the standards laid down in the plan. Failure to build within a period which varies from place to place (generally 2 or 3 years, renewable in certain cases) renders him liable to expropriation (with compensation on a fixed basis of past value). If the municipality does not expropriate the central government has the power to do this.

In *Taiwan*, where vacant land is also taxed at a high rate, the *Implementary Regulations of the Equalization of Urban Land Rights* provide for the compulsory development of vacant land in urban areas in 3 years (2 years in Taipei). In addition, land on which the buildings are worth less than 10% of the value of the land must be built on according to the approved scheme within 5 years. Otherwise this vacant and underused land should be expropriated.

PRE-EMPTION RIGHTS

The right of pre-emption, or the right of first priority, offers public authorities the opportunity to acquire land when a landowner is interested in selling. The landowner must first offer his land to the public authority; should the public authority not be interested in acquiring the land, the owner may sell to a private party. The formal pre-emption procedure is based on an announcement in the land register. The public authority must announce its interest in the land within a period of time imposed by regulation.

The pre-emption rights allow the public authority to control the land market and to create land reserves without being obliged to buy large land areas in a short time. On the other hand, the pre-emption right may restrain the activity of land market since landowners—afraid that the pre-emption will be invoked and followed by expropriation—may not offer their land for sale. The pre-emption right policy may bring more positive results if it is connected or combined with an active purchasing policy of public authority to buy and supply the necessary land to the market. In France the pre-emption right is largely used in the planned areas of ZUP, ZAD and ZAC.

Basic regulations fix that in special planned, declared zones (which are larger than such needed for implementing the long-term urban development scheme) land transactions are restricted. The landowner may sell his land if the public authority is not ready to buy, but both parties are free to accept or reject the price offered by one of the interested parties. The landowner is also free not to sell his land even if the public authority agrees to the price the landowner asks.

On the other hand, the public authority is free to decide after a period of some months that it is not ready to buy at all, and the landowner can then sell privately. If there is no agreement over a price, and if both parties are interested in the transaction, the price may be fixed by the court. The public authority may also begin the expropriation procedure if it is interested in buying the land and there is no agreement about price, or if the owner is not ready to sell. But there is a regulation which restricts the pre-emption right to some fixed period of time (4 years in ZUP and 14 years in ZAD). Such time restrictions may negatively influence the market mechanism because some landowners may not be interested in selling their land, preferring to wait until the time when the pre-emption right is over. It may be suggested that if the pre-emption right were not limited by time it would favourably influence landowners to sell and thereby improve the land market mechanism. The pre-emption right is considered as a very appropriate measure for an efficient land policy. This is the proposal of the experts' committee in Switzerland and some other countries. For agricultural land *Switzerland* has a very extensive pre-emption right; Cantonal and Federal legislation gives priority rights to the farmers of a village to buy land if someone from their village is interested in selling his land.

In *Sweden* this right permits a municipality, under defined conditions, to take the place of buyers in sales of real property. The provisions on pre-emption are contained in an Act and Crown Regulations which came into force on 1 January 1968.

Prospective sellers of land are required to make their intentions known publicly, thereby appraising the municipality at an early stage. This requirement enables the local authorities to keep up with events on the real estate market (price movements, changes of tenure, etc.) and makes it easier for them to conduct a policy of land acquisition.

In testing whether a condition exists for the exercise of pre-emption under the terms of this provision, the direction of future community growth and the need of land for different purposes shall be assessed.

If the area is one for which a master plan has been prepared and adopted by the municipal bodies concerned and the subject land is set aside under the plan for residential or industrial development or such purposes as traffic ways, public places, recreational areas, etc., the conditions for exercising pre-emption should be usually in hand.

The assessment should turn out the same way if the area has been set aside for specified purposes in an adopted regional plan. Should a district plan or subdivision plan for the area be in preparation, this fact ought to constitute sufficient grounds for the municipality to pre-empt the land the plan is intended to encompass. Even if the planning work has not proceeded to the point where a master plan or regional plan has been drafted or proposals for a detailed plan are in hand, pre-emption should be exercisable if the land (having regard to its location and the growth of the municipality) can be assumed as necessary for the purposes in question. Demands on the municipality to establish the probability of future use as grounds for pre-emption are not made unduly excessive. On the other hand, a contention that is not sustained by inquiry that certain land is required for urban development is, of course, inadequate. In cases where neither comprehensive general plans nor detail plans are in hand, an assessment may be appropriate based on, for example, population forecasts, house-building programmes, or industrial investment plans. Over and above the importance of the foregoing, there is not cause to restrict pre-emption because of the time that may elapse until land is to be developed. If future growth can be foreseen for a considerable time to come with a sufficient degree of probability, pre-emption should be exercisable even though a long time may pass before the change in land use arises. Pre-emption may be exercised if the property is located within municipal jurisdiction. It may also be exercised outside the local limits if the property is located within the municipal bloc to which the greater part of the municipality belongs, and provided the affected municipality gives its consent.

Exempted from pre-emption are parcels smaller than 3000 m² (about 32,300 ft²) and with a rentable value below SRr 200,000 ($40,000).

The committee of experts in *Finland* suggested making it obligatory that the landowners inform the municipality in advance of any intended transfer of real property. But the committee considered that there was insufficient reason to grant municipalities first option in the purchase of real estate for sale. The desired effect would be achieved through obligating an advance notification of an intended sale, and through a simplification of the expropriation procedure which municipalities can use. In the Federal Republic of *Germany* there has been submitted a proposal to the Parliament to introduce the pre-emption right in all urban regional areas.

The pre-emption right gives public authorities the priority in buying land from a landowner interested in selling. Also, such a procedure leads to better information about the land prices existing in different areas.

The pre-emption rights allows authorities to exercise influence on the land market through purchasing limited quantities of land in different areas. Such land transactions in some areas create a basis for compensation at unexaggerated prices for land expropriated at a future date.

EXPROPRIATION FOR PUBLIC PURPOSES

The traditional view of land as a public trust is the justification for expropriating land needed for urban development. Legislation usually places upon the expropriating authority the responsibility to prove that condemnation is necessary to achieve community goals. The individual's property rights are, in turn, protected by regulations that ensure the owner an opportunity to question the expropriation order and to demand a fair compensation price.

In most countries, expropriation is restricted to land needed for public purposes. The term "public purposes" does not, however, imply the same uses in all countries. In some countries, uses for which land may be condemned include essential public services, such as roads, schools, and other buildings of public utility, but not housing. In other countries, the law clearly empowers local authorities to expropriate land needed for housing. Differences from country to country as to the permissibility of expropriation indicate, therefore, that disputes over the legality of condemnation focus not on whether expropriation contradicts individual property rights, but on whether the intended use of the land in question is defined as essential to community welfare.

Each country must determine in which cases the needs of all the citizens have priority over individual rights. Thus countries that must purchase land for housing on the open market do so not because private property rights take precedent over housing programmes planned and executed by the government, but because the provision of housing by public authorities is not deemed essential to community welfare. Housing constitutes a legitimate cause for expropriation in the Netherlands, Italy, Norway, Sweden, France (since 1958) and Spain (since 1962). A proposed law to permit condemnation for housing met with defeat in Denmark, and Danish authorities are forced to buy land for housing on the open market. In the Federal Republic of Germany, expropriation is possible only if the realization of the purpose for which expropriation is to be carried out is impossible in any other way.

Jurisdictional Authority for Expropriation

Each country must determine which public agencies shall have the authority to expropriate land. Municipalities must often act as the condemning authorities since the local governments are usually responsible for providing essential public services to the community. The growing phenomenon of spread-out metropolitan areas which consist of many independent local governments has raised new problems concerning planning and jurisdiction. Land reserves needed for future development of a city may encroach on the territory of another local government; yet, the law permits expropriation only within an authority's jurisdiction. Despite their interdependency with neighbouring localities, some municipal governments may be opposed to comprehensive development programmes whose realization depends upon the coordinated exercise of condemnation powers by each of the governments involved.

These obstacles to the achievement of planned urban development have led to different administrative approaches to expropriation. Alternatives include placing the administrative responsibility for expropriation at the national or regional or local level (with the permission of the central Government). Some of the approaches used are as follows:

Belgium. In 1962 a law giving a wide interpretation of expropriation purpose was introduced. Local and regional authorities have the possibility of compulsory purchase of all real estate needed for implementing schemes in a local and regional framework.

France. The Land Orientation Law of 1967 allows expropriation by different public authorities: the central Government, regional representatives of the central Government (Prefects), local authorities and regional or local mixed public enterprises. This law also introduced the possibility of expropriation for setting up land reserves—without a framework of an approved development scheme. If a long-term town-planning development scheme is approved, however, the land reserves must first be provided in the framework of that scheme.

Italy. An approved town-development scheme (the General Regulatory Plan) is equivalent to a declaration of public utility and allows for expropriation of land needed to carry out the scheme.

Spain. Since 1962, a special land directorate within the central housing ministry has been authorized to expropriate land needed for the National Housing Programme.

The United Kingdom. Rights of expropriation traditionally belong to local authorities; but the new-town corporations have expropriation rights for purposes of providing land for erecting a new town. The Land Commission was given the power to compulsorily purchase land for land reserves, although, in practice, this possibility is limited because beginning the expropriation procedure requires a development permit issued by the local authority. The amendment of this condition was discussed.*

Singapore.† The Land Acquisition Act vests the government with very wide powers of compulsory acquisition of private land. This power may be invoked not only for a "public purpose" but for various

---

* UN, *Urban Land Policies and Land Use Control Measures,* Vol. III: *Western Europe,* New York, 1973, p. 40.

† UN, *Urban Land Policies and Land Use Control Measures,* Vol. II: *Asia and the Far East,* New York, 1973, p. 79.

other wide-ranging purposes and even on behalf of private persons. This is evident from section 5 which provides that any land may be compulsorily acquired if needed for any of the following purposes:

"(a) For any public purpose;

(b) By any person, corporation or statutory board, for any work or any undertaking which, in the opinion of the Minister, is of public benefit or of public utility or in the public interest; or

(c) For any residential, commercial or industrial purposes."

Expropriation Procedure

There are two main reasons for the long period of the expropriation procedure. Sometimes the landowner tries to appeal the necessity of expropriation for public purposes according to existing legislation. The usual reason, however, is that the negotiations and the legal procedure in fixing the compensation are very time-consuming. Therefore, clearness in town-planning legislation which automatically allows the public authorities to expropriate may shorten the expropriation procedure. Obviously, the negotiations for the rate of compensation must take time; therefore, the ability to take possession of the land with the declaration of a public-utility order for expropriation, without waiting for the result of a compensation decision, is very important.

Although it is difficult to transfer land-use rights without knowing the exact price which must be paid, being able to take possession of the land without a long procedure allows construction firms to begin development schemes immediately.

The procedures followed in several countries are, in brief, as follows:

The Netherlands. The expropriation procedure takes from 3 to 4 years to execute after the decision to expropriate has been taken. It is possible, however, to take possession of the land immediately after the decision without waiting for the whole of the expropriation procedure to be completed. Nevertheless, because of the complications involved, municipalities prefer, where possible, to try to arrive at a mutual understanding with the owners and are even prepared to pay more than the market value of the land in order to avoid using the expropriation procedure.

Sweden. In certain situations, it may be necessary to take possession of object property before the expropriation process runs its course. If the matter is of extreme importance for the expropriator, a court of law may order what is known as "simple prior occupancy", which confers a defined right to make use of the property.

The United Kingdom. The Act of 1946 is still available for the compulsory-purchase procedure. The compulsory-purchase order must be announced in the local press, and individual owners and leaseholders must also be informed. After the date of the press announcement, one has a period of 6 weeks in which to object to the legality of the order and to apply to the court. Discussion about the amount of compensation may take some years to settle; but the acquiring authorities can, in fact, take possession of the land before the compensation is finally paid. They must, however, pay interest for the amount fixed by the court as a compensation from the date on which the land was taken into possession.

Japan. The expropriation system in Japan comprises a general and a special law. The general law is the Land Expropriation Law (Law no. 219 of 1951) promulgated to enable the acquisition of land needed in the public interest. The special law is called the Special Measures Law Concerning Acquisition of Land for Public Uses (Law no. 150 of 1961). It is applied where land is required by such developments of high importance as roads, water conservation and utilization facilities, railways, electric power sources or for projects recognized as special public projects by the Public Use Land Council, an advisory organ of the Ministry of Construction. It has been ruled since 1964 that all projects carried out under the direct jurisdiction of the Ministry of Construction should in principle apply for recognition as projects to which the special law is applicable. The basic difference between the two laws is that the special law provides a considerably shortened and simplified procedure as compared to the one given in the general law.

Korea. The main points in the procedure of expropriation briefly are that any promoter of a public work must first get his public work approved by the Ministry of Construction.

Within 2 years of this announcement the promoter is required to apply to the local governor for the expropriation of the land. The local governor announces the specifications of the land to be expropriated or used and also notifies the landowner and other interested persons. After the governor's announcement no changes in the character of the land or structures on it which might create an obstacle to the projected work are permitted without his prior permission. The promoters can then enter the land for survey, investigation, etc. They are required to prepare and sign a document about the measurements and title, etc., and have it signed by the owner and other interested persons. If the owner or any other interested person refuses to sign it, the promoter may approach the appropriate authorities. The law requires the promoters to conduct negotiations with the owner and other interested persons. If these negotiations succeed, the promoters apply to the Land Expropriation Committee to confirm the agreement. But if they do not, the promoter may ask the committee to adjudicate.

As soon as an expropriation committee receives an application it is announced and copies of the announcement are placed for public inspection for a period of 2 weeks. Within this period the landowners or other interested persons may submit their views to the committee. The committee's deliberations start immediately after the period of public inspection is over and the promoters, owners and other interested persons are notified of the date and place of such deliberations. Within 2 weeks of the announcement of deliberations, the committee is required to adjudicate on the matter.

Compensation System

In most countries the criterion for evaluation is the market value; some countries specifically declared this to be so in their constitutions. In virtually all countries that use market value to determine compensation, compensation procedures take a long time. The actual method for computing market value remains to be fixed.

The guidelines commonly used to ascertain value are the transactions made in recent years on comparable sites in the area of greatest proximity to the site in question. The difficulty is that the value of an individual site is influenced by diverse factors (e.g. frontage, position on street, location in the area). Thus, the exact value of the particular site is open to debate. Fixing the compensation price and then allowing the owner to appeal are time-consuming tasks.

Simplification of the compensation process is an aim of the expropriation authorities in virtually all countries. Modification of existing programmes has the combined objectives of shortening the procedure and making it more efficient, and assuring the payment of fair compensation awards which are not computed on the basis of the value resulting from the authority's decision to expropriate. Compensation procedures have, of course, evolved somewhat differently in different countries:

Federal Republic of Germany. Compensation is based on the open market value at the time of expropriation. Sometimes the price paid for the expropriating authority is higher than the market price. The landowner may ask for land in another location instead of cash compensation.

Finland. In 1965 the Government introduced a bill in the legislative body which would have given the communes a right to expropriate land for housing, for instance; with compensation to the owner for a reasonable market price, while the normal compensation had been based on the market price as such; but the bill was not passed. The change from compensation based on "full market-price" to "reasonable market price" was considered by jurists not to comply with the principle of "full compensation" implied by the Constitution.

France. Until 1962 French law provided that land values should be determined by a tribunal according to the prevailing market prices. This procedure gave rise to a situation in which the announcement of expropriation plans led to speculative increases of land prices for the surrounding area. At the end of a long legal dispute, the public authority was forced to pay a compensation price far in excess of the market value of the land prior to the decision to develop the area. The Law of 1962 specified that evaluation of land for the purpose of compensation must be done according to its value 1 year before the public announcement; but even for that period, it need not take into account the increased value resulting from the announcement of the development schemes or the changes in land-use regulation. In practice, it was difficult to evaluate the value of expropriated land and to establish the increased value resulting from development schemes. Judges were therefore inclined to fix compensation at a higher value. The Law of 1965 introduced two corrections: (i) the evaluation should take into consideration the normal increase of land prices (not resulting from development schemes); (ii) in case of an appeal, the basis for fixing compensation is the value that existed one year before opening the expropriation procedure—the same basis of evaluation made by the first court.

Italy. Compensation, based on the Naples Law of 1885, is calculated as an average between the market value (not resulting from the impact of development schemes) and 10 years' accumulated rent; in the absence of a rent, the average is made on the basis of assessable value declared for the purpose of taxation.

Netherlands. Compensation to landowners (mostly farmers) is based on the market value plus 10 years' income; and from this latter sum, the income of the interest of the cash compensation is deducted.

Spain. Both land authorities of towns with more than 50,000 population and capitals of provinces are obliged to publish revised assessments of land values every 4 years. The tables serve as the basis for taxation and compensation. The added value of the land resulting from the economic and social development of the area is taken into consideration in the periodic revision of the assessments. The landowner is thereby guaranteed part, but not all, of the additional value of his property due to development.

Sweden. The Expropriation Act does not contain any general rule as to the point of time to which valuation shall refer. According to legal usage, that time is most commonly the date of the final judgement in the expropriation case. But if the expropriator has already taken possession of the property by then, no allowance shall be made for any change in the property value that has arisen after occupancy.

Republic of Korea.* Where adjudication does take place compensation is based on the market price at the time of adjudication, taking into consideration the prices of land transaction of neighbouring lands and the rent or income accruing from the expropriated and neighbouring lands. However, the normal government practice is to give 70% of the market value as just compensation though one or two recent court cases have decreed in favour of full market value. Appeals against the award of the Land Expropriation Committees can be made to courts of second instance. It is also pertinent to mention that in actual practice a very large majority of expropriation cases are mutually negotiated, most often at prevailing market values.

In cases of expropriation, compensation should be paid not only for the land but also for buildings, structures and things over or attached to it and losses and damages owing to the removal of residence, business or articles from the land. As stated earlier, the amount of compensation has to be first negotiated between the promoter and the owner. Only when such negotiations fail is compensation adjudicated by the Land Expropriation Committee.

Singapore. The principles to be followed in determining the amount of compensation in Singapore are as follows:
  (a) The market value at the date of the publication of a preliminary notice provided that such notification has been followed within 6 months by the declaration of a final notice but in other cases the market value at the date of the final notice.
  (b) Increase in the value of the owner's other land likely to accrue from use to which the acquired land will be put.
  (c) The damages resulting from the severance of or injurious affectation to the owner's other land.
  (d) Reasonable expenses incidental to change of residence or place of business in consequence of the acquisition.

* UN, *Urban Land Policies and Land Use Control Measures*, Vol. II; *Asia and the Far East*, New York, 1973, p. 78.

(e) Restrictions imposed under the Planning Ordinance.*

In practice it has been found impossible to distinguish between (a) and (b).

Japan. The basis of compensation provided by law is payment at current market value. An expropriation committee or commission of seven members determines the amount of compensation.

The standards for compensation of losses arising out of the acquisition of land varied in the past from project to project. In 1963 "Standards for Compensation of Losses Arising Out of the Execution of Public Projects Under the Direct Jurisdiction of the Ministry of Construction" were promulgated to provide uniform and adequate compensation.

A major difficulty is that these laws require compensation to be given on the basis of market values, which are extremely high because they include unearned increases in land prices which have resulted either from the execution of public works construction or anticipated potential development values. High compensations hinder the smooth acquisition of land for public purposes. The Government is therefore contemplating a drastic revision of the land expropriation laws with a view to rationalizing the basis for the payment of compensation.†

Remarks

Different experts have expressed views that even the strongest measures and evaluation for expropriation purposes are not sufficient to control final notice land speculation in a market economy. The real problem is not to neutralize the additional value created in the expropriated land, but to formulate a land policy that will not allow the creation of additional value. This is possible in a market economy only by providing a sufficient quantity of land ready for construction in areas where there exists a demand for land. One of the difficulties in carrying out the expropriation procedure on the basis of former Land-use value and not according to the new value created is re-

---

* *Ibid.*, pp. 79, 80.
† *Ibid.*, p. 74.

sulting in injustice caused by the exproportion law. While one owner must sell his land which is expropriated at the lower prices, his neighbour is free to sell his land at speculative prices on the free market. Thus, it is rather difficult to introduce low prices for expropriated land without taking from other landowners the additional value deriving from public-authority decisions.

One of the arguments against expropriation methods is the injustice occurring when some landowners must sell while others are free to keep the land. Freezing all land prices in an area at a given date may create a situation where all landowners have the same rights and the same obligation when eventual expropriation occurs. Obviously, such a price freeze must be adjusted in order to ensure the real monetary value of land. Such price-freezing as a basis of compensation may limit the purchase of land for speculative reasons, since in the case of expropriation, the land would be compensated for on the basis of the former frozen land price. Such a system, of course, must be connected with taxation methods which ensure that the additional value deriving from urban growth and decisions by public authorities shall be transferred to the community.

ADMINISTRATIVE PROCEDURE IN LAND-USE POLICY

The results of land-use policies are influenced to an important degree by the administrative methods employed.

The necessity of acquiring building permits from the authorities is one of the main means of efficiently regulating land use. Generally the landowner or contractor receives a permit to build in accordance with existing regulations, while the authority checks to see that the land was used according to the permits.

The procedure of getting a building permit is connected with the relationship between the local authorities and the citizens, and with the local authorities and the central powers. On the one hand, there is a desire to shorten the time needed by the citizen to obtain a permit; on the other hand, the central authority is interested in more closely supervising land-use allocation by the local authority. This control is needed so that local vested interests do not force misuse—as in allowing a more intensive land use than legislation permits—and also to defend the citizens from a local authority which makes acquiring a building permit difficult even when the citizen planned to build according to legislation. The control by the central authority should prevent the local authorities from keeping a request longer than the time needed to investigate its merits.

Different countries introduced a regulation allowing the citizens to appeal to the central authority or the court if he believes that the local authority misused its power. The procedure of issuing and controlling building permits is of the highest importance for the efficiency of town-planning legislation. Without efficient procedure the best planned legislation will not achieve the aims of ensuring urban development according to the needs of the population.

The *United Kingdom* introduced a system of carefully organized planning machinery, based on issuing a development permit for each change of land use. The planning authorities are limited to a period of 2 months for their decision. The citizen has a right to appeal to the Minister of Housing if he is convinced that the decision of the local authority is unfair. The Act of 1968 allowed housing inspectors investigating the appeal to make a definitive decision.

Italy established very careful control by representatives of the central power over local authorities issuing building permits. In certain cases, representatives of the central government may even cancel permits given by the local authorities if the conditions of the permit do not correspond to building regulations. The Law of 1968 even fixed the norms of land use for different zones of a town. The local authorities have no right to change their norms without authorization by the central government.

In *Spain* the central government not only mandates town planning legislation but also controls the activities of local authorities. The representatives of the provincial government may issue building permits if the local authority does not answer the request of a citizen in a given time. Alternatively, the representative may cancel the permit issued by the local authority if the conditions of the permit do not correspond to legislation.

Central government intervention is especially important in countries without a long tradition of democratic, local government. But such intervention is important in all countries, since the local authority was elected directly by the town's citizens, and future re-election depends on the satisfaction of the citizens. Difficulties with local vested interests may hamper the activities of the local authorities. Therefore, supervision and control by the central power may be of help to the local authorities in realizing town-planning legislation.

Legislative measures imposing use of land for construction purposes within a fixed time period, combined with the declaration of some city areas as zones of frozen development, might be sufficient to force the use of vacant land in urbanized areas. Generally, the lack of such legislation forces large segments of the population to look for housing in areas far from the cities, while, within the urbanized area, there exists enough space to satisfy the needs of the growing population. Such legislation may also reduce the costs of infrastructure provision, which generally are lower in cases of concentrated development than in fragmented and dispersed areas in a large city region.

CITIZEN PARTICIPATION IN PLANNING

The increased educational level of the population and the active role of large population strata in the public life of countries has posed the problem of a way to permit active participation of the population in elaborating development schemes.

Comprehensive urban and rural development requires more and more intervention by public authorities. Rapid urban development requires long-term planning; but the plan must account for major technological changes and the changing needs of the population. There is a contradiction between the needs of an individual and his family, the needs of a population within a locality or region, and the needs of a country. Planning must be based on an estimation of all needs, taking into account the magnitude of factors influencing the needs.

One may ask, however, what are the criteria for formulating the needs; in what way the real needs of the population can be estimated. One of the ways is through studies carried out by public authorities and by research institutes—interviews with citizens whose attitudes may be the basis for measuring the population's needs.

Recently, there has been an increasing trend towards finding new ways of citizen participation in elaborating development schemes directly concerning the population. In some cases, the law demands publication of the development schemes and asks citizens to formulate their remarks. The scheme may be approved by the central or local authority only after investigation of citizens' objections.

It may be, however, that the most important question concerning citizen participation is not the formal regulation allowing citizens to formulate their remarks, but the method by which information about the scheme's details is disseminated. Knowledge of the problem connected with the development scheme may be of the highest importance in allowing citizens to formulate their remarks. If the importance of citizen participation were sufficiently appreciated, a better way of informing the public would be found. Citizens' experience and knowledge of everyday needs might help the planner in elaborating development schemes. Obviously, there are always alternative solutions with advantages and disadvantages; and active participation of citizens might be of help in finding the best solution. Moreover, the knowledge that citizens were participating and investigating objections might influence planners to account more carefully for various vital needs which are sometimes neglected in theoretical schemes. Some examples in various countries are provided below.

France. In France regulations provide that all urban plans must be made available for public scrutiny at the local town hall and in the departmental office of the ministry responsible for urban planning. This provision is similar to those concerning expropriation, the purpose of which is to protect the rights of any person whose interests might be affected. In 1960 the Ministry of Building recommended, with the aim of associating the public with both the preparation and the approval of urban plans, the establishment of a local committee, representing the various social and professional classes, which would be kept informed concerning preliminary studies and work, and consulted on the choice among various alternatives. It was hoped that the posting of the draft plan at the town hall might be accompanied by an effort to popularize the solutions adopted, e.g. in the press or by means of exhibitions. This recommendation, unfortunately, has seldom been put into practice, since local authorities feared that many difficulties might be caused by such wide publicity given to plans, especially if the plans were disliked by the public-at-large.

Italy. Among the objectives of the social services in Italy is the encouragement of the people to take an interest in helping to formulate and implement development schemes; indeed, it constitutes the main purpose of social centres in the south. Similar objectives are pursued by district councils and local campaigns initiated by political parties or social-action groups. The ILSES, in particular, employs this procedure both through social centres and through social workers who have been active in the aftermath of recent disasters. The national legislative body is also formulating plans with a view to decentralizing the administration of large municipalities.

The Netherlands. In the Netherlands, the population of a quarter or a town often is informed of social measures to be adopted within the framework of the development plan. The community-development method is used for activities the purpose of which is the social development of the community; thus, when the central government makes grants for urban development, it is often stipulated that the population also must participate.

The United Kingdom. In the United Kingdom, town-planning meetings are open to the public for consultation and participation before the submission of plans to the central authorities for final approval, which is granted only after meetings of representatives of the various ministerial departments concerned. Changes have recently been made in the degree of publicity given to development plans. In the past, observations made on them by the public were not published. Today, however, publicity is given not only to the observations of critics of the plan, but to the report of the Inspector of Planning on those observations and to any decision taken by the Minister concerning the Inspector's action.

Local planning authorities are increasingly using public meetings to determine support for, or criticism of, general planning policies. In this connection, the Birmingham Conference, organized in 1965 by the Permanent Conference of Social Service Councils, stressed the following points: (a) the need to improve communications between planners and citizens seeking to be better informed, concerning not only what will happen to them, but the place where they are going to live and the facilities they will find there, and (b) the desirability of making young people of school age familiar with development plans, as it is they who will be affected by them, thereby also better integrating the young people into the adult community.

CONCLUSIONS

The general purpose of the detailed macro- and micro-planning schemes discussed is to avoid undesirable development, for example to prevent fragmented development with vacant land in areas of urban development, to preserve recreational land and good agricultural land in the vicinity of the city, and to keep land reserves for future development. But even the best planning schemes cannot ensure that development will actually take place; this needs more active measures. Land-use planning in the absence of more positive government intervention also does not change the conditions operating in the private land market, but merely shifts speculation from planned to unplanned areas, even assuming controls within the planned areas are stringent and detailed enough to prevent speculation.

The experience of different countries suggests that in order to implement efficiently a comprehensive land-use planning scheme new regional institutions are generally necessary. These must be able to effectively prevent local authorities from changing the detailed land-use plan. On the other hand, there must be effective coordination and cooperation in drawing up the original plan between the appropriate local, regional and national authorities.

Sometimes where it is impossible to introduce legislation which affects the country as a whole, it can be extremely useful to introduce stringent land-control measures in specific development areas. This procedure of freezing development in a certain area can give the government time to assemble the needed financial resources before a chaotic development becomes fixed. However, it must be kept in mind that if the area of frozen development is too small, this will only serve to encourage speculation in adjacent areas.

The restrictions on the issuing of building permits (e.g. for offices) has had some desirable effects but unfortunately has not been co-ordinated with New Towns policies. It must be understood that if development is to be slowed down in the city centre this must be compensated for in the city region by the provision of planned communities including commercial, residential and industrial developments. Otherwise such a policy encourages fragmented development in the region and high prices in the city centre.

One of the most important innovations recently has been the introduction in Spain and Taiwan for the first time, of land-use legislation which *requires* use of vacant land for particular purposes according to plan (rather than just prohibiting certain uses). Though still in its early stages, this procedure is of the highest importance for the future, as it implies a change in the concept of land ownership from a right to a duty.

REFERENCES

Amsterdam Public Works Dept., *Town Planning and Ground Exploitation in Amsterdam*, 1967.

Cullingworth, J. B., *Town and Country Planning in England and Wales*, London: G. Allen & Unwin, 1964.

Danish National Planning Committee, *A Survey of Danish Planning Legislation*, Copenhagen, Apr. 1965.

Darin-Drabkin, Haim, "Control and planned development of urban land: towards the development of urban land policies," UN Interregional Seminar Paper, Madrid, Nov. 1971.

Haar, Charles, *Law and Land: Anglo-American Planning Practice*, Cambridge, Mass: Harvard University Press, 1964.

Hall, Peter and Clawson, Marion, *Planning and Urban Growth: An Anglo-American Comparison*, Baltimore, 1973.

Jagmetti, Prof. R. L., *ETH, Neue Tendenzen im Zurcherischen Bau-und Planungrecht, Sonderdruck aus dem Schweizerischen Zentral-Blatt für staats- und Gemeindeverwaltung*, Band 66, Zurich, 1966.

Lichfield, Nathaniel, *Economics of Planned Development*, London: Estates Gazette, 1956.

United Nations, *Urban Land Policies and Land Use Control Measures*, Vol. VI: *Northern America*, New York, 1973.

The Use of Land: A Citizen's Guide, Report of the Rockefeller Brothers Task Force, New York, 1973.

Watson, Michael and Haywood, Jack, *Planning, Politics, and the Public Interest: the French, British, and Italian Experience*, London: Cambridge University Press, 1975.

CHAPTER 11

Taxation on Land

1. TAXATION METHODS

Taxation in its simplest definition represents a compulsory contribution to the public authority to cover its expenses. Taxation ensures income so that the collective needs of the individual and the society can be supplied.

A major task of taxation is to link the collective resources to the most productive aims in accordance with the agreed-upon criteria of productivity and social efficiency. These criteria are, of course, determined by the social and political structure of the community and its values. Most taxes also have specific aims, and their efficacy is measured by the degree to which these aims are achieved. A side-effect of taxation is its impact on the redistribution of income and wealth. Colin Clark* underlines that "every statesman designing a system of taxation has to take into account three quite different considerations, which may often lead to conflicting conclusions, namely social justice, economic efficiency and administrative practicability. . . . The principles of efficiency applied to taxation require first that it should be as little discouragement as possible to people's willingness to produce: and further that it should 'distort' production as little as possible, i.e. should not encourage producers to produce more which consumers want less at the expense of such other commodity which the consumers want more."

According to Colin Clark a tax is effective to the extent that it does not compromise the goal for which it has been fixed. Thus income taxes are effective to the extent that they do not injure the efficacy of

---

* Colin Clark, "Land taxation: lessons from international experience", in *Land Values*, edited by Peter Hall, London, 1965.

work, as too high tax rates discourage people from working too hard and the fiscal aim is not realized. Differential rates of taxation of capital investment and profits above a certain level in particular areas make one investment more profitable than another. In a perfectly free market with free capital movement, there is an average profit on capital investment and economic activity.

An exaggerated level of taxation of labour and capital may diminish the expected income from the taxation and restrain the economic activity. In a society with an open economy and free relations with other countries, capital investment can find its way from a country with a high taxation rate to one with a lower rate. Labour has no such a freedom of movement, but is able to restrict work to the absolute minimum necessary for existence on an appropriate level without investing any additional effort to produce more if the income from that extra effort is taken by taxation for the collective needs and not kept by the worker as additional income.

It is a fact that in a society with a high standard of living, a considerable part of the individual's needs are supplied by the public authorities (health, education, etc). Therefore, the level of taxation in such countries is generally higher than in less-developed countries. The efficiency of a taxation system is measured by the degree of participation of different income groups and owners of capital in the general revenue of the public authorities budget, and the way in which the needs of different population strata are supplied by the public authorities.

The criteria of efficiency cannot be measured only quantitatively. They are a function of a social structure. Some countries with a very high level of economic development consider the individual's effort to increase his income as a means towards general economic productivity, and therefore reduce public expenditures on some services.

In USA the country with the highest GNP *per capita* in the world, a considerable part of health and education is financed by the individual and not by the public authorities. On the other hand, England, France and the East European countries are ensuring health, education and housing as a part of general public expenditure. The social results of a taxation system is therefore one of the essential criteria of efficiency.

The land taxation system may be evaluated as other systems according to economic and social efficiency, which can be measured mostly by the impact of taxation on supply of land needed for urban development.

Colin Clark is mentioning "among the range of practicable taxes there is none which is so economically 'efficient' as land tax.... Any one, whether wage worker, salaried worker, manager or proprietor, who is taxed at a rate which he thinks is too high, may work less energetically, or take more leisure, or possibly emigrate. A piece of land can do none of these things. On the contrary, its owner is likely to administer it with more skill and care, and put it to the best possible use, if he has to pay a substantial tax on it anyway. And, unlike savings, land is not the fruit of past human effort.... The amount of land available for agriculture and mining is determined by natural factors, and for urban use (in almost all cases) by the activities of people other than owner of the land himself" (page 126, *Values*).

A high tax does not really conflict with economic efficacy, as the land exists and will continue to exist, even if the taxes continue to get higher. However, as Clark suggests, the real criterion of efficacy in taxing land lies in the extent that the tax contributes towards ensuring a land supply to the market, according to demand for building and other uses.

2. LAND TAXATION AND LAND PRICES

One of the essential criteria of land taxation efficiency is the impact of taxation on land supply to the market. It may be suggested that taxation which reduces the demand for land and increases the supply to the market may be evaluated as an efficient taxation system.

Generally, a high rate of tax in comparison with the value of a good will increase the price of that good. Taxation of land, on the contrary, may lead to a lower level of land prices. Taxes on land do not automatically affect land prices in one particular direction.

The impact of taxes on land price formation results from the nature of land value. The value of most goods, in a perfectly functioning free market, is based on their production costs and their profitability to the owner of the means of production. The level of profit and the level of production costs are regulated by competition on the free market.

The peculiar character of land affects its value and price. Land cannot be produced and has no cost of production. The costs of infrastructure works may be seen as the costs of production of urban land. But there is generally no relationship between the (high) prices for urban land and the (low) costs of infrastructure works. Land has value because of the revenue which may be expected from structures built on the land now or in the future. The expected profit is therefore influenced not by the production costs but by the capital investment (public and private) in structures for services, roads, etc., which are influencing the economic, social and cultural value of one location more than another. The location factor is therefore the essential basis for creating land value and land rent. The land rent may be formulated as a part of the land value which is created as a result of favourable location. The scarcity of land in desirable locations leads to the high level of urban land prices.

The prices of land in some locations are therefore a result of a high level of urban land rent and not of high production costs. A high level of land taxation in areas where the land rent is the essential factor in land value may not influence the land price, which is high in comparison with land prices in the location far from the focus of urban life, but will diminish only the level of urban land price or land profit. In such cases land taxation may influence the redistribution of national wealth, taking a part of the additional value created by the urbanization process from few landowners and transferring to the urban society in order to cover the permanently growing urbanization costs and investments, which are the basis for permanently increasing land value.

But under some conditions a taxation system may lead to land-price increases. A very high level of taxation of land profits at the time of transference of land ownerwhip may reduce the supply of land to the market, and in such a way increase the land prices. Different results may be achieved if the additional land values created as a result of the urbanization process is *collected not at the time of land transfer but is paid by all landowners periodically, thus increasing the maintenance costs of holding land.*

Obviously, the impact of a taxation system on land prices is different for vacant or built land. In the case of vacant land, a high level of property tax and an additional value tax collected periodically increases the costs of capital investment in land property and diminishes the attractiveness of land as a source of capital investment of a high interest level. A lessened demand for land as a capital investment may ease land prices and thus the high maintenance costs of vacant land may increase the supply to the market.

The impact of a high taxation of built land depends on various factors. It may reduce prices because of the restricted attractiveness of real estate with high maintenance costs, but it might not have much effect if there is a high demand for dwellings and commercial buildings; in such a case the high level of taxation just leads to a higher price for residential and commercial buildings. The taxation in this case will not redistribute wealth but will be an additional burden on the majority of citizens. But even in such a case, investment in real estate may be less attractive if the taxation level is high and in the long term the demand for real estate in the free market might be reduced.

Generally, the taxation methods are influenced by the general outlines of socio-economic policy. In most countries taxation methods, being a part of land-use policies, are trying to prevent land prices rising faster than housing costs generally. This is especially so as land prices are an essential part of housing costs, and for a social policy which is aiming to ensure an appropriate level of housing services for every citizen. But in some countries in a certain stage of development land speculation is seen as one of the factors in economic development. In such countries the public authorities are not interested in keeping a low level of land prices; on the contrary, it is suggested that high land prices are an important stimulus for economic development. Taxation methods in many countries are influenced by such an approach and the rate of land taxes there is generally low.

But very often there exists a contradiction between the declared general policy of social welfare, and the taxation methods which encourage land speculation and hamper planned urban-development (because of a low level of land taxes). Such a situation exists in many developing countries where the government is trying to carry out a progressive social policy, but the pressure of influential landowner groups does not allow it to introduce taxation methods corresponding to these aims.

In some countries we see high taxation of income from labour and economic activities and low taxation of land property, or high taxation of profits in general and low taxation of profits from land. This often results from underestimating the role of urban land in national wealth, and especially of the importance of high land prices in affecting urban growth.

One of the difficulties in establishing the efficient land-taxation methods is the contradictory effects of taxation in comparison with other goals of socio-economic policy.

A detailed examination of taxation methods may show that their efficiency is related to other items of land-use policy. The institutional aspect of land taxation is of the highest importance. The interrelationship between the central, regional and local authorities and the general financing policy of these authorities exerts an essential effect on land taxation results.

Types of Land Taxes

There are different taxes in respect of land values. We will try to give a survey and analyse the effects of different types of land taxes on the land market and thus on urban growth. The two main tax categories are *property taxes* and *taxes on land profits* or on the increased value created by urban growth. The impact on the land market is a product not only of the actual taxation system, but also is greatly affected by the system and method of evaluation of land prices. Therefore a special section is devoted to evaluation systems.

3. PROPERTY TAXES

Taxation of land property has deep roots in the past. In Athens and other countries in ancient times, land was taxed. In the historical period when agriculture was the basic factor in the national economy, the taxation of land was the main source of fiscal revenue for the ruler of the state. In some countries the size of land properties was not only the basis of a tax but also the basis on which a number of soldiers had to be supplied for the army.

A property tax on land as well as on buildings has mostly a fiscal aim:

to provide the financial means for municipal and central government authorities to cover permanently growing urbanization costs. At the same time, the taxation of land property and real estate generally also has social and planning aspects. The method and rate of property taxation may serve in the redistribution of wealth, and may achieve some planning purposes if the tax is differentiated according to different land uses in urban areas.

The difficulty in introducing efficient taxation methods appropriate to the new urban situation has various causes. One of them, and a very important one, is that land ownership is in the hands of an enormous number of citizens for whom land is a kind of life security. These landowners are opposed to high taxation. Existing taxes are mostly fiscal in character, although some of them also have social aspects; while some countries have recently introduced taxes for planning purposes.

One of the difficulties in taxation is that the effect of a tax which has one purpose may in time be different from the expected ones. For instance, a high tax on land profits during land transfers, with a diminishing tax rate over time (to discourage speculators but encourage those who have saved land), may lead to further speculative holding of land (as the longer held, the lower the tax). Taxation methods, in order to be efficient, have to be taken into account for possible unforeseen side effects.

Different countries use different systems of land property taxation as well as a different administrative structure to evaluate and to collect property taxes. The administrative structure of the country and the patterns of public finance, including the relationship between central, regional and local authorities, have an impact on the methods of taxation employed.

Higher taxes on land than buildings may influence higher taxation of buildings where the role of land is higher than where the role of land is lower and therefore higher taxation of commerical services than residential. Site value taxation, separate from buildings, will benefit owners of dwellings or firms located at the periphery of the city while imposing a higher part of taxation on commercial sites in the city centre.

It has to be discussed whether the rate of property tax should be equal for built sites and vacant land. There is also a question of whether a progressive tax on vacant land according to the value and size of a site should be introduced—this would be in order not to impose a high rate of taxation on land belonging to the low- or middle-income socio-economic groups who are trying to ensure land to improve housing conditions for themselves or their children. A differential rate of taxation on vacant land may allow a high rate of tax on land for speculative purposes, and a low rate for prospective homeowners.

It may be suggested that a differentiated rate of tax on improved sites could also be introduced distinguishing between commercial and residential buildings.

Also, it has to be discussed whether in the case of taxing vacant urban land there should be tax reductions where there is no public plan for construction schemes. In such cases the landowners are not using their land for construction purposes, not because of speculation, but as a result of a lack of planning schemes.

There also exists the problem of the taxation of land in an agricultural use within areas classified as urban. Should such land be taxed at agricultural or urban value? Are the public authorities interested in encouraging use of such land for agricultural purposes, or in forcing the landowners to use it for urban purposes (as a result of high taxation)? This problem has recently been discussed in Denmark, Israel, in some states of the USA, and in some other countries.

The USA

The property tax plays the dominant role in financing the budget of local authorities. In 1968 this tax provided 68% of general municipal income from local sources. The rate of tax varies according to different states and different local authorities. It is from 0·5% to 2·5% with an average of 1·4% for the whole United States.

The importance of the property tax in the local government budget has led to a long and deep discussion about different aspects of the experience of this system. Sometimes there is a feeling that because of the important role of the property tax in the local government revenue, the public authorities are not opposed to land-price increases because this ensures a higher income for the local authorities.

The high fiscal importance of the property tax results from the administrative and financial structure of the public authorities in the USA. The federal system and the basic role of the local government in the administrative machinery leaves the care for providing the essential social services such as health, education and social welfare mostly to the local authority. The permanently growing expenditure exerts an impact on the budget structure. The administration of the property tax, which is based on the local government administrative structure, leads to the certain evaluation of the property tax and collecting the income in the framework of small administrative units—the counties. Therefore, there exist differences in evaluation between one county and another and big differences in income from the property tax according to the income level of the citizens. The social and planning effect of such a tax administration creates enormous differences between the level of services between one county and another, according to the level of income from the property taxation. The negative aspects of this system is expressed by the efforts of each county to encourage the establishment of enterprises which may ensure a high income for the investors and a high income from the property tax for the local governments, while at the same time such enterprises may have negative social effects.

Some of the states have introduced a centralized system of assessment in all these counties of the state. Hawaii represents an example of such a centralized system, where the state administration nominates the assessors. In some other states such as Kentucky and Maryland, the assessment function is a state responsibility; thus the assessment is carried out by an elected or appointed county assessor who is paid and supervised by the state.

Differential Assessment

One of the most discussed problems of the taxation system as it exists today is the question of differential assessment (both of land and buildings and urban and agricultural land). Only two states, Pennsylvania and Hawaii (and some counties in California), have introduced a separate rate of taxation on land and buildings. Agricultural land near the cities is generally taxed according to the agricultural value and not on the basis of the market price, which contains some part of the future urban value. Some states have introduced a differential system of taxing such land. The USA Congress report on land use (published in 1974) discusses different proposals for the improvement of the property-taxation system.

Differential Assessment of Land and Buildings

Pennsylvania enacted a law, the graded tax law, in 1913, allowing separate assessment of land and buildings and for the gradual reduction of tax rates on buildings over a period of about 10 years, until buildings would be taxed at half the rate applied to land. This law applied to Pittsburgh and Scranton.

There is general agreement that this tax system has encouraged the recent rebuilding of the downtown areas, though credit must also go to urban renewal efforts. Speculation in land was decreased as the plan went into effect and studies have shown that the average homeowner pays a lesser tax bill than if land and improvements were taxed equally.

In 1963 the Hawaii legislature passed Act 142, the Graded Property Tax law. The tax rate on improvements was established at 90% of the tax rate on land. Then, the law provided for a gradual reduction of tax rates, in improvements to 40% of the rate on the land value, through reductions every 2 years over a period of 10 years. The lowering of the improvement tax factor every 2 years could be deferred for 2-year periods by the Governor.

The law has become the subject of public debate in Hawaii. At present over 6 years after taking effect, the improvement tax factor is 80% of the land value tax rate, as there has been some deferment of its reduction. The Department of Taxation recommended repeal, arguing that the benefits to be gained from the graded tax system have been achieved and that a single, but higher, tax rate would be most advantageous now. The state legislature, however, voted to continue the graded tax law. If there was a changeover to a land-value tax system, that process in itself would change the current value of land and raise a serious question of equity for present landowners.

Differential Assessment—Agricultural Land

The issue of differential assessment of farmland has attracted more and more interest as cities have continued to expand into the surrounding countryside. The US Department of Agriculture has estimated that taxes per acre on farms in Standard Metropolitan Statistical Areas average 5 times as much as those on farms in rural areas. In order to protect the farmer who wishes to continue to plant, but who cannot afford taxes based on metropolitan assessment levels, a number of states have enacted laws providing some form of differential treatment. There has been some question, however, as to whether these laws have not benefited speculators more than farmers.

Differential assessment laws fall into three broad categories: preferential assessment, deferred taxation and restrictive agreements. Preferential treatment places the least demands on the landowner. It simply allows that land devoted to agricultural use shall be assessed on the basis of its value as agricultural land. The most in the way of requirements is the stipulation made by a few states that the land shall have been in agricultural use for 2 or 3 preceding years. Preferential assessment laws are in effect in nine states: Alaska, Colorado, Connecticut, Delaware, Florida, Indiana, Iowa, Maryland and New Mexico.

In deferred assessment, taxes are charged according to the land's assessment for agricultural use until it is diverted to other purposes. At that time the additional taxes which would have been due had the land not been differentially assessed are collected for the preceding 3 to 5 years. Five states, Minnesota, New Jersey, Oregon, Rhode Island and Texas, have laws providing for deferred taxation. Only Oregon charges interest on the deferred revenue.

Laws authorizing restrictive contracts and agreements provide the state government with a power it lacks under the other two forms of differential assessment; the state may determine which parcels of land should be given the benefit of the differential treatment and thus be encouraged to remain in agricultural use, and which might better be encouraged towards development.

Such laws are now in effect in Hawaii, California and Pennsylvania. The Hawaii law requires the landowner to petition the state to have his land declared as dedicated to specific agricultural uses. If the petition is approved, the land is assessed according to the permitted uses for a minimum period of 10 years. After the fifth year either the owner or the state may give 5 years' notice of cancellation. If the owner puts the land to any other than the specified uses, the special assessment is cancelled and the additional taxes are due, retroactive to the date of petition, with interest. The California law is similar except that the contract is between the landowners and the local government.

The restrictive agreement laws of Hawaii, California and Pennsylvania seem the best of the differential treatment arrangements. Deferred assessment, especially with interest, at least provides for the refunding to the community of revenue from increased value of land. Simple preferential treatment, with no stipulations except that land be, in some general sense, in agricultural use, seems almost an open invitation to speculators.

The United Kingdom

The property tax is a local authority tax based on rates which are levied on the basis of rental value of a property. "The basis of assessment for rating was first set out in precise terms by the Parochial Assessment Act 1836, which defined the annual value as the rent at which the (hereditaments) might reasonably be expected to let from year to year free of all tenant's rates and taxes...and deducting there from the probable annual average cost of the repairs, insurance and other expenses, if any, necessary to maintain them in a state fit to command such a rent. Broadly speaking, this basis still holds good, although it has been subjected by later statutes to various exceptions and to detailed rules. The statutes concerned have been consolidated in the General Rate Act 1967."*

The local authority fixes the local rate, which is in pence per pound of rentable value of each property in the local authority area. All occupied properties are taxed with a reassessment every 5 years. Non-occupied property, which is not providing income, is not taxed. Therefore vacant land in not subject to taxation in spite of its high capital

---

* *Report of the Commissioners of Her Majesty's Inland Revenue, for the year ending 31st March 1968.*

value in the urbanized areas. Even commercial buildings, if they are not occupied and therefore not providing revenues, are not taxed. The rates are generally low in comparison with the capital value of the property. This system of taxation is criticized by some experts because it encourages landowners not to use vacant land for building purposes according to the urban development schemes.

In a country where income from economic activity is taxed at a high rate in the top income brackets, the regulations which exempt non-occupied property from property tax have led to the strange fact of non-occupied office buildings being constructed in the heart of London, in spite of a high demand for office space, as a result of a lower rate of capital gain tax than income tax or property tax.

France

Land taxes are the basis of local government taxes. They are collected from both built and non-built land, and the evaluation is based on rental value. The tax rates are fixed by the local authority and roughly on the average $0.3\frac{1}{2}$–0.7% from the capital value. The land-use legislation in 1962 suggested introducing a higher level of tax. The Ministry of Housing proposed a law allowing the municipality to fix the rate at 1–3% of capital value. This proposal was not accepted by Parliament. Other regulations were introduced in order to encourage the financing of development works in newly urbanized areas. But such regulations are not a substitute for the property tax which had to ensure the financial means for urban growth expenditure and at the same time to serve as a means to restrain the land-price increase.

Taiwan

The land-value tax is the basic tax of the government in order to keep a part of increased urban-land values for the use of the public authorities. It is collected annually by the central, regional or local authorities for urban land or for land planned for future urban development. The rate of this tax is graduated, from 1·5 to 7% of assessed value, according to the value of the site. Small landowners of built properties are taxed at the lower level of 0·7%. Urban land in agricultural use is taxed at 1·5%, while land designated for green space at only 1%. This tax is combined with a specially high rate of taxation of vacant urban land which is not used for building purposes according to the planning schemes. The rates of the vacant land tax vary from three to ten times the ordinary land value tax. This method of higher taxation of unused urban vacant land may be seen as an example of using taxation methods for achieving planning purposes.

Sweden

The property and land-value tax is collected as a part of the wealth tax at a rate of 1%–2·5% of the capital value, although properties under 150,000 crowns ($40,000) are exempt.

4. TAXES ON LAND PROFITS

Taxes on land profits include taxation of the additional value created through "normal" urban growth and general price increases as well as of the profits resulting from specific public authority development works and planning decisions.

Legislation in some countries distinguishes between these two categories and has a special tax on increases in value connected directly with the carrying out of development works. In some cases this is called a betterment tax, and is based on the collecting by the public authorities of a part of an additional value resulting from planning decisions, but not necessarily as a direct result of infrastructure works. There are special categories of taxes on the profits resulting from public decisions to change land use from agricultural to urban, or to allow more intensive use of land through fixing higher building densities than accepted in the planning schemes.

Other countries use the term land increment or land profit tax, which is based on collecting a part of land profits without defining the cause of increased land value. Such a tax includes the collecting of a tax on land profits resulting from the impact of "normal" urban growth as well as those due to the public authorities' planning decisions. It is based on the general concept of capital gain taxation.

It might sometimes be difficult to separate the additional land value resulting from public authorities' investment and planning decisions, and that increase caused by the general price increase, inflation and urban growth process.

It may also be suggested that different effects on value may be caused by the direct and indirect impact of development works on a site or on a large space. Generally, public capital investments influence the aggregate values of land in areas being affected by the new improvement in different ways.

But there some public authority decisions whose effect on price land increases might be measured easily. The planning decision to change land use from agricultural to urban, or from residential to commercial, or increase the building densities leads to such a high rate of price increase that it is comparable to creating a new land value. Such a planning decision, being a result of urban growth, creates an additional value sometimes defined as an economic rent.

Generally land price increases resulting from population growth and urban development are seen as "normal" profits or "normal" capital gain in comparison with land-value increases resulting from public authorities' decisions or public capital investment. A more detailed analysis may cause some doubts about this assumption. Generally population growth creates a higher demand for dwellings and in such a way leads to a higher demand for land. But the higher demand for housing does not affect the price of building materials as much as land prices, as the supply of land is not so easily increased. The peculiar nature of the urban land market therefore leads to a state in which even the "normal" increased land value has an element of "unearned increment".

Therefore, it might appear astonishing that in some countries with a high level of land prices the taxation on land profits is lower than on other kinds of capital gains. This may be explained by the fact that land profit taxation stems from a time when urban land prices were not increasing at such a high rate as in the last 20 years.

The patterns and the rate of land profit tax depends on the socio-economic structure of a country, the general structure of public finance and planning, on the society's view of land as a factor in human settlements and the political approach to equity and the redistribution of wealth.

The United Kingdom

The United Kingdom is an example of a country where land profit taxation is a result of a general approach of comprehensive planning and of an attitude regarding social justice and the redistribution of income and wealth. The history of the betterment tax in the UK is a history of political changes and differing political views. During the Second World War different committees prepared schemes for post-war society based on principles of planning, nationalization and social justice. In 1942 the Uthwatt Committee published a report advocating overall planning (national, regional and local) of economic activity and urban and rural development. For land policy, the report suggested that the most efficient way to ensure land use for future development was nationalization. But the authors of this report did not propose complete dissolution of property rights, keeping in mind the probable opposition of public opinion and therefore the inability of the government to carry out such a programme. The Uthwatt Committee therefore recommended nationalizing development rights to use the land instead of nationalizing the land itself.

On the basis of this recommendation, the Town and Country Planning Act of 1947 introduced a taxation rate of 100% of the additional land value created through development. The theoretical justification of such a high rate of tax was that the planning process is creating a new land value as a result of the development and, therefore, this additional value belongs to the community whose activity is the source of the new land value.

1. Planning was subject to central control. All plans had to be submitted to the Minister for his approval. This made planning national in character.

2. All development rights were vested in the state. In future if an owner wished to develop his land he had to obtain permission from the planning authority to do so. At the same time as planning permission was given, a development charge was levied calculated as the difference between the present and the future use value of the site. This was intended to ensure that all land would change hands at existing use value. Then the problems of compensation and betterment would not arise, because all development values accrued to the state.

3. A Central Land Board was set up to handle the claims for compensation and appeals about the new development tax. This overcame certain problems of changing values.

4. Planning authorities and other statutory authorities were given wider powers of compulsory acquisition in order to make sure that land was available for suitable development; but it was not intended that these powers should be used as a general rule.

5. A new basis for compensation was provided in the event of compulsory acquisition—this was the existing use value.

6. A fund of £300 million was set up to meet cases of hardship arising out of the loss of values that existed on the enacting date.*

The provisions of the 1947 Act did not achieve the expected results. Landowners were not interested in selling their land if they had to pay all the profit resulting from its development. The transactions which were actually realized were based on the payment of the betterment tax not by the landowners but by the buyers, thus increasing the land prices. The real importance of the new regulations was mostly for the public authorities, whose compulsory purchases were now on the basis of the former land value (based on pre-war prices) and not on market prices (representing the expected values after development).

The Conservative government (elected in 1951) eliminated the 100% betterment tax but left unchanged the compensation provisions of the 1947 Act. The result was that landowners who sold their land on the private market received the full market price (including the full development value), while the landowners who were obliged to supply their land to the public authorities only got compensation according to the low former land value (without any part of the development values).

The 1959 Act changed this ridiculous situation by introducing payment of the full market price for land bought by public authorities by compulsory purchase.

The return of a Labour government in 1964 again led to change in betterment taxation. In 1967 a development levy was introduced to start at 40% of the realized development value increasing to 50% in 1968. This tax level was higher than the ordinary capital gain tax of 30% (applicable to land profits not due to development). The Conservative

* *Land Values*, edited by Peter Hall, London, 1965, pp. 64–65.

government abolished the special betterment levy in 1971 applying the ordinary capital gain tax (to a maximum of 30%) to all land transactions.

Recent proposals are influenced by the general approach of the new Labour government programme, which is to nationalize all land designated by development schemes for future urban growth. The proposed rate of betterment tax is 80%. This rate is very high, but lower than the 100% introduced by the 1947 Act, as a result of the failure of the 100% rate to take all the additional development value from the landowners. The purpose is to take for the benefit of the community a considerable part of the extra development value, but to leave to the landowners a part as an incentive to sell the land so as not to eliminate the functioning of the land market.

> ... In the cases of compensation and betterment the conflict is between taking away the gains of development value from benefited owners on the one hand, and keeping the market working on the other. An owner will only sell his land for development provided he obtains for it more than it is worth to him in its existing use. If for reason of equity, or saving in cost to the public, or on any other grounds, the extra value is taken away from him he will not be willing to make his land available and the market will break down. This means that the choice of solution to the problems depends in the first place upon how much importance is attached to the continued satisfactory working of the market. If the market is held to be indispensable to the allocative process a very different kind of solution is likely to result from that where the market is deemed to have outlived its usefulness.
>
> In this connection it is possible to take one of two views. Either we can argue that the market is an anachronism because the job of allocating land to its various uses has been taken over by the planning machine, or we can say that the market is still necessary because it secures that land is utilized most efficiently within the use limits laid down by the plan. Each of these views is tenable on its own assumptions and this is part of the difficulty. A final solution is hard to find, because the holders of these opposite views tend to divide along the lines of the two major political parties.*

It might be suggested that beside these two opposite views there exists a third alternative. Besides dependence on a well-functioning market and allocation of land resources only by public authorities, there might be a possibility of an effective mixed mechanism based on a deciding role by the public authorities in the allocation of land for different purposes, but leaving some areas (and especially built-up areas) to the functioning of market mechanism.

* *The History of Compensation and Betterment since 1900, pp. 54–55.*

The experience of the history of the betterment tax in Britain may show that a high level of betterment tax without a high level of property tax and other land-use policy measures may not achieve the planning and social policy objectives which were the basis for the recommendation by the Uthwatt Committee.

Different countries have introduced in recent years high levels of land profit taxes. Norway, Sweden, Denmark, France, Taiwan and South Korea are countries where land profits are taxed at the level of 60–80%. There are differences in between each of these countries in evaluating land profits and in the way of collecting this tax. Generally, it is connected with the differences with the overall taxation system of the country.

Denmark

This tax is elaborated in the act called "Act on Special Income Tax". It has been amended several times since it was first introduced in 1960. The most important new amendments are as follows: the tax is levied on the difference between a final amount (the selling price, with regulations for private mortgages) and the basic amount; if the property has been bought after 1 January 1966 the basic amount is the price at which the seller has acquired the property; but if the property has been bought before 1 January 1966 the seller can choose the total value at the 1965 general valuation as basic value instead.

The regulated basic amount is calculated as 30% plus 6% for each year between the original purchase and the sale to account for inflation. The first 6000 Kr of profit more than the actual payment value is exempt from tax. There are additional exemptions for small value property. The levy on the regulated profit is 65%.*

France

Land profits resulting from transactions of buildable land held less than 5 years are treated as profits from commercial transactions and are subject to general individual income taxation rates. Profits achieved

---

* *Valuation and Taxation of Real Property in Denmark*, p. 14.

from selling land after 5 years are taxed at a rate of 60% of the difference between the selling price and the original price paid for the land. The calculation of the original price is adjusted by 25%, and by the increase in the cost of living; for each year of land maintenance an additional increase of 3% is added to the calculated purchasing price.

Norway

In Norway profits on the sale of land are normally taxed as income. In the case of sales of relatively large tracts of land, which the owner has kept for some time, this is very significant, since much more than half of his profit may be taken as income tax. For people who have a high income from other sources, this may happen even if only a small piece of land is sold. Because of the gradually rising general price level, the sale of the land may even lead to a loss in real value when the tax is deducted. Generally, taxing profits as income leads to some withholding of land from the market. The reluctance to sell is supported by the fact that the general taxation of fixed properties is low, so that it does not cost very much in taxes to keep land, even within or near a built-up district. In 1960 the tax on built-up land was between 0·4% and 0·8% of assessed value, varying in different municipalities. Exempted from taxes are houses financed by the State Housing Bank, municipal properties and, sometimes, houses more than 20 years old.

Sweden

Until 1968 profits accruing from land transactions were taxed only if the land had been held in ownership for less than 10 years. Property that had been held in ownership for more than 10 years and subsequently sold was exempt from this tax. This system had a negative effect on the land market and hence on revenue from taxation as landowners waited for at least 10 years before selling their property in order to avoid payment of this tax.

The legislation of 1968 changed this situation by stipulating that profit from any transaction of land was to be taxed irrespective of the length of time that the land had been held in ownership by the vendor.

Property sold after less than 2 years of ownership is taxed on 100% of the profit while property sold after 2 years of ownership is taxed on 70% of the profit. The profit made is calculated as the difference between gross income and the purchase price (on the part of the vendor), bearing in mind the continuously declining purchasing value of money. The calculated amount of profit is therefore adjusted according to the increase shown by the Consumer Price Index during the period from the year of purchase to the year of sale. Additionally, the amount spent on improvements to the property during the period of ownership is deducted from the calculated gross income. For residential property there is a further deduction of 3000 crowns (US$600) for every year of ownership. Therefore, tax on profits from transactions of residential property is less than that on property in commercial use. The deductions applicable to developed land are not applicable to vacant land. For a property which has been in ownership for a very long time, there is a possibility of choosing one of two ways of assessing the purchasing price:

(a) on the basis of the estimated value 20 years before the sale occurred, *or*

(b) as 150% of the assessed value in 1940.

The rate of tax on profits from land transactions is usually based on the General Income Tax because this profit is considered to be a revenue and is therefore included in that which is taxable by the General Income Tax.

South Korea

Land profits are collected on the basis of the Real Property Speculation Check Tax which was introduced in 1967. The aim of this tax was to restrain land speculation by collecting the profits from land transfer. The rate of tax is 50% from "net assessible marginal profit". The profit is calculated as the difference between the selling price and the acquisition costs. The purchasing price is adjusted by the wholesale commodity index. Also, the cost of capital improvements and land maintenance and the expenses in connection with the land transaction are included.

Taiwan

The land profits resulting from transactions are taxed by the "Land Value Increment Tax" (LVIT) introduced in 1964. The land profit is calculated on the basis of the difference between the selling and purchasing price. The acquisition price is adjusted to the rate of inflation and the cost of improvements. Rates of LVIT are 20% of land-price increment if the increment is less than 100% of the parcel's previous value; 40% of the part of the increment between 100 and 200%, 60% on that part between 200 and 300%, and 80% of any increment over 300% of the parcel's previous value. A special rate of 10% applies to the sale of small owner-occupied plots. For industrial land which will continue to be used as a factory site after transfer, LVIT rates are reduced by 50% (above a certain point). No LVIT is levied in the case of land acquired by government on a compulsory basis.

The common features of the tax system in some of the above investigated countries are not only a relatively high rate of land profit taxation. Of special interest is the way of evaluating land profits which aims to exclude the impact of inflation on land-price increases. Some countries with a very high level of inflation (such as South Korea, Taiwan and also France) are calculating the acquisition price adjusted for the increase in the cost of living. Denmark, in order to avoid the complicated calculation of adjusting for inflation, adds 30% to the purchase price, along with 6% yearly as a fair return on the invested capital in land.

There are some countries with a policy of taxing land profits at a lower rate of taxation. These countries are mostly interested in ensuring incentives for capital investment in land. Real estate business in such countries is seen as an important factor in economic progress. Generally, the low rate of capital-gain taxation is accomplished not so much by a lower rate of taxation but by deducting different expenses for land which reduces the taxable amount of profit. In real estate, as well as for industrial enterprises, a high rate of depreciation has been introduced. Such methods may be justified for estimating the decreased value of machines and buildings with time and maintenance. There is no such justification for land—land does not deteriorate with time. On the contrary, in a period of rapid urbanization its value in general is increasing. It may be that such an approach results from the time when land ownership was a sign of social status and an economic necessity for a citizen. In such countries the rate of tax is higher when land is transferred in a short or medium period of time, and lower for land transfers after a long period of ownership.

Finland

In Finland, the communities collect taxes mainly on income, while the federal government collects taxes on income and property as well as a number of indirect taxes such as a sales tax. There is both an income and a property tax on land. The property tax is of lesser importance. Income derived from land is taxed on the basis of: (a) normal profit, e.g. rent income; (b) sales profit, unless the land has belonged to the same owner for at least 10 years; and (c) professional selling of building-lots if the person or persons concerned are professionally selling lots. The assessment in points (a) and (b) means that the profit is added to the total taxed income which is taxed by the government, the commune and the religious community. In some cases, the "professional" seller may be exempted from the tax if the buyer is a commune. This provision has made public land acquisition somewhat easier (and has decreased the return of taxation).

Switzerland

In Switzerland, each canton has autonomous powers for levying taxes on land profit. The common basis of taxation in all cantons is the fixing of progressive rates of tax on land profit and the reduction of the rate with a long period of ownership. The highest rate on profits is in the canton of Zurich, where it reaches 40%, with an additional 50% (60% of the total profit) if the transaction is made within 2 years of ownership. However, the tax diminishes by 70% if ownership has been established for more than 25 years, meaning that owner will only pay 12% at the highest level. In some cantons, the land profit is not taxed if the land is owned for longer than 10 or 15 years, as in Geneva and Valais.

Israel

Land transaction carried out within 2 years of purchase are taxed as normal commercial transactions on the basis of income tax rates reaching 70% in the highest income brackets (though recently reduced). Land transactions on land owned for more than 2 years are taxed at between 20–40% of land profit. The land profit is calculated on the basis of deducting from the selling price the acquisition prices and also the cost of improvements and the taxes paid during the time the land was held. The rate of tax varies with the length of ownership. For each year of land maintenance 3% is deducted from the taxable amount.

The USA

Land profits are taxed on the basis of the general capital-gains tax, which is 50% lower than the income-tax rate. The highest income-tax rate has been 50%, while capital gains as well as land profits are taxed at most at 25%. The real level of the tax on real estate profits is lower, because of many deductable items which reduce the taxable amount.

The reduced rate of taxation of land profits after a longer time period of land holding has a negative impact on land supply to the market in countries using such a system. Landowners are interested in keeping land as long as possible in order to pay a lower rate of taxation. Obviously, such a taxation system is not the only reason for the reduced supply to the market. The permanently increasing land prices resulting from rapid urbanization and the expected price increases in the future are also influencing the land market in countries where there is a fixed rate of taxation on the land profits without regard to length of ownership. It may be suggested that the timing of the payment of the tax on additional value may have an impact on the supply of land to the market.

5. TAXES TO FULFIL PLANNING GOALS

One of the problems affecting negatively the implementation of plans is the existence of vacant land in the urbanized areas; therefore some countries have introduced taxation measures which aim to make it expensive to hold unused land, and to prevent more intensive land use than according to plan. At the same time some taxes aim to put land on the market by collecting taxes on the increase in land value due to planning decisions at the time of that decision.

Taxation of Vacant Land

For urban development purposes, special importance should be attributed to the taxation of vacant land in urbanized areas. For example, some countries have introduced a higher rate of taxation on vacant land than on improved land. The purpose is to make the maintenance costs of vacant land more expensive, in order to influence landowners to use the site for building purposes. Such taxation on unbuilt property in urbanized areas has already been introduced in some countries. *Spain* introduced a special tax on vacant land in areas declared as urbanized. After declaration as an urbanized area, the rate is 0·5% of the market value, or of the expected value after development. After provision of infrastructure, landowners must then pay a rate equal to 2% of market value, and after 5 years, if landowners keep the site unused for construction purposes, they must pay a rate of 5% of the market value.

Syria introduced a differential rate of property tax on vacant land according to the value of the site. The intent of the regulation is to keep the tax low on small low-valued sites which, for instance, owners are holding for housing construction for themselves or their family. The rate increases with increases in site value so that owners keeping land vacant in urbanized areas for speculative purposes will pay more. The regulation of 1966 introduced the following rates according to the site value:

less than $12,050	1%
$12,051–$24,100	2%
$24,101–$73,100	3%
$73,101–$124,500	4%
$124,501–up	5%

Also according to this regulation, the municipality is entitled to put a site up for public auction if the landowner does not pay taxes for a 3-year period. Of course, such a regulation is designed to influence the landowners to use the land themselves or sell to someone else who will use it for construction.

Another example is in *Taiwan*, which introduced a progressive rate of taxation on vacant land of two to five times the basic property tax rate, again with exceptions for small landowners wanting to build their own home.

There is also a municipal tax on vacant sites in urban areas in *Chile*. The tax takes effect 5 years after a detailed planning scheme has been approved, and is levied at an increasing rate each year (starting at 1% of the assessed value and rising by 1% each year to 6%) until the land is used for construction purposes.

Taxes Forcing Compliance with Planning Schemes

Some taxation policies also have relevance for effectuating planning goals. For example, in 1967 a *French law* introduced a tax of 90% (it has recently been proposed to fix this rate at 100%) to be paid on land used more intensively than allowed by the land use coefficient. For example, if, because of pressing needs, a municipality permits a 10-storey building where only 5-storeys are allowed, the landowner pays a tax of 90–100% of the value of that land used more intensively.

A variant of a "planning tax" is the *Spanish* tax on vacant sites, which is applied according to the stage of the development scheme. Additionally, the Spanish Land Law of 1956 allows municipalities to apply a planning tax specifically on vacant land in city centres, land under compulsory sale, and on buildings of insufficient height (below permitted storey level according to the planning scheme). This particular ordinance is significant because most taxes and land-use regulations apply only to the actual use of the development plan. The 1965 law also introduced a measure permitting the public authority to expropriate land in new urbanized areas when it is not used according to the development scheme.

Taxes on Land in Order to Pay Development Costs

Some countries introduced a system of payment of land-price increases not at the time of purchase, but either periodically or when a land-use change occurs as a result of public authority decisions.

Denmark introduced recently a land value tax when land is transferred from agricultural to urban use. The tax rate is 40% for the first 200,000Kr ($50,000) of land profit and 60% for any higher amount. The tax is collected after a public authority to change land use. The municipal council is obliged to buy the land if the owner is not interested in keeping the land (since he has to pay the tax). The owner may obtain a delay of up to 4 years in paying the tax. He may also get a mortgage to pay the tax over 12 years.

The estimation of the taxable additional value increase is based on the published evaluation of all land properties in Denmark carried out by the public authorities every 4 years.

Denmark also had a tax of 4% on all additional land value, paid periodically after each evaluation. This tax was abolished as a result of public opposition in a referendum in 1965.

Australia also has a tax on the land-value increase resulting from public authority decisions to change use, to be levied immediately after such a decision has been taken. The rate of the tax is 50%. The taxable amount is based on a difference between the evaluation of planned urban price and former agricultural price. In order to defend the interest of the small landowners, agricultural land up to $15,000 is exempted.

Taiwan levies a high rate of tax (graduated to 80%) on the increase in value of land that is held more than 10 years of ownership. These measures have the aim of increasing the land supply to the market, by imposing an additional land tax on landowners if they have not sold their land after many years (for speculative reasons).

South Korea. The government introduced a tax of 30–40% in the metropolitan area of Seoul on land changed from agricultural to urban use. The collection of this tax has to provide the financial means to carry out the infrastructure works in the new urbanized area.

It may be suggested that the taxation of the additional land value created by urban growth periodically, rather than at the time of transfer of ownership, may increase the supply of land to the market and also provide the public authorities with the needed means to finance development schemes. Increasing the maintenance costs of holding land vacant as a financial investment and improving the financial position of the public authorities (enabling them to carry out more development works) may be seen as one of the most efficient means of increasing the supply of land to the market and thus restraining land prices increases.

6. VALUATION METHODS

The effectiveness of land taxation is in large measure dependent on the evaluation system. The rate of tax on profits may be very high, but if the evaluation system does not function appropriately the actual tax rate (based on the difference between the original purchase price and the selling price) may be far lower.

An ineffective evaluation system is also likely to be an unfair one. Where there is no system which limits the freedom of an evaluator to rate property as he sees fit, and also allows public comparison of the evaluations of different properties, there is no guarantee that every citizen will be paying the tax equally. This problem of equity in turn creates resistance to payment.

In order for tax methods to be efficient, a periodic public evaluation carried out by the same system for the whole country would be appropriate. This would ensure that there was a check on the decisions of individual evaluators (who in the current system are under great pressure to change their evaluations in order that owners should avoid high taxes), and would also show all citizens that they had the same rights and the same obligations. It would also be extremely useful for determining compensation in the case of public appropriation procedures.

The importance of such a uniform, systematic, periodic and public evaluation system cannot be underestimated. Some principles of land tax administration have been drawn from the UN report on that subject.

There are three criteria which a system of property valuation must meet if it is to provide a satisfactory and practical source of revenue from taxation. It is essential that the system be based on valuation arrived at uniformly, appraisals that result in equalized values and a relatively inexpensive cost of administration. To fulfill these requirements, a system that employs the three basic approaches of sales analysis, income capitalization and replacement cost has been developed that is based primarily upon appraisal by comparison. This process of appraising property for purposes of taxation is referred to as the mass appraisal approach.

To facilitate the process of comparing properties, they are classified and the values are reduced to area or frontage standard units to establish a common denominator which eliminates the many variations characteristic of individual parcels and therefore provides a valid basis for making the comparison.

The establishment of standard units of value for the parcels of known value and then the extension by comparison of the units of properties of unknown value establish the value of the parcels as if they were standard; but many parcels are not standard. The system of valuation by the mass appraisal approach provides rules, formulae and factual tables for the modification of standards units and standard parcels that are applicable to all types of urban parcels.

Sales data, which is generally considered the best evidence of value if enough reliable data are available, can be used to appraise both improved and unimproved land. It is the only approach that lends itself to the appraisal of vacant parcels because such property does not produce income—at least not in accordance with its highest and best use—and since there is no building or other structure the replacement cost approach is inapplicable. Both sales analysis and income capitalization are adaptable to the appraisal of urban land with improvements on it only if used in conjunction with replacement cost, the process being to determine the value of the improvements by the replacement cost approach and deducting that amount from the sale price or the capitalized income, leaving the residue to be attributed to the value of the land.

There are five broad categories of urban land according to use—residential, commercial, industrial, institutional and recreational—which provide the basis for the classification of urban land. Residential classification refers to areas in which the predominant use is for dwellings, whether owner-occupied or leased, which eliminates such establishments as hotels, motels, hospitals and rest homes, which are primarily commercial enterprises. Commercial classification is applicable to areas in which the predominant use is for retail business. Areas devoted to light and heavy industry, usually including wholesale and warehouse districts, are classified as industrial. Property used for government purposes at all levels, schools and other educational institutions, whether public or private, hospitals and other health institutions, churches and other religious institutions, and other property similarly used is included in the institutional classification. Property devoted to parks and playgrounds, whether publicly or privately owned, is classified as recreational.*

Some examples of the problems of land tax evaluation are drawn from several countries.

Korea. Land tax administration and collective procedures, even after the 1967 property tax reforms, continue to be inadequate. Because cadastral maps are incomplete, the accuracy of self-assessment cannot in many cases be checked. Even more seriously, the few properties whose assessments are in fact checked are valued by government employees who are quite often not professional valuers, using unsystematic techniques. Public resistance to those "unscientific" valuations has been stiff. Local officials are sometimes reluctant to revalue one property when they know that all other properties in a given area also need revaluing. There is also evidence that taxes are being evaded through underreporting of sales prices.

The Real Property Speculation Check Tax has also been largely ineffective. Although it probably had a beneficial impact in the first few months of its existence, the exemption of vacant land from the tax, as well as expectations that the 1967 law might be abolished, have made it virtually impossible to enforce. Since 1969 land speculation has again

---

* *UN Manual of Land Tax Administration,* New York, 1968.

been intense, and has focused particularly on idle urban land because of its relatively lower level of taxation.

As in most other countries, expropriation procedures in South Korea are so cumbersome and time-consuming that they are resorted to only when a negotiated price becomes impossible to agree upon. These delays can be especially serious in South Korea, however, because the rapid rise in land prices can significantly increase acquisition costs.

Taiwan. The Land Value Tax (LVT) is the government's principal means of taxing the value of urban land on a recurrent basis. Levied annually by provincial or municipal governments, it is payable by the landowner. Both the Land Value Tax and the Land Value Increment Tax apply to "urban land", defined as (a) all lands located within legally established city planning areas and (b) areas not under legally established city plans designed by the Minister of Interior Affairs as sites for future commercial centres, seaports, or other urban development.

The LVT is not levied on land due for expropriation. In practice, as in the case in most other countries, compensation usually equals or is very close to full market value.

Zoning ordinances have not succeeded in preventing large-scale encroachments of commercial and industrial enterprises into residential areas, as is also true of many other countries. Furthermore, there is no effective density zoning to control excessively high densities in and around urban areas, particularly in squatter settlements.

Official assessments are often badly out of date. Except for a reassessment in Taipei early in 1968, the last general island, wide assessment of urban land took place in 1964. Much of the efficiency of the self-assessment system is consequently negative, since owners only have to declare to within 80% of a government figure that may be several years old. In instances where the landowner feels that his parcel might be expropriated (and consequently, where a self-assessment far under market value would be foolish), he will often declare a value very close to or even higher than the government's official assessment. Because tax rates are low and administration weak, he gains much more in compensation than he loses through higher taxes.

In the experience of both advanced and developing countries, fair and up-to-date assessment procedures are vitally important to the success of urban land-use controls. In Taiwan, for example, the advantages of the dual assessment system are mitigated by out-of-date official assessments. Landowners have little difficulty producing an assessed value within 80% of the low government figure.

Even though comprehensive assessments are difficult and expensive, short cuts, such as untrained valuers or revaluation of a sample of properties, may only result in bitterness and resistance. Knowledge of land prices and even of assessment procedures is spread widely throughout systems in the sample of countries examined. Real estate agents are usually well aware of the prevailing market values of properties, registered and unregistered, in their communities. In South Korea and Taiwan real estate agents are consulted by the public authorities in the process of determining official assessments. There is thus little chance that an unfair assessment will go unnoticed. Moreover, resistance is not confined to the case of one individual having a heavier tax burden than another. All landowners will often resist assessments they feel are arbitrary or capricious even though all are being treated equally.*

Australia. In Australia, land tax is assessed on the unimproved capital value of the land. The Valuer-General is required to issue at least once every 6 years for each property three valuations, viz. Unimproved Capital Value (UCV), Improved Capital Value (ICV), Assessed Annual Value (AAV). Only the UCV and AAV are used for rating and taxing purposes. Every class of land is valued including "strata" and air rights, and mineral-bearing land (mines and quarries).

The improved value of land is the capital sum which the fee simple of the land might be expected to realize if offered for on such reasonable terms and conditions, as a bona-fide seller would require.

In determining the improved value of any land being premises occupied for trade, business, or manufacturing purposes, such value shall not include the value of any plant, machines, tools or other appliances which are not fixed to the premises, or which are only so

* International Bank for Reconstruction and Development, *Social Appropriation for Betterment.*

fixed that they may be removed from premises without structural damage thereto.

The unimproved value of land is the capital sum which the fee simple of the land might be expected to realize if offered for sale on such reasonable terms and conditions as a bona-fide seller would require, assuming that the improvements, if any, thereon or appertaining thereto, and made or acquired by the owner or his predecessor in title, had not been made.

The assessed annual value of land is nine-tenths of the fair average annual value of the land, with the improvements (if any) thereon; provided that such assessed annual value shall not be less than 5% of the improved value of the land.

When the Valuer-General issues a certificate of valuation for rating purposes, which he is obliged to do at least every 6 years under the Act, the certificate sets out the valuation district, the owner's name, the address of the property, the dimensions and area of the land, the particulars of title, and if improved land a very brief description of the improvements; and then in columns the UCV, ICV and AAV with the date the valuation takes effect in the council's books, and the date of issue. One copy is sent to the owner or ratepayer, and a duplicate to the local council. An owner dissatisfied with the valuation may lodge an objection within 42 days of its issue.

When an objection is lodged, the Valuer-General will decide whether he will amend the valuation or disallow the objection. On receipt of the reply the objector has the right to request that the matter be referred to a Valuation Board of Review, which consists of three members, two of which are practising valuers. Objectors may be represented in person by counsel, solicitor or agent, witnesses may be called and submissions made in writing. The rules of evidence are not strictly adhered to, nor is evidence taken on oath. If either side is dissatisfied with the Board's decision, the matter may be referred to the Land and Valuation Court, which has Supreme Court's status, and the matter is heard as a completely new case strictly in accordance with the law and rules of evidence which is given on oath. The case is heard before a single judge without a jury, and there is no appeal to a higher Court, except on a point of law, in which the final Arbiter is the Full Supreme Court of New South Wales or the High Court of Australia.

Denmark. Denmark first introduced a periodic, variable evaluation system in 1922, with a general evaluation of all properties taking place every 4 years, though a special evaluation takes place when a property has been transferred to urban use during the 4-year period. Land value is assessed separately from the improvements on the land as since 1926 there have been two kinds of taxes: land-value taxes and taxes on improvements. It is important to note that the Danish evaluation system is based on the use of the same evaluative criteria for the whole country. Assessors are elected by the municipality and their work is supervised by appointed officials of the Ministry of Finance. It is the task of the Ministry to prepare the needed material for formulating the criteria used by the assessors to evaluate property. The transactions which take place during the 4-year period together with other factors associated with planning decisions and development works carried out during the period constitute one criterion for evaluation. The results of the tax evaluation are published as maps and made available to every citizen in Denmark. The evaluation serves as the basis for the property tax, for compensation in case of expropriation, and as a basis for collecting the benefit tax of land transactions.

General valuations, i.e. valuations of all properties, take place every 4 years. In between there is a valuation every year of properties that have undergone changes, e.g. by parcelling out or by investments to a certain extent. Moreover, owners can, at any time, require an additional valuation, those valuations and the annual valuations are based on the price level at the last 4 years general valuation keeping in mind the changes made after the general valuation. Finally there is a special valuation when a property has been transferred to urban zone.

The valuation organization is very democratic, being based upon participation from non-specialist citizens elected by the municipality councils or appointed by the Minister of Finance on the basis of proposals from the county boards or trade organizations and unions.

The country is divided into 1908 valuation districts: 6–13 districts are administered by 1 chairman, who, together with 2 valuers elected by the municipal board for a period of 4 years, constitute the valuation committee for each district. The chairman is appointed by the Minister of Finance on the basis of proposals from the county board. The chairmen are again united in supervisory boards or committees, 1, 2 or 3 in each county.

Prior to a general valuation, a preliminary valuation is performed based on a sample of various categories of property chosen by the district committee assisted by the supervisory board. The preliminary valuations are checked and revised by the supervisory board, and after having been examined by the assessment directorate they are used as a basis of negotiations between each supervising board and the assessment directorate and members of the assessment board.

As a basis for examination of the valuations the following material is available:

1. A questionnaire in which the owner has given certain information about the property: the area, the buildings, improvements, public and private investments. The owner also has the option of giving his proposal for the valuation of his property in the questionnaire but this option is little used and of little importance.
2. Information on sales of real estate property in the region. To ensure that information about sales is as complete as possible. A buyer must deliver a completed questionnaire containing information on the size of the purchase money paid and the method of payment. The information about sales is, of course, of fundamental importance to the valuations, and is being continually prepared for statistical information.
3. Valuation maps are made to various scales according to the needs in different areas. The maps show the assessed land values per hectare or m^2, which makes a comparison with valuations of neighbouring properties very easy; moreover, the maps contain information on sale prices of unbuilt land in areas where a number of such sales take place.

When the valuation is completed information on the land valuation in the urban district together with the land-value maps are deposited for public inspection. Owners as well as the municipal councils have the right of objection and appeal within 4 weeks, the owners being able to object not only to their own assessment but also to those of others. Appeals must be directed to the Taxation Court.

The periodical evaluation system with published evaluation maps aids the efficient collection of the property tax and at the same time serves as a basis for estimating land profit in the case of land transfer and compensation in the case of expropriation.

SUMMARY REMARKS

The efficiency of taxation methods might be measured by their effect on the financing and planning of urban growth. Taxation on land, like other types of taxation, has a fiscal purpose to assure income for the public authorities; at the same time in some countries the additional aim of taxation is to serve as a means to redistribute income and wealth in order to reduce inequality. Taxation on land has two additional aims: to give the community the additional value created through public authority planning decisions and investments, and to serve as a means to increase the supply of land needed for urban development.

The review of various taxation methods adopted in various countries shows that there are various attempts to adjust the taxation system to the growing needs of public expenditure on urban services which are permanently increasing in cost. But it may be suggested that in no country has the taxation system succeeded in collecting the major part of the additional value created through the urbanization process. Experts in different countries have made estimates of the size of this additional value. Colin Clark has estimated the increase in urban land values in the UK over a 7-year period as £16,000 million. In the Federal Republic of Germany it was estimated that the gain in urban land value in the post-war years amounted to DM100,000 million ($25 billion). This is in countries where the increase in land prices has averaged around 10% per year. In the less-developed countries price increases have been 20–30% yearly.

It is suggested by some experts that the land-price increase may be slowed through the introduction of some taxation methods which reduce the possibility of gaining high profits from land. One of the reasons for the high rate in land price increase is the restricted supply of land in areas where there is a high demand. Therefore it may be suggested that a taxation system which makes it expensive to hold land vacant may increase the supply of land to the market and hence reduce land prices. The introduction of a high rate of tax on vacant land, with an increasing rate for each year the land remains unbuilt, may lead to an increase in supply of land to the market. Obviously it is necessary to collect this tax regularly and to expropriate the land of those owners who avoid the tax. Of additional importance is the exact evaluation of land at its current market value in order to avoid the payment of taxes based on an outdated (and very low) price for that land.

Another useful device is the differential assessment of land and buildings in order to encourage the use of land to the fullest extent possible according to planning regulations. For example, buildings may be taxed at half the rate of land.

An additional factor influencing the efficiency of tax collection and discouraging excessive land price increases is the payment of a tax on the additional value created through planning decisions not at the time of transfer of land ownership, but at the time the public authority decision to change land use was made. Such measures may ensure a considerable income for the public authority and at the same time should diminish the attractiveness of capital investment in land, holding it unbuilt after a change in planning regulations. Payment at the time the planning decision is made may influence the use of land for development purposes. It may be suggested that a 60% rate of betterment tax payable at the time of planning decision may allow the public authority to collect a larger amount than a tax rate of 80% collected at the time of change of land ownership.

Agricultural land where planning permission for a change to urban use has been given presents a special problem. If there is such a betterment tax as described above (which today only exists in Denmark) then it is suggested that agricultural land may be taxed only on the basis of its agricultural use value, as the additional value due to a prospective change in use will be received by the public authorities through their betterment tax. But if this is not the case it may be suggested that the system of deferred payment of the full rate of tax (which would be collected after a number of years retroactively when the land changed in use) may help to keep land in agricultural use as long as possible.

One of the major problems of urban growth which the taxation system has not been able to solve is the gap between the large expenditures necessary by the big city in order to provide services for the population of the entire city region and the income of the large city which is derived solely from those living within its administrative boundaries. The relationship between the city, the city region and the central government concerning the division of urbanization costs has not found a proper expression in the taxation system. Some attempts have been made to introduce a municipal income tax, usually as part of the national income tax. Such a system involves an extraordinarily large payment of a proportion of the income tax to the big cities which have the largest expenses. There have also been adopted in some parts of the USA income taxes of the city payable by all those who work in the city; additionally a special sales tax is collected on all goods sold in the city.

The method of taxation in the city and city region is related to the general structure of a city-regional government which does not effectively exist in almost all city regions of the world. The lack of such an authority with overall responsibility for urban-growth expenditures leads to planning decisions being taken by some local authorities based on short-term fiscal necessities which are in conflict with long-term planning goals (for example, decisions to allow higher densities in order that a developer will give some land to the local authority for community use).

Taxation of land is part of the general taxation system which is ultimately an expression of the socio-economic structure of a country. The growing responsibility of the state for providing essential services has led to the strengthening of the public sector of the economy and also to a higher proportion of taxation in total GNP. Therefore it might seem astonishing that such an important part of the economy as the urban land market, in which there has been such a large increase in value during the last 20 years, has not found an appropriate expression in the taxation system, especially given the growing cost of urban growth for the public authorities. This has occurred in a period when the large amount of untaxed profit on land has exercised a considerable pressure on the financial market (i.e. adding inflationary pressures to the economy). Probably one of the reasons for the lack of an effective property tax system is that land is widely held by many small investors as security in a time of permanent inflation. The attempt in some countries to overcome the opposition of the large strata of property owners to a high rate of taxation has led them to fix a graduated rate of tax on property, whereby those who only own a small amount of property pay a lower rate than those with large land holdings. Measures of this nature may be useful in overcoming the political opposition to effective land-taxation systems.

Obviously one of the basic factors leading to successful implementation of taxation policy is the existence of an efficient evaluation system. The experience of different countries using particular evaluation systems is that a system of periodic and public evaluation is relatively inexpensive in relation to the advantages that such a system has. When landowners perceive that the system of evaluation is fair and based on common criteria, there is less evasion of taxes and less scope for corruption than when decisions about evaluation are made relatively arbitrarily.

The linking of the revenue from land taxation with the expenses for the essential services connected with urban growth may help to eliminate the opposition of the majority of the population to effective land-taxation methods.

REFERENCES

Archer, R. W., "Site value taxation in central business district redevelopment", *Urban Land Institute Research Report* 19, 1965.

Cheo, I. K. "A preliminary study of taxation on urban vacant land in Taiwan", in *Land for the Cities of Asia, op. cit.*

Clark, Colin, "Land taxation: lessons from international experience", in *Land Values*, edited by Peter Hall, London, 1965.

Hady, Thomas F., "Differential assessment of farmland on the urban rural fringe", *American Journal of Agricultural Economics*, Vol. 52 (Feb. 1970).

International Bank for Reconstruction and Development, *Social Appropriation for Betterment*, May 1972.

Lichfield, C. O., *A Valuation for Rating and Taxation*, London, 1968.

Netzer, Dick, *Economics of the Property Tax*, Washington, DC, 1966.

Ontario Commission on Taxation, *Report*, 1967, 2 volumes.

Pickard, Jerome Percival, *Changing Urban Land Uses as Affected by Taxation*, Urban Land Institute, Washington, DC, 1962.

Prest, A. R., *Public Finance in the Developing Countries,* London: Weidenfeld & Nicolson, 1975.

Suh, Young Chul, "How land speculation profit is taxes in Korea", International Tax Program, Harvard Business School, 1970.

Turvey, R., *Economics of Real Property*, London, 1957.

United Kingdom, *Land* (White Paper), 1975.

United Nations, *Manual of Land Tax Administration, including Valuation of Urban and Rural Land and Improvements*, New York, 1968.

——, *Urban Land Policies and Land Use Control Measures,* vol. III: *Western Europe*; vol. VI: *Northern America*; vol. II: *Asia and the Far East*, New York, 1973.

United States Senate, Committee of the Interior, Hearings on S.268, *The National Land Use Policy and Planning Assistance Act*, vol. IV, Washington, DC, 1973.

CHAPTER 12

Patterns of Land-Acquisition Policy

The socio-economic structure of a country, its rate of urbanization and its patterns of central and local administration are influencing factors in the formulation of a public land acquisition policy. In addition, the role assumed by the government in supplying the housing needs of its citizens is a deciding factor in the patterns of a public land-acquisition policy. In countries where housing is viewed as a vital public service, much like health and education, which the government must provide, the public authority administering the land-acquisition policy must supply the land needed for public housing projects.

In almost all countries of the world the state has taken the responsibility for supplying the land required in the development of the infrastructure. A solid infrastructure of national roads, railways, water and sewage lines, etc., is an essential factor in the economic development of a country and an essential condition for urban development. Public authorities are required to provide the land needed for infrastructure projects. This land is acquired by forcing landowners of areas being developed to supply the required land for infrastructure works as a condition of approval of a private development scheme, by acquiring the land in the free market or by expropriating the land from the landowners.

Urban development and the growth of public services resulting from the general increase in the standard of living has generated increased demands for public buildings. The provision of land needed for such buildings has been one of the tasks of the public authorities and a force generating public land acquisition.

Thus, public land-acquisition policies and procedures have developed in response to the land requirements of public housing projects, the development of a sound infrastructure and public utility projects. Since most countries are involved in at least one or more of these three activities it is possible to suggest that some kind of public land-acquisition policy exists in almost all countries.

Public authorities are trying to influence urban development by preparing development schemes and establishing land-use regulations. The goal of these policies is to create a legislative framework for urban development. Major differences exist in the planning methods and degree of public intervention used by various countries.

Land-use regulations are designed to enforce the development schemes. Building regulations and land-use schemes may control the types of activities at specific locations but they are unable to influence the timing of land-use changes.

In most cities of the world, private land ownership and the holding of vacant land has created a paradox; while there is a lack of land in the market, there is enough vacant land in cities to carry out the development schemes. This situation is especially obvious in metropolitan areas where high-density districts are surrounded by large vacant tracts of land and construction activities are carried out in response to the land available in the market rather than to the urban needs. The shortage of land required to complete the formulated development schemes pushed building activities into fringe areas where the land required for urban development is readily available.

Pressure to carry out housing projects and to provide land for industrial development and public services motivated public authorities in different countries toward taking an active role in supplying land needed for urban development. Some countries pursue an active acquisition policy, acquiring land which is then supplied to developers in accordance with a development scheme. In most countries public authorities have the power to acquire land and in situations where the land is needed for public purposes they have the power to expropriate the land.

Although most countries have similar compulsory powers, big differences exist between definitions of public purpose. These differences result from the different socio-economic structures of the countries. In countries where the state assumes large responsibilities for the provision of vital services needed by the population, the public purpose has a broad definition. In those countries where public intervention is kept to a minimum, public purpose is restricted to providing land for infrastructure projects.

In some countries the provision of housing is viewed as a vital public service, in which case the public authorities must provide housing for the population. In some countries, on the other hand, the role of the public authority is limited to the provision of financial assistance for public housing. Many efforts have been made to find methods of reducing the cost of public housing. Different methods were introduced which tried to achieve higher productivity, better work organization and improved planning methods. All of these methods were attempts to reduce the cost of public housing. The growing demands on housing by large population strata have induced public authorities to strengthen their role in providing land for public housing projects. It has been the experience of those countries which play a limited role in acquiring land for public housing that the public authorities are spending large sums to acquire land on the free market and paying higher prices as time goes on. As a result, their efforts to reduce costs through higher productivity, etc., have been ineffective.

After some years of experience in providing land for housing projects, the public authorities have found they cannot limit their activities to providing land for present housing needs. As a result of the housing projects carried out, a high percentage of the population was able to improve their housing conditions. They moved from substandard units into new facilities with modern equipment. At first these new units satisfied the desires of the population. As time went on, they had the feeling that a better dwelling unit was not sufficient for their needs. Some of the housing projects provided only a small number of housing units. They did not provide the related schools or cultural facilities. In most cases, the housing projects were built on cheap land located far from the city centre and places of employment. Thus the population moving into the improved housing was required to spend increased travel time when moving to work or to the city centre where vital services were supplied.

On a larger scale, urban development policies are planning larger urban settlements containing dwelling units, service centres, areas for industry, commerce and large networks of public utilities. The planning of these large-scale developments in different countries has resulted in new communities, new urban settlements and new towns in different regions of the countries. At the same time, existing urban districts were redeveloped by adopting the existing land uses to new demands and providing land for public services, recreation and transport. The goal of these planned communities was to improve the housing conditions of the population. In addition, they were viewed as an efficient tool for implementing policies for planned urban growth and balanced population distribution.

While land was being provided for housing projects, the growing demands of industrial development presented the problem of providing the land required for new industries and developing commercial activities. In those countries where the public authority was limited to the provision of housing, there was no connection between the location of new industrial and commercial centres. In many cases, employment opportunities and commercial facilities were located far from the new housing areas. As a result of the increase in land prices in the metropolitan areas, industries were unable to acquire needed land at locations which could supply the needed manpower and distribution centres. In response, some of the public authorities took the responsibility for providing land for industrial and commercial activities. This responsibility gave the public authorities the opportunity to place industries in areas where more rapid development was desired. The United Kingdom, France, Spain, Italy and the Scandinavian countries, Singapore, Hong Kong and some states in India are presently carrying our policies which locate industries to control development.

Increased incomes and higher standards of living have resulted in increased demands on public authorities to provide land for recreational purposes and additional different purposes. Legislation has been amended to allow public authorities to use the power of compulsory purchase to acquire land not only for short-term needs but also for *future* urban development. Some countries (Sweden, Norway, Finland, the Netherlands) have been acquiring land for future urban development during the last 20 years. Other countries (Spain, France, Italy, India, Chile) have introduced legislation in recent years allowing for advance acquisition.

Legislative power which limited public authorities to acquiring land for present needs proved inadequate. The investments by public authorities and urban growth brought an increase in land prices. Housing projects, public facilities and plans prepared for new urban settlements caused large increases in the land prices of land adjacent to the new developments. Thus the public authorities had to invest money to carry out development schemes and then pay higher land prices resulting from the influence of the previous development. In addition, land ordinarily available at a cheap price in the land market became difficult to purchase when development schemes were implemented and even announced because the landowners preferred to hold the land vacant rather than sell it for public development. In response, some countries instituted a policy of advance acquisition by purchasing land in agricultural use which might be used for future urban development. The experience of countries practising advance land acquisition shows that such policies economize public spending and also provide an efficient tool for carrying out development schemes. Policies providing for the acquisition of land needed for long-term development have been introduced in recent years in France, Spain and Sweden. The United Kingdom has a long tradition of acquiring land for new towns and housing projects. Yet, the lack of national authority to acquire land for long-term development forced the local authorities to acquire land solely for immediate housing needs.

Land-acquisition policies are carried out in different patterns as a result of differing political and historical backgrounds in various countries. Land-acquisition policy is related to control measures and legislative sanctions which permit the implementation of advanced acquisition. The impact of acquisition policy on urban development and the land market depends on several factors. The administration, the method of selecting land uses, and the financial means play an important role in defining the impact. In addition, the institutional framework for land acquisition and land administration which are connected to the general government administrative network, and the relationship between local, regional and national authorities influences the impact of public land acquisition on urban development. The land-acquisition policy is a part of a national growth policy and serves as an efficient tool for carrving out national development schemes.

CATEGORIZATION OF LAND-ACQUISITION POLICIES

This survey of public land-acquisition policies will show a wide range of methods and scope of land acquisition. They vary from land acquisition for some purposes and some locations as in the USA, Canada, Singapore, Hong Kong, Chile, India—to more extensive programmes in the Netherlands, Sweden, Israel and Spain.

Most of the surveyed countries require land for carrying out social housing projects, but some include in the purpose of land acquisition the space needed for new towns development (UK, Israel, France, India, Australia). Some countries are leading the land-acquisition policy towards erecting new industrial centres combined with housing projects. This is the aim of erecting "polygones" in Spain for decentralizing the economic activity of Madrid and Barcelona. Also, some of the new towns in India have such housing projects attached to the new industrial centres.

There is a difference in the role of the planned new towns in different countries. The UK and France are developing new towns in large city regions in order to restrain the high rate of growth of the big city. For other countries, new town policy is one of the measures to influence a rapid development of the less populated regions of the country (this is the case in Israel and the example of the new capitals of Brasilia in Brazil and Canberra in Australia).

New towns should be distinguished from new neighbourhoods and new communities. The land-acquisition policy of different countries and cities is aiming to encourage the creation of new planned communities and planned neighbourhoods, which are based on combining housing projects with all needed services for a community, and also trying to develop some employment opportunities for the inhabitants of the planned neighbourhoods or communities. Such planned human settlements are based on a close connection with an existing big city which provides for the inhabitants of the planned communities the majority of employment and high level services. The effect of such new neighbourhoods on urban growth depends on the ability of such communities to absorb urban population growth, avoiding a fragmented development and insuring a comprehensive city region development. The best examples of such a development are in the cities of the Netherlands and Sweden, while this has not happened in France, UK, Israel and Spain despite a policy of extensive public land ownership.

The following survey is intended only to show some of the outstanding examples of advance land-acquisition policies that have been adopted in some particular locations. It begins with examples of more comprehensive acquisition policies as a part of an overall goal of planned new communities. The most important examples of successful, large-scale advance land acquisition programmes (in the Netherlands, Sweden and France) are discussed separately in subsequent chapters.

The UK. The most important experiments in the creation of complete New Towns have been carried out in the UK since 1947.

The New Towns policy was seen as an efficient way of planned redistribution of the population, and especially as a way of decongesting metropolitan areas. By September 1967, twenty-four new towns were erected in Great Britain. According to the official report on the implementation of the New Towns Act, since the late 1940s more than half a million people moved into new towns, which now have a total population of some 950,000. By the end of 1968 some 186,500 new houses, flats and maisonettes, more than 950 new factories, some 620 new offices, nearly 3000 new shops, and about 370 new schools had been built. The necessary services and facilities— such as water, gas, and electricity supplies, roads, youth parks, and public transport—were also provided.

The achievement of the New Towns scheme consists mostly in erecting communities on the basis of socio-economic planning which provide the new population with housing, jobs and services. The planned size of the New Towns (50,000–70,000) was based on the conceptions and technological conditions of the late 1940s. The rise in the standard of living, and the development of high-level services, brought a change in the "size" considered desirable.

A population of 100,000–200,000 for a new town is now seen as the most desirable. For instance, the newly planned town of Milton Keynes has an ultimate planned population of 250,000. In addition to size, the newly erected towns depend not only on building activities of public authorities, but also on private construction which is expected to account for about 50% of the dwellings.

The extensive length of time it takes to create a new town and the difficulties involved in creating the new community, led to the policy of extending small or medium-sized towns, which would combine the advantages of large-scale new building with the benefits of a continuing urban tradition. The Town Development Act of 1952 enabled local authorities of small and medium-sized towns to encourage rapid development, so as to receive population from nearby overcrowded cities.

Land is acquired for New Towns by a Development Corporation which is an autonomous body responsible for the development of the needed infrastructure of the New Town. It is supposed to operate on an economic basis, returning loans received from the central government for land acquisition and development by the sale of plots. In 1964 the New Towns Commission took over the land-acquisition tasks of all the separate development corporations (many of whose functions had been transferred to newly established local government authorities).

In 1965 the government created the *Land Commission* charged with the task of securing that the right land was available at the right time for national, regional and local development plans. This Commission was intended to help local authorities acquire land; it had powers of appropriation of land planned for development and received a working capital of £45 million (as a loan from the central government) for this purpose. However, in practice it seems that there has been a contradiction between the large-scale purposes of the Land Commission and the size of its financial resources (in comparison, land authorities spent £145 million on land acquisition in 1964–5). The Land Commission in 1967–8 had approved proposals for the acquisition of 1500 acres valued at £5·7 million. The Land Commission was abolished by the new government in 1970.*

Australia. Some of the most interesting experiments in public land acquisition have been carried out by various cities and states in Australia. First, the City of Canberra (the federal capital) was planned from the beginning on the basis of public ownership of all land in

* UN, *Urban Land Policies and Land Control Measures*, Vol. III: *Western Europe*, New York, 1973, pp. 296–7.

the city, with leaseholds granted to private individuals at open public auctions. The leases usually run for 99 years, and the land uses permitted are specified in a detailed manner as part of the lease. Land for public purposes (recreation, schools, etc.) is allocated as required to the appropriate public or non-profit agency (e.g. church). This system has succeeded in allowing private development of the city with the exact control over land use that most land use zoning schemes seek to approximate, while at the same time supplying the land needs for public and community purposes without using the private market. One problem has been that the open land kept as a reserve for future development in the city tends to become used customarily as parkland; and there is local opposition to using it for development purposes, even according to planned schemes, to meet the expanding needs (population growth of 10% p.a.). Thus in recent years a nearby suburban town which does not use the Canberra plan has begun to absorb some of the overspill growth.

Another important experiment in public land acquisition has been the South Australia Housing Trust, established in the 1930s and charged with the responsibility of providing cheap public housing in order to encourage industrial development. The Trust, a semi-independent body, has in the post-war period become a massive developer offering low to middle-income housing for both sale and rent, and has built more than one-third of all the land it needed by negotiation (powers of eminent domain were not used). Its most spectacular achievement has been the construction of a complete satellite city of 60,000 people some 15 miles north of Adelaide. It is suggested that land and housing prices have risen to a lesser degree in the Adelaide metropolitan area than in other Australian cities which have been experiencing rapid growth (Adelaide was growing in population by 4·6% per year in the early 1960s).

A third significant Australian example is the Perth Metropolitan Region Planning Authority. Perth has been experiencing a speculative land boom in recent years, with land prices increasing by 15 to 22% annually and land being withheld from the market. This has been due in part to the well-laid-out plans of the Metropolitan Planning Authority for areas of future development, which pinpoints rural areas of interest to speculators. Therefore, since 1965 the Metropolitan

Region Planning Authority has been given the power to acquire land compulsorily for any purpose consistent with the Metropolitan Plan. It has been suggested that the Authority should undertake the major responsibility for future development of land; however, in order that this does not result in large profits for the current speculative holders of land in the path of future development, it has been suggested that compensation should be payable by the Authority to landowners only on the basis of existing use value (i.e. equal to rural prices in distant areas).*

Israel. In Israel a very high percentage of the total land is in national ownership. There are 888,000 hectares of publicly owned land, 150,000 hectares of privately owned land, and 1,000,000 hectares of non-utilized land (mostly desert). However, 47% of the land in or near urban settlements is in private hands; and it is this strategically located land which influences the urban land market.

Therefore there are quite different factors in operation affecting the growth and development of new planned communities in the less populous regions where the land is publicly owned, and the already existing urban regions, where the private land market is the dominant influence.

Public policy has aimed at a more balanced regional development by creating new towns and new settlements in the less populous regions. Regional planning has allowed the creation of comprehensive schemes of agro-industrial development. In one area a network of twenty-five rural cooperatives was established with a new town in the centre and smaller towns for each five villages. In the last 25 years some thirty new towns and 350 new rural collective settlements were established which absorbed 30% of the population growth for that period. New neighbourhoods were also built near the big cities on publicly owned land.

But the interesting aspect of the Israeli situation is that the extensive programme of public land development did not exert any essential influence on the private land market in the big cities. The rate of land-price increase in Jerusalem and Tel Aviv have been

* Peter Harrison, "Urban land policy: some Australian experiments" in *Land for the Cities of Asia, op. cit.*

some of the highest in the world. Because of its location, privately held land had the decisive impact on land prices.

It may be suggested that the high land prices are a result not only of the separation of the private and public sectors of land market and the strategic location of private land, but the result of a lack of an appropriate and comprehensive urban land policy. The taxation system has encouraged the holding of vacant land in urban areas by not taxing land profits as other profits. This has led to a lack of land on the market in the urban areas, and consequently price increases of 20–30% yearly with resulting high suburban densities. At the same time the restriction in the size of private sector due to extensive undeveloped public land holdings have also encouraged speculation.

The example of Israel may serve to show that extensive public land ownership without an appropriate overall land policy is unable to influence land prices in the big city regions, although influencing urban growth patterns in less-developed regions.

Spain. Spain has undergone rapid urbanization and industrialization in recent years, causing a great strain on existing resources and leading to very steep rises in land prices in urban areas. In response to this situation, the government created a central land authority, the *Gerencia de Urbanizacion*, with the duty of acquiring the land needed for new industrial and residential centres. Legal powers already existed for the municipalities to carry out this task, including expropriation and limited compensation rights, but they were not taking advantage of these powers. This land authority carries out policy in accordance with National Development Policy, which includes a National Housing Programme and the planned regional development within the urban regions of Madrid and Barcelona, in order to decentralize and disperse the population concentrations in the central city areas by creating "polygones"—outlying neighbourhoods with industries located there. The authority has succeeded in acquiring 25,000 hectares (of the estimated 33,000 ha. needed to carry out the planned 15-year housing programme) from 1961 to 1969, and has developed and built some 250 estates.

However, the policy has been less successful in influencing the existing urban land market in the big cities. This results from the fact that the land acquired has generally been at some distance from the city, and at the same time not in large enough parcels to allow the creation of major alternative service centres which people from the large cities would prefer to live near.*

India. The most interesting experiment in land-acquisition policy in India has been the experience of New Delhi. In 1959 the Delhi Development Authority was created with the task of the large-scale acquisition, development and disposal of land in Delhi in accordance with the new Master Plan. Some 50,000 acres were frozen pending action by the DDA. Compensation was payable on the basis of existing market value at the date of preliminary notification of compulsory acquisition (with some small additional solatium). Under this scheme the Delhi Development Authority developed and sold a large number of plots through public auction at high rates and alloted a number of plots at low rates to low and medium-income groups on a lottery basis (subsidizing these by the scale of the high priced plots). All plots were sold on a leasehold basis. In 1969 a massive programme of house construction for low-income groups was launched, both through direct construction by the DDA, financing through the newly created Federal Government Housing and Urban Development Corporation, and by means of loans for middle-class housing from the Life Insurance Corporation of India.

The basic weakness in the New Delhi programme of land acquisition, according to a UN expert,† was that it was not properly coordinated with the housing construction programme.

It is stated:

> While it is highly profitable to invest in land, it is not equally profitable to invest in housing, especially middle class housing, let alone housing for low income groups. As a result, there has been a growth of luxury housing in Delhi at the expense of middle class and lower class housing.... The DDA has, by its policy of auctioning land at high prices, facilitated the construction of

---

* UN, *Urban Land Policies and Land Control Measures*, Vol. III: *Western Europe*, New York, 1973, pp. 145–6, 303–4.

† Ashish Bose, "Some aspects of rising land prices and land speculation in urban Delhi", UN Regional Preparatory Conference, *Habitat*, 15 May 1975, pp. 17–19.

luxury housing in Delhi.... The question therefore arises whether it is possible to have an urban land policy for disposing and developing land with a grudging attention of low-cost housing.... If our ultimate objective is housing, the cost of land and the cost of housing as well as the returns on each must be considered together and not piece meal as is done today.

It should be noted that legally land leased by the DDA had to be built on within 2 years or the lease was invalid; due to shortages of building materials, however, this has not been enforced.

Singapore. In order to effectively implement the housing programme of the Singapore Housing and Development Board, in 1966 a Land Acquisition Act was passed which gave the government wide powers to acquire private land on a compulsory basis. Compensation is payable for the market value of the land in its existing use (i.e. the intent was to exclude the effects of the expectation of a future change in use). Squatter settlements are not treated as part of existing use value. In addition in Singapore approximately one-third of the land (one-quarter in the central areas) is state-owned, though much of this is in existing public and military installations. Another substantial proportion is held on lease from the government; it is now the policy that all new leases given out are for only a short period (20 to 33 years).

The Housing and Development Board is responsible for the land acquisition, development or redevelopment, planning, and construction of public housing. The Board acquires land through use of the compulsory powers mentioned and through reclamation of coastal waters. Resettlement of squatter settlements and the housing of the lower-income groups were its primary aims, though it has been intended that the development of industry and services should go hand-in-hand with the development of new public housing estates. The Singapore housing programme has had one of the highest rates of housing construction in the world—over 54,000 units constructed between 1960 and 1965, and 65,000 more until 1970. The third Five-Year Building Programme calls for the construction of 125,000 units (increasing the yearly rate of construction from 15,000 to 25,000). The Housing and Development Board has acquired some 2900 acres of land between 1968 and 1972 to accomplish this task, paying approximately US$18 million in compensation. In addition, over 1200 acres were acquired through reclamation. Densities of the new housing projects have been high, averaging some 650 persons per acre.*

Chile. According to a UN report, the Chilean Urban Development Corporation (CORMU) represents the most important of public land-acquisition agencies that has been created in Latin America.† CORMU was set up in 1964 as part of the newly created Ministry of Housing and Urbanism, along with the National Planning Office and the Housing Corporation (CORVI). It has its own funds and is autonomous in character, with a governing board appointed directly by the President and funds allocated to it from general revenues (as well as money derived from its own resources through the sale or lease of land, the issuance of loans, or received from general housing funds). The main function of CORMU was acquisition and development of urban land in conjunction with local authorities and CORVI projects for the development of social housing and infrastructure works. It was also in charge of all zoning and proposed changes in land use. Part of the land acquired was to be used as a land reserve for future urban development. In order to acquire land, CORMU was given wider powers of condemnation than previously existed—expropriation could be undertaken on all property considered necessary for the implementation of urban development schemes. Compensation could be in the form of land already owned by CORMU, securities, or other assets.

From 1964 to 1967 CORMU succeeded in acquiring approximately 1500 hectares per year, about half by direct purchase and half by expropriation. About half the land acquired was a land reserve for future urban development. The evaluation of the UN report is that:

> ...CORMU was operating as an effective regulating body in the real estate market. It has been in a position to compete with the traditional housing and

---

* International Bank for Reconstruction and Development, "Urban land and public policy: social appropriation for betterment", unpublished, May 1974, pp. 45–49; K. R. Chandra, "Urban renewal in Singapore", in *Land for the Cities of Asia* (edited by Woodroff and Brown), Hartford, Connecticut, 1971, pp. 134–5.

† UN, *Urban Land Policies and Land Use Control Measures*, Vol. IV: *Latin America*, 1973, New York, pp. 60–62.

urban development corporations and is able to provide land at lower prices than these private concerns, which produces an automatic drop in the market prices. On the other hand, since its resources still depend on general revenues and it has no definite way of obtaining funds outside the national treasury, its action is fettered and it cannot operate as a real mechanism for providing the necessary land to carry out housing development plans and to regulate the urban development process.

Hong Kong. As a British Crown Colony, all land in Hong Kong is legally owned by the government. However, as in Singapore much of the land is virtually privately owned by being held under a very long lease agreement with the government. There is a private market in land rights, since leases are sold at auction to the highest bidder (and can also be transferred). The state monopoly of land ownership obviates the need for public acquisition of land. Under the Land Resumption Ordinance of 1900, land can be "resumed" into Crown use, either through negotiation of a mutually acceptable compensation to the lessee or else compulsorily (with compensation set by an independent Board). Compensation is on the basis of current market value, but the government does not have to compensate immediately (as long as it pays interest on the compensation sum). Acquisition can also be in the form of exchange of parcels of land. Finally, in recent years the government has acquired a good deal of undeveloped land through the reclamation of shallow bays and inlets.

Using these methods of land acquisition, the government of Hong Kong has undertaken in recent years an extensive housing programme to resettle people from the vast squatter settlements. By the end of 1968 some 1 million people had been resettled in 466 public housing blocks, and it was estimated 2 years later that 40% of the population lived in publicly built housing. The housing plan announced in 1972 aimed at constructing some 180,000 units annually over the next 10 years. Thus Hong Kong has been able to undertake one of the most extensive rehousing programmes in the developing world. It should be noted, however, that due to the absolute shortage of land in the territory of Hong Kong, densities even of the new public housing have been very high. There have been some attempts to construct satellite neighbourhoods in the adjacent New Territories (that part of the mainland of China under Crown lease).*

Canada. There are two land-acquisition programmes noteworthy of attention in Canada, firstly the land-acquisition powers given to municipalities as a part of the national housing programme, and secondly, the advance land-acquisition policies that have been carried out by a few Western Canadian cities. The 1949 National Housing Act provided that the Federal government would assume 75% of the cost of buying and servicing vacant land needed for urbanization. Under this programme over 23,000 acres had been acquired up to 1969. All land had to be used for public housing. This amount of land represents only 5% of the total increase in urban land during the period, and it has been suggested that municipalities were reluctant to assemble raw land because of the possible expense and because of their lack of experience and fear of political opposition to such procedures. However, certain cities in Western Canada have been carrying out advance land acquisition since the 1930s under Provincial legislation. Saskatoon (population 130,000) first acquired land through tax default in the Depression. By holding on to its land in the post-war period, it has been able to maintain a land bank with enough reserve land for 20 years future development, and to successfully plan the allocation of new land, including sufficient recreation space. Red Deer, Alberta (population 35,000) realized in the early 1950s that rapid projected population growth (its then population was 9000) needed comprehensive planning of future development. A land-use plan was prepared, and strategic lands on the fringe were quietly acquired. As the city had not yet laid basic infrastructure works, landowners had an incentive to sell to the city. This policy has virtually eliminated land speculation and has assured efficient land use, with enough green

---

* International Bank for Reconstruction and Development, "Urban land and public policy: social appropriation for betterment", Bank Working Paper No. 179, May 1974 (unpublished), pp. 50–52; S. S. Hsueh, "Urban land value and taxation in Hong Kong", *Land for the Cities of Asia*, edited by A. M. Woodruff and J. R. Brown, Hartford, Connecticut, 1971, pp. 296–7.

space in the city and no waste of good agricultural land until needed for urban development.*

The *USA*. There have been a number of programmes in the United States that have sought to create a more efficient acquisition of land for various public purposes. The three most important such purposes (all federally aided) have been the construction of highways, the redevelopment of central city areas, and the provision of recreational space. The Federal government pays 50% of the costs of state highway construction (and 90% of Interstate Highway System costs), including land-acquisition costs. Recently advance acquisition of land on the right-of-way of future highways has been advocated in order to reduce costs. California has the most extensive programme of advance acquisition of highway rights-of-way, saving an estimated $25 million a year.

The Urban Renewal programme has, since 1949, meant that the Federal government will pay two-thirds of the net costs to local authorities of acquiring, redeveloping and reselling to private developers tracts of land in the central cities in slum conditions. The local authorities can use the power of eminent domain to acquire land, but must pay compensation at market prices for it. On average the land-acquisition costs have accounted for 64% of gross project costs; up to 1964 some 36,400 acres of land had been acquired by 970 separate Urban Renewal projects.†

In recent years there has been increasing concern in the USA about the preservation and provision of land for recreational needs. Spurred in part by public concern, the amount spent by the states on recreational land acquisition increased fourfold between 1960 and 1970 to about $80 million a year. Federal agencies spent an additional $240 million on open-space acquisition between 1966 and 1970. However, needs have been growing faster than acquisition: between 1950 and 1970 attendance of state parks increased by 300% while their

---

* UN, *Urban Land Policies and Land-Use Control Measures*, Vol. VI: *Northern America*, New York, 1973, pp. 70–79.

† UN, *Urban Land Policies and Land-Use Control Measures*, Vol. VI: *Northern America*, New York, 1973, pp. 67–68.

acreage only increased by 80%; for national parks, acreage increased by 29% and attendance by 400%.*

Finally, there have been several experiments in a more comprehensive land-acquisition policy. Encouraged by Federal loans for large-scale urban development, private developers (financed by a consortium of banks) have built two complete planned communities as suburbs of Washington, DC. In order to be profitable these communities have been primarily middle class, with a high level of services but no independent economic base.

The state of New York in 1968 created the Urban Development Corporation with the power to over-ride local zoning ordinances in order to assemble land needed for development on a planned community basis. The UDC can borrow money directly for its own purposes, and also relies on the resources of already existing programmes, but must be ultimately self-financing by reselling the land it has assembled to private developers. In 1970 and 1971 the UDC initiated close to $700 million of development in the state, including a new community and a town-in-a-town.†

IMPACT OF LAND-ACQUISITION POLICIES ON PATTERNS OF URBAN GROWTH

The effectiveness of land policies may be measured by the allocation of land for different purposes according to the needs of a society and by their impact on the land market. The main factors influencing the measure of effectiveness are the following:

(a) the goals of land acquisition;
(b) the institutions of land acquisition;
(c) the methods of administration of public-owned land;
(d) the interrelationships between relevant governmental agencies;
(e) the financing methods;
(f) the mobilization of human resources for land-development works.

---

* *The Use of Land: A Citizen's Policy Guide to Urban Growth* (Rockefeller Brothers Task Force on Land Use and Urban Growth), New York, 1973, pp. 107–111.
† *Ibid.*, pp. 259–60.

Goals of Land Acquisition

In the case where the purpose of land-acquisition policy is restricted to only some land-use purpose, the results are also restricted,
and are not able to influence the patterns of urban growth. The
concentration of efforts on erecting social housing projects may lead
to solving the short-term needs of ensuring housing for the low-income
population, but in such a case the result is the creation of some
housing complexes without the needed services and sometimes in
locations far from work and high-level services. In most cases, keeping
in mind the restricted financial means of the public authorities, the
land is acquired far from the city frontiers (where it is cheap). Such
land development in new areas far from the city has a negative impact
on the land market, increasing the land prices of large areas of vacant
land between the new development and the previously urbanized areas.
The negative social results are increased travel time to work and
services, as well as social segregation.

The supplying of cheap land needed for new industrial enterprises
in a new industrial centre may solve the short-term needs of space
for the growing industrial sector, but it may lead in the future to
obstacles to continuous, efficient industrial growth. Industrial enterprises need auxiliary services, and good transport connections for the
supply of raw materials and distribution of production goods to the
consumer centres. New high-technology enterprises need highly qualified manpower, which is not always willing to live in small settlements
or in housing projects near industrial enterprises without high-level
services. There are a lot of examples from different countries that
show that industrial development in new areas did not succeed, if such
development was not integrated within a comprehensive human settlement scheme of a size ensuring high-level services and variety of
employment sources (thereby creating a socially mixed development).

It has to be kept in mind that it is generally more difficult to
create a new independent human settlement, including all the needed
city functions, than it is to extend an existing small or medium-size
town or to erect new small settlements in an existing developed city
region. It should be underlined that a new town is not only a new
economic enterprise, but a new society. It is easier therefore to extend

an existing sociological settlement unit than to create a new one. One of the obstacles to extending existing human settlements or to using the land within the framework of the existing urban and rural settlements in a more efficient way is the land-ownership relations. The legislative measures and the institutional aspects of land acquisition may influence in a decisive way the purpose and the results of the land acquisition policy.

The Institutional Aspects

The purpose of land acquisition, and the role of the central and local public authority in the governmental structure affects the character of the land-acquisition agencies. In a country with strong central governments there were established national land-acquisition and land-development agencies. This is the case in France, Spain, Israel, Singapore and Hong Kong. The countries with a long tradition of local government autonomy have developed municipal land acquisition agencies, as is the case in the Netherlands, Sweden and the UK. The experience shows that the lack of regional land-acquisition and land-development agencies is a serious obstacle for carrying out not only national and regional land-use development schemes, but even an efficient land-development policy of a city with a long tradition of land acquisition (as in the case of Dutch cities).

The transformation of the city function from the city to the city region makes a separate city acquisition and development policy quite impossible. Urban growth occurs mostly in the city region. The lack of regional land-acquisition and land-development agencies may be seen as one of the obstacles for the further development of human settlements in countries with long public land-acquisition experience (the Netherlands, Sweden, Norway and Denmark).

The experience of the UK shows also that the lack of coordination between the former Land Commission and the municipal authorities, and the lack of regional land-acquisition agencies (with participation by the municipalities), is one of the major weaknesses in the government's land policy (which is being perpetuated in the newly prepared legislation). The experience of Israel shows that the operation of a national land authority administrating public land, without coordination with municipal authorities and without establishing regional land authorities, may involve a contradiction between the needs of the urban growth and the fiscal vested interests of the Land Authority.

The regional land-acquisition and land-development agencies in France, which have the participation of the municipal authorities in the region, as well as the representatives of some private economic institutions, may serve as an example of such a regional executive. But at the same time the French example, with its exemplary administrative structure, may show that the results of land policies are not solely affected by the method of organization. The permanently high rate of urban land-price increase in France shows that for efficient land policy there is a need for a coordination and inter-relationship of different factors influencing the land policies. Especially, it should be kept in mind that the land-acquisition policy in France is restricted to some areas of the future development only, and only some areas of urban renewal, leaving the majority of land for present and future urban development to the play of free market forces.

But in some cases, and especially in countries with restricted financial means and an insufficiently strong (both economically and administratively) public sector, even some restricted public acquisition and development agencies are important.

The programme of the agencies for land acquisition and development works, such as CORMU in Chile, the Delhi Development Agency for land acquisition and similar agencies for land acquisition, development works and housing projects in Singapore and Hong Kong are examples of policies which have restricted purposes which have been successfully achieved by means of land-acquisition policies.

One of the examples of an efficient framework for land acquisition for restricted purposes is the New Towns Development Corporations in the UK. Their purpose is to acquire land and develop it, as well as carrying out the needed planning for erecting housing projects, public and private services, and industrial enterprises in the New Towns.

ADMINISTRATION OF PUBLICLY-OWNED LAND AND THE COORDINATION BETWEEN AGENCIES

The method of administrating publicly-owned land may be seen as one of the factors influencing the effectiveness of the land-acquisition policies.

The use of the publicly-owned land is connected with the establishment of criteria for land values which allocate land for different purposes, without the market mechanism, and the establishment of relations between the public land authority and the users of the land (residential, commercial, industrial), and between the public agencies and the construction and housing companies. The relationship between the public land authority and the other governmental agencies, especially the planning authority and the financial departments, are of the highest importance in the administration of the publicly-owned land.

The basis for the evaluating land prices in the new planned area of land acquired by the public authority is varying from one country to another. Generally, it is admitted that the calculation of price should be based on the costs of land acquisition plus the investment in the infrastructure costs. In some cases also the investment in the social infrastructure (public utility institutions) are also included in the costs. Also, the interest in capital investment for paying the loans for land acquisition and the infrastructure investment is added to the costs.

One of the problems of a cost and benefit calculation of public land acquisition is connected with the distribution of these costs according to the different land uses and land users.

Generally, in most countries the price of land for low-cost housing is based on the costs of the public authority, and in some cases the price is estimated to be lower than actual cost on the basis of a special subsidy from the central government for low-income housing.

In a case where the land authority is supplying land not only for social housing, but for middle-income groups and also for commercial enterprises, there are different approaches in different countries. The Netherlands and Sweden evaluate land cost the same for residential purposes, without distinction between levels of housing standard, with the price differences based on location and density of use. Australia (Canberra) fixes a low price for social housing and leaves to competition among builders the price for high-level residential use. In Israel the price of land for residential purposes is fixed administratively by the land authorities, establishing lower prices in new towns and less-developed regions and higher prices for residential use in the big cities and in already developed urban areas.

Commercial land prices are established in most countries by competition, but some countries fix them administratively lower than the market price in order to attract commercial services to new areas. Such a system may aid the development of commercial services in the new areas, but it may also result in discrimination in favour of some commercial enterprises who succeed in locating in an attractive area. On the other hand, if there is not the prospect of a sufficient turnover in a new area, even low (administratively set) prices will not be attractive enough. Some cities have adequately solved this problem by erecting needed commercial services in new areas by public or co-operative institutions directly, subsidizing prices at first and establishing higher land prices and rentals after some time. An interesting example of fixing criteria for commercial land prices in new towns is the French legislation for new towns' centres. It is suggested that the commercial enterprise should pay land rental not on the basis of land value, but as a part of the turnover. This system is based on an assumption that commercial land prices are influenced by the location and by the size of the human settlement (which influences the turnover). Therefore the commercial services would pay a lower rent than actual land cost in the first period of new town development, and a higher rate in further stages of development.

One of the most discussed problems of public land administration is the question of leasing or selling the land to users. In the Netherlands and Sweden some municipalities are using the system of leasing and others of selling land. In Sweden, the government gives preference to leasing by fixing better terms for loans for land acquisition when land is leased. In France, generally, the land acquired by the public land-acquisition agencies is sold to the developers. Israel has a long tradition of leasing land, but in some cases Parliament allows land to be sold. There are obviously pros and cons in each of these systems. The leasehold system allows the public authority to keep for the community the permanently increasing urban land values.

But this system required more investment of public capital than when land is sold. The leasehold system should allow the public authority to obtain more easily land for changing needs and consequent land-use changes. On the other hand it is suggested that efficient land-use legislation and taxation methods, that control development may serve as a partial substitute for public leaseholding of land.

The system of selling land acquired by the public agencies may create more money for additional land acquisition, and at the same time still allow the assembling of large land parcels for carrying out future development schemes. In France financial groups together with the public authorities participate in large-scale land acquisition. This is done in the framework of public mixed societies with at least 50% public capital. The system of selling publicly owned land has the disadvantage not only of losing for the community the prospective additional land value, but also losing flexibility in the case of changing future land-use needs. It is desirable even when land is sold by the municipality, not to transfer rights to the land until the land is used for building purposes (in order to prevent the holding of vacant land). One of the advantages of public ownership is the ability to fix the timing of land use according to development schemes. Public land ownership is not only to ensure the immediate needs of human settlement, but to create the needed land reserve for future development, including such a vital need as recreation (e.g. national parks) which have no commercial importance. Therefore the system of selling public land may influence only short-term needs and is less in keeping with long-term development.

It may be suggested that the essential factor in the choice of system is the method of financing land acquisition, and especially the appreciation by the public authorities and by public opinion in general of the role of land as an essential factor in establishing the patterns of urban growth and the quality of urban life.

The financial factor also plays an essential role in the method of administrating the publicly-owned land. In countries where the land authority is autonomous and even independent financially, it may attempt to demonstrate its efficiency by showing large financial surpluses. It can happen then that the public land agency is acting as a small vested interest in contradiction to the planning requirements of other public institutions. The examples of the land authority in Israel, the Delhi development agency, and the French implementation agencies for ZAD (zones of concentrated action) show what might be the dangers of a public agency activity if its policy is not part of a comprehensive development process closely coordinated with other public authorities.

There are several well-known examples which received much public criticism, such as the changing of the face of Paris by allowing extra-ordinary high-rise building along the Seine, and the high-rise building erected on the hills of Jerusalem. One of the deciding factors in these public decisions was the higher immediate income for the public land authority from a decision allowing higher densities than fixed by the planning authorities. In such a way these public agencies are carrying out a policy based on short-term profit, which is the basis of the private economy, and neglecting the destructive effect on urban growth patterns of such policies. Some experts in France and Israel suggest that this short-sighted financial policy by the land authorities does not increase (even the short-term) government revenues, but only increases the revenues of big private financial interests by giving them conditions more favourable than those formerly possible on the basis of free competition.

On the other hand, the example of the Amsterdam municipality, as well as Stockholm, may show what positive urban growth pattern is possible when the land authority is a part of the same municipality, acting in coordination with the planning department, the financial department and the public works department. Obviously, coordination does not mean no conflicts, as there might always be different approaches by different agencies dealing with specific fields of action. The deciding factor influencing the implementation of the planning process is the ability to narrow the differences in the conflicting short-term interests of the different agencies by a dominant public authority, which should draw the lines of compromise between long-term plans and short-term needs.

FINANCING AND THE MOBILIZATION OF HUMAN RESOURCES

Financial difficulties are often seen as the main obstacle to the implementation of a public advance land-acquisition policy. Those countries with a long experience of public land acquisition have financed their programmes through normal municipal budget sources, with the assistance of long- and medium-term loans from the central government (Sweden, the Netherlands). France and Spain have financed land acquisition directly from national government revenues allocated to the national land-acquisition agencies, with additional funds from private financial groups interested in participating jointly in development schemes. In the Netherlands and Sweden as well, it is sometimes the case that private builders will transfer land to the public development agencies in order to participate in development schemes.

The experience of the Netherlands and Sweden shows that an advance land-acquisition policy economizes public money by supplying land for building when needed on the basis of prices paid many years earlier. The rate of price increase of land in urban regions in nearly all countries is considerably higher than the capital costs of loans to finance advance land acquisition. A comparison between the costs of infrastructure works (which obviously affect prices of the land on which development has been carried out) and the cost of raw land acquired many years before development works are started shows that in some countries the price of raw land for 10 years' needs is the same as the expenditure for development works for a single year.

A more detailed study may suggest that some of the difficulty in financing advance land acquisition is a result of a lack of understanding of the importance of such a policy for urban growth patterns, and not purely a result of financial difficulties. It may be suggested that the vested interests of developers and land-owners—interested in continuing to get high profits from the permanent rise in land prices resulting from reliance on the private market to supply land— should not be neglected as a factor creating an unfavourable climate of opinion for advance land acquisition.

An understanding of the importance of the role of advance land acquisition in assuring more desirable urban-growth patterns may lead to the mobilization of greater financial resources to carry out such a policy, not only from general revenues but also by collecting a proportion of the increase in land prices throughout the city as a result of the development of new areas. In addition, it might be possible to institute a greater degree of partnership between landowners and the development agency, whereby landowners put their land at the disposal of the public development agency, and in return get either shares in the public agency or construction rights on a piece of land equivalent to what they previously held (with some addition for the increase in value due to development).

There exists another alternative method of financing the acquisition and development of land, especially appropriate to countries with a low level of economic development and a high percentage of underutilized manpower. By giving each family the right to a certain plot of land, on the condition that they carry out development works themselves (with the assistance of the public authorities supplying tools and organization), large manpower resources may be mobilized and a large number of minimally developed sites may be created. It is probably more important to ensure every person land for housing in the future on the basis of planned development than it is to carry out complete development which, given the limited financial resources of the authorities, will not supply enough housing for everyone. Many examples of such site preparation by less-advanced methods in some of the developing countries show that such a policy may ensure a basis for future housing schemes and the development of new human settlements on a planned basis. The examples of the self-help housing schemes based on a cooperative organization of labour in Cuba and Spain, where the public authorities supply building materials and tools, show that such schemes are possible given more than one political orientation.

SUMMARY REMARKS

The evaluation of land-acquisition policies is difficult because of the comparatively restricted experience of application of such a policy. Only in Sweden, the Netherlands and Israel (and in Canberra, Australia) has there been any long-term experience. In other countries such policies have only begun in earnest in the last 10 years—a short period for evaluating policy and particularly too short a perspective for a proper estimate of the ultimate costs of financing such programmes. However, it is the view of many experts from different countries, including the UK Land Commission, various UN reports, and others, that the growing needs for land in urban areas can be more efficiently met through such policies of public land acquisition than through the traditional taxation and land-use control measures. The lower rate of land price increase in those countries, such as Sweden and the Netherlands, which have such a policy is an indication of the truth of this assertion.

On the other hand, the experience of Israel, France, India and other countries has shown that a policy of public land acquisition or land-ownership *on its own* does not necessarily affect the urban land market, and may not even supply enough land for the growing areas of urban concentration. It may be suggested that the effectiveness of a land-acquisition policy mostly depends on the extent of land acquisition in comparison with the size of the needs. The most important part of a public land acquisition policy is that it allows the public authorities to fix the timing of land-use development precisely, and thus they are able to effectively implement a long-term development scheme.

All land-use planning measures play a role in preventing undesirable development by putting restrictions on land use. But these schemes are unable to impose development according to plan at a certain time. Therefore the development scheme is implemented when landowners are willing to use their land for construction purposes. As they are mainly interested in obtaining a high profit from the sale of their land, they prefer to wait until land prices rise before allowing development. The result is that only some part of the needs for land are satisfied, while the operation of land market leads to higher land prices. Thus the present system produces fragmented instead of continuous development.

The policy of public land acquisition is expected to lead to the municipality playing the dominant role in the execution of the development scheme, by acquiring land on a large-enough scale to serve as the basis for supplying the needs for the entire future expansion of the urban population.

In cases where public land acquisition is restricted to some purposes and some locations only, it has no effect on the land market and urban growth patterns. There is a danger that the public authorities (including the planning authority) may use their powers to adapt the planning scheme not to the needs of the growing urban community, but to the needs of public vested interests (i.e. in order to promote specific schemes by functional authorities).

On the other hand, it has been argued by some experts that there is a risk for the public authority in committing itself to such a large-scale land acquisition over a long time period, as urban growth patterns and needs may be very uncertain over such a period. This may be correct for private land acquisition for long-term needs. There is uncertainty in forecasting the exact location of future growth. But it is possible to forecast the quantitative needs for different land uses over time in a large city region. New transportation technology may influence the location of expansion, and may (with a reduction in the energy consumption of the consumer society) change urbanization patterns and lead to more concentrated development. This would mean a reduction in the use of the private motor car. It may be suggested that these developments would not be in opposition to a policy of large-scale land acquisition. On the contrary, the close co-ordination of the land acquisition and planning authority in the same government agency would greatly diminish the risk, as the land acquired could be used either for urban or for recreational purposes.

The cost-benefit calculation for the Stockholm region showed that land acquisition even 20–30 years before actual development is economically viable and allows a considerable degree of long-term flexibility.

But it must be understood that there is at present a lack of knowledge of how to allocate land without the market mechanism. There is a danger of bureaucratically administered decisions about the allocation of publicly-owned land without taking into account the real views of the citizens. There are, of course, difficulties in deciding how to take into account public views, as there are conflicting interests between local and city region needs, and also between different strata of the population. One of the main difficulties in land allocation is the conflict between the short-term needs of housing stock and the long-term development scheme for an integrated, planned city region. Large-scale land acquisition could reduce this conflict by making available land for housing purposes in the context of an overall planning scheme which properly developed infrastructure and public services at the same time.

The allocation by the public authorities of sufficient funds to carry out comprehensive development of all land has a decisive effect on the land market. In cases where the publicly-owned land is used only for low-income housing schemes, the land-acquisition policy only has a limited impact on the land market. Land used for commercial purposes in suburban areas, and land with favourable accessibility to the city centre or favourable environmental features is still high-priced. On the one hand, the comprehensive development of planned new communities on publicly-owned land for all population strata, providing high-level services, good transportation connections, and some luxury housing, may lead to a restrained rate of increase of land prices in the vicinity of the city. This has occurred to some extent in Sweden. On the other hand, the construction of housing projects and even new towns in the Paris region, as well as in Israel, the UK and Spain, have had no effect on the high rate of land-price increases in the city region.

The extent, location and variety of land uses on publicly-owned land is the decisive factor in the effectiveness of the public sector in influencing the private land market. Only if the public sector does not isolate itself from certain sectors of the land market will it have a great economic impact. Obviously the methods of administration and financing of publicly-owned land has a considerable effect on the use of land according to the plan. More favourable conditions of leasing public land for development by the authorities, and frequent re-evaluation of land prices (to collect part of the incremental increase as tax), may strengthen the financial structure of public land-acquisition agencies, enabling them to finance future land purchases from income from publicly-leased land, and collecting for the community the additional value created by the urban growth process.

Efficient expropriation and compensation legislation, as well as appropriate land-use planning measures, may be helpful for creating large reserves of land for future development if payment for acquired land is made at existing use value (i.e. excluding the additional value created through an expectation of a change in use from agricultural to urban).

A comprehensive land policy using different measures, combined with an extensive public land-acquisition policy, may create a basis for ensuring land for future urban growth according to the changing needs of society. Obviously the results of such a policy are affected by the institutional structure of the responsible public agencies and their ability to effectively coordinate their activities in the common interest—to rise above their particular public vested interests.

REFERENCES

Armstrong, Alan, "Emerging land policy in Canada", notes for a colloquy on National Land Policies, American Society of Planning Officials, 1970.

Brodeur, David, *Survey and Analysis of Large Developments and New Communities Complete or under Construction in the United States Since 1947*, US Department of Housing and Urban Development, Community Resources Development Administration, Feb. 1969.

Darin-Drabkin, Haim, *et al.*, *Patterns of Land Use and Land Tenure in Israel, op. cit.*

Government of Australia, Commission of Inquiry into Land Tenures, *First Report*, Nov. 1973.

Harrison, Peter, "Urban land policy: some Australian experiments", in *Land for the Cities of Asia, op. cit.*

Hsueh, S. S., "Urban land value and taxation in Hong Kong", in *Land for the Cities of Asia, op. cit.*

Ministerio de la Vivienda, Government of Spain, *La Descongestion de Madrid, analisis de una experiencia en curso*, Madrid, 1967.

Neutze, G. Max, *The Price of Land and Land Use Planning: Policy Instruments in the Urban Land Market*, OECD, 1973.

Shoup, Donald C. and Mack, Ruth, *Advance Land Acquisition by Local Government*, Washington, DC, HUD, 1968.

United Nations, *Urban Land Policies and Land Use Control Measures*, 7 volumes, New York, 1973.

The Use of Land: A Citizens' Guide to Action, op. cit.

CHAPTER 13

Land Acquisition in Sweden and the Experience of Stockholm

THE FRAMEWORK OF SWEDISH LAND POLICY

General Background

Sweden is the fourth largest country in Europe, having an area of 444,793 km² or 175,000 ml². However, in spite of its size, most of Sweden's land has remained relatively unpopulated.

Of the total land area 59% is forest, 11% farmland, 29% other land, and only about 1% urban settlements. The population density is only 44 inhabitants per square mile. Historically, the Swedish population has concentrated in three regions: the plains of the south, the lakes region, and at the river mouths along the northern coast. Today more than 86% of Sweden's population of 7·7 million live in urban settlements of more than 2000 people, two-thirds in settlements of 10,000 or more. Roughly one-third of the urban population lives in the three settlements with populations of greater than 200,000: Greater Malmo with 300,000; Greater Göteborg with 600,000; and Greater Stockholm with 1·3 million. The greatest growth has occurred in medium-sized settlements (pop. 10,000–100,000). The larger metropolitan areas have increased very little in size, while small urban settlements have even decreased. Concurrent with the development of decentralized urban settlements, rising industrialization has produced an influx of population from the northern agricultural and forest regions to the urban centres of the south, placing a great strain on social services. This trend is expected to continue as a result of the changing structure of commerce and industry.

Sweden is a constitutional monarchy with a parliamentary form of government. There are twenty-five provinces or counties including Stockholm which are decentralized administrative units of the central government. These are administered by a county board presided over by a governor appointed for life by and responsible to the national government. Representative government in each province rests with the popularly elected council (*landsting*) which meets once a year. In Stockholm, which has the status of a province, all duties, both provincial and municipal, are carried out by municipal officials. Town planning, education below the university level, and social welfare fall by law to the responsibility of the municipalities. The municipality also is responsible for buying and selling real estate.

One historical reason why Sweden may have a vigorous public land policy is that before the nineteenth century virtually all land in Sweden was owned by the Crown or by local governments.

Policy Framework: Land Acquisition as part of Housing Policy

The principal reason for municipal land-acquisition policy is the construction of dwelling units in accordance with government housing policy, which is one of Sweden's welfare state measures. The responsibility undertaken by public authorities of providing housing for almost all sectors of the population inevitably affects land-policy measures, as the implementation of the Housing Programme requires a guaranteed supply of land.

Experience has shown that solutions to the problem of housing should not be seen merely as the provision of a projected number of housing units, but rather as part of a general environmental policy concerned with the provision of services in answer to social, cultural and economic needs.

The government, the county councils and the municipalities work closely with each other with regard to housing policy. The financing of the Housing Programme is primarily the responsibility of the government, while some municipalities provide additional means of subsidizing the Housing Programme. The municipalities are also charged with the administration of applications for government loans. The government is responsible for planning both the long- and short-term national and regional housing programmes on the basis of housing programmes submitted by the municipalities and the county councils. The government also controls the execution of the housing programmes and uses its planning and financial role to control and influence housing costs, the quality of housing, land costs and the location of housing projects.

By law the area of responsibility of the municipality is the following:

(a) The municipalities are entrusted with the planning and organizing of a housing production which is sufficient for the entire population.

(b) They can expropriate ground for housing purposes.

(c) They have the right and duty to control building so that well-planned and healthy housing areas are created.

(d) The municipalities can to a very large extent through taxes, fees and loans independently finance land acquisition and development works and public services in housing areas. They have their own right to tax incomes of private persons and companies, and levy minor taxes on houses.

(e) The municipalities can start their own enterprises for production and administration of housing.

(f) Alongside government measures they can subsidize housing for special groups who otherwise would not be able to acquire good housing units.

(g) It is the duty of the municipalities to arrange government loans and contributions for housing.*

The government through their National Housing Board prepares a long-term housing programme. The recent programme for 1964–75 aimed to provide 1 million dwellings. The national planning programme is based on 5-year housing schemes submitted by each municipality. Each 5-year scheme is revised annually in relation to changes which have occurred and which are forecast. Each municipality is required to submit a 5-year scheme before it qualifies for financial aid in housing from the government. In this way, the government ensures that municipalities acquire land at prevailing market prices in advance of

* Enrst Michanek, *Housing Standard and Housing Construction in Sweden,* Stockholm: The Swedish Institute, 1965, p. 19.

the actual implementation of their housing programmes, thus keeping land costs relatively low. Financial assistance from the government is limited to a stipulated maximum price, for land above this price the municipality has to find other sources of finance. The general aim is to prepare land reserves for housing needs forecast for the next 10 years. In order to ensure that housing is erected where it is needed and not merely in areas where cheap land is available (i.e. usually on the peripheries of towns) the government also controls the location of land for housing through the activities of the county councils.

The coordination between the government and the municipalities is also expressed in the techniques of planning. The financial programme for housing is drawn up annually by the government but the municipalities, in order to plan their housing activities, require information and a guarantee of long-term financial assistance from the government. Recently, therefore, some improvements in planning techniques were introduced. The planning programme now consists of two parts:

1. The minimum guaranteed subsidy for the amount of housing planned for the coming 5 years, and
2. a reserve programme for 1–3 years.

The period for the guarantee is longer for a rapidly growing urban area but is restricted to 1–2 years for slowly growing areas.

Implementation. The implementation of the Housing Programme by the municipalities is based on close coordination between the developers and the building societies. The municipalities do not limit their activities to the planning and control of housing but have created tools to influence in an efficient way the implementation of the Housing Programme. One of these tools is the municipal building societies which act as non-profit societies where the management is nominated by the municipalities. The foundation capital is provided by the municipalities but the societies act as autonomous units competing in the building market with the private corporate sector.

In 1969, 44% of all housing units were built directly by the municipalities through municipal building societies or non-profit building companies (only 14% were built by cooperative housing associations and 39% by the private sector). These societies, in which the municipalities hold all the shares and appoint the directors and board of managers, own and administer for the municipalities all the dwelling units which the societies construct themselves or contract to be constructed. Non-profit companies operate in a similar manner with the exception that the cities do not own all the shares. In addition to apartment houses, the Housing Programme includes some one- or two-family houses which are financed in part by a prospective owner either through his own labour or a cash down-payment. The municipal building societies are also primarily responsible for the construction of community services such as shops, libraries, cultural institutions, social services, etc., in residential areas. In addition to the active role in residential construction, some municipalities (such as Stockholm) also have an office for distributing dwellings whether municipally, cooperatively or privately constructed. The policy of land acquisition by Swedish municipalities may be seen as a further dimension of the public authorities' responsibility for providing adequate housing for all inhabitants. Just as they deem it necessary to provide such vital public services as water, sewerage and other infrastructural works, so they are also responsible for providing adequate and suitable land for residential building.

ADVANCE LAND ACQUISITION IN SWEDEN

Methods of Land Acquisition—Planning Procedure

A municipality that seeks to pursue a land policy in accordance with central government recommendations must prepare itself for a considerable expenditure of administrative and financial resource. If these resources are to be used optimally, long-range planning must govern the conduct of land policy. Priorities must be ordered among different areas of expansion as well as between new development and redevelopment.

The planning of land policy requires investigations of future land needs, directions of expansion, and alternative timetables for new development and urban renewal. Just how much work should be put into the planning of land policy depends on the state of comprehensive general planning in its physical and economic aspects, as well as how up to date and inclusive it is.

Action programmes. The results of municipal planning for land acquisition and disposition are then compiled in a land-policy action programme running for at least 10 years. Such a programme states how much land the municipality has to acquire each year in tracts of new development and redevelopment as well as specifying deadlines for the commencement of negotiations to acquire land and for any coercive measures that may have to be taken in the form of expropriation, etc. The methods of financing land acquisitions are also indicated.

Use of Different Instruments: Acquisitions by Voluntary Agreement

The pre-enactment legislative materials on expropriation assume that municipalities will rely mainly on voluntary agreements with landowners to acquire needed land. If such a course proves impossible, the municipality then has grounds for resorting to expropriation.

It was observed earlier that acquisitions should be made well ahead of a building project (about 10 years). However, it is also important to carry out the acquisitions in proper sequence.

The planning monopoly. An important aid in the building programmes of the municipalities is their right to decide where and when building will occur and how it should be shaped, the so-called municipal planning monopoly.

Correctly utilized, the planning monopoly is the most important aid of the municipality for achieving a suitable utilization of land from the point of view of community building.

For instance, in order for the land to be utilized for building, it must have been considered suitable for the purpose from the general point of view during the planning process. Legal regulations also stipulate that building may take place only after a detailed plan has been established. A municipality can also decide how its building shall take shape.

Expropriation. If other means fail municipalities can resort to expropriation "to ensure that land is available on reasonable terms for urban development and otherwise to transfer to municipal ownership undeveloped land for disposal on leasehold tenure". They could expropriate land if it could be shown that the landowners themselves were hardly in a position to exploit it or that any such exploitation would not imply reasonable land prices for the purchaser. Expropriation was also possible without such proof, when the municipality declared its readiness to make the land available afterwards on a leasehold basis. The instruments thus have goals relating to both planning policy and price regulation.

These expropriation measures have been applied to a moderate extent. The main effects have been indirect, the mere threat of expropriation prompting landowners to conclude "voluntary" agreements with the local government.

By virtue of amendments in the Act that have been in force since January 1972 it is no longer necessary to prove that the landowners themselves are unlikely to be capable of exploiting the land on reasonable conditions. It suffices now for the local government to show that the land may be required for planned community development. In principle, the municipalities have thus gained priority right to all land needed for this purpose, and also the legal means of acquiring it at an early stage.

The law existing until recently did not fix exactly the date of land-value evaluation for paying compensation. Generally it was understood that the market value prevailing at the time of the court decision was the basis of compensation. The expropriation procedure took place over a long time of 3–5 years and therefore the municipalities had to pay an increased price for land.

An important improvement was introduced by the new amendment to the expropriation Act of 1 January 1972. According to this amendment the compensation for the expropriation should be based on the market value 10 years before the expropriation was decided by the municipalities.

According to this amendment the public authorities should not pay the additional value created during the 10 years before the expropriation. For a transitional period of time it was decided that this regulation will be realized gradually. Until 1981 the compensation will be based on the price prevailing on 1 July 1971. This regulation will require the municipalities to pay until 1981 compensation based on less than 10 years but for the future the landowner and the potential land investor might not be interested in keeping land unused or to invest in land purchase for expected land price increases.

The ability to pay compensation according to the land price prevailing a long time period before expropriation may influence the landowners to be ready for a voluntary agreement with the municipalities, instead of starting a long expropriation procedure.

Priority purchase right. Municipal priority purchase right implies that the municipality, under certain conditions, has the right to take the place of the buyer at the sale of real estate.

The priority purchase right aims at improving the possibilities of the municipalities to acquire, at an early stage, land that is needed for the development of the community. As an aid in the municipal land-acquisition politics, priority purchase is a complement to voluntary acquisitions and acquisitions through expropriation.

The provisions for compulsory reporting gives the municipality early information about ·land sales. Thus it is possible to follow the happenings in the real estate market (price development, changes in proprietor conditions, etc.) which helps the municipality to plan its land-acquisition policy.

In order to keep land prices in check, it is important for the municipality to acquire the land before expected building causes an increase in value. For the same reason the municipality should also offer a sufficient amount of land prepared for settlement well before building commences. Otherwise there is a risk of price-raising competition over the raw land.

Fields of application. The municipality has priority purchase right over such real estate as is required for planned future development.

The ability of the municipality to exploit priority purchase rights is in no way limited by stipulations that the land be used for development within a certain time limit. If there is a sufficient degree of likelihood that the land will be used for future development, the amount of time elapsed between purchase and utilization is immaterial.

Excluded from priority purchase right are such real estate that have an area under 3000 m² and a taxation value lower than 200,000 Sw. Cr.

Procedure. In order to stimulate the real estate proprietors at intended sales to give the municipality the first opportunity to acquire needed property, there is a provision in the law for home bidding. A home bid is made when a proprietor offers the municipality, in writing, an estate at a certain price and on other stated conditions. If the municipality wishes to accept the home bid, the seller must be informed of this decision within 3 months.

Public Ownership of Land

The leasehold system. Most land acquired by public authorities in Sweden is held by themselves indefinitely under a leasehold system. Leaseholdership was first introduced in Sweden in 1907 to foster sound residential conditions by providing private citizens with land for building, without surrendering title to the land. The retention of land in public ownership was meant to have the increase in land values accrue to the community at large and to make it easier to allocate land to other uses at some future time. Leaseholdership has gradually evolved into an instrument of land policy with extended applications to social investment.

Contracts of leaseholdership enable a municipality to control land uses more actively than is permitted by building and planning legislative measures. Problems involving land assembly are more flexibly solved under leaseholds than by freeholds. It becomes easier to carry out major readjustments when land is held under lease. The most frequent subject of controversy, expectations of future values, is then largely eliminated. When a municipality grants the use of land under leasehold, it reserves the right to claim a substantial proportion of future increments in the capital value of land. In the long run, therefore, leaseholds ought to be of great importance for municipal finances.

According to the 1908 law the leasehold terms were from 26 to 100 years. Stockholm introduced the term of 60 years for residential land, 26 years for commercial land and 5–7 years for industrial land. Since 1953 leasehold is vested for an indefinite period, not for a fixed term of years. Unless a longer time is agreed upon, the first period runs for 60 years and every successive period for 40 years. If a leasehold is granted for a land use that is not mainly residential (commercial or industrial), agreement may be reached for shorter time-periods, though not for less than 20 years.

The basic rule is that the rent shall be paid at unchanged amounts over specific time periods. Unless a longer time is agreed upon, each period runs for 10 years. This is according to the law of 1968. Until that time (according to the law of 1953) the conditions of rent could be changed every 20 years for residential land use and 10 years for commercial. Before that time the rent conditions could only be changed with the expiration of leasehold terms, i.e. often 60 years for residential leases and 26 years for commercial ones. During the penultimate year of each period, both the lessor and the lessee are entitled to call for readjustment of ground rent. If this right is not exercised, an unchanged amount of rent is payable in the subsequent period. If the contracting parties cannot agree on changing the rent, the amount for the following period must be fixed by an expropriation court with reference to the land value at the time of review. The appraiser of land value considers the purpose of leasehold tenure and the detailed regulations with which the lessee must comply as concerns use of the lot and building thereon. When a leasehold expires, the lessor is required to pay for buildings and other property which constitute appurtenances to the leasehold, i.e. everything that, under law, would have been attachable to the lot had it not been leased.

Land acquisition from the state. As concerns prices and other conditions for a conveyance, it is postulated that these are primarily a matter of substantive negotiations between the parties. The bargaining position of municipalities has been strengthened to give them essentially the same opportunities to acquire state land as to expropriate private land. In the event that the municipality and the land management fail to agree (in cases where the latter is empowered to decide independently on alienations) the issue is referred to a newly established body, the State-Municipal Land Board. This board consists of a chairman and two other members, of whom one represents the state and the other the municipalities. The decisions are binding on the state-seller and cannot be appealed. The Board is required by its directives to ensure that no further obligations shall be imposed on the municipality than would have been considered had the land been acquired by expropriation.

Advantages of leasehold system. If the advantages of the leasehold system are judged from the municipal point of view, it is, above all, the importance of owning the land in connection with the town planning that must be considered. For the planning of a functional and systematic development of a large city, it is essential that the municipality be able to decide in which order different areas are to be built, where the traffic routes have to be situated, and the way in which the land is to be divided among industries, shopping centres, offices, blocks of flats and one-family houses. The necessity of dealing with a varying number of private landowners is a hindrance to a timed construction and a rational distribution of the ground. These circumstances are probably acknowledged everywhere; but there are many who advocate that the land should be sold when the city has decided upon the way in which it is to be used and the town plan is formulated. It is, however, impossible to deny that the leasehold system is more fit to enable the municipalities to realize the schemes in conformity to their wishes. The leasehold system makes it easier to arrange transport and other common facilities in connection with modern and often complicated shopping centres. The arrangement of the small local streets in the garden suburbs is also facilitated.

The leasehold system is, without doubt, of great importance for the construction of the new suburbs.

The possibility of reclaiming land from leaseholders for other purposes was, from the beginning, looked upon as one of the advantages of the leasehold system. In spite of the contracted period which must be taken into account it is nevertheless easier to take the land back than it would be in the case of private ownership. And it is certainly less expensive, as the city already owns the land. Furthermore, it means that the city has influence on the ground value and can counteract unreasonable rises. The increases of land prices that still occur can consequently be utilized by the municipality itself.

The importance of municipality ownership of land has become obvious, especially in connection with the reconstruction of the centre of the inner town. It is much easier to reconstruct the inner town if the ground belongs to the city. Every scheme and every detail which has to be executed on private land entails time-consuming discussions about exploitation, density, necessary traffic junctions, common facilities, etc.

It may be asked whether there are no disadvantages connected with the leasehold system; the answer is that there is one principal disadvantage, namely the problem of *financing*. Considerable capital must be at the disposal of a municipality for the acquisition of land, often long before this land can be planned and built on; and the investments must remain after the exploitation of the ground. It is a difficult municipal problem which probably needs the assistance of the national government.

Methods of Financing

Leasehold loans. To improve the ability of municipalities to finance leaseholdership and thereby encourage the greater use of this instrument, they have been permitted since 1965 to borrow from state funds.

A loan bears interest from date at the same rate as for a housing loan (6·25% for 1969). The term of a loan is 40 years, of which the first 10 years are amortization-free, followed by 30 years of repayment at equal annual amounts.

The loan programme is administered by the National Housing Board and county housing committees.

Loans for land acquisition. To make it easier for municipalities which do not lease land to acquire land for urban development or associated facilities to accommodate their future growth, the government has made available a new class of loans for this purpose as of 1 July 1968.

Preference in granting these loans goes to the acquisition of land for new development. No loan is granted if the price for a piece of land exceeds a reasonable level as defined by the appraisal criteria for expropriation.

The maximum amount of a loan is set at what the municipality has paid or is to pay in cash for an acquisition. No collateral is required. Interest is payable from the purchase date at the same rate as a housing loan. The loan matures in 10 years, and exemption from the repayment of principal may be allowed for the first 2 years.

Loaned amount. Loan funds for land acquisition have been supplied from 1968 at 30 million Kr a year, in 1971 at 50 million Kr and in 1972 at 75 million Kr. This figure may be evaluated as insufficient in comparison with land acquisition costs—300–400 million Kr in 1972 for 100,000 dwellings built per annum.

Taxation methods. The municipalities can also finance land acquisition out of their general revenues. One of the important features of the taxation system is the degree of financial autonomy exercised by the municipalities through their receipt of a part of the revenue from income tax reserved for municipal activity. The main taxes connected with land policies are the following:

1. municipal income tax;
2. real estate municipal tax;
3. real estate property tax (as a part of the wealth tax);
4. tax on land profit.

The most important source of income from taxation is the municipal income tax which provides about 40% of funds to cover municipal expenditure. This tax is paid as a certain percentage of the taxable general income of each citizen or of each juridicial person. The rate of taxation is usually about 15% of the general income but varies between different municipalities, sometimes reaching 20%. Hence, the rate is not a fixed one. Each municipality decides annually on the rate of tax for the current year according to financial conditions.

The real estate municipality tax has existed since 1861 and is based on the assessed value of the real estate rather than on the income from rental. This tax is usually calculated as a given percentage of annual income from rental. There is, however, a guaranteed minimum revenue from taxation: should the amount of income from rental fall below 2% of the assessed real estate value of the property, then the tax is calculated as the given percentage (as mentioned above) of 2% of the assessed real estate value.

Adaption of the Leasehold System and Effect on Finance*

Those communities that acquired land far in advance and did not subsequently sell it now have an effective additional source of revenue in income from leasing land. In January 1964 the Land Evaluation Committee made an inquiry of all cities and towns in Sweden, concerning the application of the leasehold legislation. It is mainly the largest cities that lease land to a considerable extent. Seven cities, among them the three largest in the country, began to apply the leasehold system during the years immediately after the law was enacted (1908–12).

In order to illustrate that on a long-term basis the purchase of land will be financed to a considerable extent by inflowing leasehold money, the summary given below was made from information on five towns that have applied leasehold for a long time. It should be mentioned, however, that part of the payments accruing to leasehold are required for interest on and amortization of outstanding loans required for the purchase and development of land that has been leased under leasehold. The ratio of the cost for land purchase to payment for leasehold should, however, be encouraging for the leasehold system in the long run (Table 13.1).

TABLE 13.1.

Town	No. inhabitants 1·1·63	"„ of leased land	Applics. leasehold since	Expenditure of the municipalities per year for purchase of land for lease-hold purposes mainly (average of land acquired 1959–63) (Sw. Cr)	Amount of inflown leasehold payments during 1963 (Sw. Cr)
Stockholm	802,124	85	1908	9,902,200	26,786,992
Goteborg	410,681	93	1912	19,505,000	10,763,000
Malmo	237,517	49	1912	4,141,800	2,761,144
Landskrona	29,102	65	1909	204,580	276,641
Engelholm	13,075	90	1913	146,500	165,900

* Data taken from C. G. Carleson, "Inquiring concerning leasehold", *Statens Offentliga Utredningar, 1966:24* (Stockholm, Justitie-departementet, 1966).

The municipalities that do not extensively lease land under leasehold were asked for their reasons. Ninety cities answered this question; of these, only ten stated that the question about application of the leasehold system had not been topical. Financial problems are the reasons most frequently given for not using the leasehold system. Approximately fifty cities gave this reason alone, or in conjunction with others, for not introducing leasehold.

When comparing the replies of larger and smaller towns, it appears that the question about introducing leasehold has been much more vital for the larger towns than for the smaller ones. The answers support the contention that the question usually does not arise in a small built-up area, but does emerge when an area has reached a certain size or is about to expand greatly.

The questionnaire solicited general points of view on the leasehold system, as well as suggestions for reform; fifty-seven cities and twenty-nine towns responded to this item. Concerning the cities in general, a positive attitude to the leasehold system can be observed, as well as a belief that the system is an effective instrument for capturing increases in land values for the municipality. The financing question was also dealt with, and different suggestions for coping with it were made. Thus, many municipalities suggested improved loan possibilities in order to facilitate the municipal purchase of land. Many others suggested that the municipality should be granted the right to draw one-time amounts to cover the exploitation costs of the municipality. A shortening of the payment regulations period was also considered to be a desirable reform.

It should be stated that the possibility of retaining increases in land value for the municipality through the leasehold system, in its current form, are limited and depend upon the time for redemption of the land by the municipality, after a period of leasehold.

Another point mentioned was that clear guidelines for stating land and building values at redemption are lacking. Lastly, the periodic change in leasehold payments are of importance in this connection.

Evaluation of Leasehold System

The investigation shows that cities which introduced a policy of land acquisition and a leasehold system during the period 1908–13 now have an efficient instrument for city planning and urban growth.

The experience of the three largest cities—Stockholm, Goteborg and Malmo—as well as two smaller ones—Landskrona and Engelholm —shows that after the same period of using the leasehold system all have income from leasehold land which serves as an important basis for continued finance of land-acquisition policy, although the replies to the questionnaire about the condition of leasehold show that the success of such policy may be dependent on active financial support from the central government.

The recent improvements in financing conditions of the government loans for land acquisition by the municipalities, however, shows an increased awareness by the central government of this problem.

STOCKHOLM'S LAND-ACQUISITION POLICY

The City of Stockholm

Stockholm, the capital of Sweden, is situated at the point where the waters of Lake Mälar flow into the Baltic. It is built partially on the mainland of Upland and Sodermanland. To the east lies the Stockholm archipelago, composed of thousands of islands.

The centre of the city is the island of Stadsholmen (City Island) where the old city was founded. Immediately to the north of it is the old commercial and industrial area of Lower Norrmalm in and around which are concentrated much of the retail, wholesale and industrial activities of the city.

The population of Stockholm has increased since the middle of the nineteenth century from 90,000 to 300,000 in 1900 and 815,000 in 1950. Greater Stockholm now has about 1.3 million people. The town proper is planned now for 900,000 people, of whom 360,000 live in the re-developed central area and 540,000 in the suburbs.

The Stockholm Municipality Land-Acquisition Policy

At the beginning of this century, the Stockholm Municipality introduced a policy of land acquisition to supply land for urban

Plate 1. View of the Farsta Centre, Stockholm.

Plate 2. View of the Farsta Centre, Stockholm.

Plate 3. View of the Vällingby Centre, Stockholm.

Plate 4. View of the Vällingby Centre, Stockholm.

development. The municipal authorities saw as their task the acquisition of sufficient land to supply all the land required for future urban development.

The first important acquisition (Enskede estate with an area of 610 ha.) was ratified by the City Council of Stockholm in the spring of 1904. In the autumn of the same year, four properties were purchased in Bromma (Traneberg, St. Angby, Akeshov and Ulvsunda), with a total area of 1360 ha. The City Council thus bought nearly 2000 ha. in less than a year. In comparison, the total built-up area at that time was about 1700 ha.

A point of interest is that these very extensive land acquisitions, costing in all 3·6 million Kr, which was at that time a considerable sum, were accepted by the City Council with almost a full majority.

In the case of Enskede, the vote was almost unanimous. Concerning the Bromma properties, there were 82 votes for and only 12 against the purchase. In the following years the discussion became livelier, as was the case when a motion was raised in 1912 in the City Council proposing the purchase of Farsta, a farm of 645 ha. Many members of the Council found this a rather doubtful investment, or at least thought it unnecessary to buy up land so far from the built-up area, a point of view which was quite understandable in those days. It was not until the fifties that this estate was finally exploited.

One of the councillors who first emphasized the importance of land acquisition for the further development of the capital was the bank director, K. A. Wallenberg, who finished his contribution to the discussion about the above-mentioned Farsta property as follows: "Those who believe that our City is going to stagnate ought to vote against it. Mr. Chairman, I believe in the future and I vote for the proposal of the preparatory Commission."

Of course opposite opinions were also expressed. In 1931, for instance, when two estates (Beckomberga and Racksta) comprising a total area of 500 ha. were bought, the newspapers ran headlines such as "Expensive superiority complex" etc.

In the 1930s the City continued to buy up practically all available land on the outskirts and had by then acquired 12,600 ha. of the 15,000 ha. total area outside the inner-town.

The construction of flats on a larger scale in the outskirts began in the 1930s, and with that, the city also began to let out ground for multi-family houses. The first residential area of this kind was Traneberg. where construction was begun in 1934. The idea of *leasing* land for blocks of flats was, however, rather new at that time. It is therefore not surprising that at the same time a considerable amount of land in the inner town was sold by the city for the construction of flats (for example, in the neighbourhood of Norrmalarstrand, and at Erikslunden, Kristinberg and Fredhall).

Recently, the city has had to buy back some of these properties (at Fredhall) for the construction of the new ring-road (Essingeleden). It was not until 1938 that the authorities decided to stop advertising any municipal ground for sale.

An extensive housing construction programme has been carried out in the outskirts of the capital during the last decades. The result of this is that a large portion of the dwellings in Stockholm are situated on leasehold ground.

The total number of dwellings on the outskirts was about 166,000 in 1966; 117,000 of these (70%) were built on leased land. In the inner town, there were 176,000 dwellings, 2·7% of which, or only 4800, were built on leasehold land. However, the main importance for the municipality of maintaining land reserves under the jurisdiction of a single authority is that it allows effective implementation of an urban development plan according to a time schedule based on the needs of urban growth.

Cost of Advance Land Acquisition

For the purpose of measuring the economic cost of advance land acquisition, we shall compare the price paid by the municipality for land with the consumer price index and calculate the cost of the capital invested over the period from the purchase date until the land was planned for development. In this way we can obtain a rough estimate of the costs to the municipality of a policy of acquiring land in advance of when it is actually needed for development. To the capital costs must be added the cost of administrating the land until it was used. In addition, the current income from the lease of land must be taken into account when figuring the actual cost of advance land acquisition. The prices paid by the municipality will then be compared with current open market prices for land in the same location (keeping in mind that purchase prices for the municipality include capital costs and are adjusted according to the consumer price index).

In order to minimize differences in price due to location value, we shall consolidate the land purchases into groups according to different time periods. In this way we can establish the average price paid for land during each time period and compare it with average trends in the consumer price index.

It is impossible, given the present data, to eliminate the factor of location value since the sample is so small and the differences in location value so large. Consequently, it must be kept in mind that in the comparisons between the consumer-price index and the land-price index, differences in location value will inevitably influence the land price index.

Table 13.2 shows those figures in current prices and 1966 fixed prices.

A comparison of the average Swedish consumer price index and average prices paid for land by the municipality shows that in the years 1905–12 and especially in 1916–19 the land price index was considerably higher than the Consumer Price Index. The difference between the general price increase and the land price index reached its highest point immediately after the First World War (from 1916 to 1919) during a period of inflationary pressure on the market.

In the 1920s and 1930s the difference between the land price and consumer price indexes again became smaller. In this period the level of the land price index is similar to the period of 1905–12.

It must be noted here (Table 13.3) that the lower price of the land acquired during the 1920s and 1930s was due to the fact that these lands were located further from the centre of Stockholm than those lands purchased in 1905–12. In these years the municipality acquired more than 3000 ha., including lands for the future development of Vällingby.

The post-Second World War period shows a high rate of increase in land prices while the consumer price index rose but much less sharply. This trend is similar for almost all other countries as well.

Before 1939 several factors helped to keep the cost of raw land at a

TABLE 13.2. Land Acquired by Stockholm Municipality in Years 1904–66 Located within City Borders

Year of acquisition	Name of area	Location	Space (in ha.)	Price (Kr/m²)	Total amount	Consum. price index	Price Kr/m² fixed in 1966
1904	Enskede	South	610	0·32	1,952,000	100	1·88
1904	Traneberg	West	28	0·7	196,000	100	4·10
1904	St. Angby	West	160	0·07	112,000	100	0·41
1904	Akeshov	West	585	0·07	409,500	100	0·41
1904	Ulvsunda	West	587	0·15	880,500	100	0·88
1905	Alsten	West	181	0·16	289,500	101	0·95
1905	Svedmyra	South	131	0·12	157,200	101	0·70
1905	Mossen	South	137	0·13	178,100	101	0·75
1905	Arsta	South	380	0·60	2,280,000	101	3·48
1908	Lillsjonas	West	130	1·60	2,080,000	108	8·68
1908	Appelvikon	West	75	1·70	1,275,000	108	9·22
1908	Gubbangen	South	76	0·27	205,200	108	1·46
1912	Sodertorn	South	645	0·15	967,500	115	0·76
1916	Orhem	South	193	0·12	231,600	139	0·50
1917	Hammarby	South	360	1·00	3,600,000	191	3·07
1919	Johannelund	West	40	4·15	1,660,000	308	7·90
1922	Smedslatten	West	40	3·00	1,200,000	215	8·18
1922	Skarpnack	South	670	0·36	2,412,000	215	0·98
1930	Alvsjo	South	500	0·14	700,000	187	0·44
1930	Harrangen	South	130	0·20	260,000	187	0·63
1931	Hasselby	West	1000	0·31	3,100,000	180	1·01
1931	Racksta / Beckomberga	West	510	0·32	1,632,000	180	1·04
1935	Vastberga	South	426	0·38	1,618,800	176	1·27
1937	Langbro	South	160	0·38	608,000	184	1·21
1938	Enebyberg	West	22	1·25	275,000	187	3·92
1938	Balsta Flysta	West	157	1·50	2,355,000	187	4·70
1938	Nokenavgen	South	78	1·25	975,000	187	3·92
1939	Nynohov	South	67	3·75	2,512,500	193	11·39
1945	Skarholmen	South	110	0·46	506,000	266	1·00
1947	Blackberg	West	100	3·35	3,350,000	275	7·14
1947	Karrtorp	South	27	5·87	1,584,900	275	12·51
1950	Orby	South	400	2·10	8,400,000	297	4·14
1961	Satra	South	500	6·00	30,000,000	502	7
1966	Jarva	West	1600	9·00	144,000,000	586	9

TABLE 13.3 Land Purchase by the Stockholm Municipality

Land situated within the town

Year	Area/ha.	Average price Kr/m²	Index of land price	Index of cons. price	Average price in 1966 Kr/m²	Amount in current prices (1000 Kr.)	Amount price in 1966 1000 Kr
1904	1,970	0·18	100	100	1·06	3,546	20,882
1905–12	1,755	0·42	233	107	2·34	7,371	41,067
1916–19	593	0·96	533	188	2·56	5,693	14,669
1922	710	0·51	283	215	1·39	3,621	9,869
1930–39	3,050	0·46	255	187	1·59	14,035	48,495
1945–50	637	2·17	1205	279	4·43	13,840	28,219
1961–66	2,100	8·28	4600	565	8·29	174,000	174,000
Total	10,815					222,106	337,201

Land situated in the suburbs of the town

Year	Area (ha.)	Total cost (Kr)	Price (Kr/m²)	Average Kr/m²
1961	1,460	32,400,000	0·25–5·90	2·21
1962	950	3,400,000	0·36	0·36
1963	2,936	29,980,000	0·38–38·90	1·02
1964	4,855	36,336,000	0·11–11·50	0·75
1965	6,593	73,970,000	0·72–1·65	1·12
1966	3,853	37,725,000	0·70–1·16	0·98
Total	20,647	213,811,000		

relatively low level. The acquisition of large quantities of land permitted a constant supply of low-priced land to the construction sector to fill housing needs. Additionally, the policy of giving low-interest loans for housing projects built on low-cost land helped to restrain the demand for expensive land. This, then, acted as a deterrent to land speculation which would drive land prices up. A third influential factor was the generally low level of commodity prices during this time.

After the Second World War the increase in land prices was the result of two primary factors. The first was a general rise in consumer prices as expressed in the level of the consumer price index. The second factor was a sharply increased demand for land, brought about by the rapid urbanization which occurred after the war.

Within the Stockholm municipal borders, land prices were especially affected during this period. This was due to the fact that high prices prevailed for land in more heavily built-up areas which had been resold by the municipality, as well as for the generally freely marketed raw land in the city region. However, in spite of the various locational differences in land prices within the Stockholm region, it may be suggested that the advance land-acquisition policy helped to keep land prices at a relatively low level, by supplying land for development according to the demands of urban growth.

Cost-benefit calculation. Some aspects of the economic advantages of advance land acquisition may be demonstrated by a hypothetical cost-benefit analysis of the purchase in 1938 of all the land actually acquired by the municipality between 1947 and 1966. By comparing the results of this analysis with current, prevailing free-market prices for raw and developed land, a measure of the public funds saved by advance land acquisition can be achieved.

We will set the hypothetical 1938 purchase price at $1.59 \, \text{Kr/m}^2$. Capital costs will be set at 7% per annum—6% for interest on invested capital and 1% administrative costs for maintaining the lands during the period they remained undeveloped. (The estimated interest rate and administrative costs have been intentionally exaggerated.) Over the period of 23 years capital costs increased 4·7 times, over 28 years, 6·6 times. Thus by 1961 lands hypothetically purchased in 1938 should be worth 7·47 Kr/m² and in 1966 they would be worth 10·49 Kr/m².

At these prices it would seem that advance land-acquisition costs were approximately the same price paid for land by the municipality in 1961 and 1966, 6 Kr/m² and 9 Kr/m² respectively. But the importance of advance land acquisition is that, as well as lower cost, it enables the municipality to ensure that urban development will be planned and without wasted space, and furthermore it serves to restrain the pressure on land prices in the free market.

The Effect on Stockholm's Development: the Creation of Planned Neighbourhoods

The acquisition of land needed for future urban development by the municipality has given it the effective means of carrying out its general development plans in accordance with changing needs. The general plan for Stockholm's development in this century began with the idea that the central area should have high density, with a zone of multi-family housing surrounding the business centre, and the suburban region outside this zone should have uniformly low density, consisting mainly of one-family houses. Over the past 20 years the Stockholm planners' concept of a desirable arrangement for the suburbs has changed considerably. At the end of the Second World War the influx of population to metropolitan Stockholm was much greater than had been expected, and the density of population in the suburbs began to build up. The planners, therefore, proposed the development of suburban units (which may be called "neighbourhood units" or semi-satellite towns). Each unit would have its own shopping centres and cultural facilities and most neighbourhoods would be connected to the centre of the city by extensions of the local railway system.

The development during the whole post-war period has been guided by a master plan, which has been in operation since the last year of the war. The main concept was the preservation of Stockholm's mono-centric character and the dominating position of the central business district. The master plan rejected the continuation of the pre-war development process of spreading one-family houses and blocks of flats over the whole outer town area as well as satellite town planning. It recommended a kind of compromise between these two extremes with

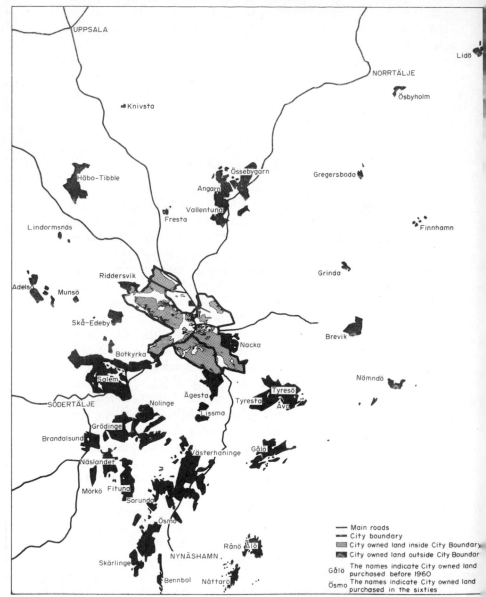

Fig. 13.1. Plan of Stockholm, 1970. (By courtesy of Stadskollegiets Informations-
kommitte/Esselte Tryck.)

the inner area of Stockholm's outer town (which on the whole comprised the already developed areas) more or less of a "dormitory suburb" character and the more peripherical parts of the outer town containing both dwellings and a substantial amount of places of work.

In 1960 a census showed that there was a total of 217,000 economically active inhabitants in the outer town. Out of those, 51,000 (24%) worked in their own district, 116,000 (53%) in Stockholm's inner town and the remaining 50,000 (23%) worked in other parts of the outer town or in other communes. Evidently, the planners have not been able to provide the outer town with a sufficient number of places of work in accordance with the master plan, which was built upon the sociological concept of "neighbourhood planning".

The master plan's application of the new ideas was the following hierarchy of settlement units: housing groups with 500–700 inhabitants, neighbourhood groups with 1000–3000, residential areas with 7000–15,000 and town districts with 25,000–50,000 inhabitants.

The settlement units were to be kept rather small with maximum radii from 200 m (housing groups) to 1500 m (town districts), and three-fourths of the dwellings were to be situated in multi-family houses. This proportion came closer to the wishes of Stockholm families (as expressed in answers to an investigation, where about one-third of the households preferred one-family houses) than the actual proportions built in the first post-war years, as more than 90% were blocks of flats.

By concentrating construction of new apartments, small houses, shopping centres, public facilities, and industry around subway and railway stopping points, Stockholm's planners hope to create viable, semi-self-sufficient communities which give their inhabitants a sense of belonging to a neighbourhood, serve a larger shopping area, provide jobs for a significant portion of their residents and support the investments in the mass transit system.

Relationship between Stockholm and the other Municipalities in the Stockholm Region

The close relationship between Stockholm and the localities in the region created a need for a regional cooperation for institutions capable of coordinating the activity of Stockholm and the other municipalities in the region. The reality of people living in the region and working in Stockholm created a need for the establishment of a regional authority able to plan the region's activities and to execute the plans. The Stockholm region succeeding in creating a regional housing-planning association, which is a voluntary authority but one with strong influence in planning housing activities and negotiating with the National Housing Board to get the needed government loans to subsidize housing and distribute it among the municipalities of the region. This planning association acts on the basis of coordination with Stockholm and the municipalities of the region. Obviously there are some conflicting interests between different municipalities in connection with the allocation of housing needs. But these different interests are generally solved in the framework of the coordinated activity of the regional planning association.

A more difficult situation has been created regarding land supply and land use. There exist differences between the financial possibilities of Stockholm in comparison with the small municipalities. The Stockholm municipality succeeded in purchasing large quantities of land located outside Stockholm and within the administrative boundaries of the small municipalities in the region. The use of land for satisfying the needs of the Stockholm citizens depends therefore not on the available land purchase by Stockholm but on the readiness of the other municipality to use the land, on the basis of an agreement with Stockholm. Obviously there exist some conflicting interests between Stockholm and the other municipalities interested primarily in satisfying the needs of their own citizens. These conflicting interests result in the wish of the municipality to use more land for satisfying the needs of their own citizens than for Stockholm's residents. Sometimes the municipalities are not interested in growth and refuse to develop land located in their administrative boundaries. Such conflicting interests between the separate municipalities are an expression of the existing conflict between different groups of citizens and local and regional interests. Such conflict is also a result of the conflicting interest between the present generation and the needs of the future generation. The institutional aspect of this conflict may receive a solution through the establishment of regional institutions with executive power, but on the basis of the participation of the different municipalities in the regional institutions' decision-making, and with the active participation by the citizens of the region in the planning process on a basis of coordinated activity between planners and citizens.

Planned neighbourhoods. For the city of Stockholm itself in the last 25 years, seventeen neighbourhood units, with a population of a quarter of a million, had been completed by 1960. Most of these were designed and completed as relatively small clusters, numbering about 10,000 inhabitants. However, experience showed that such a community was too small to support the kind of varied life which was thought to be desirable, so four of the later units, Vällingby, Högdalen, Farsta and Skärhomen, were designed to accommodate from 20,000 to 25,000 people. Second, Lower Norrmalm, the central business district to the north of the City Island, has been extensively redeveloped to provide more efficient and aesthetically satisfying commercial and business use, and to improve the transportation network of the region, much of which is focused on this area. Third, a subway system was built and a major highway programme was undertaken in 1960. In 1962 Stockholm adopted a master plan which divided the inner city into the different zones and generally prohibited the mixture of commercial and residential uses. It was the first attempt to zone a Swedish city on such a large scale and encountered considerable opposition from business and financial interests.

The whole territory within Stockholm boundaries is almost completely developed. The planning of new suburbs is based upon a sociological concept which is itself broken down into three specific aspects: the functional, the social and the architectural aspect. This approach stresses that housing should be situated within walking distance of the schools, shops, playgrounds, public transports, and if possible, places of work. The inhabitants of a functional group eventually form a social unit.

Three main centres: Vällingby, Farsta, and Högdalen are in existence and a fourth one is in the process of being built. They have been a commercial success and attract a large number of shoppers who commute by subway and by car. The detailed examples of the achievements of two of these new neighbourhoods will serve to illustrate the advantages of comprehensive planning that can be gained when the municipality owns all the land needed for new development.

Vällingby. The distance between the district of Vällingby and the centre of Stockholm is some 12 km. Travelling time by the suburban line is about 25 minutes. In 1951, when the town plan was authorized, it was completely virgin land, and in 1954 the neighbourhood centre was inaugurated. In 1960 there were 23,000 inhabitants within a radius of 1 km of the centre, and some 85,000 in the "Greater Vällingby" area. The district is built up around two stations on the western suburban line. All land in the area is owned by the town of Stockholm, as is the case with most of the ground still available for building purposes within the town's boundaries. When built on, the land is not sold, but leased out. The municipality has been responsible for building commercial and industrial as well as residential space.

In accordance with the principles mentioned above, this new district of Vällingby has been planned with ample space for working purposes. The biggest industrial area is some 20 hectares. In and around the central area, workshops of different sizes for industries of less disturbing and more city-like nature have been planned. The town itself is erecting industrial estates and leasing the floorspace. Space has also been reserved for offices and stores. Moreover, the public institutions to be located here (hospitals, schools, old people's homes, crèches (nurseries), etc.) provide work for many of the inhabitants.

In the "Greater Vällingby" area there are 13,000 places of work. According to the census in 1960 (when there were only 9000 places of work in Vällingby) 56% of those who were employed in the area lived there, which implied that 80% of the gainfully employed inhabitants of Vällingby were working outside the area.

The greater part of the population lives in blocks of flats. In principle, the residential quarter has been concentrated near the suburban stations. The areas served by the two stations have been divided into neighbourhood units, each housing some 3000 persons. The larger part of the block of flats consist of three-storey "lamellas", with each flat cutting across the building from wall to wall. This type of building is considered to be superior to higher buildings for family dwellings, no lift being necessary and better contact being maintained between the housewife working in the home and the small children in the playgrounds. Buildings of this type are so placed in relation to one another as to form more or less closed-in yards. Other three-storey blocks will be built in the form of connected starhouses.

Groups of 10–12-storey dwellings, intended primarily for single persons and small families, will be put up amongst the other buildings, above and around the Vällingby centre proper.

The one-family dwellings are composed of villas, terrace-houses, and chain-houses. The villas consist mainly of "smastugor". These latter are small houses, erected under the sponsorship of the town, but for which the proposed occupant may take an active part in the actual building. The advantage of this is the cash payment to be made by him will then be considerably smaller.

The traffic has, as far as possible, been divided up. The highways are connected to "feeder" streets, which in their turn, distribute the traffic to the actual local streets with parking space. The latter are designed to discourage through traffic. Special paths for pedestrians and cyclists are built in the areas. Space for garages has been reserved near the residential buildings.

Grounds for ball-games and minor training fields are arranged near schools and parks. A major sports field is planned to the west of the central parts of Vällingby south of the highroad. This will be connected to the big recreation area which covers all the land to the south of the built-up area as far as the shores of Lake Mälar.

The main centre at Vällingby has several department stores and boutiques, restaurants and repair shops together with offices for different social and civic activities. It also contains several kinds of cultural institutions, such as a theatre, a library, a cinema, assembly rooms, conference rooms, churches and so on. In close proximity to this centre, a secondary and high-school is planned with indoor swimming pool, gymnasium, sport-hall and assembly hall.

This centre also acts as chief centre for the neighbouring suburbs, each of which has a smaller centre of its own. Certain of its facilities will therefore be available to the new suburbs housing some 60,000 people (or 100,000 if surrounding areas already built-up are included).

The provision of local shops and social services is taken into account in the general planning. The neighbourhood unit is built up around a minor centre which provides lower-level consumer services.

The smallest unit is represented by a number of houses or buildings around a children's playground, a sanded playground for younger children and a place for baby carriages—all near the houses and surveyable from their windows. Of such groups of homes is formed a greater unit with nursery (crèche) and large playground apparatus. This greater unit (a neighbourhood unit) is laid out in a way that keeps all pedestrians well away from roads and especially from the highway.

The town plans are so arranged that the residential section has contact with the local street system on one side and with the park on the other.

Farsta

Farsta is located about 6 miles due south of the centre of Stockholm. It, too, was built on wholly municipally owned land, starting in 1958. Here, the developer of the shopping centre was a private concern. It was designed along the same general lines as Vällingby with respect to the grouping of residential areas, the location of the shopping centre, the segregation of traffic, and the aim of achieving a certain degree of economic self-sufficiency. The architects for Farsta's shopping centre, who also designed Vällingby's, were able to profit from the experience in the older area. While the two centres are about the same size, considerably more space is devoted to parking at Farsta, which has over 2300 spaces. The population of Farsta is about 30,000 and some 150,000–200,000 people are within easy driving distance.

The square is surrounded by commercial buildings, three of which are occupied by department stores. The centre has about fifty shops. There is also a restaurant, five banks, a savings bank, a library, a cinema and a medical and dental clinic. The centre has a theatre, a youth centre, a kindergarten and two churches.

Several point-blocks are located close to the centre with slab-blocks farther out, much the same as at Vällingby.

The erected new communities, sometimes called new towns, have to be seen as the first step in realizing the Stockholm regional development plan which is based on development of new centres in the region.

According to the regional plan, ten local centres of the Vällingby–Farsta type were to be built in the surrounding communes. One of them, Solna, was opened in 1966; another, Täby, is under construction. The remaining centres are smaller, have less traffic segregation and are less equipped with parking spaces, cultural and social institutions, etc. But still, they are on the whole designed in accordance with the principles which have guided the planning of Stockholm's outer town.

It is a widespread belief that the population increase in Stockholm from the present 1·2 million inhabitants to perhaps over 2 million in the year 2000 will necessitate satellite towns. On the other hand, the great majority of those who are responsible for traffic planning and re-vitalization of the city core are convinced that the present structure will be able to serve an even larger population than 2 million, if underground, railway and motor-way construction is allowed to go on according to present, but enlarged plans, and if the city core will be allowed to expand into its immediate vicinity and divest itself effectively of all kinds of routine industries.

A Cost-Benefit Analysis of Advance Land Acquisition in Vällingby and Farsta

Vällingby. The majority of the land for Vällingby was acquired in 1931: 1000 ha. at 0·31 Kr/m² and 510 ha. at 0·32 Kr/m². The development plan, however, was not instituted until 1951. Since it was necessary for the acquired land to be held for 5 years before it could be planned for development, the calculations will be based on a 15 year period instead of the actual elapsed time of 20 years. Capital costs will be set at 7% per annum—6% per annum interest rate plus 1% per annum administrative costs. At 7% per annum compound interest rate, prices will increase 3·87 times over 20 years. The average price paid per square metre in 1931 was 0·313 Kr and therefore the value in 1951 of land acquired in 1931, based on 7% per annum capital costs, will be 1·21 Kr/m². This is 58% less than the actual price of 2·10 Kr/m² paid by the Stockholm municipality for land acquired in 1951. The difference in location value between land acquired in 1931 and in 1951 might be higher considering that in 1951 the acquired land was generally further from the centre than in 1931.

Farsta. In Farsta 645 ha. of land was acquired in 1912 at a price of

$0 \cdot 15 \, \mathrm{Kr/m^2}$. Development of the area began in 1958 on the basis of a development plan initiated in 1952. Over 40 years and at a rate of 7% per annum, the value of the land increased by 15 times to $2 \cdot 25 \, \mathrm{Kr/m^2}$. The Stockholm municipality, on the other hand, paid $2 \cdot 10 \, \mathrm{Kr/m^2}$ for land in 1950.

For this it can be seen that, in spite of the high costs of capital invested over 40 years (which are admittedly exaggerated), the price of land acquired in 1912 is not significantly different from the price paid by the municipality in 1950 (again taking into account differences in location value). But the advantage of having held the land for 40 years gave the municipality the opportunity to plan and supply land for the construction of an entire community, an opportunity it probably would not have had if the land had not been held by the municipality.

Some additional data for the cost-benefit analysis may be obtained by comparing land prices in Vällingby and Farsta at the time of establishment of these neighbourhoods with prices prevailing in similar locations today. The prices on the outskirts of Stockholm in locations less favourable that Vällingby and Farsta were 80–120 $\mathrm{Kr/m^2}$ in 1974. If we calculate the price of the developed land in Vällingby and Farsta by adding the cost of infrastructure works (approximately $25 \, \mathrm{Kr/m^2}$) and the interest costs on capital investment for land purchase until 1974, the value of the acquired land is about $40 \, \mathrm{Kr/m^2}$; this is 2 to 3 times less than in other locations in the region.

The Effect on Land Prices in the Stockholm Region

A further demonstration of the economic advantages for the municipality of advance land acquisition and their impact on free market prices may be seen from the following studies of free market land prices in various scattered locations in Stockholm and the Stockholm region. A study of land prices in Sweden was undertaken by the Ministry of Justice in 1966. Although the study was limited to a reduced number of purchases and sales and to certain regions only, the results are significant for the land-prices development. The study shows that during the period 1957–63 the building sites for one family-housing increased in the county of Stockholm by 46% or 6·5% yearly, in Uppsala by 39% or 6·1% yearly, in Sodermanlands by 30% or

5·4% yearly. A higher price increase is shown for land for summer houses in Stockholm (8·8% yearly price increase); in Uppsala the price increase was 6.2% and in Sodermanlands 7.2%.

The higher price increase for summer houses is explained by the building of these houses on free market land and not on land purchased by the municipalities. An additional reason is the extreme pressure on the market for this kind of housing.

The other important criterion for land policies is the role of land in housing costs. It has been 6·3% in Stockholm for social housing for multi-family houses and 10–15% for one-family and semi-detached houses (in the years 1960–62). This figure did not change in the following years. In the UK the figure for social housing was 14–20% (at a density of 10 dwellings per ha.); it was increased for the co-op building societies from 10% in 1958 to 30% in 1965. In the Paris region it was 19·3% in 1962, 22·6% in 1966. In Spain it was 28% in 1964 (10–12 km from Madrid).

The development trend of prices in the city of Stockholm are significant for the impact of land acquisition. The following figures show the price development trend: from 1967 to 1974 land prices on the outskirts have increased from 52 Kr/m^2 to 150 Kr/m^2, or 7% yearly. For land in central residential areas from 400–800 Kr/m^2 to 1200 Kr/m^2 or 6·5% yearly; for land in the CBD from 2000–3000 Kr/m^2 to 3000–4000 Kr/m^2 or 7% yearly.

Such a rate of increase of about 6–7% yearly is relatively low in comparison with other countries: Germany 1962–68, 11%; France 1950–66, 18%; Italy 1950–62, 15%; Spain 1950–69, 20%; Israel 1950–68, 20%.

Obviously the level of land prices and the trend of land-prices development are influenced by many factors and not only by land policies; but keeping in mind the very high rate of GNP increase in Sweden and the rate of population increase in the Stockholm region, it might be suggested that land policy played a dominant role in the relatively slow rate of land price increase and the low level of land in housing costs in comparison with other European countries. In the Stockholm region, as in other cities, the highest *rate* of land-price increase is to be found in the newly urbanizing areas on the outskirts of the city. As there exists some information on land-price trends in some of Stockholm's suburbs, it will be useful to present this data in order to contrast it with the situation obtaining in the new neighbourhoods mentioned above that were developed by completely public authorities on the basis of public land ownership.

Hasselby and Brankyra. The results of a study in Hasselby and Brankyra as well as in Solna show the major effect on land prices of planning decision changing use in a location where there is no public land acquisition. Hasselby and Brankyra are two municipalities located in Stockholm's suburbs. These areas show a similar pattern of changes in the price of land for the construction of one-family houses.

Hasselby embraces an area of commercial kitchen-gardens and an area of multi-family houses, but only the southern part (of one-family houses) was the subject of study. Brankyra is entirely composed of one-family houses.

The study is based on 271 purchases of land designated for construction, of which 77 are in Hasselby and 194 are in Brankyra. The total area (Hasselby: from 600 to 2400 m^2; Brankyra: from 600 to 1000m^2) was divided into different plots during the period of time studied.

The land price increase more or less follows the same curve in the two communities. In Hasselby the average price increased between 1960 and 1964 from 27 Kr to 41 Kr and in Brankyra from 24 Kr to 44 Kr. The land-price index varied for Hasselby, from 100 (1960) to 150 (1964) and for Brankyra, from 100 to 180. The yearly price increase was 10% for Hasselby and nearly 17% for Brankyra, whereas the consumption expenditure index increased by only 3·3% during the same period.

Solna. The development of land prices in Solna illustrate well the effect of changes in land use. The area studied was Lily Alby, located south-west of Solna, near a beautiful Stockholm suburb and surrounded by many lakes. Between 1900 and 1940 the area only contained small houses. From 1940 a few tracts near the lakes were industrialized.

Two Town Plans, the first in 1949, the second in 1958, brought a complete change to the character of the community. The Town Plan (in 1949) designated a part of the land for small houses and industry;

the General Town Plan (in 1958) designated the whole area for industrialization (thereby entailing the destruction of the small houses).

The expectation of a different use of the land caused a price increase. Since the Town Plan of 1949 was accepted, the yearly price increase has been 10%. From 1940 to 1950 the average price increased from 20 to 40 Kr/m^2 (i.e. a yearly increase of 7·2%). After 1958 the price increase is significant and in 1960 it reached 150 Kr/m^2 (i.e. a yearly increase of 14%).

A comparison of the formation of land prices in different locations within the Stockholm region shows that there are large differences in the rate of price increase according to different locations and uses. Thus, although overall Stockholm region land prices are relatively low compared to the rest of Western Europe, within the region there is quite a bit of variation in land prices, which is in some cases quite extreme (witness the rates of increase in Hasselby, Brankyra and Solna). An important factor, in these cases, and on Swedish land prices in general, is planned changes in land use. Whether for industry or for summer houses, land that is not publicly supplied is subject to a higher rate of increase than in cases where the land is municipally supplied.

These limited examples, then, emphasize the important role which advance land acquisition can play in regulating the land market.

SUMMARY REMARKS AND EVALUATION

Land acquisition policies have allowed the Stockholm municipality, as well as other municipalities in Sweden, to create a land reserve for future urban development. There still is the problem that certain other municipalities lack the funds to carry out a policy of large-scale land acquisition.

Recently, the government increased the amount of loans for advance land acquisition, but the rapidly growing land needs for different purposes resulting from an increased standard of living require further financial sources for land acquisition.

The private sector cannot afford to invest in the uncertainties of future development, but through the institution of advance land acquisition it is possible for the public authority to create a large enough land reserve to minimize the risks of planning for future development: the larger the reserve the smaller the risk. A large reserve is necessary, because the larger the land reserve the more options are open for changes in location of various land uses, and the less disruptive it is likely to be when a particular area is changed from one use to another.

Therefore, if the planning authority is at the same time the land-owning authority, it is possible to interchange one land use for another as the changing needs of growth become evident. However, the enactment of planning legislation or land-acquisition policy is not enough by itself to ensure effective land use. These measures must be combined with an effective procedure for expropriation of land required for urban growth. Only together do they form an effective framework for preventing unplanned, and stimulating planned development, by giving the municipality a virtual planning monopoly.

The regulations for expropriation, based on payment according to former land use reduces the amount of compensation by eliminating purely speculative land price increases resulting from prospective land use change.

The right of the municipality to take possession of the expropriated land before completion of the expropriation procedure helps to shorten the procedure and encourages the acquisition of land on the free market, since landowners have no hopes of retaining property ownership through delayed or extended court proceedings. Several recent legislative changes have also been introduced which further encourage land acquisition and increase the ability of the municipality to plan effectively; these include priority rights of the municipality in the acquisition any property, and government assistance in land acquisition for leasehold purposes.

Obviously there are problems which even the most effective planning and acquisition cannot solve, although they can to a certain extent moderate their effects. The foremost of these problems is that of transportation which, due to the topography of the Stockholm region, presents many obstacles to planned development.

Stockholm recognizes the problems which it faces with regard to transportation, and it has already planned measures which, it is hoped, will lessen the strain on the centre city. These include the creation of new suburbs in the region around mass transportation facilities, where commuting on these facilities will be the optimum means of getting to and from work. In this way Stockholm will know how far it can expand its boundaries, and at what population density in order to maintain a healthy urban structure.

By acquiring large amounts of land, Stockholm has assured itself of more than enough land to plan these new neighbourhoods, as well as the possibility of providing recreation areas on the lands which remain uncommitted to another specific use.

The land purchases by the Stockholm municipality over a long period of time have allowed not only the preparation of a town-planning scheme but also the timing of urban development as the land needed for development was already under municipal ownership.

A cost-benefit analysis of the advance land acquisition shows that such a policy has given the municipality not only the benefit of planning but has also saved public funds by acquiring land for future urban development while it was still in agricultural use, and, therefore, was acquired at low prices.

Hopefully, this 70 years of experience in advance land acquisition may serve as a guide for other countries, too.

Obviously the evaluation of the achievements of a land-acquisition policy should not neglect the complicated problem of the administration of publicly-owned land. There exists a problem of fixing proper criteria for the estimation of costs and for the allocation of land to different uses according to the present and future population needs. Sometimes there are differences and even conflict between the financial department and the planning department over the attempts of the former to recover the development costs over the short term. Such investments might be better seen as part of the essential long-term development investments made by society. Obviously the present calculation of costs is related to the methods of financing currently in use, whereby the municipality must take out loans for land acquisition, paying interest at the prevailing market rates. Although central government assistance is available to procure better terms for the loans, there is still a problem if the land investment gets no return over the medium term.

The high-density, high-rise buildings in some new neighbourhoods have been criticized by the residents who would like more family houses and one-storey units. The unsolved problem of social equity and economic efficiency in land-use planning requires the establishment of new methods of investment which would allow a solution to the conflict between short-term and long-term needs, and which would mean that the time was available to ensure the proper long-range land-use planning.

REFERENCES

Carlsson, C. G., "Inquiry concerning leasehold", *Statens Offentliga Utredningar,* 1966; p. 24 (Stockholm: Justitiedepartement).
Hamrin, Eva, and Wiren, Erick, *Town and Country Planning in Sweden Today,* Stockholm, 1964.
Government of Sweden, Memorandum prepared for the 35th Session of the ECE Committee on Housing, Building and Planning, 1974.
——, Paper read before the 2nd Nordic Meeting of Housing Ministers and the 15th Nordic Conference on Housing Administration, Copenhagen, 16–18 June, 1969.
Land Policy Commission, *Kommunal Markpolitik,* Report I, SOU, 1964.
Land Value Committee of 1963, *Markfragen I & II,* SOU, 1966.
Michanek, Ernst, *Housing Standards and Housing Construction in Sweden,* The Swedish Institute, 1963.
National Swedish Building Research Institute, *Municipal Land Policy in Sweden,* D5; 1970.
National Swedish Building Research Institute, *Urban Land Policy in Sweden.*
Odmann, Ella, "Some views on land ownership in urban planning and house production in Sweden", *Geoform* 13/73.
Odmann, Ella and Dahlberg, Gun-Britt, *Urbanization in Sweden,* National Institute of Building Research, Stockholm, 1970.
Pass, David, *Vällingby and Farsta—From Idea to Reality,* National Swedish Building Research Institute, 1969.
Pahlman, Ake, Stockholm municipality, personal communication, 14 June 1972.
Stockholm Regional Planning Commission, Skiss 1966 till regionplan for Stockholm-straketn, 1967.
Stockholm City Planning and Building Office, *Land Acquisition and Leasehold in Stockholm,* Dec. 1967.
Strong, Anna Louise, "Land banking in the Stockholm region", unpublished paper, 1974.

CHAPTER 14

Advance Land-Acquisition Policy in The Netherlands: the Amsterdam Experience

The experience of Amsterdam demonstrates that a policy of advance land acquisition, carried out over the long term, enables a city to carry out a policy of balanced, planned development without sprawling, fragmented development and, at the same time, to control the land market without any special taxation measures. The fact that the municipality has established a virtual monopoly on the purchase of land needed for future urban development, has led to it being able to influence the urban land market and restrain price increases. The system of leasing rather than selling land has enabled land to be efficiently used in planned new neighbourhoods.

The interesting feature is that in spite of a high rate of population growth and GNP, the Netherlands has the lowest rate of land-price increase among all the industrialized and developing countries. Such a situation may be evaluated as the result of the land-acquisition policies of the municipalities and legislative measures which have made the municipalities the dominating factor in the urban land market, supplying land needed for general urban growth and for private as well as public housing.

BACKGROUND TO POLICY

The territory of the Netherlands consists of 41,000 km² (about

15,800 ml^2). The land area of the Netherlands may be geographically divided into three zones:

1. the coastal zone which is basically comprised of dunes which serve as a defence against the sea;
2. the large zone of land behind the dunes which is below sea level— this zone comprises 40% of the Netherland's total land area and is the most densely populated;
3. the zone of land above sea level to the east and south extending to the borders of Germany and Belgium—this zone is generally less economically developed and is furthest from the coast, which serves as the developed commercial link with the outside world.

In 1972 the population was 13·5 million, while projections to the year 2000 indicate a population of 15–15·5 million. In comparison with the most recent 15 years, the rate of population growth has declined somewhat. In 1950, 85% of the population lived in municipalities with more than 5000 inhabitants but, by 1969, this figure had risen to 91%. Also by 1969, 31% of the population lived in municipalities with more than 100,000 inhabitants. The average population density is about 330 persons/km^2 (about 1000/ml^2) while in urban areas the average density is 2400 persons/ml^2 (although densities do exceed 7000 persons/ml^2 in some urban areas).

NATIONAL LAND POLICY

Historically, the high population density, rapid urban growth and difficult topographical conditions (with most land in urban areas below sea level, land filling is necessary before development, thus making small-scale development uneconomic) have all led to an active land policy by the Dutch government. Operating in a framework of local autonomy, national legislation has ensured the legal framework and financial means for carrying out policy such as advance land acquisition. The control of finance by the central government (municipalities receive much of their income as the part of national tax revenues returned to them in proportion to their population, with an extra amount for the large cities with special problems) has given them a means of influencing the municipalities to adopt comprehensive land-policy schemes. The provincial governments must approve any planning scheme produced by the municipalities, and this provides another check in the direction of proper long-term land-use planning. Land acquisition has emerged as one of the principal means by which the large growing cities can ensure the execution of an efficient land-use scheme.

Procedure of Land Acquisition

The Dutch land-acquisition procedure is based on the Expropriation Act which gives municipalities the power to expropriate land located in an area of an approved extension plan. While the purpose of the Expropriation Act is to ensure the availability of land needed for future development, it also protects the property rights of landowners. Compensation for expropriated land must be paid on the basis of existing market prices. Generally, the approach of market-price compensation is common to the expropriation procedures in most countries of the world.

The basic difference between the Dutch compensation policy and others lies in the area of land-market-price formation. Generally, transformation of agricultural land use to other uses near urbanized areas affects the formation of high land prices, even for land remaining in agricultural use. Therefore, the public authority in most countries has to pay relatively high compensation costs according to the principal of market prices. The Expropriation Act in the Netherlands, based on the original 1851 legislation, influenced agricultural land prices in a different way. The knowledge that future land planned as urban extension would be expropriated did not encourage speculative investment in land. Rather, the planning procedure (i.e. the provincial government's right of approval of local development plans and its control of building permits) created continuous rural areas near the city frontiers, without urban extension into these areas. Thus, the planning procedure, by controlling the direction and location of growth, effectively kept some land in agricultural areas outside the building market. The net result was to create a situation where the municipalities themselves became the biggest land purchasers and developers. The municipality's monopolistic advantage in the suburban land market thus prevented payment of exaggerated prices.

Where expropriation of agricultural land is required, the methods of compensation take into account payment not only for land in agricultural use, but compensation for the loss of the owner's income source as an agricultural producer. This additional compensation is equal to 10 years of income from agricultural production. From the combined total compensation, an amount equal to the interest on this amount in government bonds is deducted. For example, if the value of an acre of agricultural land is $200, the rate of income from agricultural production of this acre is 10%, and the bond rate of interest is 6%. The owner will be entitled to the following additional compensation: 10% from $200 is $20 of yearly income, multiplied by 10 years will be $200. From this sum is deducted the bond rate of 6% annually over the 10-year period, or $120. Thus, the owner will receive an additional $80 per acre to the $200 in market value. Generally, the long tradition of public land acquisition has created a favourable understanding of land expropriation for future urban development in that the municipality is able to acquire the needed land from owners through negotiation. Only a minority (about one-third) of the landowners apply to the court in order to fix the just compensation.

Land Development and Calculation of Costs

A general principal in calculating costs is that all land-acquisition and development costs of the area are to be included in the costs of construction of buildings erected, including housing, commercial and others. Costs assignable also include the interest on the invested capital from the time of acquisition till the date of supplying the land for construction.

A particular problem in the cost calculation is the method of charging the general costs on individual sites according to different land uses (i.e. residential, commercial or industrial) as well as different types of dwellings (one-family, multi-storey houses, shops, and offices in multi-storey houses and so on).

One method of cost calculation is the so-called "x" method, where a typical dwelling unit is chosen as a standard. To this typical unit, coefficients are applied which make other units of the same space either more or less expensive. The overriding principal is that the general evaluation of the entire area must cover all the invested costs. Rents are then derived from these cost calculations, with the exception that for low-income dwellings there is a special government subsidy. There are considerable differences in evaluating the land for housing and commercial enterprises.

Obviously, the peculiar topographical characteristics of the raw land in most of the big cities makes the development works quite expensive, but there is criticism of the method of calculation of the costs, even charging interest for the time land is held while executing the development works as part of the costs of development works. It is suggested by some experts that the capital investment in acquiring land and carrying out the development works should not be charged interest. Differences of opinion concerning the calculation problem are connected mostly with the relationship between the central government and the municipalities (and similarly for the way of financing the land acquisition and land works). That is, as the municipalities have none of their own financial means for these tasks, they have to receive loans from the national government. Such loans are given for a medium term at an interest rate near to the rate existing on the financial market.

Another possibility is that there exists some connection between the regularly high development costs (resulting from the topographical character of the land) and the high charges in the housing projects. Perhaps it would be more equitable to spread some of the costs over the total population of the city rather than only to the inhabitants of the new neighbourhoods. The general belief is that the municipalities are looking too much for an economic return in the new developments and have limited financial means to adjust rents to the payment possibilities of low-income groups. Thus, although there exists a system for subsidizing the housing costs of the lower-income groups, the problem of calculating and covering development costs should be associated with the general costs of urban development and urban growth.

Administration of Publicly-Owned Land

It is the policy of the Amsterdam municipality to rent publicly-owned land rather than sell it. Other municipalities such as Rotterdam, the Hague and Utrecht both rent and sell public land.

Land rentals are based on a long lease system first introduced in Amsterdam in 1896, which specified that land be let on lease terms to a maximum of 75 years. Upon expiration of the lease, both the land and attendant structures reverted back to municipal ownership without the municipality being obliged to pay any compensation for the erected structures.

Several changes in this legislation have been introduced since its inception. In 1915 a perpetual leasehold for residential buildings was introduced. According to this new legislation, the lease could be extended after the initial term of 75 years for a succeeding period of 50 years. At the end of each lease term, the municipality has the right to fix a new ground rent as well as to revise the conditions of the lease for the new term.

In 1966 an important change with respect to the financial conditions of the lease was also introduced. According to the former leasehold conditions, the evaluation of land value as a basis for paying the rent could be changed only at the end of the leasehold term (75 or 50 years period). This condition was changed and redefined so as to fix land values. But a new term of annual ground term was introduced. In connection with the permanently declining power of money, an adjusted rent term was introduced which must be fixed every 5 years in order to adjust the "fixed-value" rent to the real purchasing power of money. The adjustment was based on the average price level of the net home product published by the Central Statistical Office every year which represents the total value of produced goods and services in the Netherlands during a 1-year period. Use of this method adopts the basic rent value to the real purchasing power of money every 5 years. The rate of the land rent is 4–6% according to different uses: 4% for social housing, 6% for private residential building and 6% for commercial and industrial.

AMSTERDAM'S LAND-ACQUISITION POLICY

The history of Amsterdam starts at the beginning of the thirteenth century. In terms of site and locational characteristics, marshy sur-

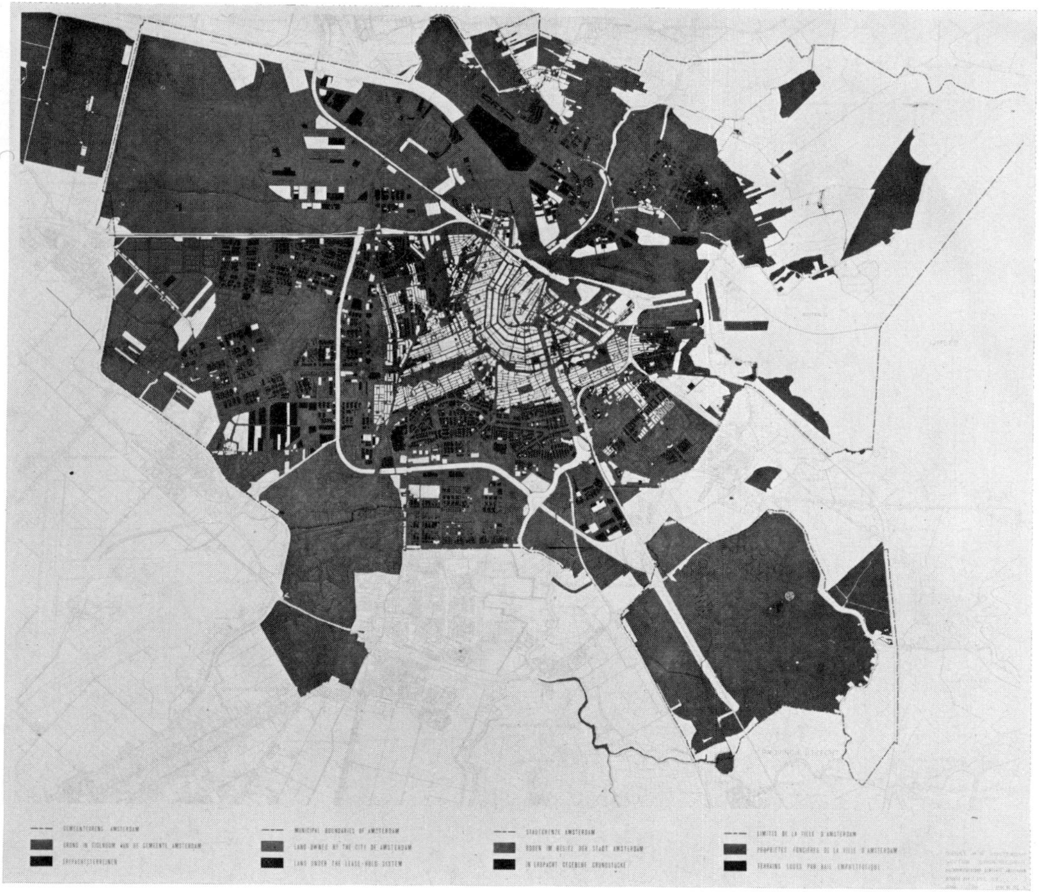

Plate 5. Plan of Amsterdam.

Plate 6.

Plate 7.

Plate 8.

roundings, water and low ground had a great influence on the patterns of the city's initial development. That is, as the city had such weak subsoil, it was built on piles at a very high density. Indeed, the peculiar character of the city's environment influenced the active role of the municipality in physical planning.

At the end of the nineteenth century renewed rapid development began, primarily associated with the opening of the North Sea Canal (1876), which brought increased economic activity and population growth. In the last 30 years of the nineteenth century, Amsterdam's population doubled to 510,000. One of the consequences of this rapid development was a shortage in the supply of required land for future building activities. As a result, land prices increased considerably. It was at this time that the municipality decided to take responsibility for guiding future urban development. As a first step, the municipal council took control of enterprises which were vital for the city's development and which were previously operated by private concerns (e.g. utilities). In 1896 the council decided to retain in public owner-ship the land needed for future urban development by introducing a long-lease system for land acquired and prepared for development by the municipality. Using the national guidelines established by the Federal Housing Act (introduced in 1901) and a new building code (1905), construction of the first public housing project was begun in 1907. At the same time, it was decided to prepare an extension plan for the south section of Amsterdam. An extension plan for all of Amsterdam was completed in 1935 and approved by the Crown in 1939 (Plate 5).

The Dutch Planning Legislation, after approval by Provincial authority, gives the Amsterdam municipality the power to expropriate land for residential, industrial, commercial and recreational require-ments included in the extension plan. This legislation permits con-tinued re-evaluation of the plan to incorporate major changes in development trends of population and economic growth. During the execution of the overall extension plan, many such changes have been necessary. For example, the amount of land needed for total residential requirements was significantly higher than that forecasted initially. The basic reason for this departure was the decline in the average household family size per dwelling. Instead of the 3·4 household size per dwelling forecasted for the year 2000 (3·7 existed in 1935) the average decreased to 3·2 in 1960 and to 2·6 in 1973. The net result of this change produced a demand for 26% more dwellings per 1000 persons. Similarly, increased standards of living increased demand for more living space per person. Thus, the planned density initially forecasted by the plan (55–70 dwellings per hectare) decreased in the newer neighbourhoods to an average of 40 dwellings per hectare. In terms of scale, the Amsterdam land-acquisition scheme has resulted in the addition of 6200 hectares to the municipality's size over a period of 20 years (1945–65). In comparison to its area of 5700 hectares in 1945, the Amsterdam urban area was more than doubled.

While development costs have been high, the Expropriation Act facilitated the purchase of raw land at relatively low prices (Table 14.1). The table shows that by the year 1961 the highest paid price was 2·70 gd/m², * about $1 per square metre, or less than $4000/acre.† Only in the 1960s have prices been above this ceiling. However, even these were lower in comparison with other European cities. It must also be pointed out that the acquired land was a natural extension of the existing city area rather than acquisition of tracts far removed from the city boundaries, which otherwise would tend to result in lower prices. It is also noted that the investment needed for infrastructural development in the municipality is higher than in most other countries primarily as a result of its peculiar topographical nature. For example, the execution of the extension scheme of West Amsterdam required 23 million m³ of sand to fill a low area of about 3000 ha.

Generally, the combination of planning legislation and the land acquisition policy of the Amsterdam municipality permits a continued, progressive expansion of the city which avoids large, fragmented suburban areas with associated high percentage of vacant land. The latter is the reality and a major problem for most other cities in the world today. In the case of Amsterdam, the acquired land reserves for future urban development by the public authority not only induced the municipality to prepare detailed development plans, as do other

---

* 2·60 guilders = $1.

† $4000 is high, but only 40% higher than in purely rural areas. This is primarily due to high capital investment costs associated with Dutch farm land.

TABLE 14.1. Land Acquisition of Amsterdam Municipality in the Period 1947–74

Year	Hectares	Amount (guilders)	Price (guilders/m^2)
1947	72·7	549,300	0·75
1948	5·5	130,400	2·38
1949	53·7	670,200	1·24
1950	106·2	787,200	0·74
1951	95·6	901,300	0·94
1952	96·2	1,396,300	1·45
1953	141·3	1,363,000	0·96
1954	95·7	1,857,700	1·94
1955	242·8	5,647,300	2·32
1956	432·9	7,090,500	1·63
1957	441·7	8,026,400	1·81
1958	273·1	5,863,600	2·14
1959	715·0	11,056,900	1·54
1960	210·7	5,700,200	2·70
1961	83·7	5,081,900	6·07
1962	389·8	17,345,900	4·45
1963	464·0	23,660,700	5·09
1964	512·6	18,835,600	3·67
1965	291·1	12,092,900	4·15
1966	194·3	9,351,700	4·81
1967	99·0	8,708,700	8·80
1968	269·8	8,745,200	3·24
1969	1163·3	30,324,500	2·61
1970	546·4	40,430,300	7·40
1971	95·0	13,560,000	14·27
1972	77·6	9,071,900	11·69
1973	69·9	7,613,600	10·89
1974	71·4	5,280,600	7·40

municipalities in the world, but also to execute these plans within the time framework forecasted. This was primarily possible because the essential basis for executing the development plans, i.e. land, was in the ownership of the planning authority, thereby making the execution of urban-development schemes easier and more efficient. However, by itself, advance land acquisition cannot automatically solve the difficult problems which result from high rates of urban growth and ever-changing population needs. The difficulty is created by the need for constant re-evaluation and improvement of development plans during their execution, which results from the changing relationships between land-use requirements for individual needs. At the very least, uncertainty in planning is reduced when land ownership is within the same framework as the planning authority.

Effect of Large-scale Land Acquisition on Planning

The large-scale land-acquisition policy of Amsterdam municipality allowed it to build planned communities as part of the extension of the city for a long time. The authors of the first Extension Plan were initially influenced by the Garden City movement. In reality, however, they erected new planned neighbourhoods with a high percentage of green space. The first step of the Extension Plan was the development of the west part of Amsterdam (about 3000 ha.) as well as one neighbourhood in the south. The second plan developed was for the extension of North Amsterdam. The third was for the south-east extension (also about 3000 ha.), which included a scheme for the expansion of a neighbouring municipality of Amsterdam, Amstelveen, to 70,000 inhabitants. The south and west extension scheme, which is now in the final stage of completion, is based largely upon providing land for residential needs. The programme for the south-east extension, which is carried out in cooperation with the municipalities of Amstelveen, Ouder Amstel and Diemen, is a more mixed development of the total 1750 ha. included in the extension plan, 900 ha. is for residential use, 250 ha. for industrial use, 200 ha. for special uses, and 400 ha. is for recreational use.

The overall regional development scheme (for an eventual population of 2 million) is based on the extension and growth of such small towns near the city (up to 20–25 miles) such that each will achieve a size of about 100,000 inhabitants. In terms of employment increase, the development scheme for Amsterdam is based on the assumption that 70% of the working population will be employed in the service sector. Thus, its requirements must be partly supplied through urban renewal programme and partly by developing service subcentres outside the city. Also, foreign trade and port oriented growth must be accommodated near the port area along the North Sea Canal (for a projected employment increase of 150,000–200,000 workers). Another 100,000–150,000 would be employed in industry and services in the subcentres.

Obviously, a high percentage of those employed in Amsterdam will have to commute to work daily from subcentres in the region. Therefore, a good transport network is an essential precondition for an efficient, comprehensive regional development plan. In particular, the transportation plan assumes that the number of commuters employed in Amsterdam will increase from 50,000 daily in 1961 to 100,000 during the next 15–20 years. The proposed solution centres on the reorganization of public transportation in order to provide a subway which will be based on underground traffic in the central area and mostly above-ground traffic in the outlying areas. For automobile traffic, the plan proposes a network of motorways which interconnect the regional system with the urban, using tunnels near the centre of the city for connection between the north and south. Parking space will be provided in zones near the city centre, but not actually in its heart, thus requiring use of public transportation for commuting to centre city work places. Additionally, traffic arteries are integrally connected with the planned neighbourhoods, thus ensuring good access to the neighbourhood's centre while at the same time attempting to avoid placing major roads inside the residential areas.

Some neighbourhood examples. The first step in carrying out the extension plan was the successful creation of new planned neighbourhoods with a total of 50,000 dwelling units. Land acquisition largely took place in the years 1949–51. By 1955 almost all the needed land was acquired. Actual construction works on the first neighbourhood commenced in 1952, and by 1965 almost all dwellings were constructed (48,000).

The planned development of new communities ensures needed environmental features, especially space for recreational activities. The initial extension plan fixed a recreation standard on the basis of prevailing patterns, i.e. $4 \cdot 6 \, m^2$/person outside of the residential neighbourhoods. However, the standard was increased during the execution of the plan to $7 \cdot 5 \, m^2$/person. Perhaps the most interesting feature of the new neighbourhoods is the provision of a high amount of green space inside the dwelling spaces in spite of a relatively high gross density (averaging 54 m^2/person within the residential neighbourhoods for parks, playgrounds and common gardens).

A comparison of the density of structures in Amsterdam with those of the new neighbourhoods illustrates the role of integrated land-use planning in providing a high level of residential quality. The eight newly erected neighbourhoods in Amsterdam extensions (six in West Amsterdam) are used as examples (refer to Tables 14.2 and 14.3). Of the 50,835 planned dwelling units in the eight neighbourhoods, 48,000 were constructed by 1965. Of the 48,000 completed units, 21% are one-family houses, 60% are 3–5 storeys, 9% are 6–8 storeys and 10% are 9–14 storeys. By comparison, in Amsterdam, one-family houses represented less than 6·7% of the total dwelling units. Here the predominant type of dwelling was a 4-storey unit (without elevators). The goal of the extension plan in the new neighbourhoods was to achieve a proportion of one-family houses of 33%. In reality, this goal was reached only in the first three planned neighbourhoods, where the proportion of one-family houses is 30–33%.

The social goal of the extension plan was to ensure a population of mixed-income groups living in the same neighbourhoods. With one exception, the dominant social groups are working and middle-income classes. In the neighbourhood of Buitenveldert, the dominant social groups are of middle- and upper middle-income class. Generally, although all neighbourhoods are based on the same planning guidelines, an effort was made to ensure some individual character.

A short review of the highlights of six of the eight new neighbourhoods demonstrates some of the planned patterns.

Slotermeer. Slotermeer is a garden city of 10,000 dwellings which is subdivided into seven sections, each with its own commercial centre. The main commercial centre is in the middle of the neighbourhood. Two belts of green space divide the neighbourhood from west to east. The prevailing types of dwelling units are three to five storeys high (58% of total). Some high-rise buildings of nine to fourteen storeys, residential as well as office buildings, dominate the landscape. An interesting feature of the planning of the different types of house is the separation of the one-family units from the multi-storey units, thus creating continuous areas of one-family houses. This segregation was

TABLE 14.2. Neighbourhood Dwelling Unit Types

Neighbourhood	Total dwellings	Type of dwelling								Total (%)
		One-family		3–5-storey		6–8-storey		9–14-storey		
		Number	%	Number	%	Number	%	Number	%	
Slotermeer	9,920	3,100	31·3	5,770	58·1	410	4·1	640	6·5	100
Geuzenveld	4,560	1,480	32·5	3,010	66·0	70	1·5	—	—	100
Slotervaart	5,430	1,700	31·3	3,280	60·4	400	7·4	50	0·9	100
Osdorp	12,180	2,335	19·2	6,710	55·6	705	5·8	2430	19·9	100
Overtoomseveld	3,140	160	5·1	1,780	56·7	640	20·4	560	17·8	100
Westlandgracht	1,610	90	5·6	1,110	68·9	410	25·5	—	—	100
Buitenveldert	8,823	1,225	13·9	4,920	55·7	1694	19·2	984	11·2	100
Nieuwendam-Noord	5,172	503	9·7	3,687	71·3	288	5·6	694	13·4	100
Total	50,835	10,593	20·8	30,267	59·5	4617	9·2	5358	10·5	100

TABLE 14.3. Development Schemes for the New Neighbourhoods

Neighbourhood	Period of land acquisition	Period of development works execution	Dwellings constructed until end of year									
			1952	1953	1954	1955	1956	1957	1958	1959	1960	1963
Slotermeer	1940–2	1948–52	93	2679	6488	7983	8,358	8,566	9,093	9,238	9,238	9,575
Geuzenveld	1949–51	1949–53	—	—	—	396	1,685	3,314	4,200	4,433	4,434	4,485
Slotervaart	1951–2	1952–5	—	—	—	136	1,252	2,251	3,661	4,592	5,145	5,250
Osdorp	1953–6	1955–8	—	—	—	—	—	—	116	1,787	3,497	8,920
Overtoomseveld	1952–3	1954–60	—	—	—	—	—	—	172	1,206	2,234	2,580
Westlandgracht	1953–5	1957	—	—	—	—	—	—	—	—	754	1,470
Buitenveldert		1955–9	—	—	—	—	—	—	—	419	906	4,750
Nieuwendam-Noord	1958–60	1956–61	—	—	—	—	—	—	—	—	—	400
			93	2679	6488	8515	11,295	14,131	17,242	21,675	26,208	37,430

planned in order to create a more quiet environment for people interested in living in such dwelling units. The population of the neighbourhood is mixed, comprised mostly of working and middle-income classes, and with both young couples and retired citizens.

Geuzenveld. This neighbourhood is located west of Slotermeer (construction started in 1954 and finished in 1965). The commercial centre is characterized by a high-rise residential building with shops on the ground floor. The multi-storey houses are concentrated in the centre of the neighbourhood, while the single-family houses (33% of total dwellings) are constructed on the fringe, thus creating a graduation into the adjacent rural area. Although the neighbourhood is not a large one (4658 dwellings) different segments of the neighbourhood were planned by different architects in order to avoid an exaggerated uniformity of structure.

Slotervaart. This neighbourhood (5430 dwellings) enjoys the most favourable location, being near the pre-Second World War city, on the border of a lake and a park, as well as in close proximity to a railway, which connects it with the entire metropolitan area. The main commercial centre is in the middle of the neighbourhood, incorporating the majority of the high-rise buildings, office buildings and public services.

Osdorp. This is the largest of the seven new neighbourhoods (12,063 dwellings were built by 1965). The Osdorp neighbourhood has a high percentage of 3–5-storey houses (60%) and a relatively high percentage (20%) of 9–14-storey dwellings. The remaining 20% of the dwellings are single-family houses. A special feature of this neighbourhood is the commercial centre, which is not located in the middle of the neighbourhood, but rather on the fringe of the neighbourhood, near the border of Lake Sloterplas. This commercial centre serves other neighbourhoods of Amsterdam West as well as Osdorp. The centre is planned for pedestrian traffic with a road located around the centre. The other unique feature of this neighbourhood is the concentration of different types of schools, including high schools, technical, and art schools.

Nieuwendam-Noord. This neighbourhood, erected to the north of Amsterdam, must be considered as part of the future of Amsterdam's northern expansion. It is connected with an existing garden village, Nieuwendam, and with vacant areas of land which will be developed in the future. The neighbourhood is largely composed of 3–5-storey houses which comprise 72% of all dwellings. This is the neighbourhood with the lowest proportion of one-family houses (less than 10%).

Buitenveldert. This is one of the more "exclusive" neighbourhoods. This neighbourhood is south of Amsterdam (near the pre-Second World War city) and is divided by a narrow green space. It is also near a large park. The population of this neighbourhood is composed of mostly higher-income groups. Most of the units are not more than three storeys high in order to avoid the need for elevators. The one-family houses are mostly luxury villas. On the north-west side of the neighbourhood, 70 ha. are provided for one of the two Universities of Amsterdam. One of the University Hospitals is also located there.

Land-use patterns in the new neighbourhoods. The experience of the Amsterdam new neighbourhoods shows that by efficient planning it is possible to build communities of high density which have as much green space per person and even as high a proportion of single-family houses as less well-planned developments in other countries with much lower gross densities. Obviously the allocation of green space is more collective (i.e. high rises surrounded by parks) than individual (though there are private gardens). Recently there was some opposition when a new planned neighbourhood included what was considered too much collective green space and not enough land for private gardens.

The location of 48,731 dwellings on 1256 hectares means that housing construction has proceeded at an average density of about thirty-nine dwellings per hectare (15·6 dwellings per acre). All neighbourhoods are characterized by a considerable land allocation for public parks and playgrounds; the average is 58 m^2/dwelling or 18 m^2/person. More impressively, the green space allocated as common gardens (outside the private garden attached to the house) within the residential areas is on the average of 36 m^2/person.

Generally, there are small differences in the gross densities for the six neighbourhoods; gross density varies between 38·6 and 44·0 dwellings per hectare. Only one neighbourhood, Buitenveldert, shows a lower density of 31·8 dwellings per hectare. Here there is a higher land allocation for public open space (81·4 m²/dwelling in comparison with 41·2 to 63·6 m²/dwelling in the other neighbourhoods). This is primarily a result of the special feature of this neighbourhood in that there is land allocated for the Free University as well as a large sports stadium.

In terms of comparisons among neighbourhoods (Table 14.4), for the three neighbourhoods of Slotermeer, Geuzenveld and Slotervaart, the percentage of one-family houses varies between 30–33% as compared to Osdorp (20%) and Nieuwendam-Noord, where one-family houses are only 10% of the total dwelling units. In terms of space allocated for dwelling area, the first three neighbourhoods vary between 25–32 m²/person, as compared to 21 m²/person for the other two neighbourhoods. In terms of allocation for public parks and open spaces the amount allocated in Osdorp and Nieuwendam-Noord is higher than in the other three neighbourhoods. As a result of the combined effects of such different land-use allocations there is only a small difference between the gross density per hectare, 39–44 dwellings per hectare in the three neighbourhoods with a high proportion of one-family houses, in comparison with 41–44 dwellings per hectare in the neighbourhoods with the low proportion of one-family houses (Osdorp and Nieuwendam-Noord).

Of course, differences do exist in terms of net density of both categories of neighbourhoods: 77–79 dwelling units per hectare for Osdorp and Nieuwendam-Noord, in comparison with 55–65 dwelling units per hectare in the three neighbourhoods with a high percentage of single-family houses.

The most impressive conclusion may be taken from the comparison of the locations of the new neighbourhoods. As they are really a continued development of the existing city, the lack of vacant land between these new developments and the existing city ensures good traffic interconnections to work places as well as easy access to the complete range of services available in the existing city.

A comparison between the gross density of the Amsterdam planned

TABLE 14.4. Land-Use Allocation in Amsterdam's New Neighbourhoods (m²/person)

Name	Slotermeer		Geuzenveld		Slotervaart		Overtoomse		Osdorp		Buitenveldert		Nieuwendam-Noord	
Area in hectares	248		254		259		235		243		314		228	
Number of dwelling units	9923		4658		5310		2672		12,063		8782		5323	
Gross density	43·98		39·25		38·75		42·59		41·44		31·84		43·89	
Net density	65·09		60·84		54·75		74·33		77·47		64·65		79·5	
	m²/p	%	m²/p	%	m²/p	%	m²/p	%	m²/p	%	m²/p	%	m²/p	%
Area for dwellings	9·16	11·8	8·87	11·1	9·40	11·8	6·46	8·8	7·12	9·3	10·1	10·3	7·4	10·4
Area for private gardens	5·34	6·8	5·71	7·3	6·09	7·6	2·46	3·6	4·03	5·3	5·9	6·0	2·4	3·4
Area for group gardens	11·84	15·3	17·31	21·6	9·53	11·9	9·37	12·7	9·43	12·5	11·8	12·0	10·9	15·1
Area for shops and parking	0·38	0·5	0·56	0·8	0·56	0·8	0·56	0·8	0·59	0·8	0·8	0·8	0·6	0·8
Total	26·72	34·4	32·45	40·8	25·58	32·1	18·85	25·9	21·17	27·9	28·6	29·3	21·3	29·7
Public services	7·21	9·2	5·34	6·8	5·93	7·4	9·65	13·1	4·53	5·9	5·5	5·6	3·5	4·9
Trade and comm.	0·88	1·2	0·44	0·6	1·56	1·9	0·71	0·9	0·59	0·8	0·7	0·8	0·6	0·8
Total	8·09	10·4	5·78	7·4	7·49	9·3	10·36	14·0	5·12	6·7	6·2	6·4	4·1	5·7

TABLE 14.4 (*Continued*)

Name	Slotermeer		Geuzenveld		Slotervaart		Overtoomse		Osdorp		Buitenveldert		Nieuwendam-Noord	
	m²/p	%	m²/p	%	m²/p	%	m²/p	%	m²/p	%	m²/p	%	m²/p	%
Roads for dwellings	21·28	27·4	18·9	23·7	31·1	39·0	23·15	31·4	19·15	25·4	19·5	19·9	18·8	26·1
Roads for public building	2·56	3·3	2·06	2·6	2·0	2·5	2·59	3·5	1·56	2·0	2·5	2·6	1·2	1·8
Roads for trade	0·84	1·1	1·06	1·4	0·56	0·8	0·59	0·8	1·03	1·3	1·0	1·0	0·7	0·9
Roads for open space	1·38	1·8	1·65	2·0	0·12	0·2	0·12	0·2	2·06	2·7	1·9	1·9	2·3	3·2
Access roads	—	—	—	—	—	—	—	—	5·93	7·8	12·6	12·9	4·4	6·0
Total	26·06	33·6	23·67	29·7	33·78	42·5	26·45	35·9	29·73	39·2	37·5	38·4	27·4	38·8
Public parks	10·93	14·1	13·03	16·3	8·8	11·1	12·9	17·7	14·4	19·0	17·7	18·1	10·7	14·8
Playgrounds, sports, and school open space	1·66	2·1	1·22	1·6	1·68	2·1	2·46	3·4	1·93	2·6	1·4	1·5	2·4	3·3
Water	4·12	5·3	3·40	4·2	2·31	2·9	2·28	3·1	3·5	4·6	6·2	6·3	5·6	7·7
Total	16·71	21·5	17·65	22·1	17·79	16·1	17·64	24·2	19·83	26·2	25·3	25·9	18·7	25·8
Total area (m²/person)	77·58	100	79·55	100	79·64	100	73·30	100	75·85	100	97·60	100	72·50	100

neighbourhoods with some communities in the USA indicates the significance of the role of planning and socio-cultural patterns on land allocation and residential environment. The average gross density of the seven Amsterdam neighbourhoods is 39 dwelling units per hectare or 15·6 dwelling units per acre. The gross density in the planned community of Reston, Virginia, is 3·5 dwelling units per acre for 2–8-storey buildings. Higher densities than those existing in the new neighbourhoods of Amsterdam relate to multi-family housing projects financed by F.H.A. One of these projects, Fresh Meadows, Queens, New York, has a density of 21 dwelling units per acre (for 13–21-storey buildings). These examples may serve to show the advantages of a single authority acting simultaneously as planner, landowner and land developer.

Comparison with Urban Renewal Policy

The importance of a policy of advance land acquisition and a planned development of new communities becomes clearer when one considers the problems associated with redevelopment of decaying, already built-up areas.

Existing conditions in the old part of the city require urgent, basic renewal. The problem involves not only the demolition of some of the older houses, but also a considerable improvement in the overall residential environment, socio-cultural facilities, recreation areas and traffic connections. Generally, the constant changing of social needs requires higher living standards which are expressed in terms of increased dwelling space per inhabitant and more space per inhabitant and more space for recreation, educational facilities and social services. As the area of the existing city must also provide additional space for commercial services and light industries, it will be impossible to provide the same quantity of new residential units to replace those demolished. Thus, some part of Amsterdam's inhabitants must be relocated outside of Amsterdam. This creates a special problem, especially for some of the more aged inhabitants who have long been accustomed to their existing residential environment. Generally, there exists strong opposition by dwellers and homeowners in the old parts of the city to the renewal projects. A good example of the reasons for their opposition is found in a recent symposia discussion paper:*

> ...Our four large cities contain high percentages of very small and decrepit old dwellings, the sole attractive feature of which is the low rent. These houses are still partly inhabited by aged peoples who need little dwelling space and who cannot afford the luxury of moving to new residences, and partly by younger people in the age group of 20 to 25 and 30 years, who possess low means of support so far, and who in most cases have not yet started a family.... For these two age groups, the older "fixed ones" as well as the young very "mobile" ones, the low rent of the ramshackled old dwellings and their central situation are a definite advantage. It is these same age groups precisely, especially the younger people among them, which are extremely opposed to the pulling down and to the renovation of dilapidated city districts.
>
> Neither the aged people, nor the younger ones, who regard their stay in older districts as a brief adventure, nor the house owners who, in the majority of cases, derive no appreciable profits from their property, are willing to invest in the maintenance of the aged temporary buildings. As a result, these homes are increasingly used for the settlement of economically weak people.
>
> However, there are indications that the push element is prevailing and that what is important for those who leave for suburbia is ultimately not the dwelling and the direct residence surroundings, but the quality of the total living environment. The departure from the city to remote rural municipalities entails also, disadvantages for those involved. One of these drawbacks is the time and cost requirement as a result of the daily trips to and from work and school.

In terms of urban renewal costs, the financial burden is increased by the high costs of land acquisition in the urban renewal area. Estimated costs of land acquisition of redeveloped land in urban renewal areas compared with the land costs of the new neighbourhood extensions in the west, south, north and south-east shows that 1 square metre of land in the urban renewal area will cost 600 guilders/m^2 ($200) in comparison with 60 gd/m^2 in the south-east extension ($20) and 37·5 gd/m^2 ($12) in the west-south and north extensions.

The high expenditure needed for urban renewal is also demonstrated by comparing the total investment associated with acquiring and developing 5200 ha. of the urban extension (2·4 billion guilders), compared with the 3·0 billion guilders (more than 1 billion dollars) needed for investment of 500 ha. for urban renewal. The financial problem is further complicated by the low-income levels of inhabitants in the renewal areas. Recent municipality data show that the average

* *The Large City as a Problem Area* (Amsterdam: Contributions by the City Development Directors of Amsterdam, Rotterdam, The Hague and Utrecht to the discussion regarding the Third Space Planning Note, 1973), pp. 5–9.

annual income of renewal area inhabitants is not more than 10,000 gd, and that 30% of the heads of households have incomes of less than 8000 gd annually ($2700). It is suggested that a reasonable ratio of rent to income for families with an average annual income of 10,000 gd should be 17% which results in a monthly rent of 140 gd. Such limits upon the ability to pay rent would necessarily require a large public expenditure for rent subsidization. According to the existing subsidy policy of the national government, public housing for low-income groups is subsidized up to 200 gd monthly (not including personal rent subsidy). Such a subsidy, however, will be insufficient to finance urban renewal construction. Thus, a higher subsidy for urban renewal rehabilitation will be needed.

A comparison of the total costs of the new construction in urban renewal areas and rehabilitation costs with the costs of new construction in the Bijlmermeer extension of the south-east development area shows that the actual rent cost per month (prior to subsidies), for the same amount of dwelling area (80 m^2/dw) in the new neighbourhood, will be 625 gd monthly, while for urban renewal new construction it will be 675–900 gd per month. For urban renewal rehabilitation dwellings of 72 m^2/dwelling area it will be 460 gd monthly.

It must be underlined that the high costs of new construction in the urban renewal area are based on a density twice as high as that of the new neighbourhoods, 80 dw/ha. in comparison with 40 dw/ha. Tables 14.5 and 14.6 compare the details of the housing costs in the new neighbourhoods with those of the urban renewal area and the public subsidy needed according to the different rent expenditure possibilities of different income groups.

Certainly, the method of financing urban renewal is an international problem, a problem for which a variety of solutions have been postulated. While renewal is socially a very advanced policy, it does result in high public expenditure for the permanent subsidy of low-income dwellers. Thus, in some countries, new construction and rehabilitation in the renewal area is directed toward higher-income groups, as well as for offices and commercial services, all of which are able to bear the burden of high renewal costs.

One possible, partial solution is to allocate for residential uses some of the space in the central areas of the city allocated to office

TABLE 14.5. Comparison of Housing Cost of Urban Renewal and in the Bijlmermeer Extension

	Bijlmermeer extension	Urban renewal new construction	Urban renewal rehabilitation
Net area per dwelling in m²	80	80	72
Number dwellings per hectare	40	80	80
Number parking places per dwelling	1·35	1·2	1·0
Land acquisition costs per dwelling (guilders)	15,000	20,000–50,000	15,000
Building costs per dwelling (guilders)	50,000	50,000	30,000
Parking cost per dwelling (guilders)	10,000	10,000–15,000	10,000
Project cost per dwelling including parking (guilders)	75,000	80,000–115,000	55,000

TABLE 14.6. Subsidies Needed for Low-income Inhabitants for Urban Renewal and Bijlmermeer Extension

	Bijlmermeer extension	Urban renewal new construction	Urban renewal rehabilitation
Project cost per dwelling (including parking)	75,000	80,000–115,000	55,000
Actual rental cost per month	625	675–900	460
Rental price levels established by policy:			
(a) 150 guilders monthly			
actual rent cost	475	525–750	310
Subsidy needed	69,000	74,000–109,000	45,000
(b) 200 guilders monthly			
actual rent cost	425	475–700	260
Subsidy needed	62,000	67,000–102,000	38,000
(c) 300 guilders monthly			
actual rent cost	325	375–600	160
Subsidy needed	48,000	53,000–88,000	24,000

buildings. Such a measure may improve the overall environmental conditions of the centre through mixed land-use planning, while, at the same time, imposing on those firms wishing to locate offices in the centre the obligation to pay for part of the costs of residential construction.

ECONOMIC RESULTS OF LAND-ACQUISITION POLICY

The comparison of land prices paid by Amsterdam's municipality during the years 1941–66 with the development of land prices on the urban fringe in other European countries illustrates some of the economic advantages of a public land-acquisition policy.

An important point is the small difference between the price of land in agricultural use near the city frontiers and the price in the rural areas. The prices near the city may be only 30–50% higher than the land in the purely rural areas. In comparison with other countries these differences are insignificant. For example, the prices of agricultural land near big cities and at a distance of 10–20 miles are about 20 times higher in the Federal Republic of Germany, 10 times in Italy, 15 times in Switzerland and 30–40 times in Spain. Certainly the value of agricultural land *not near* urban areas is influenced only by the intensity of its use and the income derived from its use. For agricultural land *near* urban areas, however, it is more common to find land-price formation strongly affected by the prospects of future urbanized values.

In most countries the rate of increase in the price of raw land in newly urbanized areas is sometimes higher than the increase of the building costs. Thus, during the last 10–20 years the role of land in general housing costs increased. In the Netherlands the yearly increase of raw land during the years 1945–63 was only 2·6%. During the same time there was a considerable increase in development costs, but this corresponded to the increases in building costs. In Italy the yearly increase of urban land price cost was 12–19%, in Spain $11\frac{1}{2}$–28% and in France 13–21%.

As a result of the relative stability of land prices, the Netherlands is one of the few countries in the world where the role of land in housing costs has not changed (1951—20%, 1969—20%). In comparison to pre-Second World War figures, the role of land in housing costs has actually diminished (it was then 33%). It is noted that the land costs in total housing costs is high compared to the low prices of raw land. The reason for this relates to very high land-development costs which reach a level of $15–20/m². In terms of land-price development within the city, prices have not increased at nearly the same rate as in other European cities. The average real estate price in 1947 was 169 gd/m², and in 1964, 464 gd ($155)/m². Table 14.7 shows the percentage increase of the above values. The general price increase during the 17 years was 175%, or about 6% yearly. If prices are calculated as "fixed" prices, as the consumer index increased by 47% over the period, this fixed price increase is decidedly less. In both cases, these increases must be considered very moderate in comparison with other European cities.

TABLE 14.7. Land Price Development in Amsterdam from 1947 to 1964 (yearly average)

Year	Price per m² in guilders	Index 1953 = 100
1947	169	100
1948	181	107
1949	205	121
1950	185	109
1951	183	108
1952	172	102
1953	169	100
1954	206	122
1955	242	143
1956	261	154
1957	277	164
1958	283	167
1959	300	178
1960	356	211
1961	373	221
1962	419	248
1963	446	264
1964	464	275

According to a more recent information, average residential land prices are between 200–300 gd/m² ($70–100) and, in some of the more exclusive areas, prices range from 300 to 600 gd/m². In contrast, commercial land prices in the central area reach 2000–3000 gd/m² ($700–1000), while the highest commercial value (in Leidenstaat) was

9000 gd in 1971 ($3000). Comparing both sets of land prices to those in the new neighbourhoods, which are approximately 100 gd/m² ($35), we may arrive at the conclusion that the land policy of the Amsterdam municipalities had some impact on land prices in residential use, but is without influence on the commercial land-use prices in the central area of Amsterdam.

TABLE 14.8. Real Estate Price Development according to Town Sections
(guilders/m²)

Year	0	1	2	3	5	Average
1947	172	163	162	181	133	169
1948	178	250	173	140	183	181
1949	206	226	220	114	—	205
1950	182	219	176	—	—	185
1951	188	183	193	140	—	183
1952	172	156	181	153	197	172
1953	168	181	204	123	122	169
1954	209	216	210	164	221	206
1955	265	243	220	185	194	242
1956	281	238	268	177	236	261
1957	291	251	279	186	193	277
1958	307	256	283	199	152	283
1959	340	239	284	202	217	300
1960	407	311	320	255	283	356
1961	391	375	371	279	307	373
1962	442	393	432	300	346	419
1963	471	424	470	315	385	446
1964	481	384	543	363	424	464

CONCLUSIONS

Generally, the small difference in land prices near the city frontiers compared with land prices in rural areas has a decided impact on the patterns of urban development. That is, the ever-increasing extension of urban space has and continues to influence the price of land far from the urbanized area (regardless of use).

One of the achievements of Amsterdam's land-acquisition policy can be measured in terms of the effects on the social structure. The ability to acquire land at relatively inexpensive prices near the city frontiers permitted the provision of needed housing for low-income groups. However, as noted previously, such a policy also needs some additional subsidization because high development and building costs make housing too expensive for low-income groups.

Another of the advantages of the administrative structure associated with Amsterdam's land acquisition policy is its ability to shorten the time periods of both land acquisition and construction. Table 14.3 indicates that no more than 6–8 years passed from initial land acquisition until completion of housing construction. Certainly, the combined authority of the municipality's planning division, land-acquisition department, and division for development works within the same organization framework has been a positive factor in shortening the time needed for total execution of development plans. It is also noted that shorter time periods from land acquisition to completed construction permits an economizing of capital in land acquisition.

The favourable experience of the last 25 years of the Amsterdam municipality's acquisition policy is, of course, primarily based on the planned development *within* its municipal jurisdiction. In the future, there may be difficulty in planning future extension because much of the land needed for new development schemes is located in the broader city region, and including land within other autonomous municipalities. Therefore, new development plans will require close coordination with those of the other municipalities. Such regional coordination may not come easy, however. The basic problem centres on the need to take a regional development approach without the regional institutions and authority to do so. Close coordination does take place at the provincial level, where each of the seventeen provincial governments coordinates the activities of the municipalities in their respective provinces. The provincial governments cannot, however, initiate and direct the municipalities to execute provincial development plans. As the provinces have no agencies for land acquisition or implementation, all plans must be executed by the separate municipalities.

Most of the small municipalities have no appropriate qualified staff to deal with land acquisition and land administration. Regional land agencies with participation of representatives of local authorities may be helpful for implementation of national urban land policies.

The need for a regional land-acquisition and land-use authority is becoming an urgent problem, a problem which will require further adaptation of the existing administrative structure so as to better respond to the new needs resulting from the extension of the city's functions into a broader city region.

REFERENCES

Government of the Netherlands, Ministry of Housing and Physical Planning, *Second Report on Physical Planning in the Netherlands*, 2 Parts, 1966.

——, *The Randstad: The Urbanized Zone of the Netherlands*, 1970.

——, *Town Planning and Redevelopment in the Netherlands*, 1970.

——, *The Development of the South-west of the Netherlands*, 1971.

——, *Abridged Report on Housing*, 1972.

——, *The Residential Environment*, 1969.

——, *Amsterdam's South-east Extension*, 1971.

Municipal Real Estate Policy in the Netherlands, Haagseveer 35, Rotterdam.

Municipality of Amsterdam, *Town Planning and Ground Exploitation in Amsterdam*, Department of Public Works, 1967.

Statistiek van het grondgebied naar gebruik in de gemeente Amsterdam.

Zuidhoek, G. J., *Het Amsterdamse bouwblokonderzoek*, 1970.

CHAPTER 15

Urban Land Policy in France

France has succeeded in creating some of the most efficient administrative instruments for implementing land policies. The French experience will serve to demonstrate at the same time the limits of the efficiency of organizational structure operating in the context of limited policy objectives. As most land policy in France has been aimed at specific economic planning goals, the results have had limited impact on overall urban growth patterns, although achieving impressive results in the areas of policy action.

FRAMEWORK OF POLICY

Land policy in France has been greatly influenced by the system of general economic planning established in the post-war years. At the same time it has responded to the increased state responsibility assumed for the provision of housing, education and other welfare services in the period since the end of the Second World War. In particular, since the 1950s the state has assumed responsibility for building much-needed housing.

The system of economic planning used in France is based on long- and medium-term forecasts of various sectors of the economy. It is a system of directive planning which tries to allocate state funds to those areas in which future growth is desired. Urban development plans are part of the general planning process. Land policy necessary for the execution of urban-development schemes therefore becomes a concern of government policy. The specific measures adopted depend on the particular planning goals and are adjusted continually to achieve the planning goals. These goals in themselves are subject to revision; however, the general aims of policy can be stated.

1. To enhance the position of France in Europe and the world through a high rate of economic growth. This includes both promoting higher efficiency in industry and services, and strengthening Paris as a world financial centre.
2. To achieve a more balanced regional development within France.
3. To organize society with more regard for social equity as well as increased efficiency.

The execution of national planning goals in France is facilitated by the existence of a highly centralized administrative structure. The central government is represented in each department (there are ninety-five in all France) by the Prefect, who is responsible for carrying out government policy in his department, and at the same time is responsible for bringing local interests to the attention of the central government. Local government is fragmented among some 38,000 communes. The Planning Commissariat (CGP) is the national body responsible for the preparation of the Five Year Plans and the supervision of their implementation.

Since 1964 regional development has become a more important part of overall planning policy with the creation of the Delegation for Regional Development (DATAR) as the central administrative body responsible for regional planning. France was divided into twenty-one regions, made up of several departments, with the prefect of the largest department serving as regional prefect. In addition, in each region a Regional Economic Development Commission (CODER) was created. This was a consultative body of about fifty members, composed of representatives of trade unions, chambers of commerce, farmers, etc., and also local community representatives. In theory regional policy was to be made in consultation with this body. However, the attempt to make regional policy at the regional level (through CODER) rather than at the national level through the planning instruments of the state (particularly DATAR) has not been wholly successful. In 1972 CODER was abolished and its functions split into two bodies, one made up of economic interest representatives and another of local officials.*

* Pierre Gremion and Jean Pierre Worms, "The French regional planning experiments", *Planning Politics, and Public Policy*, edited by Jack Haywood and Michael Watson, 1975.

Regional planning in France has had a strong influence on planning for urban development, both in terms of goals and in terms of administrative structure. The principal factor in France's regional imbalance has been the attraction of Paris, where salaries have consistently been well above the national average. Therefore a policy of restraining the growth of Paris and strengthening other regional urban centres was adopted in the Fifth Plan (1966–70). DATAR designated eight metropolises (Lille, Nancy, Strasbourg, Lyon, Marseille, Toulouse, Bourdeaux and Nantes) as "counterbalancing metropolises" in which high-level cultural and commercial services (universities, modern transport and telecommunications facilities, central business district redevelopment, etc.) were to be created. The object was not to compete with Paris as a world financial and commercial centre, but to restrain migration from the regions to Paris by providing attractive regional centres.* In the latest planning concepts, this policy has been expanded to include the strengthening of the small towns in the less-developed regions by the provision of better primary and secondary infrastructure (improved transport, more techincal schools, etc.). DATAR allocated some 400 million francs for regional development in 1974.

DATAR, in conjunction with the Ministry of Regional Development, Housing and Public Works (a recent amalgamation of two ministries), has been responsible for initiating more comprehensive planning through the creation of coordinating study groups (OREAM) for metropolitan region planning schemes. In addition, DATAR has directly proposed and coordinated with different central government ministries the planning and execution of new town schemes for the dispersal of population from the large city centres and the creation of new growth centres within the urban region (particularly Paris).† Thus the goals of regional policy—agricultural modernization, industrial decentralization and restraint on the growth of Paris both through strengthening the regions and through decentralization within the Paris region—have led to increasing state interest in urban development.

---

* R. Arrogo, *Les Problems Fonciers et leur solutions*, Editions Berger-Levrault, Paris, 1969, pp. 46–47, 89.
† François d'Arcy and Bruno Jobert, "Urban planning in France", in Haywood and Watson, *op. cit.*

URBAN-LAND POLICY

Urban-land policy has changed with changing planning goals. At first in the post-war years emphasis was on the construction of social housing projects (HLM), which were built both for sale and rentål. (Before 1940, there had been little public housing, though some co-operative projects and rent control existed.) Land was acquired by the local authorities for use for housing projects; actual construction was by private firms. Recently planning objectives have shifted to more comprehensive urban-development schemes, including the erecting of new communities and city centre redevelopment schemes. In addition, it has been a consistent policy goal to coordinate efforts between state and private capital in executing urban-development schemes, in order to aid economic (and particularly commercial) growth, to ease the burden on state finances, and to establish a scale of priorities where efforts should be concentrated. Urban development plans are generally formulated in the framework of the overall Four Year Plan. The aims of urban land policy may be set out as follows:

1. To ensure the needed land for urban growth.
2. To mobilize the financial means to execute the infrastructure works.
3. To transfer to the public authorities the additional value created through public development programmes.

To these ends, French policy has created a range of institutions specifically concerned with different urban policy goals. The most interesting aspect of the French experience is that these institutions have generally been in the form of public land development companies, which are mixed companies in which local authorities are represented together with private interests. These companies were created in order to secure greater flexibility and greater financial resources than development through the conventional government agencies. They are given powers for the acquisition of land through negotiation or expropriation, the clearing of the area, allocation of different land uses, and the siting of industrial buildings. Every stage of the company's activities comes under close public inspection, and must be coordinated with the regional development plan. Generally, private participation is limited to 50% of total capital.

Mixed economy companies for urban activity also exist for construction purposes (particularly of social housing), where public participation is usually more limited. Such companies are limited in the amount of profit they can make; in return, they are granted especially favourable terms of credit. Finally, urban renewal activities can also be undertaken within the framework of a mixed company, whereby the owners of slum areas contribute their land to the company and the municipality undertakes the rehabilitation of the area.

The object of the mixed companies is to cut through administrative delay and mobilize resources for specific development projects, including the securing of more favourable financial terms for loans for development works. The mixed company formula appears to have been successful in France. By 1966 over 300 such companies had been organized for construction purposes alone.

Another instrument through which the French government attempted to increase the useful participation of private interests in urban development schemes was the plan for the leasing of land from private owners. Under a law enacted in 1964, and in view of the delays inherent in expropriation procedures, the public authorities have the right to conclude a leasing agreement with a private landowner for a limited number of years (18 to 70) for building rights on his land, for housing or infrastructure works. The public authority may pay the lessor either through rent (linked to the building-cost index) or securities; or they may place part of their construction project at his disposal. The lessee undertakes to maintain the buildings for the period of the lease and restore full ownership rights to the land after its expiration.

Another part of this law provides for the joint participation of landowners in urban renewal schemes in the framework of the mixed companies for urban renewal described above. The law now provides for notification and publication of the detailed scheme for the redevelopment of an area. A choice is then presented to all affected landowners between expropriation or participation in the urban-development project through a mixed company. If they choose the latter, landowners are paid an annual fee for the use of their land. The mixed companies for urban renewal are solely for the management of the land, and negotiate with builders for the needed construction, with the land leased from the landowner through the intermediary of the company. Thus the landowner receives rental income as well as shares in the company. He may also receive part of the buildings put on his land. However, as these companies are still quite new the value of their shares is not always obvious to the landowners.

Regional Land Acquisition Agencies are, in the mixed company framework, one of the most important policy instruments for supplying land. The first was established in Paris in 1962, and two others have been created in Basse Sene (le Havre) and recently in Lorraine (Nancy). The Paris Regional Agency, which has a great deal of experience, may serve as an example of an efficient method of land acquisition, supplying land for the growing needs of the Paris region.

The Real Estate and Technical Agency of the Paris Region (l'Agence Fonciere et Technique de la Region Parisienne) was founded in accordance with the Decree of 14 April 1962. The purpose of this industrial and commercial establishment is to proceed, within the Paris region, with the purchase (if need be through expropriation, or through the legal right of pre-emption) of the land necessary for the various urbanization operations, and to carry out these operations themselves.

The mission of the Agency is twofold: as a real estate agency, it purchases land; as a technical agency, it is empowered to proceed to the improvement, equipment or renovation of buildings required for the carrying out of urbanization of any kind, or necessary for the installation of public services or facilities.

The land purchases of the Agency are made either on behalf of the Agency itself (only in the areas appointed by the administrative head of the Paris Region), or on behalf of the state or of other public bodies.

In addition to the juridicial means at the Agency's disposal, such as sales by private contracts, through expropriation for public purposes, or through the right of pre-emption established by the law of 26 July 1962, the Agency possesses financial means based on the loans granted by the National Fund for Real Estate Improvement and

Urbanization—Fonds National d'amenagement foncier et d'urbanisme (FNAFU); to this must be added the district loans, and the loans and financing operations on the part of the future users of the grounds.

The board of directors consists of 22 members, 11 of whom represent the state (senior officials of the Ministries of Economy and Finances, of Equipment and Housing, of National Education, of the Interior, of Welfare, and of Transportation) and 11 represent the local public bodies: 2 for the city of Paris, 2 for the District of the Paris Region, and 7 for the administrative subdivisions of the Paris Region.

Hence, the Real Estate Agency is a service that can be used by the state, by the local public bodies and by the district. However, it is with the district that the Agency entertains closer relationships, since the Agency can operate only in the sectors assigned by the administrative head of the Paris Region, or with his agreement, the administrative head assuming also the function of General Delegate to the district by the Decree of 10 August 1966.

Up to 30 June 1968, the Agency had acquired 2851 ha. of which 930 ha. were for itself, 1144 ha. for the state, and 777 ha. for the Agency as a service-rendering institution. The acquisitions undertaken or those for which preliminary steps have been taken, represented on 1 July 1968 altogether 920 million Francs. It is interesting to note that 2526 ha. out of the 2851 ha. acquired were purchased on a private contract basis. By 1973, 20,000 ha. were acquired (8600 ha. purchased for new towns and the rest had been for infrastructure works, recreation, etc.).

LAND-USE PLANNING MEASURES

Land-use planning controls have been used very successfully in France as tools of land policy. In particular, public authorities have been given wide and flexible powers which in theory should set both overall planning norms to control unwanted development and also allow the planned development of designated areas by special regulations.

The 1967 Land Guidelines Act introduced the two new overall planning measures that became obligatory: the Urban Development

Master Plan (SDAU) and the detailed land-use plan (POS). The general plan has to fix the outlines of urban development for the next 20 to 30 years. It is adjusted in coordination with the future forecasting of the relevant government ministries in connection with the 5-year plans and approved by DATAR. However, it is only of an indicative nature, as operational commitments are not made over such a long time period.

The detailed land-use plan (POS) is legally binding and sets allowable land uses and building coefficients for all sites in an urban area for both public and private use. Local authorities are required to draw up detailed plans, keeping in mind the long-term development plan (SDAU). There has been considerable delay in effectively drawing up POS plans at the local level, attributed in part to influence of property interests at the local level.* As a result many land-use coefficients in central city areas are set at a high level (allowing high densities). Therefore the government's urban reform programme this year (1975) introduced the maximum land-use coefficient as 1·5 for Paris and 1·0 for the rest of France, with all the additional value created by any construction exceeding these limits to be transferred to the community.

French land-use legislation has increasingly recognized the need for special measures in areas designated for development. The first such attempt was the creation of priority urbanization zones (ZUP) in 1958 in order to concentrate the development of social and private housing projects together in designated areas. Under the ZUP regulation private housing of over 100 units had to be built in the designated zone (where the authorities were attempting to concentrate infrastructure works); no large-scale building could take place outside these zones. Within the ZUP land prices were frozen and the state had priority rights to purchase any land offered for sale.

The ZUP was used on a large scale when it was first introduced. In 1959–60 over 400,000 units of HLM (publicly subsidized low and moderate income housing) were built. In subsequent years about 60,000–80,000 units of public housing a year were constructed in ZUP areas, out of a total of about 300,000 public housing units yearly. In

---

* d'Arcy and Jobert, *op. cit.*

all, to 1968, 770,000 units of public housing had been built under ZUP. The ZUP provided a framework for a policy which was dictated by short-term housing needs; with time, the need for larger-scale housing projects which could properly be provided with services became obvious, and thus the size of ZUP areas was increased. While the ZUP provided the advantage of concentrated housing construction, it also fueled speculation on the outskirts of the zone.

In 1965 larger "zones of deferred development" (ZAD) were authorized in order to create areas where the state could acquire land cheaply for some specific purpose in the framework of the national plan. Land prices within these zones is frozen for 8 years (later increased to 16 years) and the public authorities (including public companies) have priority purchase rights on any land offered for sale. Within ZAD areas compensation for expropriated land is payable only on the basis of use value as of 1 year before the declaration of the zone. Land acquired by the state may be temporarily leased for specific uses. The ZAD areas are intended to provide reserves for the future development of new towns, tourist centres, and industrial and commercial sites. But by freezing development and invoking pre-emption rights over a large area the state is able to control prices without purchasing a great deal of land itself.

A ZAD area is declared by the prefect in connection with the national and regional planning framework, and approved by the central government. The average size of such a zone in 1970 was 556 ha. In all the following land area was declared as a ZAD:

	1967	1972	1974
Paris Region	57,982 ha.	136,218 ha.	—n.a.
The Provinces	69,393 ha.	312,212 ha.	—n.a.
Total	127,375 ha.	448,430 ha.	534,000 ha.

Of this total 68,650 ha. were for new towns. There are significant differences in the distribution of this figure between Paris and the Provinces, however. In the Paris region 26% of total land in ZAD areas was for new towns; in the provinces, 22%. Conversely tourism made up 57% of provincial ZAD area. This figure is influenced by two very large ZAD tourist areas: the Cote Acquitaine (SW Atlantic Coast) proposed tourist area, of 125,000 ha., and the Languedoc-Rossillon scheme of 23,000 ha.

While a ZAD cannot affect prices of land or buildings outside a zone, it has been able to limit land prices within the zone through its controlled market. Average prices of land offered to the public authorities (under priority purchase rights) decreased from 2·5 times above forecasted public spending in 1966 to 1·5 times public bids in 1970. What is significant is that this occurred without any widespread public purchase. The public authorities declared their public interest in 2107 ha. of land in ZAD areas in 1970, exercised their pre-emption rights on 1391 ha., but only actually purchased 577 ha. total in the ZAD areas of some 384,000 ha.

Thus the ZAD is a policy of selective restriction of the free market in land in areas of future development. It has not been applied to new building within the zone, however; therefore it is of great advantage to developers who are buying land at controlled market prices and selling building space at free-market prices on the basis of competition.

The newest legal instrument of French land policy is the zone of concentrated development (ZAC). This was created in 1967 as a replacement for ZUP in order to encourage coordinated and concentrated urban development, particularly in central city areas. Normal building regulations (POS) are suspended in a ZAC area. The ZAC area can be part of a scheme for either private, public, or mixed development, including housing schemes, service centres, new commercial developments, universities, etc. The ZAC provided the instrumental framework for an operational scheme for land acquisition and the execution of infrastructure works, and also for the mobilization of financial resources. If development is private, the local authority must approve the proposed plans. In reality ZAC has been extensively used for commercial redevelopment based on higher land-use coefficients, in return for financial concessions and assistance to the state. In 1971 there were 217 ZACs declared, of which 148 were for housing schemes (mainly public) and 102 of which were initiated by private interests. The distribution of the housing schemes was as follows:

	Number	Dwelling units	Area (ha.)
Paris	44	56,215	2598
Provinces	104	104,374	4558

The Minister of Equipment (the amalgamation of Housing and Public Works) stated that he was opposed to too great a use of the ZAC procedure. His arguments were that the local authorities would be able to exercise too much control over commercial development and force developers to pay too great a share of urbanization costs.

The framework of ZAC may serve as a good example of the possibilities of involving private capital in financing public development schemes. But at the same time it may show that an administrative framework is not in itself adequate to guarantee that the implementation of such a scheme will be desirable for urban development. This depends on the amount of influence the public authorities choose to exercise in opposition to private plans, and also the socio-economic goals of the development scheme. The Arrondisement Italie (Paris) scheme is a classic example of how a ZAC area was developed economically but with negative social consequences. The land-use densities in the Italie development are three times their former level. At the same time the amount of social housing (HLM) included in the scheme was reduced from 3500 units originally planned in 1966 to 1750 units in 1972. The poorer strata who had formerly lived in the area were replaced by white-collar and professional workers. The amount given to families for relocation (15,000 Fr.) was not enough for relocation, even in HLM housing. According to the Urban Commission of the VI Plan, only one-third of the planned HLM housing was actually built; more importantly, the majority of those displaced could not afford the replacement housing offered and their relocation rights were purely theoretical. A large number left their apartments before the date of relocation.* But it should be underlined that ZAC has been responsible for the construction of some very impressive commercial centres, as in Maine-Montparnasse, Defense and others.

* Claude Pottier, *La Logique du financement public et l'urbanization*, Paris, 1973.

LEGAL MEASURE OF LAND ACQUISITION: EXPROPRIATION AND COMPENSATION

Before 1953 it was only possible to expropriate land if it could be shown that the private owner did not intend to carry out the proposed development scheme himself. This provision was removed in 1953 for infrastructure works (primary and secondary, i.e. including schools, hospitals, etc.) and in 1958 for all land needed for an approved urban-development plan (including housing, industrial development and tourism). This shortened the time needed for expropriation, but the procedure is still a long one (beginning with the declaration of the public purpose of expropriation and then soliciting objections). In 1967 the government proposed that the prefect be given the power of expropriation without appeal, but this was rejected by Parliament. However, under the law of 1935 expropriation by the prefect had been allowed in cases of extreme national urgency. While originally this was mainly applied to military fortifications, with time it was extended to national roads, and in 1970 urban development was included. This power has been extensively used; it is not a legal expropriation, but gives the public authority the right to take possession and to start planning while the expropriation proceedings are going on.

According to the laws of 1958 and 1962, compensation is payable according to the market price averaged over transactions for the last 5 years (except in ZAD areas where it is 1 year before the ZAD area was declared). Generally this results in lower prices for those whose land has been expropriated than their neighbours who have not, since prices of adjacent land in an area where a public development scheme is carried out usually rise greatly. As a consequence judges have often interpreted the law rather liberally, in order to take into account the injustice done to those who could not sell their land on the free market. On the other hand, the state administrative organs would like to limit the freedom of the judges to set compensation payments. The problem of compensation is still unsolved. The contradiction between the freedom for some to make large profits from land sales and the restraints on a few has created a feeling of unfairness and an unfavourable climate of public opinion for the introduction of more restrictive legislation regarding compensation. This may serve to show that a policy that expropriates large areas (e.g. advance public land acquisition) is less unjust than a policy expropriating only some small areas.

FINANCING METHODS

The financing of urban development is one of the integral features of land policy in France. At the same time the central government subsidies serve as one of the principal tools of control ensuring the proper execution of the planning process. Subsidies to local government and public corporations are of two types: global subsidies and subsidies for specific, detailed projects (it was estimated for 1975 that global subsidies will be 30% of specific subsidies). In general the state finances some 30% of infrastructure works. In addition the state makes available loans for land acquisition and development works for 6–10 years (at 6% interest since 1964) to the local authorities. This is to enable them to meet the high capital costs of acquiring land which is then sold to construction firms. Thus the local authorities bear the major burden of public spending on urban development. It was estimated that out of a net national product of 1016 milliard Fr., 163 milliard Fr. was for buildings and public works. Of this some 33 milliard Fr. was public investment, divided between 10 milliard Fr. spent by the central government, 19 milliard by the local authorities, and 4 milliard provided by the semi-public development agencies.[*]

To provide the means for the local authorities to pay for infrastructure works, the Urban Commission of the V Plan proposed one of the two following taxes:

1. a tax on all new buildings according to its built surface;
2. a tax of land value as the basis of the construction surface allowed by the planning regulations.

The 1967 law allowed local authorities to impose a higher rate of property tax (from 1% to 3%, rising to 5% in special circumstances), but this power has not been widely used. Thus most construction has been financed by borrowing from the special public banks. In 1975 Urban Reform proposals of the government included making the higher

---

[*] *Conception et Instruments de la planifications urbaine,* Centre de Recherché d'urbanisme, 2nd edition, Paris, pp. 77–80.

property-rax rate mandatory. The Ministry of State also subsidized the interest on loans made by the public banks for infrastructure works to the local authorities (reducing the rate of interest from 6% to 3%). In 1967 infrastructure works were financed as follows:

1. Loans with subsidized interest   668 million Fr.
2. Loans without subsidy for land acquisition   386 million Fr.
3. Loans without subsidy for other development works   914 million Fr.
4. Local budgetary resources   200 million Fr.
5. Central government resources for development   478 million Fr.
6. Total   2646 million Fr.

Thus financing in France is a combined effort of private interests (who actually carry out construction), state and local government. Due to the financial weakness of the local authorities, the state-planning instruments (which include the Urban Investment Commission of the Planning Commissariat and the Programme of Modernization and Investment—PME—prepared for each metropolitan area) have significant leverage, though up until now their coordination has been inadequate.*

AN EXAMPLE OF LAND ACQUISITION IN PRACTICE

The Languedoc-Rousillon Corporation

Operating Languedoc-Rousillon and the method of executing a planning scheme in this region may be a classical example of how a policy of land acquisition may be successful and save public funds by proper timing. It was decided by the government planning authorities to develop a big tourist region in the south-west Mediterranean in Languedoc. The proposal was to erect a new tourist centre, build roads, new hotels, prepare the beach and in general to create a large recreation area. The task was to acquire approximately 5000 ha. to implement development works, and after making the area ready for construction to lease or to sell the land to other builders. In order to acquire the land at the low price existing in that region, the operation

* François d'Ardy and Bruno Jobert, *op. cit.,* pp. 304–6.

was held secret and the task of buying the land was given not to local officials but to a few officials in the central government who bought the land sometimes even through non-government companies.

As the first step to realizing the programme in 1963–4 an area of 24,700 ha. was declared as ZAD ("zone d'amenagement differe"). The extent of ZAD was larger than the area needed for executing the project, thus allowing the planning authority freedom in its choosing the needed area for carrying out the project, and not creating a situation where an area very close to expropriated or bought land within ZAD would be incompatably lower in price than prices existing in neighbouring free market areas.

Thus, in a short time the authorities succeeded in acquiring 4472 ha., of which 3213 ha. were acquired by May 1968 at a cost of 47,529 francs—or an average of $1\frac{1}{2}$ Fr/m². Of this area, 2200 ha. were acquired as a result of real negotiations and 1000 ha. on the basis of expropriation. To implement all the schemes, the authorities had to acquire another 1259 ha. To acquire the additional land and to avoid land speculation near the tourist region, the authorities declared 5429 ha. as land designated for public use, where expropriated procedures could be used if there is no freely reached agreement on price.

This example of Languedoc shows how it is possible to avoid spending public money if the land is acquired at the right time, in the right place, and by the right procedures. It is significant that in some places in this region the land is now valued at 200 Fr/m². (Information from Prefect of Paris Region.)

PARIS REGION DEVELOPMENT: THE RESULTS OF LAND POLICY

The present situation of the Paris region may be summarized as overcrowding inside Paris and a large region of fragmented development divided among some 214 different local authorities. New development in the region has been characterized by the erection of several small housing projects in each local authority district without adequate services. As a result the dispersed housing erected by public and private building has been far from Paris, without needed commercial and public services, and without good transportation connections to

Paris. About 10,000 ha. (equivalent to the previous urban surface of Paris) has been used for public housing at a density averaging 20 d.u./ha.

The aim of the Paris regional development scheme is to concentrate development in a few urban centres—New Towns which will carry out all city functions and provide a high percentage of employment for local residents, high-level commercial services, education and other public services, and a variety of industrial enterprises. The New Towns will be constructed in a framework of a regional land-use planning scheme, ensuring enough land for recreation and developing a transport network based on a combination of public (Metro, bus and train) and private transportation.

The New Towns are planned to eventually include 200,000–300,000 people and serve as a centre for a population of 1 million each. Thus they are planned to accommodate the entire projected growth of the Paris region for the next 30–40 years (estimated as 4–5 million increase). This is in contrast to the previous scale of housing developments, the largest of which contained 30,000 units.

The New Towns are being constructed around existing small villages located some 25 km from Paris. Five new towns are planned: Evry, Marne-la-Vallee, Melun-Senart, Cergy-Pointoise and Saint-Quentin-en-Yvelines. At the present the development of the first of these towns (Cergy-Pointoise) has just begun, with 6000 units of housing constructed. But 6120 ha. of land for all the towns had been acquired out of the planned 10,000 ha. by 1971. The infrastructure works are financed 55% by the state and 45% by the local authorities.·

The new city of Cergy-Pointoise, located on a loop of the Oise, in the middle of a riverside park of 150 ha., may serve as an example of the new towns being built in the Paris region. It is planned to have a total population of 200,000 inhabitants with 60,000 housing units on 600 ha. of land. It is planned to have jobs for 120,000, including 800,000 m² of office space. The district of Cergy-Pointoise was created in 1969 and the first residents settled in 1973. By 1975, 6000 units of housing had been build (92% of them social housing). Also established have been government, commercial, administrative and financial services including a 200-room hotel, a swimming pool, four cinemas, a skating rink and a telecommunications tower. The originally planned aerotrain connecting Cergy-Pointoise with Paris has been abandoned but a rail link is being built (to be ready by 1978).

The interesting point about the development of these New Towns is the important role played by the Paris Regional Land Development Agency, a public company, in acquiring land. It spent the following amount for land acquisition for new towns:

> 1966—49 million Fr.
> 1967—21 million Fr.
> 1968—61 million Fr.
> 1969—33 million Fr.
> 1970—40 million Fr.
>
> ———————————
>
> 204 million Fr.
>
> ———————————

The Paris Regional Development Agency shows that an efficient land-acquisition policy can best be carried out on a regional basis.

Recently the population of the Paris region has begun to slow its rate of increase (increasing at a yearly rate of 0.95% from 1968 to 1975 compared with 1.5% from 1962 to 1968). Paris proper decreased in population by 300,000 inhabitants during this period while the region increased by 612,000 (as compared with 781,000 in the previous census period). Most significant is the decrease in the net population migration to the Paris region: 700,000 from 1954 to 1962, 377,000 from 1962 to 1968 and only 87,000 in the last 7 years. These figures include an out-migration of 20,000 per year.

The newly prepared Paris Regional Development Plan has been adjusted to take into account these figures. The new scheme is based on a lower population growth estimate than the 1965 plan. It is now forecast that the population of the region in the year 2000 will be 12 million rather than 14 million as previously estimated (the present population is 10,350,000).

It is intended to create a poly-centred approach to the organization of urban space, avoiding the continuous extension of one large urban area. Thus it is intended to create two axes of urban growth along the major river valleys with a balanced development of overall and urban land uses. It is also intended to avoid the erection of large isolated housing projects without services or adequate transport facilities.

Therefore there is provision for an integrated public transport network in the plan. At the same time high-rise building in the densely populated Paris region has been prohibited. Finally, it is intended to increase the amount of green space available per person, which today is lower in Paris than most other major Western cities.

SUMMARY REMARKS

The results of French land policy represent both important achievements and a gap between the stated goals and the results of implementation. One of the features of French land policy is an advanced legislative and policy structure. It may be suggested that in some ways France is an example of a country with advanced land-use policy measures but restricted results due to the influence of pressure groups on actual implementation. Both the achievements and the constraints result from the major role of the state in the process of planning urban development, based on a scale of priorities and the concentration of activity in restricted areas. Within these restricted areas the results have been impressive; but at the same time it should be underlined that results in other areas have been quite limited.

It may be suggested that one of the most impressive achievements is the permanent search for better solutions to the problems posed by urban growth. New policy measures have been introduced and even policy goals have been modified when previous attempts did not show the expected results. One example is the recently adopted change in regional policy which favours the development of small and medium-sized towns. This is a modification of the previous policy of concentrating regional planning efforts mostly in the creation of eight major metropolitan areas as centres for regional developments. The transition from the concentration of housing projects in restricted areas (ZUP) to the encouragement of the development of housing schemes along with appropriate services and with accessibility to all city functions (ZAC) is another example. The development of new towns in the Paris region and in other regions of France is a logical result of such a concept. The understanding of the role of the level of services in attracting people to a new urban environment has led to public encouragement of the development of services in some of the new towns (Cergy-Pointoise) even before there is a large enough population to sustain such services (by means of government subsidies).

The recent legislative proposals limiting densities in urban areas and introducing pre-emption rights for all municipal authorities, as well as the proposals for shortening the expropriation procedure and for the introduction of more efficient planning methods in order to shorten the planning process, are additional examples of the adaptation of policy measures and methods to changing perception of needs.

The dominant role of the central government is one of the factors that permits such a policy to be carried out. This is especially shown in regard to the advanced financial methods adopted. But even the growing understanding of the planning needs by the responsible authorities (the Ministry of Environment and the planning experts) has not been able to overcome the structural weakness of urban planning, and especially land-use planning, in a society strongly influenced by the pressure of financial interests and large land owners (both as represented in Parliament and through extra-parliamentary pressure groups with a great influence on the course on economic development). The policy measures are therefore based on close cooperation with financial capital in carrying out the planning programme. Such cooperation between the public and private sector (between state capital and private capital) is not a negative approach. On the contrary, keeping in mind the restricted possibilities of finance on the basis of the general public budget, the mobilizing of private savings by means of government loans schemes may allow good cooperation between the government and private capital. But the reality of cooperation in France has meant rather the use of government institutions to strengthen private financial interests and not the mobilization of private capital for carrying out government policy goals. This has been particularly shown in the erection of the new commercial centres in Paris in urban renewal areas, where the lower-income groups have been pushed out of Paris and the city redeveloped for commerical and luxury residential use.

The policy of concentrating activity to achieve restricted objectives has resulted in a permanent land price increase, making France a country with one of the highest rates of land price increase. The reports of the Urban Commissions of the IV, V and VI Plans (1961, 1965 and 1969) all mention high rates of increase of land prices as one of the main obstacles to implementing the planned urban development schemes. On the other hand, the comparison of land price increases with the suburbs show that these prices have increased 30% a year compared with 20% in Paris. The high rate of land price increase has led to an increasing role for land in housing costs—from 16% for social housing in 1965 to 26% in 1969 (and 60% for luxury residential housing in Paris and 80% for commercial developments). The growing price of land, leading to higher housing costs, has led to the location of housing projects far from the city centre, increasing transportation expenses, travel time and travelling conditions. But it should be underlined that there is a growing appreciation by the planning and financial authorities of the need to improve the transport network through investment in public transport (the metro, regional express trains and an integrated regional and national transport network). This should ensure good accessibility for different urban and rural settlements within the large city region and between metropolitan areas.

The desired results of the regional approach to urban planning have been expressed in the recent population census in France. The population of the Paris region has shown a lower rate of increase between 1969 and 1975 than between 1962 and 1968, and the population of Paris proper a higher rate of decrease than in the previous period.

This achievement of more balanced population distribution was due to the land policies of advance land acquisition by regional land acquisition and land-development agencies, as well as to the allocation of the necessary financial means by the central and local government in participation with private financial institutions. The recent adoption by Parliament of legislation limiting densities in urban areas and transferring all the additional value resulting from the approval of higher densities by the planning authorities to the community is a further step in land policy, adapting legislative measures to the changing needs of urban growth.

REFERENCES

Agence fonciere et technique de la region Parisienne, 1967.
Cahiers de l'Institute d'amenagement et d'urbanisme de la region Parisienne, Vol. 2, 1965.

Fourastie, Jean, *Pourquoi Faire?*, Castermans, Belgique, 1970.

Grenelle, J. J., *Espace Urbain et prix du sol*, Paris, 1970.

Heywood, Jack and Watson, Michael, *Planning, Politics, and Public Policy: The British, French and Italian Experience*, London: Cambridge University Press, 1975.

Institute of Public Administration, *Urban Government in the Paris Region*, New York, 1965.

Lipiec, Alan, *La Tribut foncier urbain*, Paris, 1974.

Ministere de l'equipment, *Lez Z.U.P.*, Paris, 1966.

Perfecture de la Region Parisienne, *Documentation sur les operations d'amenagement en region Parisienne, rapport sur les propositions de modifications et lasmise en ouevre*, Jan. 1969.

——, *La Ville nouvelle de Pontoise Cergy, étude et options*, Sept. 1968.

——, *Schema Directuer d'amenagement et d'urbanisme de la region Parisienne*, Nov. 1968.

"Politique urbaine", *Sociologie du travail*, No. 2, Oct.–Dec. 1970.

Pottier, Claude, *La Logique de financement publique et l'urbanisme*, Paris, 1973.

Saint-Mark, Phillipe, *Socialisation de la nature*, Paris, 1974.

Topolov, Christe, *Capital et Proprietere Fonciere*, Centre de Sociologie Urbaine, Paris, 1973.

——, *Expropriation et pre-emption publique en France, 1950–1973*, Paris, CSU, 1974.

CHAPTER 16

Land Policies in a Market Economy

The comparison of various policy measures in different countries, and the case studies of land policy in France, the Netherlands and Sweden, show the great variety of legal and economic measures that have been employed by different countries in order to supply land according to the increased rate of urban growth. Common to all countries is the need to introduce measures which will ensure the supply of land for urban growth on the basis of the free market mechanism. The essential difficulty in all countries is the contradiction between successful activity in some restricted areas with an inability to affect the land market as a whole, due to the close interrelationship between land in different uses and different locations. The land market, in spite of its peculiar character, functions in a similar way to the market for other goods in the sense that activity in one sector affects all others. A careful control of prices in a restricted area leads to an increase in prices in the non-restricted areas, because the restricted supply of land in one area while overall demand remains high leads to higher prices. A carefully planned land-use policy which tries to prevent undesirable urban development, to ensure land for future needs for urban and recreational uses and to preserve good agricultural land in the vicinity of the city—such a policy may lead to a restricted supply of land and hence price increases in areas planned for urban development. One of the unsolved problems of present land policies is the proper timing of the allocation of land to meet both present and future needs (ensuring a supply of land for all uses).

One of the difficulties in the formulation of policy objectives and policy measures is the problem of acting at the same time to restrain the demand for land (according to the available resources) and adapting the supply to the growing needs. In à market economy and a society based on a large measure of social differentiation, the need for land and its allocation is based on the competition between individuals on an economic basis, and therefore the stronger groups are able to acquire land in locations appropriate to their needs. But the economically weaker group must pay a higher price for their poorly located land, because of the impact of the high prices for land in the best locations on land prices within a large radius of the city (due to the "chain effect").

The experience of different countries using a variety of policy measures shows that the most efficient solution has been the transfer of land ownership rights to the community; however, this has not been entirely satisfactory due to the lack of financial resources. Ideally, public finance should be available to meet the growing needs of urban growth as part of the general social investment of the society, without being dependent on an immediate economic return.

In those societies where public housing expenditure is part of the general budget for urban development, the allocation of resources for land, housing and urban infrastructure is interrelated with other expenditures according to a scale of priorities, taking into account the distribution of net national product between consumption, saving and investment. The permanent gap between the growing needs and the restricted resources requires careful and comprehensive policy using a variety of financial methods to achieve its objectives.

The experience of many countries shows that some policy results may be achieved when the three types of policy measures (land-use planning, taxation and direct intervention in the land market through public land acquisition and supply) were combined in an effort to achieve the policy goals. Land-use planning measures, which carefully allocate land for different purposes of development, thereby ensure land for future needs and concentrate development. At the same time land-use regulations which freeze land prices in a large area around the urban settlement (with priority purchase rights for the public authorities) may prevent land-price increases in areas of future urban development.

But such measures which prevent undesirable development, and even restrain land-price increases in large areas of urban extension, cannot ensure the supply of land needed for development. Therefore public authorities are often forced to change the development plans, in order to use available land for development and also to increase densities. Land prices also tend to increase in the areas outside the radius of frozen land prices. The experience of almost all countries shows that the most efficient way to supply the needed land to the market is the direct intervention of the public authorities, acquiring land, carrying out development works and supplying land for present and future urban needs. The comparison of land-price increases in different countries shows that in the Netherlands and Sweden, where land is supplied for urban development by the municipality through advanced land acquisition, the rate of price increase is among the lowest. These countries have also been relatively successful in preventing fragmented development and in providing land for recreational and other purposes as well as for urban use. But such a policy requires the allocation of adequate financial resources to acquire land and carry out development works. The lack of such financial resources is one of the obstacles to the successful execution of such policies.

A careful study of the allocation of public expenditure in various countries may serve to show that the lack of financial resources is not the essential reason for the failure to implement the policy of public land acquisition. It is rather the lack of understanding of the need to ensure a land reserve for future development on a cost-benefit basis. In addition, the pressure of landowners who want to maintain their present position in the private land market, as well as those small landowners who wish to preserve their tenuous private ownership rights, is another significant factor. In reality, given the pressure of the land market, it is likely that if present trends continue these small landowners will be acting not in their own interests but only on behalf of large financial interests.

Some countries are trying to overcome such difficulties through a policy of concentrating public effort in supplying land in certain restricted areas for some particular purpose (as in France, the UK, Israel, Chile and India). The results of such policies has been the achievement of some restricted aims, sometimes quite important ones, such as the establishment of new towns, new commercial centres and housing projects. But these policies have not influenced the overall land supply and therefore the land market in other areas of urban development. As high prices are an expression of the disequilibrium between demand and supply, the high land prices in these countries shows that they have not increased the supply of land for urban development sufficiently, despite their impressive local achievements.

Probably a comprehensive land-acquisition policy using various policy measures might reduce the necessary public expenditure to ensure a land reserve for future urban development. One of the obstacles in public land-acquisition policy is the method of compensation for acquired land to expropriation at market prices. Such a policy restricts the possibility of public land acquisition by forcing the authorities to pay high prices for land, i.e. to pay to private interests that which results from public investment in new or expected infrastructure works. The regulation recently introduced in Sweden where compensation is paid on the basis of land prices 10 years before the expropriation date may reduce the costs of land acquisition and reduce the attractiveness of land as a long-term financial investment. On the other hand, in the Netherlands, financial investment in land has been made unprofitable simply on the basis of strict control by planning authorities of land that can be used for urban development, coupled with the right of the municipality to acquire by expropriation any land needed for future urban development. The policy of declaring large areas where land prices are frozen (and the public authorities have priority purchase rights to acquire land at fixed prices) may allow them to create the needed land reserves while at the same time economizing public money. Such a method makes it unnecessary for the public authorities to actually purchase all the land needed for long-term development immediately.

Obviously there is still a problem of providing the needed land within the city for urban renewal purposes, allocating the land according to social criteria and not necessarily according to the financial possibilities of different groups. The need to influence land use within cities, and influence land prices there, is of course connected with the ability to increase the area of the city through urban extension.

Freedom of land use and land prices within the city, with control of these outside, may influence land use and land prices only in the continuous area around the city. Probably an efficient taxation policy might be able to influence land prices in the city centre. A property tax based not only on land value but on a turnover of economic enterprises and on the wealth of residential users may make land in the city centre relatively expensive, thus reducing demand there and also transferring to the public authorities some of the economic resources which are responsible for such high land prices in these central areas. In such a way it may be possible to increase the financial resources of the public authorities in order to finance urban renewal and infrastructure works within the city.

A comprehensive land policy may achieve its objectives even in the conditions of a market economy, if land can be regarded as a natural resource of limited quantity in desirable locations. Therefore the integration of different measures which allow the public authorities to fix land allocations according to growing and changing need is called for. Such a policy does not mean the immediate transfer of all land into public ownership, but the restriction of the individual land property rights of a small strata in order to assure the land-use rights of the whole population according to the needs of urban growth.

PART FOUR

Towards Land Policies for Future Urban Development

CHAPTER 17

Land Needs for the Future

The estimates of probable land utilization in the future are of the highest importance in understanding the seriousness of the problem of land as a resource existing in limited quantity and needed for various purposes. Decisions about land use today and in the near future are fixing the pattern of life for future generations. The evaluation of land needs for the future should be based on estimates of future population growth: land is needed both for urban growth and for agricultural production for a growing population. At the same time the land needs for recreational space, and the land reserves needed for ecological and climatic balance (forests, Arctic, etc.), cannot be neglected.

LAND NEEDS FOR HUMAN SETTLEMENTS

Land requirements for urban uses have been discussed in detail in a previous chapter, and it has been seen that there is a great variation in the present pattern of land utilization in urban areas, ranging from 850 m²/person to 27 m²/person (in Calcutta). The general estimates of present land use, according to the available data from different countries based on land classified as urban, may show the major differences between present and future land-use requirements (taking into account the need for a better quality of urban life in the future). It is possible to estimate land needs by comparing the total space of urban settlements with the total population. These comparisons will result in big differences between countries and cities, because of differences in land allocation and differences in the definition of urban areas. Some figures from the industrialized countries

403

are: USA, 740 m²/person; England, 440 m²/person; Federal Republic of Germany, 514 m²/person; the Netherlands, 270 m²/person. The amount of urban land compared to the total land area is: USA, 1%; England, 7%; FDR, 10%; the Netherlands, 7%. Such variations exist also in the developing countries. Urban land requirements vary in Latin America from 566 m²/person in Porte Alegro, to 428 m²/person in São Paulo, to 58 m²/person in Buenos Aires.

Keeping in mind that the land requirements for urban use have increased as a result of the dispersal of population from the city centre (and the present fragmented development of the metropolitan area—which uses large quantities of land), and also keeping in mind that densities are much lower in small human settlements (where land uses are mixed), it may not be an exaggeration to estimate that land needs for human settlements average 500 m²/person over the whole world. This would mean that today, with a world urban population of 1·5 billion, there are 750,000 km² in urban use. This is only 0·6% of the total surface of the earth (134 million km²) or 1% of the arable surface area (excluding mountains and the Arctic) of 75 million km².

In comparison, with planned urban land use the same land surface in use today may be sufficient for double the present urban population. One must also take into account the amount of land surface used by the rural settlements totalling 2·5 billion people today. There are no detailed figures available which separate the mixed uses of agriculture and settlement space in rural areas, but it might be assumed that the space is not less than that needed for urban settlements (more for housing, and less land used for other purposes). Therefore the space used for settlements by the world rural population may be estimated as 1·25 million km² (2·5 billion × 500 m²/person). Thus the total space of human settlements today would be 2 million km².

The land needs of future urban growth are difficult to estimate, depending as they do on whether development is carried out according to comprehensive planning or whether under only the current regulations. Planned urban communities, as we have estimated earlier, would require 285 m²/person; with the addition of land needed for national recreational and transportation purposes, 500 m²/person would be adequate (i.e. similar to present *per capita* use for urban areas alone). Therefore a population of 10 billion would need about 5 million km²; a population of 20 billion would need 10 million km². The significance of these figures may be better grasped by comparing them with the amount of land needed to produce food and currently in agricultural use.

LAND NEEDS FOR AGRICULTURE

Today there are about 14·5 million km² in agricultural use in the world, as compared with 2 million km² of human settlements. Thus future needs for urban space for a population of 20 billion would be 80% of present cultivated area. The FAO has estimated that there are reserves of land for future agricultural use of some 18·5 million km². These are located mainly in Africa and Latin America. There are wide variations in the intensity of land use in different parts of the world (over 30% of land surface is already cultivated in the most densely populated areas, Asia and Europe). The cultivation of these areas would require large-scale investments over time, in order to clear forests, irrigate deserts and increase water resources through desalination. In the shorter term it has been estimated by Klatzmann that more intensive use of the existing agricultural area may allow an increase in production by 100%.

Clark and Malin have both made estimates, which roughly agree, that about one-quarter hectare (2500 m²) per person "with adequate utilization of existing scientific data and modern equipment" is enough to supply a Western-type diet (meat and dairy products). Clark's calculation includes forest land of 250 m² per person adequate to supply the developed countries' standard of hardwood use. Clark has additionally estimated the amount of land needed to produce a minimum subsistence diet (i.e. all cereals) as 640 m²/person (using the most productive conditions, e.g. as in Japan). By also taking a lower figure for wood consumption (as in the case of Asian countries today) we arrive at a minimum estimate of 680 m² per person.

The potential agricultural land available in the world varies greatly according to whether we are considering land that could be easily farmed now by current methods (as much again as that currently in use); land that could be cultivated with additional investment (mainly in irrigation), estimated by Malin as an additional 26.7 million km^2; or the total potentially cultivatable land on the earth's surface, estimated by both Clark and Malin as around 100 million km^2 of the 134 million km^2 of total usable land surface on the earth (i.e. excluding the Arctic regions). Taking this latter figure along with the estimates of the land needed to support one person, they calculate that there is land available to support a world population of from 50 billion (Western diet) to 150 billion (minimum diet).

The crucial problem is handling the medium-term transition. In the long run the potential exists for feeding a large population, according to Clark, if the majority of the earth's surface is put into cultivation. It is the division of the costs of carrying out such projects that is uncertain; hence, there is a problem of the allocation of resources in the long run. The timing of investment for changing unproductive land into agricultural land greatly influences the average costs (i.e. how rapidly such major projects must be carried out). The timing, in turn, is connected with the rate of population growth. (The rate of population growth also affects the speed of investment needs in urban infrastructure and land for human settlement.) Population growth at the same time is increasing the possibility of the rational mobilization of human resources for the execution of development works needed for agriculture and for urban growth. But the realization of such a potential is connected with the planned use and management of land as other natural resources to meet human needs, and the balancing of population growth and agricultural production.

Looking into the distant future, the central problem is that of the next generation, of the 25 years to the year 2000 and the subsequent 25 years to 2025. This may be the crucial period needing careful planning of population growth and land use. A population growth rate of 1% a year, as in the USA and USSR today, means a doubling of the population every 70 years. At this rate a world population of 10 billion would not be reached for 92 years. But at the current world population growth rate (2%), with population doubling every 35 years, population would reach 8 billion in 2010 and 10 billion in 2022. But Latin America, which has the highest growth rate today of 3%, would increase its population from the current 300 million to 1.3 billion in 50 years, and would reach 7 billion in 100 years, virtually what the entire world population would grow to at a 1% rate. Taking into account the tendency of population growth rates to decline recently in more developed countries, and therefore, estimating the yearly rate of population increase over the next 25 years as 1·7%, world population would reach 6 billion by the year 2000.

CONCLUSIONS

Our calculations have shown that there is enough land for a population of 50 billion with increased investment and efficient use of land resources, which will be sufficient for the foreseeable future, perhaps 200 years. In this time span it is difficult to forecast what actual population growth might be and also what new technologies (including the use of outer space) might emerge. The experience of the previous 200 years may lead us to expect some rather major alterations in both of these variables.

Our estimates of future land supplies only make sense, however, if one realizes that it is the human factor that is of paramount importance. It is within our technological power to fulfil these estimates; but what is needed are changes in the current organization of society in order to allow the needed investments in agriculture (which are large in current terms, but minimal in terms of their long-term effect). Also fundamental is proper planning on a world-wide scale without regard for national boundaries. As both potential land resources and current human and technological resources are not equally distributed in different countries, this would be a rational use of available resources. For example, at a level of 50 billion people it is crucial that urban land space (estimated at almost 20% of total land surface) does not encroach on too much good agricultural land.

Today unplanned urban sprawl is consuming large quantities of good agricultural land. Proper planning of urban growth would reduce this wastage. For example, if all urban development was on the California model of 1000 m²/person, then a population of 20 billion would consume all the world's presently cultivated land. This figure does not take into account transport or recreational land needs. On the other hand, planned development for the same population would use a space of 10 million km² for human settlements and related needs. In order to feed such a population, a space of 40 million km^2 would be needed with the best available techniques. Such a space is more than the potential agricultural land that the FAO estimates is available in the world. This calculation shows how land needs for human settlements and for agricultural use are closely interrelated. To sustain a world population of 20 billion it would be necessary to economize the limited land surface potential by efficient use in order to ensure the future of mankind.

Obviously all these estimates are based on present technology, while the experience of the last 40 years has demonstrated that the present generation has been able to estimate neither the positive nor the negative effects of a high rate of technological progress. Therefore our estimates have only an orientation value, showing the close inter-relationship between different types of land uses. This is analagous to a living organism where the exaggerated growth of one part leads to the atrophy of the others; therefore there is a need for well-balanced use of the limited resource of land.

REFERENCES

Bosselman, Fred and Calles, *The Quiet Revolution in Land Use*, Council on Environmental Quality, 1973.
Bruton, Michael J., *The Spirit and Purpose of Planning*, London, 1974.
Denman, W. R. and Sylvia Prodano, *Land Use*, London, 1972.
Ehrlich, Paul, *Human Ecology: Problems and Solutions*, San Francisco, W. H. Freeman & Co., 1973.
Gilli, J. P., *Redéfinir le droit de Propriété*, Centre de Récherche d'Urbanisme, Paris, 1975.
Klatzmann, J., *Nourir Dix Milliards d'hommes*, Paris, 1974.
Mesaravic, Mihalo and Pestel, Edward, *Mankind at the Turning Point*, The Second Report of the Club of Rome. London, 1975.
The Use of Land: A Report of the Rockefeller Brothers Task Force, New York, 1973.
United Nations, *Urban Land Policies and Land Use Control Measures*, Vol. III: *Western Europe*.

CHAPTER 18

Towards a New Concept of Land Ownership

The concept of land ownership is associated with the social, economic and political structure and the level of development of a country. The concept of land ownership changes with the changing role of land in the economy and society. It is very different now from the time when people were not settled and moved from place to place, living from hunting before settled agriculture existed. The different types of agricultural systems influenced the land ownership concept. The concentration of people in urban settlements, technological progress, the rate of industrialization, and the growing needs for urban land are all factors which influenced the land ownership concept. But the ownership concept, which is connected with juridicial and political values, has changed more slowly than socio-economic changes.

PATTERNS OF TRADITIONAL-COMMUNAL LAND OWNERSHIP

In the early stages of human development, when the individual's economic activity was an integral part of the community and his existence was dependent on that community, land was seen as a good belonging to the community which gave the right of land use to the individual. With time this communal ownership expressed itself in traditional religious forms. The Islamic law (expressed in the Ottoman land legislation) as well as the land tenure systems in some African countries are based in a great measure on a traditional-communal approach to land ownership.

The basis of all land law in countries of the former Ottoman Empire is the Land Law of 1858, which synthesized the land practices which had developed over the course of the Empire. This law divided all land into four main categories which are still used. These are *mulk, miri, waqf* and *musha. Mulk* land is that which is owned by an individual and over which he has full ownership rights. *Miri* land is that which is owned by the state and which carries *tassruf* (usufruct). This right to use of the property may be sold by the usufructruary, or it may be let, mortgaged or even given away. It may also be transmitted to the usufructuary's heirs, although the land could not be divided among them. The state retained ultimate ownership and, if there were no heirs, the property reverted to the state.

Also, the state had the right of supervision over all transactions pertaining to the transfer of usufruct and any such transfer had to be certified by the state. *Waqf* land is land which cannot be divided or alienated, but continues in perpetuity to the descendants of the original owner. The *waqf* is a form of endowment unique to Islamic countries. The word itself means "stop", and the legal document drawn up for the *waqf* contains the full expression *Mawquf lilah* meaning "stopped for God". Originally it was meant as a charitable endowment for the establishment of schools, mosques, libraries, hospitals and other institutions, or for the care of indigent families, whereby the interest was given to particular designees while the capital was given to God. The *waqf* was soon turned into an institution for the preservation of property from extravagant heirs or from an acquisitive state. *Musha* land is land which is owned collectively. It originated from the tribal practice of dividing the arable land on which the tribe settled between its members. Since both extent and quality were taken into consideration, members were given pieces of land in different zones of the village. Also, to maintain equality, the land was reallocated at intervals. The practice still obtains although it is falling into disuse because of settlement of title which requires registration of title to a definite area. Cultivators thus became owners of permanent holdings. Two of these land institutions, namely *waqf* and *miri*, are of particular importance in understanding urban land problems and policies in some countries in the Middle East and North Africa.

In the African countries, the land-tenure systems on the continent are as complex and diverse as its climate and social groups. These differ in accordance with socio-cultural histories of the different tribal groups, the stability of traditional kingdoms, the density of population and the impact of colonial administration.

Landholding practices common throughout a greater part of sub-Saharan Africa are neither communal nor private, but are of a more "corporate" character which ensures that the rights of individual members coexist with those of the group at large. In other words, individuals are permitted to possess parcels of land for farming, building etc., but they do not have the absolute right of ownership. Furthermore, customary practices permit the direct descendants of a landholder to inherit his rights without losing these rights to the larger group. The "permissive individualistic aspect" of the customary land-tenure practice is contrary to the misconception that African chiefs and community leaders have absolute control over community lands. Most customary land codes in different parts of sub-Saharan Africa dictate that the chiefs, as traditional heads, serve in administrative capacities to ensure that various clans and kinship groups, families and individuals receive their due share. The basic tenurial framework could be understood better if it is realized that in African jurisprudence there is no clear-cut division between property and possession as is the case in English jurisprudence.

It should be emphasized that the emergence of proprietary ownership of land, *vis-à-vis* "corporate" ownership, is the result of the high economic value currently attached to land and the population pressure on land. Due to the emphasis on proprietorship in "imported" land laws, especially the English Common Law and Napoleonic Land Law, and the ever-increasing value of land as a major source of wealth for all classes of landholders, customary landholding practices are fast giving way to proprietorship as a more convenient tenure system in conditions of a market economy.

EVOLUTION OF THE RIGHTS OF LAND OWNERSHIP IN THE WEST

The right of private ownership of land is an integral part of the legal structure of most of the Western countries. Its roots are in the Roman law and the *Code Napoleon*. Article 554 of the *Code Napoleon* defines ownership as "the right to absolutely free enjoyment and disposal of objects provided that they are not in any way contrary to the laws or regulations". Ownership rights are seen as a part of the elementary rights of the individual and part of individual freedom. Such a conception of private ownership arose in opposition to the rules of feudal society, where a feudal lord had supreme rights of ownership, especially land ownership, and all tenants in the area paid him fees. In feudal society, an individual exploiting land had the right of land use, but not the right of ownership. It is for this reason that rights of private ownership—especially of land—are so carefully defended today by such large part of the population.

With the socio-economic development of the nineteenth and twentieth centuries, absolute ownership rights of land began to be in conflict with the new needs of the society and economy. In agriculture, the right to dispose of land freely resulted in the excessive parcelling of plots by the joint heirs surviving the owner. In many countries and in most cases, parcelling brought about agricultural units too small to be used for a farm. Parcelling thus became one of the most important problems needing solution. Recent legislation in most countries limits the right to divide land and allows for intervention of the public authority to reorganize such property in order to set up efficient agricultural units.

The high rate of urban growth posed the problem of the close interrelationship of different land uses and the need by the public authorities to provide land for general public purposes. The growing role of the state in the economy and society led to greater intervention in different fields of economic and social development, and therefore to controlling land use during rapid urbanization.

With the period of rapid urbanization the liberal concept was restricted, as it became necessary to take into account not only the rights of the individual but the needs of the society. These two essential factors are the basis for the concept of landownership that is followed in almost all countries. But there exists important differences in the relationship between these two factors. The socio-economic structure of the country and the rate of urbanization and industrialization influence which is to be the dominant factor. Most of the countries with centrally planned economies introduced collective landownership but also insured individual land-use rights. Countries with free **market** economies emphasize private landownership as a basis for legislation, but insure the right of the state to limit the private ownership rights of the individual if the land is needed for a public purpose.

The constitutions of developing countries are influenced by several factors. Among the most common are the impacts of traditional, communal or tribal landownership which are sometimes mixed with the modern concepts of state ownership of natural resources. On the other hand, also exercising an influence is the liberal concept prevailing in the free market countries about the individual's right to private property, including landownership.

The former colonial rulers and the concepts which existed in the home countries created a heritage in some of the developing countries which has influenced patterns of landownership. The former British colonies used the system of leasehold, where most of the land still belonged to the Crown. This concept where the Crown represented the collective needs of the society is mixed in Moslem countries of the former Ottoman Empire with the concept of *miri* land. According to this concept lands which are not cultivated for 3 years are returned to the state.

The mixed concept of combining individual rights on land with the need to use land for public purposes prevails in almost all countries. However, differences exist among nations as to which of the two elements is emphasized. Even in countries with centrally planned economies, there are some differences in the way in which the needs of society and the rights of the individual regarding land use are expressed. The Constitution of the USSR established that *all* land belonged to society, and that society should decide about the rights of land use. This law liquidated individual rights of urban landownership. On the other hand, some countries in Eastern Europe decide about collective landownership only on plots of land which are larger than a given minimum, as in Poland and Hungary. In Yugoslavia collective landownership is understood to be ownership by the community (urban or rural settlement) but not by the state. All countries with centrally planned economies have introduced a system whereby the individual has the right to use land for building a house for himself. Also in existence is a system of paying compensation (mostly by ensuring the right to build another house) if for reasons of urban development a house must be destroyed.

In the free market countries of Europe and North America, the recent process of rapid urbanization and the growing role of the state in providing essential services for society influenced the concept of urban land ownership. The Constitution of the *Italian Republic*, 22 December 1947, exemplifies the double character of land as it recognizes the freedom of private economic initiative and private property only in so far as these do not conflict with the public interest (Article 41–42). Moreover, the Constitution establishes the right to enact legislation to control and limit these freedoms in such a way as to insure the social function of land. In particular, Article 44 states that "with a view to a rational exploitation of the soil and the establishment of equitable social relations, the law imposes obligations and restrictions on private land property". Also Article 30 of the *Spanish* Constitution of July 1945, after declaring that "private property is recognized and protected by the State as a natural means of accomplishing the aims of the individual, the family and society", adds that "all forms of ownership are subordinate to the needs of the Nation and of the common welfare".

The Constitution of the Federal Republic of *Germany* articulates the two concepts of land ownership in Article 14 which reads: "The rights of ownership and of inheritance are guaranteed. Their content and limits shall be determined by the laws"; "Property imposes duties. Its use should also serve the public weal."

The differences in the concept of landownership in some countries are expressed mostly by emphasizing either the rights of the individual or of the society. The Constitutions of Taiwan, Indonesia and Chile express the limits on individual rights and consider land as a natural resource of the nation.

The *Taiwan* Constitution indicates that all land within the territorial limits of the Republic shall belong to the Chinese people as a whole, except for land whose ownership is lawfully acquired by any private individual. Thus, although the Constitution allows private ownership, it also restricts it.

In *Indonesia* the Basic Agrarian Act of 1960 states that "All rights on land have a social function". Article 2 provides that the earth, water and air space, including the natural resources contained therein, are "in the highest instance controlled by the State". The right of control encompasses the state's power to regulate the utilization and reservation of land, to determine the legal relations affecting property rights, and finally to annul or expropriate property rights.

The social character of landownership is emphasized in the Constitution of *Chile*. Number 10, of article 10, of the Political Constitution of the state states that:

> Law will establish the way of acquiring, using and disposing of property and the limitations and obligations which will permit its social function to be assured, and its accessibility to all guaranteed. The social function of property comprises all aspects related to the interests of the state, public utility and health, best use of water resources and power generation as a public service, and to the improvement of the standard of living of the people as a whole.
>
> ... No one can be deprived of his property except by means of a general or special law authorizing the expropriation for reasons of social interest or public utility laid down by the legislature. Whoever is subject to expropriation has always the right to indemnity; the amount and conditions of payment of which to be determined, protecting the interests of the community and the persons concerned.

Attention to the social character of land in the constitutions of Taiwan, Indonesia and Chile has had an impact on expropriation procedures and on the payment of compensation. In these countries, as well as in those where the social aspects of landownership are accepted, it is possible to expropriate land needed for executing urban development schemes in a short time by paying a fair compensation to the landowners. Not included in the compensation, however, are payments for increases in land value stemming from the proposed developments.

The real concepts of landownership are expressed more in the actions of public authorities in the fields of expropriation and compensation than in constitutional formulations. In some countries the public character of land is explicitly defined, but these did not indicate nor spell out how the needed land for urban development is to be supplied. On the other hand, a number of countries are pursuing a very active land-acquisition policy, expropriating the needed land in spite of constitutional guarantees that private property will be fully defended.

South American and *Central American* countries were influenced by America's Constitution of 1776 which formulated the absolute rights of private property. Most of these countries limit the power of public authorities to influence the land market and supply the needed land. Argentina may serve as an example of such an approach. Most of the Latin American countries are oscillating between the liberal concepts of the past and the new social concepts of the present.

Of the Asian countries, the *Philippines*, *Thailand* and *Korea* emphasize the liberal concept of landownership, although they have introduced land policies which permit extensive intervention by public authorities. In African countries, the traditional concept of communal land-ownership is mixed with the needs of developing societies so that state action is accepted as a factor in land development. Such a mixed concept based on traditional and modern collective needs may be observed in different Asian, Latin American and even European countries (e.g. Afghanistan, Mexico, Yugoslavia and Scandinavian countries).

In general, in spite of the prevailing liberal concepts frequently expressed in Constitutions, the new legislation connected with urban land policies is influenced by the concept of land as a national natural resource which should be used for public purposes.

Even in the *USA* and *Switzerland*, countries where private land-ownership constitutes a basic element of the society's values, a different approach underlining the social aspect of landownership has recently been observed.

The new approach was formulated by Fred Bosselman and David Callies in the report prepared for the Council on Environmental Quality as "The Quiet Revolution in Land Use Control". In this report they underline the new approach in the following words:

> If one were to pinpoint any single predominant cause of the quiet revolution it is a subtle but significant change in our very concept of the term "land", a concept that underlies our whole philosophy of land-use regulation. "Land" means something quite different to us now than it meant to our grandfather's generation. Its new meaning is hard to define with precision, but it is not hard to illustrate the direction of the change.
>
> Basically, we are drawing away from the 19th century idea that land's only function is to enable its owner to make money. One example of this change in attitude is that wetlands, which were once characterized as "useless", are now thought of as having "value". As we increasingly understand the science of ecology and the web of connection between the use of any particular piece of land and the impact on the environment as a whole we increasingly see the need to protect wetlands and other areas that were formerly ignored.

The idea that land is a resource as well as a commodity may appear self-evident, but in the context of our traditions of land-use regulation it is a highly novel concept. Our existing systems of land-use regulation were created by dealers in real estate interested in maximizing the value of land as a commodity.

The promoters of these land use regulations in the 1920s made no attempt to conserve land for particular purposes or to direct it into a specific use, but only sought to prevent land from being used in a manner that would depreciate the value of neighbouring land. The traditional answer to the question, "Why regulate land use?" was "to maximize land values". To achieve this purpose they sought to restrict those uses of land that adversely affected the price of neighbouring land by concentrating them in specific parts of the city. . . .
Most importantly, perhaps, numerous systems of local land-use regulation are beginning to contain regulations that recognize land as a resource as well as a commodity. Exclusive agricultural and industrial zoning preserves land as a resource for these important uses. Regulations prohibiting topsoil removal or requiring common open space find their justification in the protection of land as a resource for recreation and beauty. Regulations which require that a specified percentage of dwelling units in each housing development be reserved for low-income groups are recognizing the importance of land as an essential resource for housing all elements of our society.

The amendments to the Constitutions of different States as well as the new Senate Bill 268 (Land-Use Policy and Planning Assistance Act of 1973) may be seen as a first step towards a new concept of landownership resulting from the speed of urban concentration.

The primary stated purpose of S.268 is to "establish a national land-use policy, to authorize the Secretary of the Interior to make grants to assist the State to develop and implement State land-use programmes, to coordinate planning and management of Federal lands, and to establish an Office of Land-Use Policy Administration in the Department of the Interior".

In *Switzerland*, in March 1972, the Federal Assembly decided to decree and to carry out immediately some urgent space planning measures. The federal decision, which will be effective until 31 December 1975, has laid upon the cantons the obligation to determine and to convey to the knowledge of the federal authorities, a detailed land-use plan restricting development (and thus ownership rights) in areas designated for environmental preservation. This requirement has been made constitutionally binding.

One of the most important changes has been seen in the institutional field, strengthening the power of the federal government in the USA and Switzerland. In both countries the local authority is the basic element of the society's administrative structure. The freedom of the local authority to decide about land use became an obstacle in ensuring a land-use policy according to the development needs of the society. The interrelationship between different land uses in different locations and the externalities of the effect of some land-use policies on other land uses require a comprehensive regional and interregional approach to land-use policy.

THE DUAL NATURE OF LAND RIGHTS

The recent amendments to the Constitution of different countries are an extension of growing understanding of the new concept of landownership. But there still exists a gap between the new collective needs of the society and the individual rights of landownership. The understanding of the role of public authority decisions creating urban land value and the double aspect of land as a natural resource of the nation and as an economic good is important for formulating the new concept of landownership.

The recently introduced amendments and the land-use planning measures limiting the rights of plan use are a first attempt at legal and policy solutions to the special character of land (serving both collective needs and individual rights). Such a double aspect even found its expression in the Code Napoleon (according to the understanding of the collective needs of that period). Article 552 originally defined landownership as including all rights above and below the land surface, but 6 years after the publication of this article in 1810, Article 554 was published, limiting the rights of private property owners. This article stated that natural resources (e.g. minerals) below the land surface could be acquired by the public authorities without compensation. So already we see formulated in a clear way the limitation of the rights of absolute landownership in opposition to essential collective needs.

The expression of the need to adapt the legal concept of landownership to the new realities has been formulated by the Council of Europe. The recommendation presented by the Committee on Regional Planning and Local Authorities of the Council of Europe on 7 May 1969 included the suggestion that a modern land policy could "adapt existing national laws to the requirements of a modern land policy, having regard in particular to the fact that *the use of building space above and below ground level necessitates new rules on the right of ownership*". This recommendation was influenced by the 1969 Memorandum on Land Problems in Town Planning prepared by F. Canaux and Y. Nicolas, in which they suggested that land-ownership· be limited to the land surface, with no rights on the air-volume above that surface.

A similar concept has been formulated in a more comprehensive way by the well-known French expert on the law of public administration, J. P. Gilli. In his book *Redefinir le droit de propriété* he distinguishes between private space—which the landowner is entitled to use—and the space outside this limit which may be called public space. Such an approach means the transfer of considerable property rights of the community, leaving only the remainder to the individual. This concept is the recently proposed legislation of the French Minister of Construction which was adopted by Parliament. This limits land-ownership to building rights corresponding to the surface area only. The additional value created through more intensive land use is transferred to the community.

The meaning of collective rights to use land space has been changing with technical progress and rapid urbanization. A human settlement is a framework of space used collectively by the people living in it. The individual's living conditions must insure his essential needs not only for a roof over his head, but also by providing the services vital to everyday life. All these are based on using land for collective needs. The close interrelationship between different land uses may allow one to define a town as a space which provides a framework for people to live together and share that space.

The increasing rate of population growth which has extended the area of human settlement, the need to preserve land for agricultural use in order to provide food for the growing population, recreation needs, and the need for land for transportation purposes—all these needs are in contradiction to the old conditions of individual landownership. The private ownership of land by a small strata of the population means in reality that it is impossible for the large majority to enjoy land-use rights (including housing) which insures access to all city functions.

The liberal concept of universal application of individual rights in the sphere of land should result, due to the interrelatedness of different land uses, in the transfer of *ownership* rights to the community in order to insure for everyone individual land-use rights. Such a transfer of rights has many legal, economic, social and physical aspects. It should be realized that the result of such a process, based on the integral rights of the community (preventing undesirable development and planning the use of land according to the long-term needs of society), would be the transfer of ownership rights of all land needed for future development to the community, with land-use rights given to individuals but ultimate ownership reserved for the use of future generations. Obviously such a transfer should be done simultaneously with the creation of institutional means for allocating land-use rights for the whole population, based on established criteria of the value of space in relation to its location.

It should be underlined that the transfer of land from private to public ownership does not automatically solve the urban land problem. The ability to give the entire community rights of land use according to their needs is tied up in the complicated problem of establishing criteria for these needs and therefore for land allocation according to different uses. The method by which public decisions on land use are made should be seriously investigated, in order to establish how it is possible to prevent the allocation of land by public vested interests who often allocate land for different uses not according to common needs but in order to strengthen their own particular financial or institutional position. The institutional aspect of land allocation may be crucial in insuring that future land needs, both for settlement purposes and for agriculture, are met when the world population reaches 10 to 20 billion. An understanding of the double character of land as both a natural resource and an economic commodity will be vital in carrying out this task.

PROPOSALS FOR REFORM

Land use is a reflection of the priorities and goals of society which are ultimately set by the social structure. The following set of measures may serve as a basis for insuring the future of human settlements:

1. The transfer of land needed for urban growth from private to common ownership.
2. Methods of financing land development appropriate to the nature cf land (based on very long-term investments which give a return over many generations). The additional value created by urban growth may be seen as one of the sources of finance through an appropriate taxation system.
3. A regional approach to land allocation and administration.
4. An improved transportation system which meets the needs of all citizens.
5. The establishment of appropriate criteria for land allocation which will strike a balance between present and future needs.

The most important point, upon which the success of the others is dependent, is the first. As this is also the most controversial, it may be pointed out that in the whole history of human society the concept of private landownership has only been a prevalent category for the last centuries and for some types of land. During this time there have been many proposals for land reform. The purpose of urban land reform is not to diminish the rights of the individual to his own land space; the private land market has already done this through high prices. On the contrary, community landownership will guarantee that each individual has an adequate space in a pleasant environment and with accessibility to jobs and services.

The public ownership of land needed for future urban development will insure the proper planning of the city region as a whole. Enough land can be allocated for the recreational needs of the region's population and for new planned communities, which would not just mean housing but would include adequate employment opportunities and services. The ultimate aim would be the creation of a poly-city region, instead of the present pattern of one large town with many satellites.

An active role by the public authorities will not automatically solve all problems of future urban development. But it can create a framework of an urban land policy appropriate to the needs of society and more efficient than present methods. There will still be conflicts between local, regional and national interests. Public agencies with different functions may have their own vested interests even though private interests in land have been eliminated. The solution of such problems can only lie in the future; it can only be suggested today that they must be formulated in such a way as to .take into account the interrelationships between the individual, the community and the institutional structure.

There are few examples of such deep contradictions between the development of productive forces of the society and the ownership relations as in urban growth and urban land. The future of human settlements depends on the solution to this contradiction. Urban land should be seen as water, a scarce natural resource to be controlled and husbanded by the public authorities.

Urban land is both a natural resource and a peculiar type of good. It is a good because it is created by work and satisfies human needs. But at the same time it is a natural resource because the origin of this good is not through production. Urban land can only be "produced" by the decisions and investments of the public authorities. Therefore the value of urban land produced from raw land should be a good belonging to society as a whole.

The understanding of this double character of land is important in establishing a land policy which will insure land for development which will satisfy collective as well as individual needs.

In previous centuries there has been a long struggle for *agricultural* land reform. It may be hoped that the urgent land needs for survival may allow this generation to carry out the necessary urban land reform in a shorter time period. It took 100 years to add 1 million people to the human population some centuries ago; today it only takes 1 week. This rate of growth is such that the time it takes to realize land reform should be adapted to the rate of population and urban growth.

Further Reading

Chapter 1
Caldwell, W. A., *How to Save Urban America*, Regional Plan Association, New York, 1973.
Espaces et Societies, No. 3, Paris, 1971.
Plan Director del Area Metropolitana de Barcelona, Vols. I, II, III, Comision de Urbanismo y Servicios Comunes de Barcelona, 1966.
Regionplanlaening 1970–1985, Forudsaetniger, Vol. I, Copenhagen, 1971.
Regionplanlaening 1970–1985, Regionplanforslag, Vol. II, Copenhagen, 1971.
Shema Directeur d'Aménagement et d'Urbanisme de la Region de Paris, Premier Ministre, delegation général au district de la region de Paris, 1965.
Symposium on the *Impact of Urbanization on Man's Environment*, UN, June 1970.
Veranderung der Wohnbevolkerung and der Arbeitsplatze in der Stadt Zurich, Institut ORL, Zurich, 1969.

Chapter 3
Amato, P. W., *Urban Land Policies and Land-Use Control Measures*, Vol. IV: *Northern America*, United Nations, New York, 1973.
Danmarks statistik, Vurderingen af landets faste ejendomme, pr. 1 September 1960, Det Statistiske Departement, Copenhagen, 1964.
Darin-Drabkin, H., *Urban Land Policies and Land-Use Control Measures*, Vol. III: *Western Europe*, United Nations, New York, 1973.
Edel, M. and Sclar E., *The Distribution of Real Estate Value Changes*, Working Paper No. 4, Brandeis University, Waltham, Mass., July 1973.
Grenelle, J. J., *Espace Urbain et Prix du Sol*, Sirey, Paris, 1970.
Grenelle, J. J., *Dix ans d'évolution du Marche Foncier à Paris (1960–1969)*, Ateliei Parisien d'Urbanisme, Paris, 1973.
Grundvaerdikort over Ballerup-Maalov Kommune ved Vurderingen Pr. 1 September 1956–1965, Engelsen & Schroder, Copenhagen, 1957–67.
Grundvaerdikort over Hoje Taastrup Kommune ved 14 alm Vurdering Pr. 1956–1969, Engelsen & Schroder, Copenhagen.
Grundvaerdikort over Hersternes Kommune ved Vurderingen Pr. 1956–1969, Englesen & Schroder, Copenhagen.
Grundvaerdikort over Kobenhavn of Frederiksberg Pr. 1956–1969, Engelsen & Schroder, Copenhagen.
Hall, P., *Land Values*, Sweet & Maxwell, London, 1965.
Markfragen II, Bilagor: Statens Offontliga Utredningar, Stockholm, 1966.

424 Further Reading

Milgram, G., *US Land Prices Directions and Dynamics*, Research Report No. 13, Washington DC, 1968.

Marriot, O., *The Property Boom*, Pan Books Ltd., London, 1967.

Schmid, A. A., *Converting Land from Rural to Urban Uses,* resources for the future, INC, Washington, DC, 1971.

Statistik der Stadt Zurich, No. 53, Areal liegenschaften und Grundbesitz in der Stadt Zurich, Statistisches Amt der Stadt Zurich, 1965.

United Nations, "Seminar on Supply", *Development and Allocation of Land for Housing and Related Purposes*: "Country Monographs", Vol. I, 1965.

Untersuchen uber die Entwicklung der Grundstuckpreise in Zurich, Hochbaumt der Stadt Zurich, Zurich, 1961.

Voronof, M. L., "Land price development in Geneva and in the canton Geneva", manuscript based on data of the Evaluation Office, Geneva, 1973.

Wendt, P. F., *The Dynamics of Central City Land Values—San Francisco and Oakland, 1950 to 1960,* Institute of Business and Economic Research, University of California, Berkeley, 1961.

Chapter 4

Basic Development Plan, Calcutta Metropolitan District 1966–1986, Government of West Bengal, 1966.

Czerniavski, I., *Land and Land Policy in Israel*, Karka, No. 10, Jerusalem, Dec. 1975.

Darin-Drabkin, H., *Aspect of Land Policy and the Evolution of Urban Land Prices*, Ministry of Housing, Israel, Tel-Aviv, Aug. 1964.

Dwyer, D. L., *The City in the Third World*, Macmillan, London, 1974.

Flores, E., *Tratado de Economia Agricola, Fondo de Cultura Economica*, Mexico, 1968.

Khan, M. A., *Problems of Growth of an Underdeveloped Economy*, Asia Publishing House, London, 1961.

Master Plan for Delhi, *The Delhi Development Act, 1957.*

Prest, A. R., *Public Finance in Developing Countries*, Weidenfeld & Nicolson, London, 1975.

Report of the Committee on Urban Land Policy, Ministry of Health, Government of India, Delhi, 1965.

Sah, J. P., *Land Policies for Urban and Regional Development in the Countries of the Ecafe Region,* Economic Commission for Asia and the Far East, United Nations, 1966.

Secretaria de Obras Publicas, *Dinamica de la Poblacion en el Area Metropolitana de la Cinded de Mexico, Decada 1979–1980, Mexico, DF,* 1972.

Tokyo's Housing Problem, TMG Municipal Library, No. 5, Mar. 1972.

Vielle, P., *Marche des Terrains et Société Urbaine, Récherche sur la Ville de Tehran,* Anthropos, Paris, 1970.

Yamada, M., Expert Report on Planning Metropolitan Tokyo, Tokyo Metropolitan Government, Tokyo, 1964.

Chapter 7

Alonso, W., *Location and Land Use,* Harvard University Press, Cambridge, Mass., 1965.

Burgess, E. W., *The Growth of the City*, American Sociological Society, 1924.

Haig, R. M., "Toward an understanding of the metropolis", *Quart. J. Econ.,* 1926.

Harris, C. D. and Ullman, E. L., "The nature of cities", *Annales of the American Academy of Political and Social Science*, 1945.

Hoyt, H., *The Structure and Growth of Residential Neighborhoods in American Cities*, Federal Housing Administration, Washington, DC, 1939.

Hurd, R. M., *Principles of City Land Values*, The Record and Guide, New York, 1924.

Lathrop, G. T. and Hamburg, J. R., "An opportunity–accessibility model for allocating regional growth", *Journal of the American Institute of Planners*, May 1965.

Lowry, I. S., *Filtering and Housing Standards, A Conceptional Analysis*, Land Economics, 1960.

Maisel, Sh. J., *Background Information on Costs of Land for Single-family Housing*, Housing in California, Governor's Advisory Committee on Housing, April 1963.

Marshall, A., *Principles of Economics*, Macmillan, London, 1916.

Mayer, R., *Prix du Sol et Prix du Temps*, essai de theorie sur la formation des prix fonciers, Ministere de la Construction, Paris, Mars 1965.

Mills, E. S., *The Value of Urban Land*.

Penn-Jersey Transportation Study, Philadelphia, 1961.

Poyhonen, P., *Ekonometrinen tutkimus tontien hinnoista*, Helsinki, 1955.

Ricardo, D., *On the Principles of Political Economy and Taxation*, 1817.

Salmela, A., *Touttien Hinnat Ja Asemakaavakustannukset*, Helsinki, 1964.

von Thunen, J. H., *Der Isolierte Staat in Beziehung auf Landwirtshaft und National-ekonomie*, Vol. I, Hamburg, 1963.

Wendt, P. F., "Theory of urban land value", *Journal of Land Economics*, Aug. 1957.

Wendt, P. F., "Urban land value trends", *The Appraisal Journal*, Apr. 1958.

Wendt, P. F., "Economic growth and urban land values", *The Appraisal Journal*, July, 1958.

Wingo, L., *Transportation and Urban Land*, resources for the future, INC, Washington DC, 1964.

Chapter 8

Castells, M., *La Question Urbaine*, Maspero, Paris, 1972.

Chamberlin, E., *The Theory of Monopolistic Competition*, Harvard University, Printing Office, Cambridge, Mass., 1962.

Edel, M., "Marx's theory of rent, urban application", Discussion Paper No. 38, London, 1975.

Guigon, J. L., Aydalot, P. and Huriot, J. M., *Theorie Economique et Utilisation de l'espace*, Cujas, Paris, 1974.

Lichfield, N., *Economics of Planned Development*, The Estates Gazette, London, 1955.

Lipietz, A., *Le Tribut foncier urbain*, Maspero, Paris, 1974.

Turvey, R., *The Economics of Real Property*, G. Allen & Unwin, London, 1957.

Winnick, L., "Urban land value: a neglected subject", paper delivered at Ditchley Park (England), Conference on Regional Planning, July 1964.

Chapter 10

Denmark, Ministry of Housing, *The 1969 Reform of the Danish Land Use Legislation*, Copenhagen, 1970.

Douglas, P. H., *Problems of Zoning and Land-Use Regulation*, The American Society of Planning Officials, Washington, DC, 1968.

Efrat, E., *Changes of Physical Planning Trends in Israel*, Ministry of the Interior, Jerusalem, 1971.

Ferrero, A., *Cattedra di Materie Giuridiche*, Ranucci, P., *Appunti Esplicativi*, Instituto di Urbanistica, Facolta Architetture di Roma, 1969.
Italy, Ministero dei labori publici, Relazione all'on, Le Ministro sulla applicazione della legge 18·4·1962, No. 167, Roma, 1967.
Spain, Ministerio de la Gobernacion, Ley sobre regiment del suelo y ordenacion urbana, Madrid.
Stvan, J., *Environment Suisse une annee*, Digest 1973, Institut Ecoplan, Geneve, 1974.
Town and Country Planning Association, *The Land Commission Bill, Report of a Conference organized by the Association*, London, 1966.
United Kingdom, *The Town and Country Planning General Development Order*, London, 1963.
USA Department of Housing and Urban Development, Division of International Affairs, *Urban Land Policy: Selected Aspects of European Experience*, Washington, 1969.
USA, *Land Use Policy and Planning Assistance Act, Hearings before the Committee on Interior and Insular Affairs, United States Senate*, Washington, 1973.

Chapter 15
Agence Fonciere et Technique de la Region Parisienne, Rapport d'Activité 1973, Paris, 1974.
Baschwitz, J., *L'Urbanisme et l'Amenagement Foncier, Repertoite du Notariat Defrenois*, Paris, 1972.
Cornu, M., *La Conquête de Paris*, Mercure de France, Paris, 1972.
Lojkine, J., *La Politique Urbaine dans le Region Parisienne 1945–1972*, Mouton, Paris, 1972.
Magnan, R., *Conception et Instrument de la Planification Urbaine*, Centre de Recherche d'Urbanisme, Paris, 1975.

Chapter 17
Clark, C., *Population Growth and Land Use*, Macmillan, London, 1967.
Darin-Drabkin, H. and Lichfield, N., "A strategy for resources—land utilisation", International Symposium, September 1975, Science Policy Foundation.
Ehrlich, P., *Human Ecology: Problemes and Solution*, San Francisco, W. H. Freeman & Co., 1973.
Klatzman, J., *Nourir dix milliards d'hommes?*, Presses Universitaires de France, Paris, 1975.
Lattes, R., *Pour une autre croissance*, Seuil, Paris, 1972.
Mesarovic, M. and Pestel, E., *Mankind at the Turning Point*, The Second Report to the Club of Rome, Hutchinson & Co., London, 1975.
Sauvy, A., *Croissance Zero?*, Calman-Levy, Paris, 1973.

Chapter 18
Bosselman, F. and Calles, *The Quiet Revolution in Land Use*, Council of Environmental Quality, 1973.
Denman, D. R., *Rural Land Systems*, International Federation of Surveyors, London, 1968.
Denman, W. R. and Prodano, S., *Land Use*, London, 1972.

Lanversin, J., *La Propriété une nouvelle réglé du jeu?*, Presses Universitaires de France, Paris, 1975.

Ofori, I. M., *Pattern of Urban Landownership*, International Seminar on Urban Land Policies, United Nations, Madrid, 1971.

Reilly, W. K., *The Use of Land*, Thomas Y. Crowell Co., New York, 1973.

Saint Marc, P., *Socialisation de la Nature,* Stock, Paris, 1971.

Savatier, R., *La Propriété de l'espace*, Recueil Dalloz Sirey, Paris, 1965.

Stvan, J. and Staub, J., *Environment Suisse la nouvelle phase*, Institute Ecoplan, Geneve, 1973.

Author Index

Subject Index

Index of Place Names

Urban and Regional Planning Series

HART, D. A.
Strategic Planning in London: The Rise and Fall of the Primary Road Network (Volume 12)

STARKIE, D. N. M.
Transportation Planning, Policy and Analysis (Volume 13)

FRIEND, J. K. and JESSOP, W. N.
Local Government and Strategic Choice, 2nd edition (Volume 14)

RAPOPORT, Amos
Human Aspects of Urban Form (Volume 15)